Professional Stage

Module E

Information for Control and Decision Making

Revision Series

1730/F00

British Library Cataloguing-in-Publication Data

A catalogue record for this book is available from the British Library.

Published by AT Foulks Lynch Ltd
Number 4
The Griffin Centre
Staines Road
Feltham
Middlesex
TW14 0HS

ISBN 0 7483 4173 0

Acknowledgements

The past ACCA examination questions are the copyright of the Association of Chartered Certified Accountants. The answers to the questions from June 1994 onwards are the answers produced by the examiners themselves and are the copyright of the Association of Chartered Certified Accountants. The answers to the questions prior to June 1994 have been produced by AT Foulks Lynch Ltd.

We are grateful to the Chartered Institute of Management Accountants and the Institute of Chartered Accountants in England and Wales for permission to reproduce past examination questions. The answers have been prepared by AT Foulks Lynch Ltd.

EXAMINER PLUS - THE EXAMINER'S OFFICIAL ANSWERS

At the end of this book we include the new syllabus exams from June 94 to December 99 with the examiner's official answers, and at the end of each topic in the contents page below we indicate which of the questions from these exams are relevant to that topic.

For example, under the heading Accounting and management information systems below, you will see that as well as the bank of questions listed, question number 28, from the June 95 exam, among others, is also relevant.

CONTENTS

DECEMBER 1999 EXAMINATION

PREFACE

The new edition of the ACCA Revision Series, published for the June and December 2000 examinations, contains a wealth of features to make your prospects of passing the exams even brighter.

Examiner Plus

This book contains all the new syllabus examinations from June 1994 up to and including December 1999 plus the examiner's official answers. All the exams are set out in chronological order at the back of the book.

We have cross referenced all these questions to their topic headings in the contents pages so you can see at a glance what questions have been set on each syllabus area to date, topic by topic.

The inclusion of these questions and answers really does give students an unparalleled view of the way the new syllabus examinations are set and, even more importantly, a tremendous insight into the mind of the Examiner. The Examiner's answers are in some cases fairly lengthy and whilst the Examiner would not necessarily expect you to include all the points that his answers include, they do nevertheless give you an excellent insight into the sorts of things that the Examiner is looking for and will help you produce answers in line with the Examiner's thinking.

Features

Step by Step Answer Plans and *'Did you answer the question?' checkpoints* will be fully explained on the following two pages.

Tutorial Notes

In some situations the examiner's official answers benefit from a little extra explanation when they are to be used as a learning aid. Where appropriate, we have incorporated extra workings or explanatory notes, so that you derive the maximum benefit from these answers in preparation for your own exam.

Topic Index

The topics covered in all the answers have been indexed. This means that you can easily access an answer relating to any topic which you want to consider by use of the index as well as by reference to the contents page at the front of the book.

The Revision Series also contains the following features:

- Practice questions and answers - a total bank of around 80 questions and answers
- An analysis of the new syllabus exams from June 1994 to December 1999
- Update notes to bring you up to date for new examinable documents and any changes to legislation as at 1st December 1999.
- The syllabus and format of the examination
- General Revision Guidance
- Examination Technique - an essential guide to ensure that you approach the examinations correctly
- Key Revision Topics
- Formulae and tables where appropriate

HOW TO USE THE ANSWER PLANS AND 'DID YOU ANSWER THE QUESTION?' CHECKPOINTS

STEP BY STEP ANSWER PLANS

A key feature in this year's Revision Series is the Step by Step Answer Plans, produced for all new syllabus exam questions from June 1995 to June 1999.

Students are always being told to plan their answers and this feature gives you positive assistance by showing you how you should plan your answer and the type of plan that you should produce before you attempt the question.

Of course, in the exam, your answer Plan can be less fully written than ours because you are writing it for yourself. We are producing an answer plan which communicates the details to you the student and therefore is of necessity much fuller. However, all the detail is there, written in a way which shows you the lines along which you should be thinking in order to produce the answer plan.

You will notice that the Answer Plans start and finish with the exhortation that you must make sure that you have read the question and that you are answering it correctly. Each time you write down the next step in the Answer Plan, you must ask yourself - 'Why am I including this step?' 'Is it relevant?' 'Is this what the Examiner has asked me to do and expected me to do?'

Help with the answer

In addition, if you really do get stuck with the question and cannot see how to approach it, you may find it helpful to turn to the answer page, **cover up the answer itself!,** and start to read the Answer Plan. This may trigger your memory such that you can then return to the question itself and gain all the benefit of doing the question properly without reference to the answer itself.

Practice makes perfect

Like all elements of examination technique the time to learn how to plan your answers is not in the examination itself. You have to practise them now - every time you produce an answer - so that when you come to the examination itself these answer plans will be second nature.

It is probably a good idea to sketch out your answer plans in the way we have produced them here (but remember they can be briefer) and then compare them swiftly to our Answer Plan at the back of the book (don't look at the answer itself at this stage!).

This may indicate that you have completely missed the point of the question or it might indicate one or two other areas that you might wish to explore.

Then, without having yet looked at the answer itself, start writing your answer proper and then compare that with the examiner's own answer.

'DID YOU ANSWER THE QUESTION?' CHECKPOINTS

This is another feature included in this year's edition of the Revision Series. They are included in the new syllabus exam answers from June 1995 to June 1999.

At various points of the answers, you will come across a box headed **'Did you answer the question',** followed by a brief note which shows you how the printed answer is answering the question and encourages you to make sure that your own answer has not wandered off the point or missed the point of the question completely.

This is an invaluable feature and it is a discipline you must develop as you practise answering questions. It is an area of examination technique that you must practise and practise again and again until it becomes second nature. How often do we read in an Examiner's report that candidates did not answer the question the Examiner had set but had simply answered the question that they wanted him to set or simply wandered off the point altogether? You must make sure that your answers do not fall into that particular trap and that they do rigorously follow the questions set.

A good way of practising this aspect of examination technique is to imagine an empty box headed up 'Did you answer the question?' at the end of the paragraph or paragraphs you are about to write on a particular topic. Try and imagine what you are going to write in that box; what are you going to say in that box which justifies the two or three paragraphs that you are about to write. If you can't imagine what you are going to put in that box, or when you imagine it you find that you are struggling to relate the next few paragraphs to the question, then think very hard before you start writing those paragraphs. Are they completely relevant? Why are you writing them? How are they relevant to the question?

You will find this 'imagining the box' a very useful way of focusing your mind on what you are writing and its relevance to the question.

SUMMARY

Use the two techniques together. They will help you to produce planned answers and they will help you make sure that your answers are focused very fully and carefully on the question the Examiner has actually set.

1 SYLLABUS AND EXAMINATION FORMAT

FORMAT OF THE EXAMINATION

	Number of marks
Section A: 2 (out of 3) questions of 35 marks each	70
Section B: 2 (out of 3) questions of 15 marks each	30
	100

Time allowed: 3 hours

The Section A questions may be scenario-type questions which may draw upon many areas. The questions in Section B will focus on particular management accounting issues.

A present value table and an annuity table will be provided in the exam.

(1) MANAGEMENT ACCOUNTING FRAMEWORK

Management accounting operates in a changing environment in which management accounting techniques must be continuously appraised and reviewed. The management accounting framework must be reviewed in relation to the following areas.

(a) The evaluation of, and promotion of change in, management accounting techniques

(i) budgetary planning and control
(ii) standard costing and variance analysis
(iii) decision making including quantitative aids.

(b) Trends and developments in management accounting methods and techniques, business organisation and structure such as

(i) transfer pricing and divisionalised organisations
(ii) performance measurement and divisionalised organisations.

(c) Evaluating the impact of changes in business structure, functions and performance measures on the applicability and appropriateness of management accounting techniques and methods eg

(i) relevance of standard costing and variance analysis
(ii) use of traditional absorption costing methods.

(d) Identifying and evaluating existing and new methods and techniques and measures for management planning and control provision eg

(i) JIT (Just-in-time) procedures
(ii) computer integrated manufacturing
(iii) world class manufacturing
(iv) total quality management
(v) activity based budgeting.

(2) DESIGN OF MANAGEMENT ACCOUNTING SYSTEMS

(a) Developing/implementing an appropriate system including

(i) identification of cost units, establishing cost/profit/ responsibility centres

(ii) determining methods for recording relevant information

(iii) sources of information and recording/processing

(iv) computer based information storage and processing
(v) analysis of output information and its dissemination to relevant individuals/departments.

(b) Consideration and application of information requirements in relation to

(i) the costing/pricing of products and services
(ii) preparing plans
(iii) monitoring and controlling performance
(iv) decision making.

(c) Negotiating/agreeing information requirements taking into account

(i) influence of size and type of entity
(ii) nature of activities and output of each entity
(iii) long or short term nature of decisions
(iv) management structure and style
(v) conditions of uncertainty and risk
(vi) qualitative/quantitative nature
(vii) frequency, timing, format, degree of accuracy.

(3) INFORMATION FOR PLANNING AND CONTROL

(a) Budgeting and budgetary control

(i) budgeting as a multi-purpose activity

(ii) budgeting and behavioural influences

(iii) quantitative aids in budgeting; learning curve theory and application; limiting factors and linear programming

(iv) activity based budgeting

(v) control theory and budgeting; feedback and feedforward control

(vi) budgeting and new developments/good practice eg JIT procedures, added value activities, total quality management

(vii) uncertainty and budgeting

(viii) identification of relevance, strengths and weaknesses of budgeting and budgetary control.

(b) Standard costing

(i) use of planning and operational variances

(ii) trend, materiality and controllability of variances

(iii) uncertainty and variance analysis

(iv) identification of relevance, strengths and weaknesses of standard costing and variance analysis.

(c) Performance measurement

(i) measurement of activity, productivity, profitability, quality, service

(ii) relationship of measure to type of entity eg manufacturing or service, profit or non-profit making, centralised or decentralised

(iii) range of measures: monetary and non-monetary: use of percentages, ratios, indices

(iv) use of indices to allow for price and performance changes through time

(v) identification of areas of concern from the information produced

(vi) relationship between business performance and managerial performance

(vii) assessing management performance by reference to comparable internal and external information

(viii) performance measurement and developments in management accounting eg activity based budgeting, total quality management.

(4) INFORMATION FOR DECISION MAKING

(a) Pricing of goods and services

(i) target and minimum pricing
(ii) price/demand relationships
(iii) pricing of special orders and short life products
(iv) transfer pricing between divisions in a group.

(b) Identification and application of

(i) relevant costs (such as fixed/variable, direct/indirect, avoidable/ unavoidable, opportunity/sunk)

(ii) appropriate techniques (CVP analysis, use of limiting factors, recognition of risk and uncertainty).

(c) Selection of relevant information for decision making

(i) application and interpretation of quantitative techniques in decision making

- decision criteria
- expected value and expected profit, maximin
- decision trees, rollback analysis
- expected value of perfect and imperfect information
- linear programming
  - graphical and computer solution analysis
  - assumptions and limitations
  - shadow prices
  - opportunity costs
  - sensitivity analysis

(ii) use of indexing of costs and revenues

(iii) use of discounted cash flow techniques in longer term decision making situations.

(d) Use in a range of decision making situations: adoption of new products, product mix choice, discontinuance of products, make or buy, sell or further process, shutdown or temporary closure.

2 ANALYSIS OF PAST PAPERS

Topics	*J94*		*D94*		*J95*		*D95*		*J96*		*D96*		*J97*		*D97*		*J98*		*D98*		*J99*		*D9*	
Management accounting information	4	○															5	○	5	○	5	○		
Spreadsheet modelling	1	●			1	○	3	●	2	○														
Strategic v operational planning					6	○					5	●												
Activity based costing			1	○			2	○			1	○			2	●					3	●		
Backflush accounting and other modern developments									3	○					5	●			4	○	5	●		
Cost control and cost reduction							6	○																
TQM including quality related costs			3	●			6	●													1	○	3	○
Information and costs for decision making			6	○			4	○			5	●	6	○			2	○						
Decision making computations	1	○	3	○					1	○	2	○			2 3	○ ●	1 3	○ ○	1	○	1	○		
Linear programming													2	○										
DCF							3 5	○ ●							1	○							2	●
Risk and uncertainty	3	○	2	●																	3	●		
Pricing policy, including target costing			1	●					1	●			4	○	1	○					3	○	1	●
Incremental, activity based, zero based budgeting	6	○			5	○			2 5	● ○	3	○	1	●			4	○	3	○				
Budgeting techniques					4	○							5	●	5 6	● ○			2	○	2	○	1 5	○ ○
Budgeting - behavioural aspects													5	●			6	○					2	○
Standard costing and basic variances			2	○	3 2	○ ●							1	●	3 4	○ ○					4	○		
Planning and operational variances	5	○			3	●	1	○					5	●							2	●	1	○
Performance measurement - principles			5	○	2	●			4	○	4	○							6	○	6	○	4	○
Performance measurement applications	2	○											3	○										
Transfer pricing			4	○			2	●	6	○	6	○							1 4	● ●			6	○
Divisional performance evaluation							5	○							2	○								

Key

The number refers to the number of the question where this topic was examined in the exam.

○ This topic formed the whole or a substantial part of the question.

● This topic formed a non-substantial part of a question.

3 GENERAL REVISION GUIDANCE

PLANNING YOUR REVISION

What is revision?

Revision is the process by which you remind yourself of the material you have studied during your course, clarify any problem areas and bring your knowledge to a state where you can retrieve it and present it in a way that will satisfy the Examiners.

Revision is not a substitute for hard work earlier in the course. The syllabus for this paper is too large to be hastily 'crammed' a week or so before the examination. You should think of your revision as the final stage in your study of any topic. It can only be effective if you have already completed earlier stages.

Ideally, you should begin your revision shortly after you begin an examination course. At the end of every week and at the end of every month, you should review the topics you have covered. If you constantly consolidate your work and integrate revision into your normal pattern of study, you should find that the final period of revision - and the examination itself - are much less daunting.

If you are reading this revision text while you are still working through your course, we strongly suggest that you begin now to review the earlier work you did for this paper. Remember, the more times you return to a topic, the more confident you will become with it.

The main purpose of this book, however, is to help you to make the best use of the last few weeks before the examination. In this section we offer some suggestions for effective planning of your final revision and discuss some revision techniques which you may find helpful.

Planning your time

Most candidates find themselves in the position where they have less time than they would like to revise, particularly if they are taking several papers at one diet. The majority of people must balance their study with conflicting demands from work, family or other commitments.

It is impossible to give hard and fast rules about the amount of revision you should do. You should aim to start your final revision at least four weeks before your examination. If you finish your course work earlier than this, you would be well advised to take full advantage of the extra time available to you. The number of hours you spend revising each week will depend on many factors, including the number of papers you are sitting. You should probably aim to do a minimum of about six to eight hours a week for each paper.

In order to make best use of the revision time that you have, it is worth spending a little of it at the planning stage. We suggest that you begin by asking yourself two questions:

- How much time do I have available for revision?
- What do I need to cover during my revision?

Once you have answered these questions, you should be able to draw up a detailed timetable. We will now consider these questions in more detail.

How much time do I have available for revision?

Many people find it helpful to work out a regular weekly pattern for their revision. We suggest you use the time planning chart provided to do this. Your aim should be to construct a timetable that is sustainable over a period of several weeks.

Time planning chart

	Monday	Tuesday	Wednesday	Thursday	Friday	Saturday	Sunday
00.00							
01.00							
02.00							
03.00							
04.00							
05.00							
06.00							
07.00							
08.00							
09.00							
10.00							
11.00							
12.00							
13.00							
14.00							
15.00							
16.00							
17.00							
18.00							
19.00							
20.00							
21.00							
22.00							
23.00							

1 First, block out all the time that is **definitely unavailable** for revision. This will include the hours when you normally sleep, the time you are at work and any other regular and clear commitments.

2 Think about **other people's claims on your time**. If you have a family, or friends whom you see regularly, you may want to discuss your plans with them. People are likely to be flexible in the demands they make on you in the run-up to your examinations, especially if they are aware that you have considered their needs as well as your own. If you consult the individuals who are affected by your plans, you may find that they are surprisingly supportive, instead of being resentful of the extra time you are spending studying.

3 Next, give some thought to the times of day when you **work most effectively**. This differs very much from individual to individual. Some people can concentrate first thing in the morning. Others work best in the early evening, or last thing at night. Some people find their day-to-day work so demanding that they are unable to do anything extra during the week, but must concentrate their study time at weekends. Mark the times when you feel you could do your best work on the

timetable. It is extremely important to acknowledge your personal preferences here. If you ignore them, you may devise a timetable that is completely unrealistic and which you will not be able to adhere to.

4 Consider your **other commitments**. Everybody has certain tasks, from doing the washing to walking the dog, that must be performed on a regular basis. These tasks may not have to be done at a particular time, but you should take them into consideration when planning your schedule. You may be able to find more convenient times to get these jobs done, or be able to persuade other people to help you with them.

5 Now mark some time for **relaxation**. If your timetable is to be sustainable, it must include some time for you to build up your reserves. If your normal week does not include any regular physical activity, make sure that you include some in your revision timetable. A couple of hours spent in a sports centre or swimming pool each week will probably enhance your ability to concentrate.

6 Your timetable should now be taking shape. You can probably see obvious study sessions emerging. It is not advisable to work for too long at any one session. Most people find that they can only really concentrate for one or two hours at a time. If your study sessions are longer than this, you should split them up.

What do I need to cover during my revision?

Most candidates are more confident about some parts of the syllabus than others. Before you begin your revision, it is important to have an overview of where your strengths and weaknesses lie.

One way to do this is to take a sheet of paper and divide it into three columns. Mark the columns:

OK Marginal Not OK

or use similar headings to indicate how confident you are with a topic. Then go through the syllabus (reprinted in Section 1) and list the topics under the appropriate headings. Alternatively, you could use the list of key topics in Section 5 of this book to compile your overview. You might also find it useful to skim through the introductions or summaries to the textbook or workbooks you have used in your course. These should remind you of parts of the course that you found particularly easy or difficult at the time. You could also use some of the exercises and questions in the workbooks or textbooks, or some of the questions in this book, as a diagnostic aid to discover the areas where you need to work hardest.

It is also important to be aware which areas of the syllabus are so central to the subject that they are likely to be examined in every diet, and which are more obscure, and not likely to come up so frequently. Your textbooks, workbooks and lecture notes will help you here, and section 2 of this book contains an analysis of past papers. Remember, the Examiner will be looking for broad coverage of the syllabus. There is no point in knowing one or two topics in exhaustive detail if you do so at the expense of the rest of the course.

Writing your revision timetable

You now have the information you need to write your timetable. You know how many weeks you have available, and the approximate amount of time that is available in each week.

You should stop all serious revision 48 hours before your examination. After this point, you may want to look back at your notes to refresh your memory, but you should not attempt to revise any new topics. A clear and rested brain is worth more than any extra facts you could memorise in this period.

Make one copy of this chart for each week you have available for revision.

Using your time planning chart, write in the times of your various study sessions during the week.

In the lower part of the chart, write in the topics that you will cover in each of these sessions.

Example of a revision timetable

Revision timetable Week beginning:							
	Monday	Tuesday	Wednesday	Thursday	Friday	Saturday	Sunday
Study sessions							
Topics							

Some revision techniques

There should be two elements in your revision. You must **look back** to the work you have covered in the course and **look forward** to the examination. The techniques you use should reflect these two aspects of revision.

Revision should not be boring. It is useful to try a variety of techniques. You probably already have some revision techniques of your own and you may also like to try some of the techniques suggested here, if they are new to you. However, don't waste time with methods of revision which are not effective for you.

- Go through your lecture notes, textbook or workbooks and use a highlighter pen to mark important points.

- Produce a new set of summarised notes. This can be a useful way of re-absorbing information, but you must be careful to keep your notes concise, or you may find that you are simply reproducing work you have done before. It is helpful to use a different format for your notes.

- Make a collection of key words which remind you of the essential concepts of a topic.

- Reduce your notes to a set of key facts and definitions which you must memorise. Write them on cards which you can keep with you all the time.

- When you come across areas which you were unsure about first time around, rework relevant questions in your course materials, then study the answers in great detail.

- If there are isolated topics which you feel are completely beyond you, identify exactly what it is that you cannot understand and find someone (such as a lecturer or recent graduate) who can explain these points to you.

- Practise as many exam standard questions as you can. The best way to do this is to work to time, under exam conditions. You should always resist looking at the answer until you have finished.

- If you have come to rely on a word processor in your day-to-day work, you may have got out of the habit of writing at speed. It is well worth reviving this skill before you sit down in the examination hall: it is something you will need.

- If you have a plentiful supply of relevant questions, you could use them to practise planning answers, and then compare your notes with the answers provided. This is not a substitute for writing full answers, but can be helpful additional practice.

- Go back to questions you have already worked on during the course. This time, complete them under exam conditions, paying special attention to the layout and organisation of your answers. Then compare them in detail with the suggested answers and think about the ways in which your answer differs. This is a useful way of 'fine tuning' your technique.

- During your revision period, do make a conscious effort to identify situations which illustrate concepts and ideas that may arise in the examination. These situations could come from your own work, or from reading the business pages of the quality press. This technique will give you a new perspective on your studies and could also provide material which you can use in the examination.

4 EXAMINATION TECHNIQUES

THE EXAMINATION

This section is divided into two parts. The first part considers the practicalities of sitting the examination. If you have taken other ACCA examinations recently, you may find that everything here is familiar to you. The second part discusses some examination techniques which you may find useful.

The practicalities

What to take with you

You should make sure that you have:

- your ACCA registration card
- your ACCA registration docket.

You may also take to your desk:

- pens and pencils
- a ruler and slide rule
- a calculator
- charting template and geometrical instruments
- eraser and correction fluid.

You are not allowed to take rough paper into the examination.

If you take any last-minute notes with you to the examination hall, make sure these are not on your person. You should keep notes or books in your bag or briefcase, which you will be asked to leave at the side of the examination hall.

Although most examination halls will have a clock, it is advisable to wear a watch, just in case your view is obscured.

If your calculator is solar-powered, make sure it works in artificial light. Some examination halls are not particularly well-lit. If you use a battery-powered calculator, take some spare batteries with you. For obvious reasons, you may not use a calculator which has a graphic/word display memory. Calculators with printout facilities are not allowed because they could disturb other candidates

Getting there

You should arrange to arrive at the examination hall at least half an hour before the examination is due to start. If the hall is a large one, the invigilator will start filling the hall half an hour before the starting time.

Make absolutely sure that you know how to get to the examination hall and how long it will take you. Check on parking or public transport. Leave yourself enough time so that you will not be anxious if the journey takes a little longer than you anticipated. Many people like to make a practice trip the day before their first examination.

At the examination hall

Examination halls differ greatly in size. Some only hold about ten candidates. Others can sit many hundreds of people. You may find that more than one examination is being taken at the hall at the same time, so don't panic if you hear people discussing a different subject from the one you have revised.

While you are waiting to go in, don't be put off by other people talking about how well, or badly, they have prepared for the examination.

You will be told when to come in to the examination hall. The desks are numbered. (Your number will be on your examination docket.) You will be asked to leave any bags at the side of the hall.

Inside the hall, the atmosphere will be extremely formal. The invigilator has certain things which he or she must tell candidates, often using a particular form of words. Listen carefully, in case there are any unexpected changes to the arrangements.

On your desk you will see a question paper and an answer booklet in which to write your answers. You will be told when to turn over the paper.

During the examination

You will have to leave your examination paper and answer booklet in the hall at the end of the examination. It is quite acceptable to write on your examination paper if it helps you to think about the questions. However, all workings should be in your answers. You may write any plans and notes in your answer booklet, as long as you cross them out afterwards.

If you require a new answer booklet, put your hand up and a supervisor will come and bring you one.

At various times during the examination, you will be told how much time you have left.

You should not need to leave the examination hall until the examination is finished. Put up your hand if you need to go to the toilet, and a supervisor will accompany you. If you feel unwell, put up your hand, and someone will come to your assistance. If you simply get up and walk out of the hall, you will not be allowed to reenter.

Before you finish, you must fill in the required information on the front of your answer booklet.

Examination techniques

Tackling Paper 9

The examination will consist of two sections. The first may consist of scenario-type questions, designed to test the depth of your understanding of the syllabus. You are expected to assess the situation and include reasoned opinions. There are three questions in this section, of which you should attempt two, each being worth 35 marks.

Questions in the second section, of which you must also answer two out of three, are worth 15 marks each. These focus on management accounting issues.

Remember that in Paper 9 you need to produce a structured analysis of the data given in the questions. You must also comment on the relevant uses, strengths and weaknesses of management accounting.

Your general strategy

You should spend the first ten minutes of the examination reading the paper. Decide which questions you will do. You must divide the time you spend on questions in proportion to the marks on offer. Don't be tempted to spend more time on a question you know a lot about, or one which you find particularly difficult. If a question has more than one part, you must complete each part.

On every question, the first marks are the easiest to gain. Even if things go wrong with your timing and you don't have time to complete a question properly, you will probably gain some marks by making a start.

Spend the last five minutes reading through your answers and making any additions or corrections.

You may answer written questions in any order you like. Some people start with their best question, to help them relax. Another strategy is to begin with your second best question, so that you are working even more effectively when you reach the question you are most confident about.

Once you have embarked on a question, you should try to stay with it, and not let your mind stray to other questions on the paper. You can only concentrate on one thing at once. However, if you get completely stuck with a question, leave space in your answer book and return to it later.

Answering the question

All Examiners say that the most frequent reason for failure in examinations, apart from basic lack of knowledge, is candidates' unwillingness to answer the question that the Examiner has asked. A great many people include every scrap of knowledge they have on a topic, just in case it is relevant. Stick to the question and tailor your answer to what you are asked. Pay particular attention to the verbs in the question.

You should be particularly wary if you come across a question which appears to be almost identical to one which you have practised during your revision. It probably isn't! Wishful thinking makes many people see the question they would like to see on the paper, not the one that is actually there. Read a question at least twice before you begin your answer. Underline key words on the question paper, if it helps focus your mind on what is required.

If you don't understand what a question is asking, state your assumptions. Even if you do not answer in precisely the way the Examiner hoped, you may be given some credit, if your assumptions are reasonable.

Presentation

You should do everything you can to make things easy for the marker. Although you will not be marked on your handwriting, the marker will find it easier to identify the points you have made if your answers are legible. The same applies to spelling and grammar. Use blue or black ink. The marker will be using red or green.

Use the margin to clearly identify which question, or part of a question, you are answering.

Start each answer on a new page. The order in which you answer the questions does not matter, but if a question has several parts, these parts should appear in the correct order in your answer book.

If there is the slightest doubt when an answer continues on another page, indicate to the marker that he or she must turn over. It is irritating for a marker to think he or she has reached the end of an answer, only to turn the page and find that the answer continues.

Use columnar layouts for computations. This will help you to avoid mistakes, and is easier to follow.

Use headings and numbered sentences if they help to show the structure of your answer. However, don't write your answers in one-word note form.

If your answers include diagrams, don't waste time making them great works of art. Keep them clear, neat and simple. Use your rule and any templates or geometric instruments you have with you. Remember to label the axes of graphs properly. Make reference to any diagrams in the body of your text so that they form an integral part of your answer.

It is a good idea to make a rough plan of an answer before you begin to write. Do this in your answer booklet, but make sure you cross it out neatly afterwards. The marker needs to be clear whether he or she is looking at your rough notes, or the answer itself.

Computations

Before you begin a computation, you may find it helpful to jot down the stages you will go through. Cross out these notes afterwards.

It is essential to include all your workings and to indicate where they fit in to your answer. It is important that the marker can see where you got the figures in your answer from. Even if you make mistakes in your computations, you will be given credit for using a principle correctly, if it is clear from your workings and the structure of your answer.

If you spot an arithmetical error which has implications for figures later in your answer, it may not be worth spending a lot of time reworking your computation.

If you are asked to comment or make recommendations on a computation, you must do so. There are important marks to be gained here. Even if your computation contains mistakes, you may still gain marks if your reasoning is correct.

Use the layouts which you see in the answers given in this booklet and in model answers. A clear layout will help you avoid errors and will impress the marker.

Essay questions

You must plan an essay before you start writing. One technique is to quickly jot down any ideas which you think are relevant. Re-read the question and cross out any points in your notes which are not relevant. Then number your points. Remember to cross out your plan afterwards.

Your essay should have a clear structure. It should contain a brief introduction, a main section and a conclusion. Don't waste time by restating the question at the start of your essay.

Break your essay up into paragraphs. Use sub-headings and numbered sentences if they help show the structure of your answer.

Be concise. It is better to write a little about a lot of different points than a great deal about one or two points.

The Examiner will be looking for evidence that you have understood the syllabus and can apply your knowledge in new situations. You will also be expected to give opinions and make judgements. These should be based on reasoned and logical arguments.

Reports, memos and other documents

Some questions ask you to present your answer in the form of a report or a memo or other document. It is important that you use the correct format - there are easy marks to be gained here. Adopt the format used in sample questions, or use the format you are familiar with in your day-to-day work, as long as it contains all the essential elements.

You should also consider the audience for any document you are writing. How much do they know about the subject? What kind of information and recommendations are required? The Examiner will be looking for evidence that you can present your ideas in an appropriate form.

5 KEY REVISION TOPICS

The aim of this section is to provide you with a checklist of key information relating to this Paper. You should use it as a reminder of topics to be revised rather than as a summary of all you need to know. Aim to revise as many topics as possible because many of the questions in the exam draw on material from more than one section of the syllabus. You will get more out of this section if you read through Section 3, *General Revision Guidance* first.

This paper follows on from Paper 8 *Managerial Finance* which, as well as covering financial management, concentrates upon the planning and control aspects of management accounting. You must be familiar with all the management accounting content of paper 8 as all aspects of cost and management from papers 3 and 8 will be drawn together in this present paper. *Information for Control and Decision Making* extends the work of paper 8 into more advanced aspects of planning and control, and focuses upon decision making in some detail. This revision text, in conjunction with examination type questions in the main textbook, covers all the syllabus. Completing all the examination type questions in both texts should make you well-prepared for the examination.

1-4 ACCOUNTING AND MANAGEMENT INFORMATION SYSTEMS

You should be able to discuss:

- the nature of information (financial and non-financial) provided by accounting and management systems
- the use of information for internal and external purposes
- the types of information relevant for different purposes
- the use of information for planning, control and decision making (strategic and operational)
- the effect of responsibility accounting on information requirements, including the concepts of cost, revenue, profit and revenue centres and controllable/non-controllable costs
- the desirable attributes and principles of management accounting information
- the relevance and uses of open and closed systems, programmed and non-programmed information, feedback and feedforward control within the MIS
- the use of software packages in the analysis of management accounting information
- the advantages and disadvantages of spreadsheets and databases used within the MIS
- the preparation, layout and use in 'what-if' analysis of spreadsheet models
- the use of spreadsheet data-tables in the provision of decision making information

Refer to chapters 1 to 4 of the Lynchpin, and attempt all the questions shown under this heading on the contents page of this book

5,6 MODERN DEVELOPMENTS IN INDUSTRY AND COMMERCE, INCLUDING QUALITY CONTROL

You need to be able to:

- discuss the aims, features and merits of world class manufacturing (WCM)
- describe in outline the nature and benefits of computer aided systems
- identify and quantify value-added and non-value added activities
- explain the principles of just in time (JIT) procedures, and discuss their implications for cost systems and cost control, including the use of backflush accounting
- discuss the use of activity based costing (ABC) in product costing and cost control
- discuss the meaning and importance of quality and its management (TQM)
- explain the principles of performance measurement, training and product design within a TQM environment
- discuss the measurement, analysis and reporting of the costs of quality, and calculate them

Refer to chapters 5 and 6 of the Lynchpin, and attempt all the questions shown under this heading on the contents page of this book

7 to 11 DECISION MAKING (INCLUDING LINEAR PROGRAMMING AND DCF)

You should be prepared to

- discuss the ways in which costs can be classified for the purposes of decision making (eg by behaviour, function, controllability, relevance)
- use qualitative information in decision making
- explain the nature, assumptions and limitations of CVP analysis and apply it to given data
- prepare and interpret break-even and profit volume charts
- explain and illustrate the effect of limiting factors on decision making
- calculate solutions to problems involving changes in product mix, discontinuance of products/departments, make or buy decisions, further processing and service departments
- explain and illustrate the formulation of a linear programming (LP) model
- interpret the data output from a graphical illustration or computer print-out of a LP model
- discuss the assumptions and limitations of LP
- define and apply the concepts of net present values (NPV) and internal rate of return (IRR)
- contrast DCF methods with ARR and payback

Refer to chapters 7 to 11 of the Lynchpin, and attempt all the questions shown under this heading on the contents page of this book

12 STRATEGIC MANAGEMENT ACCOUNTING

You should have a general awareness of:

- the characteristics of strategic decisions
- the nature of the internal and external information required for strategic management, particularly related to competition

Refer to chapter 12 of the Lynchpin; this topic is generally examined as an element of questions from other topic areas, such as decision making and investment appraisal.

13,14 RISK AND UNCERTAINTY

You should have a good working knowledge of:

- the use of probability, expected values and sensitivity analysis in decision making
- the principles of maximin and maximax techniques
- the use of contingency tables and decision trees, in analysing the range of outcomes in problems involving conditional probabilities
- the meaning and evaluation of perfect and imperfect information

Refer to chapters 13 and 14 of the Lynchpin, and attempt all the questions shown under this heading on the contents page of this book

15,16 PRICING POLICY

You need to be able to

- identify and discuss market situations which influence pricing policy
- explain and discuss the variables which influence demand for a product
- use given data to determine an optimum price/output level
- discuss and illustrate the use of marginal and full costing as a basis for pricing
- discuss and illustrate the use of ABC in pricing
- discuss skimming, penetration, differential and target pricing

Refer to chapters 15 and 16 of the Lynchpin, and attempt all the questions shown under this heading on the contents page of this book

17-19 ACCOUNTING CONTROL SYSTEMS

You need be able to:

- describe the internal and external sources of information used in planning, including for preparation of the master and functional budgets
- discuss the information requirements of long term planning
- explain and illustrate the use of budgeting as planning aid
- use quantitative forecasting/costing techniques, including high-low, regression, and learning curves

- discuss the role of budgetary planning in target setting, motivation and performance evaluation and possible impact on management/staff behaviour

- explain the application of contingency theory to the budgeting process

- evaluate the strengths and weaknesses of alternative budgeting models such as fixed and flexible, rolling, activity based, zero based and incremental

Refer to chapters 17 to 19 of the Lynchpin, and attempt all the questions shown under this heading on the contents page of this book

20-22 STANDARD COSTING AND VARIANCE ANALYSIS

You must ensure you can:

- discuss the uses of standard costing

- calculate variances and sub-variances for sales, material, labour and overheads, including mix and yield/quantity and idle time variances

- discuss the possible causes and interdependence of variances

- explain and illustrate the use of planning and operational variances

- discuss the factors to be taken into account when deciding whether to investigate a variance, including the use of statistical control charts and decision theory

Refer to chapters 20 to 22 of the Lynchpin, and attempt all the questions shown under this heading on the contents page of this book

23-24 PERFORMANCE MEASUREMENT

You should be able to:

- describe the essential features of effective systems for responsibility accounting and internal control

- identify the areas in which performance measurement is required in typical manufacturing and service businesses, including the use of critical success factors

- identify, explain and give examples of financial, non-financial and qualitative measures that may be used in given circumstances, including the use of benchmarking

- discuss the key differences between manufactured and service products, and the performance aspects that are particularly relevant to service businesses

- appreciate, and be able to accommodate, the effect of inflation on performance measurement

Refer to chapters 23 to 24 of the Lynchpin, and attempt all the questions shown under this heading on the contents page of this book

25-27 TRANSFER PRICING AND DIVISIONAL PERFORMANCE EVALUATION

You should be prepared to:

- describe the circumstances in which a transfer pricing policy may be needed, and the necessary criteria for its design
- describe, illustrate and evaluate the use of market based methods of transfer pricing
- describe, illustrate and evaluate the use of cost-based transfer prices
- explain and illustrate the marginal analysis approach to transfer pricing
- explain and apply the "general rule" (based on opportunity costs) for transfer pricing
- describe, compute and evaluate performance measures relevant in a divisionalised organisation structure including return on investment (ROI) and residual income (RI)
- explain the need for separate measures for managerial and divisional performance

Refer to chapters 25 to 27 of the Lynchpin, and attempt all the questions shown under this heading on the contents page of this book

6 UPDATES

EXAMINABLE DOCUMENTS

Every six months ACCA publish a list of 'examinable documents' as at 1 June and 1 December which form the basis of the legislation and accounting regulations that will be examinable at the following diet.

The ACCA Official Textbooks published in June 1999 were fully up-to-date for these examinable documents published as at 1 June 1999.

The ACCA does not issue examinable documents for Paper 9.

7 PRACTICE QUESTIONS

1 ALTERNATIVE CHOICE DECISION-MAKING

Suggest ways in which recognition of each of the undernoted factors may assist the management accountant in providing information for alternative choice decision-making:

(a) learning curve effect
(b) risk and uncertainty
(c) timing of cash flows
(d) qualitative considerations.

(15 marks)
(ACCA June 93)

2 PRODCO PLC

Prodco plc has an annual turnover of £30,000,000 from a range of products. Material costs and conversion costs account for 30% and 25% of turnover respectively.

Other information relating to the company is as follows:

(i) Stock values are currently at a constant level being:

(a) Raw material stock: 10% of the material element of annual turnover.

(b) Work in progress: 15% of the material element of annual turnover together with a proportionate element of conversion costs allowing for 60% completion of work in progress as to conversion costs and 100% completion as to material cost. The material cost: conversion cost ratio is constant for all products.

(c) Finished goods stock: 12% of the material element of annual turnover together with a proportionate element of conversion cost.

(ii) Holding and acquisition costs of materials comprise fixed costs of £100,000 per annum plus variable costs of 10p per £ of stock held.

(iii) Movement and control costs of work in progress comprise fixed costs of £140,000 per annum plus variable costs of 5p per £ of material value of work in progress.

(iv) Holding and control costs of finished goods comprise fixed costs of £180,000 per annum plus variable costs of 2p per £ of finished goods (material cost + conversion cost).

(v) Financial charges due to the impact of stock holding on working capital requirement are incurred at 20% per annum on the value of stocks held.

Prodco plc are considering a number of changes which it is estimated will affect stock levels and costs as follows:

(1) Raw material stock: Negotiate delivery from suppliers on a just-in-time basis. Stock levels will be reduced to 20% of the present level. Fixed costs of holding and acquiring stock will be reduced to 20% of the present level and variable costs to 7p per £ stock held.

(2) Work in progress: Convert the layout of the production area into a 'dedicated cell' format for each product type instead of the existing system which comprises groups of similar machines to which each product type must be taken. Work in progress volume will be reduced to 20% of the present level with the same stage of completion as at present. Fixed costs of movement and control will be reduced to 40% of the present level and variable costs to 3p per £ of material value of work in progress.

(3) Finished goods stock: Improved control of the flow of each product type from the production area will enable stocks to be reduced to 25% of the present level. Fixed costs of holding and control will be reduced to 40% of the present level and variable costs to 1p per £ of finished goods held.

Required:

(a) Calculate the annual estimated financial savings from the proposed changes in EACH of raw material stock, work in progress and finished goods stock.

(15 marks)

(b) Suggest reasons for the reductions in the costs associated with each of raw material stock, work in progress and finished goods stock which it is estimated will occur if the proposed changes are implemented.

(8 marks)

(c) Discuss additional costs and benefits which may result from the proposed changes about which information should be obtained before implementation of the changes takes place.

(12 marks)
(Total: 35 marks)
(ACCA Dec 93)

3 SNECAS LTD

Snecas Ltd manufacture a range of products using a series of machine operations. One product type is made from steel bar. At present the factory layout is somewhat haphazard and machines are used for a particular job as they become available. Company management have decided to create a 'dedicated cell' of machines which will specialise in the manufacture of the steel bar products with specialist machine minders. The machines in the 'cell' will be grouped by machine type to facilitate a smooth flow of steel bar products. There are three steel bar products which are manufactured as follows:

Product A: saw the steel bar to size; turn the bar on a turning machine; harden in a hardening process; grind the bar on a grinding machine.

Product B: saw the steel bar to size; turn on a turning machine, grind on a grinding machine.

Product C: saw the steel bar to size; turn on a turning machine; drill on a drilling machine; harden in a hardening process; grind on a grinding machine.

Snecas Ltd currently operate a system whereby labour and overhead costs for all products are absorbed into product units at 225% of direct material costs. The direct material cost per metre of each steel bar product is £70.

This system results in the net profit or loss per metre of steel bar product being reported as £12.50 profit, £27.50 loss and £12.50 profit for products A, B and C respectively.

A study by the management accountant has resulted in the following budget data for the coming year for the steel bar product 'cell':

(i)

Machine operation	*Fixed labour and overhead (total)* £'000	*Variable labour and overhead per metre* £
Saw	88	36
Turn	110	14
Drill	108	40
Harden	320	26
Grind	154	25

(ii) Production/sales quantity

Product A	8,000 metres
Product B	2,000 metres
Product C	12,000 metres

(iii) Direct material prices will rise by 6% from the current year level.

(iv) Selling prices will be increased by 5% from the current year level.

(v) Variable labour and overhead costs will be absorbed at the budgeted rate per metre for each machine type listed in (i) above.

(vi) Fixed costs for each machine type will be absorbed at a rate per metre based on the aggregate quantity of products A, B and C budgeted to pass through each machine type.

You are required:

(a) to prepare a diagram which illustrates the layout and steel bar 'flow' of the new steel bar product machine group and shows the aggregate quantity (metres) of products passing through each machine type;

(5 marks)

(b) to prepare a budget summary for the coming year which details for each product:

(i) fixed and variable costs by machine operation (per metre and in total);
(ii) contribution earned per metre and in total for each product;
(iii) net profit or loss per metre and in total for each product.

(16 marks)

(c) to suggest ways in which the cost and revenue analysis for the amended machine layout indicates possible change in the product pricing and mix strategy.

(5 marks)

(d) to itemise and briefly comment on FIVE distinct ways in which the steel bar product dedicated cell layout may result in reductions in cost.

(9 marks)
(Total: 35 marks)
(Pilot Paper)

4 MAKE OR BUY DECISIONS

Short-term decision-making situations require consideration of (i) the cost classifications which the management accountant should use or ignore and (ii) factors which may affect the behaviour of costs and hence the accuracy of the cost analysis and the relevance of the decision.

Required:

Discuss the above statement in the context of whether a company should make quantities of a component used in the manufacture of a product or buy-in the component from an outside supplier.

(15 marks)
(ACCA June 92)

5 A HEALTH CLINIC

A health clinic is considering the implementation of a project which would extend its ability to provide specialist medical services for a period of five years. The project could be implemented by accepting one of two contracts A or B.

Contract A: the capital costs are payable to the contractor as follows:

£500,000 at the commencement of the project and £300,000 at the end of each of years 1 to 3.

Contract B: the overall capital outlay is estimated as being £200,000 at the commencement of the project and £400,000 at the end of each years 1 to 3. The contractor would share the capital costs on a 50/50 basis in return for a fee of £425,000 payable by the health clinic at the end of year 4, together with the contractor receiving 25% of the additional cash inflows resulting from the provision of the extra specialist services during each of years 1 to 4 inclusive. The contractor's 50% share would apply to each outlay.

The £700,000 of unutilised capital which the health clinic would have at its disposal by accepting contract B could be invested, in the pattern in which it becomes available, in a short-term fitness monitoring scheme which it is estimated would generate cash inflows of £250,000 during each of years 1 and 2 and £150,000 during each of years 3 and 4. The contractor would not receive any share of these cash flows.

The cash inflows accruing to the health club for the additional specialist medical services are estimated at £300,000 in year 1, £400,000 in year 2 and £600,000 in each of years 3 to 5. (All such figures are before any deduction of the contractor's share in contract B.)

Assume that all cash flows arise at year end points.

Ignore taxation.

Required:

(a) Prepare cost summaries and hence advise management whether to accept contract A or contract B in each of the following situations:

(i) Ignoring the discounting of cash flows, and
(ii) where the cost of capital is determined as 14%. **(15 marks)**

(b) Advise the health clinic management of the percentage of additional cash inflows from the specialist services payable to contractor B at which they will be indifferent as to the choice between contract A or contract B:

(i) ignoring the discounting of cash flows; and
(ii) where the cost of capital of 14% is incorporated into the solution. **(8 marks)**

(c) Comment on ways in which the cash flow structure of contracts A and B might influence the health clinic management in their choice of contract.

(6 marks)

(d) Name and briefly comment on quantitative techniques which could be used as part of the alternative choice process.

(6 marks)
(Total: 35 marks)
(Pilot Paper)

6 ANDREW MCDONALD

Andrew McDonald owns a farm on an island off the mainland of the United Kingdom. He generates the electricity for his home and farm by means of a diesel generator. The generator was installed some years ago at a cost of £5,000 and has a future life expectancy of five years. It functions more efficiently as the hourly demand (kilowatts) increases, as follows:

Hourly demand (kilowatts)	*Average running costs per kilowatt*
5	£0.25
10	£0.20
15	£0.15
20	£0.12

The above figures relate to the coming year (year 1). The running costs are expected to increase during the coming five year period whereby the costs each year will be 10% higher than the level of the preceding year. The running costs are avoidable for each hour in which the generator is not operated.

The average daily electricity requirement is 1 hour at 20 kilowatts, 2 hours at 15 kilowatts, 4 hours at 10 kilowatts and 2 hours at 5 kilowatts (there are no electricity requirements for the remaining 15 hours) for 365 days each year.

Mr McDonald is considering the purchase of an electricity generating system using a windmill which would reduce his reliance on the diesel generator. The windmill would cost £10,000 and would be operational at the commencement of year 1 with a five year life span.

Mr McDonald has gathered information which will enable him to make high, medium and low estimates of the electricity generation capacity of the windmill as follows:

Estimate	*Windmill output (kilowatts/hour)*	*Operating hours/day*	*Operating days/year*	*Probability*
High	4.25	12	250	0.2
Medium	4.00	12	200	0.6
Low	3.00	12	140	0.2

For each estimate weather conditions during the non-operating days of the year may be assumed to be unsuitable for the generation of electricity by the windmill.

The windmill-generated electricity would be stored in batteries and used to eliminate the highest cost running periods of the diesel generator. Each battery would cost £50. Mr McDonald would purchase twenty batteries at the commencement of year 1. This number of batteries should provide sufficient storage capacity whatever the pattern of windmill collection and subsequent usage of electricity. Each battery would have a life expectancy of five years.

The diesel generator, windmill and batteries will all have a nil residual value at the end of the five year period.

The time value of money should be ignored.

You are required:

(a) to prepare an analysis of the information which calculates the financial effect of each of the high, medium and low estimates of the electricity generation capability of the windmill and use an expected value approach to advise Mr McDonald on the financial advisability of installing the windmill.

(25 marks)

(b) to explain how Mr McDonald's attitude to risk may influence his decision on the installation of the windmill. Make use of relevant figures to illustrate your answer.

(5 marks)
(Total: 30 marks)
(ACCA June 91)

7 SCOS

SCOS Ltd intends to launch a commemorative product in the UK market for the next soccer World Cup. The proposed launch date is 1 April 19X3 with an 18 month product life cycle.

Required:

(a) Explain the procedures which may be followed in setting a selling price for the product where a total cost plus profit mark-up approach is used. **(5 marks)**

(b) Demand for the commemorative product is expected to be price dependent for the first six months after the launch date. Thereafter the entry of competitors into the market will lead to an agreed market price emerging, with SCOS Ltd obtaining a fixed share of the market which may be above or below its productivity capacity. SCOS Ltd intend to produce a maximum production capacity during the first six months and thereafter produce at a level to enable demand to be satisfied with stock being run down to zero if possible.

Comment on the impact of each of the following factors when setting a launch price for the commemorative product, where profit maximisation over the life of the product is desired:

(i) price/demand relationship;
(ii) market share;
(iii) opportunity cost/shadow price of stock.

(6 marks)

(c) Comment on the relevant costs and revenues to be considered by SCOS Ltd after the World Cup has taken place if it contemplates selling residual stocks of the commemorative product after the World Cup.

(4 marks)
(Total: 15 marks)
(ACCA Dec 1992)

8 DESAT ENGINEERING PLC

Desat Engineering plc has created a 'dedicated cell' machine group for the production of gas, steam and water valves. The valves are manufactured from steel bar which is subjected to a series of operations. The dedicated cell will commence operation on 1 January 1994. Before this date, valves were produced along with other products by passing all products through a series of machine groups, each used to perform specific operations on a range of products.

The budget/forecast data for the year to 31 December 1994 are subject to some uncertainty and are summarised as follows:

(i) Stocks at 1 January 1994:

Valve type	*Units*	*Stock value per unit* £
Gas	100	50
Steam	120	55
Water	80	60

Valves are valued at variable production cost per unit based on the 1993 unit cost estimates.

There are steel bar stocks of 340 metres at £70 per metre.

(ii) The steel bar input per valve is estimated as Gas: 0.3 metres, Steam: 0.4 metres, Water: 0.5 metres. These figures may vary by ±10%.

(iii) The budgeted amounts of dedicated cell net operating time per valve are estimated as Gas: 15 minutes, Steam: 18 minutes, Water: 24 minutes. These figures may vary by ±5%.

(iv) The dedicated cell machine group has a maximum capacity of 65 hours per week for 46 weeks in the year. It is estimated that non-productive time will be between 10% and 12% of gross manned hours. This non-productive time will be included in the unit valve costs as an uplift to the net operating time.

(v) The sales forecast of valves for 1994, which is thought to be subject to a variation of ±10%, is Gas: 3,000 valves, Steam: 3,200 valves, Water: 2,800 valves. Selling prices per valve for 1994 have been published as Gas: £70, Steam: £80, Water: £100.

(vi) Steel bar cost has been agreed with suppliers at £75 per metre. The dedicated cell variable costs per gross manned hour have been estimated in the range £80 to £90. Fixed costs attributable to the dedicated cell are estimated at £100,000 for 1994. This figure may vary by ±5% because of uncertainty about some of the estimates.

(vii) Closing stock of steel bar at 31 December 1994 is budgeted at 2% of the required input to production during 1994. Steel bar is charged to production on a FIFO (first in, first out) basis. No stocks of valves are budgeted for 31 December 1994.

(viii) If production capacity is not sufficient to allow the sales forecast to be achieved, the budget for production will be set by limiting the quantity of the least profitable valve type. If production capacity exceeds the sales forecast, the dedicated cell manned hours will be lowered in order to achieve a production/sales balance.

You are required:

(a) For the best possible outcome situation based on the above figures, calculate the production (units) for each valve type, indicating which valve type will have its production limited if production capacity is not sufficient.

(12 marks)

(b) Prepare a budget for the year to 31 December 1994 which shows the best possible outcome based on the above figures. The budget should be analysed by valve type in so far as the information permits and should show (i) production quantities, (ii) sales quantities and (iii) budgeted profit and loss statement. Profit and loss statement values should be rounded to the nearest hundred pounds sterling.

(15 marks)

(c) The values given to the range of variables in the forecast have a degree of uncertainty attached to them. Suggest ways in which this uncertainty may be accommodated by the methods used to process the data.

(8 marks)
(Total: 35 marks)
(ACCA Dec 93)

9 PARTICIPATION

You are required to discuss ways in which the degree of management participation in the budget setting process, as opposed to non-participation, may affect the efficiency and effectiveness of the process and the attitudes of those involved.

(15 marks)
(Pilot Paper)

10 RESPONSIBILITY ACCOUNTING

You are required:

(a) to define and outline the requirements of responsibility accounting.

(5 marks)

(b) to explain how responsibility may be shared in respect of the cost of operating the maintenance department in an organisation which has a number of production and service departments.

(5 marks)

(c) to suggest ways in which the design of the management accounting system may attempt to recognise such shared responsibility.

(5 marks)
(Total: 15 marks)
(Pilot Paper)

11 RUBBLEFLINT

Rubbleflint Ltd has a mining operation which involves the extraction of two chemicals RBF1 and RBF2. The initial extraction is in the form of chemical bearing rock. The rock is crushed and water treated at which stage the chemicals are dissolved and form a liquid solution. The dissolved chemicals are passed to a chemical separation process in which the chemicals are separated and converted into crystalline form. The residual rock left in the crushing and water treatment process is sold as base material for motorway construction. The following budget/standard information has been collected for a four week period.

Chemical extraction process:

20,000 tonnes of chemical bearing rock at a total cost of £460,000.

Crushing and water treatment process:

(a) Output yields 40% chemicals and 60% crushed rock with no losses.

(b) The chemicals in liquid form for transfer to the chemical separation process are in the ratio 1 tonne: 1,000 litres.

(c) Process costs (excluding the cost from the chemical extraction process) total £142,000.

(d) Crushed rock is considered to be a joint product and is sold for £40 per tonne. It is transferred to a crushed rock sales profit and loss account at cost.

(e) Costs are apportioned to joint products on a physical quantity of output basis.

Chemical separation process:

(a) Variable costs per 1,000 litres processed: £12.

(b) Total fixed costs: £4,000.

(c) The standard yield of crystallised chemicals is 1 tonne for 1,200 litres of input. The standard mix of RBF1:RBF2 is 30:70.

(d) The chemicals RBF1 and RBF2 are sold at £240 and £120 per tonne respectively.

(e) Costs are apportioned to RBF1 and RBF2 on a sales value basis.

Sundry administration and selling costs of the business total £650,000 for the four week period.

There are no opening or closing stocks of work in progress. All output of rocks and chemicals is sold in the same period.

Required:

(a) Prepare a budgeted profit and loss statement for Rubbleflint Ltd for the four week period.

(9 marks)

(b) Calculate the standard cost per tonne attributed to each of RBF1 and RBF2, and the standard cost per tonne of any abnormal losses which may be reported in the chemical separation process. Abnormal losses occur at the end of the process cycle.

(9 marks)

(c) Prepare the chemical separation process account for the four week period incorporating product mix and yield variances where the actual results are:

(i) 8,000,000 litres of chemical solution are transferred in from the crushing and water treatment process at £30.10 per 1,000 litres.

(ii) Chemical separation process costs are at standard/budget levels.

(iii) Output achieved is RBF1: 2,000 tonnes; RBF2: 4,000 tonnes.

(iv) Chemical and abnormal losses are valued as per the standard costs per tonne calculated in (b) above. **(9 marks)**

(d) Rubbleflint Ltd wish to evaluate a proposal that the chemical separation process be altered in order to enhance the yield of crystalline chemicals to 1 tonne from 1,100 litres of input, instead of the present 1 tonne from 1,200 litres of input.

The amended total data which will apply to the chemical separation process for these proposals are:

(i) variable cost per 1,000 litres input: £17;
(ii) fixed costs per four week period: £24,000;
(iii) process input will remain at 8,000,000 litres of chemical solution.

Evaluate the proposal on financial grounds using the above information together with relevant budget data. **(8 marks)**

(Total: 35 marks)

(ACCA Dec 1992)

12 WYMA PLC

Wyma plc produce and sell a single product in circumstances where overall demand exceeds production capacity. Production capacity available in any period may be affected by factors such as holidays, availability of materials and machines out of commission awaiting spare parts. The machines are automated and machine minder wages and other machine costs vary with gross machine hours (ie, running hours plus idle time hours).

Standard costing and variance analysis is in operation with planning and operational variances incorporated into the feedback information.

The original standard information introduced in period 1 is as follows:

Selling price per product unit	£80
Direct material price per kilo	£5
Direct material per product unit	7 kilos
Machine cost per gross hour	£30
Machine time per product unit	0.3 running hours
Machine idle time (% of gross hours)	7.5%

The budget and actual production and sales quantities for periods 2 to 5 are as follows:

	Period 2 (units)	*Period 3 (units)*	*Period 4 (units)*	*Period 5 (units)*
Budget	54,000	60,000	52,000	48,000
Actual	49,000	57,000	49,000	49,000

A trend analysis which records each variance and sub-total as a percentage of the original budget contribution for a period is shown in the Table below.

You are required:

(a) Prepare a summary operating statement for period 5 which reconciles the original budget contribution with the actual contribution and details all the variances (all figures to nearest £00 sterling), using the layout shown in the Table below. **(7 marks)**

(b) Calculate the revised standard contribution per unit for period 5 with a detailed analysis of the cost and revenue elements per unit (physical quantities and prices) from which it is obtained. **(14 marks)**

(c) Prepare a detailed analysis of the trend statistics for periods 2 to 5 (per Table that follows). Your analysis should highlight any significant trends and should include comments on the management accounting procedures in operation and their use in providing relevant analysis of the performance of Wyma plc.

Trend analysis showing all figures as percentage of original budget contribution

	Period 2		Period 3		Period 4		Period 5	
Original budget contribution		100.0%		100.0%		100.0%		100.0%
Revision variances:								
Material usage (at original standard price)	0.0%		-5.0%		-5.0%		-5.0%	
Material price (at revised standard usage)	0.0%		-6.3%		-6.3%		-15.6%	
Machine efficiency (at original std idle time)	0.0%		0.0%		0.0%		0.0%	
Machine idle time (at revised standard efficiency)	0.0%		-0.5%		-0.5%		-0.9%	
Machine expenditure (at revised standard efficiency and idle time)	0.0%		2.8%		2.8%		2.8%	
Sales price	0.0%	0.0%	0.0%	-0.9%	-5.6%	-14.6%	-5.7%	-24.4%
Revised budget contribution		100.0%		91.0%		85.4%		75.6%
Sales volume variance		-9.3%		-4.6%		-4.9%		1.6%
Revised standard contribution from sales achieved		90.7%		86.4%		80.5%		77.2%
Other variances:								
Sales price	-5.1%		-5.4%		0.0%		-2.9%	
Material usage	-2.6%		-1.1%		-2.1%		-3.3%	
Material price	-5.6%		-10.0%		-12.0%		-5.5%	
Machine efficiency	-1.7%		0.8%		1.6%		1.8%	
Machine idle time	-0.5%		-0.4%		-0.5%		-0.4%	
Machine expenditure	2.2%	-13.3%	0.1%	-16.0%	-0.1%	-13.1%	-0.5%	-10.8%
Actual contribution		77.4%		70.4%		67.4%		66.4%

(14 marks)
(Total: 35 marks)
(ACCA June 93)

13 ROCKALL GROUP

The Rockall Group has member divisions which manufacture and sell the same single product. Indices are compiled which monitor the change in cost levels for each element of cost against the levels applicable in 19X0 which is used as the base year. An index of 100 is used for 19X0 for each element of cost for all member divisions which manufacture and sell the single product.

Each member division has a set of indices and an overall average set of indices for member divisions making the single product is also compiled.

Additional information is available as follows:

(i) Summarised operating results for Rockpan Division, one of the member divisions which produces and sells the single product are as follows:

	19X0	*19X3*
	£'000	£'000
Sales/production	2,640	2,425.500
Costs:		
Direct material*	960	927.360
Direct labour*	360	354.375
Variable overhead*	90	96.831
Fixed overhead	300	368.880
	1,710	1,747.446
Net profit	930	678.054
Selling price per unit	£33	£34.65

* Variable with output units.

(ii) The 19X3 average cost indices for member divisions and the 19X3 cost indices for Rockpan Division (taking 19X0 as 100) are as follows:

	Member Division overall average	*Rockpan Division*
Direct material	124	110.4
Direct wages	115	112.5
All other costs	120	122.96

(iii) The market is extremely competitive and unit sales of this product by member divisions in 19X3 are on average 80% of 19X0 levels. On average, the group selling price of the product is 10% higher than in 19X0.

You are required:

(a) to prepare an inter-firm comparison analysis statement which compares the actual results of Rockpan Division for 19X3 as detailed in (i) above with the average expected results based on the Rockall Group member divisions' average performance in 19X3. The expected results should be calculated using the overall average indices per (ii) above and the average group sales activity of 80% per (iii) above. The analysis should evaluate the relative differences between Rockpan Division and the group average divisional performance due to:

(i) Contribution gain or loss due to volume changes. Note that group average indices should be used in the calculation of contribution per unit.

(ii) Selling price.

(iii) Overall cost effect for EACH element of cost. **(22 marks)**

(b) to comment on the differences between Rockpan Division and the group average performance highlighted in the analysis in (a), suggesting specific factors which may have contributed to the cost effect for each element of cost.

(9 marks)

(c) to suggest a further analysis of the cost indices which may be incorporated into the system in order to provide a more detailed analysis of the relative cost variances.

(4 marks)
(Total: 35 marks)
(Pilot Paper)

14 OPPORTUNITY COST

The management accountant may make use of opportunity cost:

(a) in the operation of a standard cost system.
(b) in the setting of transfer prices from one division to another.
(c) in deciding whether or not to accept a contract.

You are required to discuss the relevance of the use of opportunity cost in each of the above applications.
(15 marks)
(Pilot Paper)

15 LATRO GROUP

Divisions A, B and C which are part of the Latro Group sell, as part of their overall business activity, products Aye, Bee and Cee respectively to customers outside the Latro Group. Each product uses a fabric which is in short supply and is available from Exe Division, Wye Division and an outside company, Numero Ltd. Demand for each of Aye, Bee and Cee exceeds the amounts which can be supplied from the available supply of fabric.

The following forecast information is available for the period ended 31 January 1994:

(i) Final products:

	Aye	*Bee*	*Cee*
Selling price per unit (£)	42	62	56
Conversion cost per unit (£)	12	14	20
Fabric units per unit of final product (units)	5	6	8

(ii) Exe Division has fabric production capacity of 8,400 units at a variable cost of £4 per unit. Exe Division has an external market available for 7,000 units of fabric at a selling price of £9 per unit. It has no external opportunity available for its remaining production capacity.

(iii) Wye Division has fabric production capacity of 6,000 units at a variable cost of £4.80 per unit. Wye Division has an external market available for 4,000 units of fabric at a selling price of £10 per unit. It has no external opportunity available for its remaining production capacity.

(iv) Numero Ltd can supply up to 3,000 units of fabric at £6.60 per unit.

(v) It is current practice in Latro Group to allow divisions to transfer fabric at variable cost plus 100% markup.

Required:

(a) Determine the fabric purchase, sale and transfer policy which will maximise contribution for Latro Group in the period ending 31 January 1994 and calculate the contribution thus earned.

(All relevant workings should be shown).

(20 marks)

(b) Consider that Latro Group management now decide that a minimum of 200 units of each of products Aye, Bee and Cee must be produced and sold before the remaining fabric is used in a group profit maximising manner.

Calculate the amended profit maximising strategy and the amended maximum group contribution for the period ending 31 January 1994.

(8 marks)

(c) Discuss ways in which the degree of divisional autonomy may lead to a change in the sales (units) of fabric and Aye, Bee and Cee and the Latro Group contribution in the period ending 31 January 1994.

(7 marks)
(Total: 35 marks)
(ACCA Dec 93)

ANSWERS TO PRACTICE QUESTIONS

1 ALTERNATIVE CHOICE DECISION-MAKING

(a) The learning curve effect implies that after an initial learning period a steady state will be reached where the incremental time per unit will not change significantly. The learning curve effect may occur at different rates of learning from one situation to another. The rate of learning will affect the overall average labour requirement per unit for a particular project. In choosing between alternative projects, therefore, the rate of learning may be an important cost factor. In addition, the learning curve effect may also influence the incidence of material cost and variable overhead cost. A slow rate of learning may mean a higher level of material waste for a longer period. Where variable overhead is incurred on a time related basis, a slow rate of learning will increase the variable overhead cost of the project. This means that in choosing between alternatives, ignoring the learning curve effect could significantly distort the cost comparison information.

(b) Risk and uncertainty will exist in any decision-making situation. Alternative choice decision-making will be affected by

(i) efforts which are made to recognise risk and uncertainty and

(ii) management attitude to risk.

Risk and uncertainty may be recognised by assigning probabilities to a range of likely outcomes. This information may be used to calculate the expected value of profit for a particular project. When choosing between alternatives, management may decide to choose the alternative with the highest expected value of profit. This course of action ignores the possibility of a very high profit or the risk of a loss if a particular set of circumstances occurs. Taking the spread of possible outcomes into account allows management attitudes to risk to be brought into the decision-making process.

A risk seeking manager may choose the alternative with the highest profit possibility whereas a risk averse manager may wish to ensure that his choice is the one which will minimise the potential loss making possibility.

(c) Where the choice is between two projects which earn the same profit with the same initial investment, the pattern of cash flows over the life of the project will affect the alternative choice decision. Management may wish to choose the alternative which will pay back the initial investment in the shortest possible time irrespective of the overall cash inflows over the life of the project. This may be linked to the need to boost short-term profitability of the company. A longer term view will examine the cash flow streams over the life of alternative projects and discount the cash flows at the appropriate cost of capital rate. This will enable the choice between alternatives to be made on the basis of net present value (NPV). This may mean that the alternative chosen will have a lower total cash inflow over the project life but a higher NPV because of the pattern of cash flows.

(d) Information may be classified as being quantitative or qualitative in nature. Quantitative information can be used to compare and evaluate alternatives. For example where a limiting factor exists, the product mix which is chosen to utilise the scarce resource may be based on the ranking of products on the basis of contribution per unit of limiting factor. This will lead to a short-term profit maximising decision. It may be, however, that there are other (qualitative) factors which should be taken into account. Qualitative information is not readily quantifiable and is usually expressed in a descriptive manner. For example a product eliminated from a short-term profit maximising strategy may have a large anticipated future market share based on penetrating the market with an aggressive initial pricing strategy. This should be taken into account in deciding on the product mix which should be produced in the short term. Again, in a zero based budgeting exercise the competition for a share of available resources will require managers to give reasons for the operation of their department or service at incremental levels. Such reasons may be qualitative rather than quantitative in nature. When senior management choose between alternatives for the allocation of resources the strength of qualitative argument may be an important factor.

(Other relevant comment would be accepted.)

2 PRODCO PLC

(a) Workings:

Turnover	£30,000,000
Material element (30%)	£9,000,000
Conversion cost element (25%)	£7,500,000

Current stock levels:

(i)	Raw material:	£900,000	(10% × £9,000,000)
(ii)	Work in progress:		
	material element	£1,350,000	(15% × £9,000,000)
	conversion cost	675,000	(15% × £7,500,000 × 60%)
		£2,025,000	
(iii)	Finished goods:		
	material element	£1,080,000	(12% × £9,000,000)
	conversion cost	900,000	(12% × £7,500,000)
		£1,980,000	

The existing and amended costs of stock holding may now be calculated using the data in the question:

		Existing £	*Amended* £	*Saving* £
1.	**Raw material stock:**			
	Holding and acquisition costs:			
	Fixed	100,000	20,000	
	Variable	90,000	12,600	
	Financial charges (at 20%)	180,000	36,000	
		370,000	68,600	301,400
2.	**Work in progress:**			
	Movement and control costs:			
	Fixed	140,000	56,000	
	Variable	67,500	8,100	
	Financial charges (at 20%)	405,000	81,000	
		612,500	145,100	467,400
3.	**Finished goods:**			
	Holding and control costs:			
	Fixed	180,000	72,000	
	Variable	39,600	4,950	
	Financial charges (at 20%)	396,000	99,000	
		615,600	175,950	439,650

(b) The answer to this part of the question may be tabulated.

Possible reasons for the reductions in fixed and variable costs may be summarised as follows:

Raw material stock:

1. Reduction in the number of staff required.
2. Reduction in stores occupancy costs.
3. Reduction in material handling costs.
4. Reduction in administrative and clerical costs.
5. Reduction in losses due to damage in stores or obsolescence.

Work in progress:

1. Reduction in number of supervision and material handling staff.

2. Reduction in idle time of employees and machines leading to overall reduction in operating time and hence costs.

3. Flexibility of the workforce leading to increased efficiency and reduced overall costs.

4. Reduction in losses due to damage of WIP through movement from one machine area to another.

Finished goods stock:

1. Reduction in stores occupancy costs.
2. Reduction in handling costs of finished goods.
3. Reduction in insurance costs.
4. Reduction in administrative and clerical costs.
5. Reduction in number of staff required.
6. Reduction in losses due to damage and obsolescence.
7. Reduction in stocktaking costs.

(c) Just-in-time delivery of raw materials must be negotiated with suppliers. It is likely that the supplier will insist on an increase in purchase price per unit unless Prodco plc is a very large customer with significant leverage to negotiate either no increase or a very small increase in unit price. Prodco plc must check on the delivery record of suppliers. It will be important that late delivery does not lead to a stock-out situation which results in increases in cost due to idle capacity costs and possible loss of sales. The just-in-time system will require Prodco plc to examine its production plan in order to ensure that materials are requested from suppliers as required. This should bring the benefits of increased efficiency of operation brought about by the need for closer dovetailing of materials delivery/production requirements. There may be additional benefits from the opportunity cost of space no longer required for raw material stock. Prodco plc should investigate the opportunities for alternative use or sub-let of such space.

A dedicated cell format for each product type should improve the flow of products and enable a more efficient production/sales balance to be achieved, whereby the production system is more sensitive to demand. This should help increase turnover through Prodco plc being able to quote delivery dates more competitively. The dedicated cell format may involve additional costs in setting up the new machine groupings and in the training of employees. There should be benefits, however, in a possible reduction in the total number of employees required and in the more economical use of space in the production area. Prodco plc should investigate and quantify the impact on staffing and potential use of any space made available eg, the introduction of an additional product line.

It is estimated that the improved flow of each product type from the production area should reduce the overall level of finished goods stock required. Prodco plc must attempt to quantify any increase in sales which may accrue from being more sensitive to customer delivery requirements. The reduction in finished goods stock requirement will free space in the finished goods store. Prodco plc should investigate the opportunities for alternative use or sub-let of such space.

(Other relevant points would be accepted in (b) and (c).)

3 SNECAS LTD

(a)

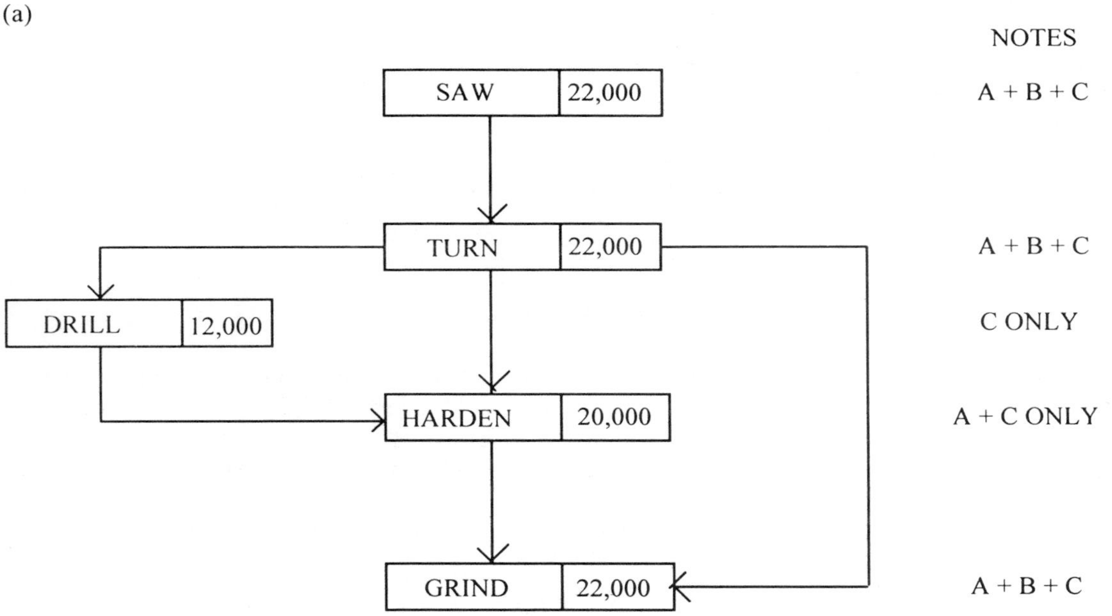

Process	Metres	NOTES
SAW	22,000	A + B + C
TURN	22,000	A + B + C
DRILL	12,000	C ONLY
HARDEN	20,000	A + C ONLY
GRIND	22,000	A + B + C

(b)

	A		B		C	
	Total £'000	*Per metre* £	*Total* £'000	*Per metre* £	*Total* £'000	*Per metre* £
Sales revenue (W1)	2,016	252	420	210	3,024	252
Direct material (W2)	(593.6)	(74.2)	(148.4)	(74.2)	(890.4)	(74.2)
Sawing	(288)	(36)	(72)	(36)	(432)	(36)
Turning	(112)	(14)	(28)	(14)	(168)	(14)
Drilling	-	-	-	-	(480)	(40)
Hardening	(208)	(26)	-	-	(312)	(26)
Grinding	(200)	(25)	(50)	(25)	(300)	(25)
Contribution	614.4	76.8	121.6	60.8	441.6	36.8
Sawing (£88/22 = £4/m)	(32)	(4)	(8)	(4)	(48)	(4)
Turning (£110/22 = £5/m)	(40)	(5)	(10)	(5)	(60)	(5)
Drilling (£108/12 = £9/m)	-	-	-	-	(108)	(9)
Hardening (£320/20 = £16/m)	(128)	(16)	-	-	(192)	(16)
Grinding (£154/22 = £7/m)	(56)	(7)	(14)	(7)	(84)	(7)
Net profit/(loss)	358.4	44.8	89.6	44.8	(50.4)	(4.2)

WORKING

(W1) Present selling prices are:

£70 + (225% of £70) + profit / – loss

= £227.50 + profit / – loss

Therefore				
	A	£227.50 + £12.50	=	£240
	B	£227.50 - £27.50	=	£200
	C	£227.50 + £12.50	=	£240

Selling prices are to increase by 5% and will thus become:

A	£252
B	£210
C	£252

(W2) Direct material costs are to increase by 6% to £74.20/metre.

(c) (1) The revised results (shown in part (b)) are as follows:

	A	*B*	*C*
Contribution per metre	£76.80	£60.80	£36.80
Profit per metre	£44.80	£44.80	(£4.20)

These indicate that all three products have a positive contribution, although product C yields a net loss. However the only relevant fixed labour and overhead cost is the drilling costs which are not used by products A and B and could presumably be avoided if product C were discontinued. At present volumes of C this amounts to £9/metre which still results in a positive net contribution; it becomes critical when output of C falls to 3,000 metres (£108,000/3,000 = £36.00 per metre).

(2) Compared to the previous system products A and B show a significant increase in profitability to the detriment of product C. This is caused by the methods used to attribute fixed costs to products. The previous system attributed part of the drilling costs to products A and B when they did not use this resource, thereby subsidising product C; and, product B was similarly charged a proportion of the hardening costs which it does not use.

(3) Product pricing is a function of demand which economists refer to as elasticity. In this question there is no information as to the elasticity of demand for each product; in the following therefore it is assumed that the demand for all three products is elastic (ie, a small change in price causes a greater proportionate change in demand). In this scenario a reduction in the prices of products A and B may be considered, together with an increase in the price of product C. The increase in demand in A and B should compensate for the price reduction and the increase in price of product C should enable the product to become profitable.

(4) The product mix decision is also affected by the elasticity of demand for each product, but also by the production capacities of each cell of machines. A reduction in product C would yield capacity which could be utilised by product A (saw, turn, harden, grind) at the expense of unused capacity (drilling). A reduction in B would only be effective if spare capacity in hardening would allow an increase in A to take place. A reduction in product A could allow there to be an increase in B, but this would leave spare hardening capacity, which could only be used by C (the least profitable product) if there is spare drilling capacity.

(d) The new dedicated cell layout should:

(i) reduce the costs of supervision by avoiding the problems of moving work-in-progress and of machine utilisation;

(ii) reduce material scrap by controlling the conversion process more closely;

(iii) reduce lost machine time, as the operators will become skilled in carrying out their own minor maintenance;

(iv) improve efficiency through teamwork within the cell group;

(v) reduce stock costs by improved production planning.

4 MAKE OR BUY DECISIONS

The basic point to be considered is whether data is relevant to the decision situation under review. Irrelevant cost or revenue data should be ignored. The main focus should be to determine whether there will be a net improvement in cash inflows if a particular course of action is implemented. The main cost sub-classifications which will be used are fixed and variable costs; directly attributable costs and general company costs; incremental costs and sunk costs; opportunity cost and historic costs. The relevance or irrelevance of the above may be considered in the context of the decision situation given in the question.

Make a component or buy-in from outside: In this situation the main focus will be on the incremental cost of manufacture compared with the cost from the outside supplier. A basic analysis will focus on the direct material cost, direct labour cost and variable overheads associated with making the component. In addition there may be some directly attributable fixed costs which are avoidable if the manufacture of the component is discontinued eg, salary of supervisor in manufacturing process. Any apportionment of costs which are not avoidable if the manufacture of the component is ceased should be ignored. Such costs will include a share of occupancy costs. The production capacity used to manufacture the component may be able to be utilised for another component or product. In this case the opportunity cost of the capacity ie, the contribution which it can earn for the firm should be added to the incremental cost of manufacture.

In addition, the cost of buying-in the component may be more than the supplier price. The bought-in component may require inspection on receipt and additional storage facilities which are not presently incurred. Another factor is the possible cost of delays or re-working in production because of flaws in the bought-in components.

The accuracy of the incremental cost of manufacture will be affected by a number of factors. The direct material cost will be based on the price of the materials used and the estimated level of process losses. It may be that bulk price discounts will be lost from suppliers if purchases of materials for this component are discontinued. The level of process losses may be based on past data which does not take into account potential reductions in such losses. The direct labour cost may not be wholly variable in nature in the short term. It may be that some of the employees would not be made redundant if manufacture of this component was discontinued nor would they be wholly utilised on alternative work. This could make labour a semi-variable cost, the fixed element of which must be estimated. Variable overheads may not be incurred solely in proportion to units of output. It may be that the component in question uses proportionately more of some variable items. This may mean that the cost driver(s) must be identified for variable cost items and used in determining the variable overheads for this component.

The estimation of which fixed costs are directly attributable to the component manufacture may be partly a subjective judgement. For example, which supervisor salaries will be truly avoidable if production is discontinued? The opportunity cost of buying-in the component will also be subjective in nature. There may be a danger of seriously underestimating the costs of re-work or production delays caused by the bought-in items.

5 A HEALTH CLINIC

(a)

Time	*0*	*1*	*2*	*3*	*4*	*5*	*Total*
	£'000	£'000	£'000	£'000	£'000	£'000	£'000
Contract A							
Capital outlay	(500)	(300)	(300)	(300)			(1,400)
Inflow		300	400	600	600	600	2,500
Net	(500)	Nil	100	300	600	600	1,100

Discount factor at 14%	1.000	0.877	0.769	0.675	0.592	0.519	
Present value	(500)	Nil	76.9	202.5	355.2	311.4	446
Contract B							
Capital outlay (W1)	(200)	(400)	(400)	(400)			(1,400)
Contractor fee					(425)		(425)
Net clinic inflow (W2)		225	300	450	450	600	2,025
Fitness inflow		250	250	150	150		800
Net	(200)	75	150	200	175	600	1,000
Discount factor at 14%		1.000	0.877	0.769	0.675	0.592	0.519
Present value	(200)	65.775	115.35	135	103.6	311.4	531.125

(i) Without discounting, A has the greater value and should be accepted.
(ii) After discounting, B has the greater value and should be accepted.

(b) The contractor currently receives:

25% of (300 + 400 + 600 + 600) = £475.

(i) Ignoring discounting the amount paid must be reduced by £100 to equate the total net flows (£1,100 - £1,000).

The percentage payable is thus $\frac{(£475 - £100)}{(£300 + £400 + £600 + £600)} = 19.74\%$

(ii) After discounting at 14% the present value of the amount paid must increase by (£531.125 - £446) £85.125 to equate the total net present values.

Let x represent the additional % to be paid to the contractor.

Year				
1:	$(300 \times 0.877)\ x$	=	$263.1x$
2:	$(400 \times 0.769)\ x$	=	$307.6x$
3:	$(600 \times 0.675)\ x$	=	$405.0x$
4:	$(600 \times 0.592)\ x$	=	$355.2x$
			$1,330.9x$

$1,330.9x = £85.125$

Therefore $x = \frac{£85.125}{1,330.9} = 6.4\%$

Therefore the contractor must be paid 31.4%

(c) The evaluations rely on the accuracy of the data used. The use of single-point estimates for each of the variables implies a degree of certainty which probably does not exist. An alternative is to use probability estimates for each variable - these then allow expected value techniques to be applied which will allow for variations in the input values. If such probability values are combined a model (simulation) can be built which using random numbers to generate a probability distribution of the final solution values.

In addition to the uncertainty, the major difference between the contracts is that B is more diversified. If the specialist services is successful then the rewards are shared with the contractor but so are any losses, thus the risk is being shared. This would presumably show a reduction of the clinic's control as the contractor would want some involvement in the decision making to compensate for the risk being taken. However, the clinic will also receive income from the short-term fitness monitoring scheme which diversifies the investment.

(d) The data given represent one set of variables which are expected to arise for each of contracts A and B. Such variables are likely to be subject to a degree of uncertainty. A number of quantitative techniques could be used to attempt to improve the alternative choice decision making process.

(i) Application of probabilities to a range of values for major variable and the calculation of the expected value outcome. This would also show the worst and best possible outcomes for each contract. The relevance of these figures would depend on the attitude to risk of the decision makers.

(ii) The use of sensitivity analysis, to test the sensitivity of each contract to changes in value of one or more variables.

(iii) Monte Carlo simulation uses random number generation in sampling for probabilities of variables.

WORKINGS

(W1) Since the outlay saved is also to be invested the total outlay occurs.

(W2) Years 1 - 4 = 75% of inflows from the clinic; year 5 inflow is not adjusted.

6 ANDREW MCDONALD

(Tutorial note: this question requires students to quantify the incremental effect on existing cost of diesel generated electricity by introducing windmill generation.

The two key points which make the question answerable are:

(i) windmill is used to eliminate high cost running periods of diesel generator (which is logical); and
(ii) windmill generated power can be stored in batteries.

The cost saving can be calculated by using the available windmill capacity to reduce the most expensive diesel generation costs as much as possible under each estimate.)

(a) **Analysis showing financial effect of windmill**

(i) **Daily requirement**

No. of hours	*No. of kilowatts*
1	20
2	15
4	10
2	5

(ii) **Output of windmill per annum**

		Kilowatt hours
High	250 × 12 × 4.25	12,750
Medium	200 × 12 × 4.00	9,600
Low	140 × 12 × 3.00	5,040

(iii) **Saving in kilowatt hours**

	High (kilowatt hours)	*Medium (kilowatt hours)*	*Low (kilowatt hours)*
Hourly demand - 5 kilowatts:			
365 × 5 × 2	3,650	3,650	3,650
Hourly demand - 10 kilowatts:			
365 × 10 × 4 = 14,600			
12,750 – 3,650	9,100		
9,600 – 3,650		5,950	
5,040 – 3,650			1,390

(iv) **Saving in running costs**

		High £	Medium £	Low £
5 kilowatts per hour:				
Year 1	3,650 @ £0.25	912		
Year 2	3,650 @ £0.25 × 1.10	1,004		
Year 3	3,650 @ £0.25 × 1.10^2	1,104		
Year 4	3,650 @ £0.25 × 1.10^3	1,215		
Year 5	3,650 @ £0.25 × 1.10^4	1,336		
		5,571	5,571	5,571
10 kilowatts per hour:				
Year 1	9,100 @ £0.20	1,820		
Year 2	9,100 @ £0.20 × 1.10	2,002		
Year 3	9,100 @ £0.20 × 1.10^2	2,202		
Year 4	9,100 @ £0.20 × 1.10^3	2,422		
Year 5	9,100 @ £0.20 × 1.10^4	2,665		
Year 1	5,950 @ £0.20		1,190	
Year 2	5,950 @ £0.20 × 1.10		1,309	
Year 3	5,950 @ £0.20 × 1.10^2		1,440	
Year 4	5,950 @ £0.20 × 1.10^3		1,584	
Year 5	5,950 @ £0.20 × 1.10^4		1,742	
Year 1	1,390 @ £0.20			278
Year 2	1,390 @ £0.20 × 1.10			306
Year 3	1,390 @ £0.20 × 1.10^2			336
Year 4	1,390 @ £0.20 × 1.10^3			370
Year 5	1,390 @ £0.20 × 1.10^4			407
		16,682	12,836	7,268

(v) **Summary**

	High £	Medium £	Low £
Saving in running costs	16,682	12,836	7,268
Cost of windmill	(10,000)	(10,000)	(10,000)
Batteries 20 × £50	(1,000)	(1,000)	(1,000)
Net (cost)/benefit	5,682	1,836	(3,732)
Probability	0.2	0.6	0.2

Expected value:			£
	£5,682	× 0.2	1,136
	£1,836	× 0.6	1,102
	(£3,732)	× 0.2	(746)
Expected benefit			1,492

Therefore, on the basis of expected value, the windmill should be installed.

Assumption

The windmill has zero operating costs.

(Tutorial note: alternatively the answer could be arrived at by calculating the total cost of diesel generation, then the cost of diesel and windmill generation. The difference would then be the incremental saving/cost from using the windmill. It is worth noting that the examiner used the latter approach whereas the 'incremental' approach used in the answer is more the 'management accounting' approach.)

(b) There are three (at least!) possible attitudes to risk (risk averse, risk neutral, risk seeker). The assumption often made is that decision-makers wish to avoid risk ie, are risk averse. In this case the 'risk' involved with the windmill is that there is a 0.2 probability of costs being £3,732 higher than under the present system. A risk averse decision-maker is likely to attach more importance to the possibility of the cost increase of £3,732 than the possibilities of saving £5,682.

(Tutorial note: it should be emphasised that this cost increase will be much higher when the time value of money is taken into account as the costs of the windmill and batteries are incurred at the beginning of year 1 whereas the savings accrue over the five years and are therefore worth less in present value terms. This could also convert the £1,836 cost saving into a loss in present value terms.)

Mr McDonald will have to decide whether the 0.8 (0.2 + 0.6) probability of saving £1,836 or more is sufficient to compensate for taking on the risk of losing £3,732. It is important also to bear in mind that all the figures are estimates including, for example, prediction of weather conditions over five years, and will therefore be subject to error.

7 SCOS

(a) When setting a selling price for a new product on a total cost plus profit mark-up basis, SCOS Ltd must consider the level of material, labour and overhead cost per product unit and the level of profit mark-up which it feels are desirable and relevant. A product cost specification should be prepared which details the material input quantities and anticipated scrap/loss levels plus the labour/machine operations and times for each department/process through which the product will pass. In addition, estimates will be required of material prices and labour rates of pay which will apply. Variable production overhead rates may already be available and may be applied to the new product. Where the new product is utilising existing production capacity, fixed production overhead will be absorbed at a rate per unit based on budgeted cost/budgeted activity. Administration, selling and distribution overheads may be absorbed on the basis of a budgeted percentage on production cost. Where it is recognised that the new product will incur specific additional overhead costs - such as an additional production supervisor, specially leased production equipment or specific advertising expenditure - the absorption of overhead costs may be altered from the rates used for existing products. The unitising of such additional costs over the life of the product will require some estimate of the total production/sales units of the product.

The level of profit mark-up to be applied in reaching a selling price must be chosen. It may be that SCOS Ltd has a standard mark-up which is used for all products which it is estimated will provide a satisfactory level of return on capital employed. Alternatively there may be a range of profit mark-up percentages which are applied depending on the type of product and the degree of competitiveness which exists in the market place.

(b) Where demand is expected to be price dependent, the launch price should be set at a level which it is estimated will maximise net income to SCOS Ltd. This procedure will be more difficult to implement because of the change in the state of the market after the first six months. At this point competition will lead to an agreed market price emerging, with SCOS Ltd obtaining a fixed market share which may be above or below its productive capacity. We are also told that SCOS Ltd intend to produce to maximum production capacity during the first six months and thereafter only to produce at a level to satisfy demand. The choice of initial/launch price will require an estimate of market share after the first six months, so the opportunity cost/shadow price of unsold stock at the end of the first six months may be calculated. Where market share after the first six months is expected to exceed production capacity, the opportunity cost/shadow price of the unsold stock at the end of the first six months is its selling price thereafter. Where the market share is expected to be less than production capacity, the opportunity cost/shadow price of unsold stock at the end of the first six months is its variable cost.

The forecast launch price at which the overall net margin to SCOS Ltd will be maximised will, therefore, be affected by the forecast market share after the first six months.

In a situation where some unsold stock is envisaged at the end of the 18 month period because of the level of market share obtained, the price at which such stock may be sold may also influence the initial launch price.

(c) The product was specifically launched as a World Cup commemorative product. It is implied that after the World Cup the market will collapse and unsold stocks will be difficult to sell. The costs incurred in producing the product are sunk costs which are irrecoverable if the market has collapsed. SCOS Ltd may be able to create some post-World Cup market by altering the unsold stocks in some way or by embarking on a supplementary advertising campaign. In any such exercise it should focus only on incremental costs and revenues when evaluating the financial viability of any proposed course of action. Incremental costs would include the advertising and product alteration costs mentioned above. A deduction from such costs would be the cost of disposing of the products (eg, transporting them to a tip) if they cannot be sold. Incremental revenue would be any price which can be obtained for the products.

8 DESAT ENGINEERING PLC

Workings

The best position values are selected for each variable and used together in order to prepare the budgeted profit and loss statement which represents the best possible outcome by selecting the best possible value for each variable.

Dedicated cell available capacity for the year = 65 × 46 = 2,990 hours

	Best position
Gross hours available	2,990
Less: Non-productive idle time	299 (10%)
Productive hours available	2,691

Hours required to meet sales forecast (after allowing for opening stock of valves):

	Best position		
	No of valves	*Minutes per valve*	*Total hours*
Gas	3,200	14.25	760
Steam	3,400	17.10	969
Water	3,000	22.80	1,140
Productive hours			2,869
Idle time			10%
Gross hours required (2,869/0.90)			3,188
Shortfall (2,990 – 3,188)			198 hours

Note 1: The shortfall of 198 hours in the best possible outcome means that the available hours must be allocated to valve types in a way which will maximise profit.

Note 2: Using Gas valves as an illustration of the workings:

(a) For the best position: sales = 3,000 × 1.1 = 3,300 units
Production = sales – opening stock = 3,300 – 100 = 3,200 units

(b) Minutes per valve = 15 mins × 0.95 = 14.25 minutes

(a) For the best possible position we have:

	Gas valves		Steam valves		Water valves	
	metres or hours	£	*metres or hours*	£	*metres or hours*	£
Unit data:						
Selling price		70.00		80.00		100.00
Less variable cost:						
Steel bar (at £75/metre)	0.27	(20.25)	0.36	(27.00)	0.45	(33.75)
Cell costs (at £80/hour)	0.2639	(21.11)	0.3167	(25.34)	0.4222	(33.78)
Contribution/valve		28.64		27.66		32.47
Contribution per cell hour		108.53		87.34		76.91
Hence ranking		1		2		3

Note: Example of workings for cell hours per unit:

$$\text{gas valve} = 14.25 \text{ min.}/(60 \times 0.9) = 0.2639$$

Using the available capacity in the profit maximising ranking order we produce the maximum requirement of gas and steam valves and use the residual hours for water valves:

	Gas	*Steam*	*Water*	*Total*
Production (units)	3,200	3,400	2,531	
Hours (net)	760	969	962	2,691

(b) Best possible outcome:

Budgeted profit and loss statement
for the year ended 31 December 1994

	Gas valves	*Steam valves*	*Water valves*	*Total*
Production (units)	3,200	3,400	2,531	
Sales (units)	3,300	3,520	2,611	
	£'000	£'000	£'000	£'000
Sales revenue	231.0	281.6	261.1	773.7
Cost of sales:				
Opening stock	5.0	6.6	4.8	
Production: steel	64.8	91.8	85.4	
cell costs	67.6	86.1	85.5	
	137.4	184.5	175.7	497.6
Contribution	93.6	97.1	85.4	276.1
Steel bar stock adjustment				1.7
Fixed costs				(95.0)
				182.8

Working notes: Using gas valves as the illustration:

(1) Sales units = production + opening stock = 3,200 + 100 = 3,300 units
(2) Sales revenue = 3,300 × £70 = £231,000
(3) Opening stock = 100 × £50 = £5,000
(4) Steel cost of production = 3,200 × £20.25 = £64,800
(5) Cell costs of production = 3,200 × £21.11 = £67,600

Also:

(6) Steel bar stock adjustment = 340 metres × £(75 – 70) = £1,700.

This is a contribution gain since production unit costs have been based on £75 per metre whereas opening stock was at £70 per metre.

(7) Fixed costs = £100,000 × 0.95 = £95,000

Similar calculations apply for steam and water valves.

(c) The calculations in part (b) show that the budgeted profit for the year to 31 December 1994 may be as high as £182,800 depending on the mix of uncertainty factors which apply to the range of variables in the model.

The sensitivity may be accommodated in a number of ways:

(i) Use a spreadsheet model. Where three variables are chosen, a data-table approach can list a range of net profit values for all combinations of the three variables (where a multi-page spreadsheet such as LOTUS 3.1 is used). For more than three variables being subject to change, individual combinations of variables data may be chosen as the basis of the 'what if' analysis and the resultant profit noted.

(ii) Probabilities may be applied to the likely values for each variable and the expected value outcome calculated. In addition, a range of net profit outcomes for various combined probability paths may be calculated. This would enable, for example, the calculation of the probability of net profit being less than £100,000 or greater than £150,000.

(iii) Monte Carlo simulation using random number generation in sampling from the probability distribution of variables may be used. This technique may now be implemented using spreadsheet software.

9 PARTICIPATION

Answer Plan

Budgets, management style, participation, budgetary slack, sub-optimisation, co-ordination, goal congruence, aspiration levels, target achievement.

A budget is a quantified short term plan (typically for one year) which is devolved from the long-term strategic plans and policies set out by the senior management of an organisation. The involvement, or lack of it, of middle management in the setting of budgets largely depends on the style of management used in the organisation.

There are two styles of management which are recognised: authoritarian and participative. Authoritarian management (referred to as theory X by McGregor) is based on the philosophy that people hate work and that they have to be forced to carry out their duties. This style relies on their being a clear distinction between those who manage and those who carry out tasks; there is no room in such a style for any blurring of this division and consequently budgets will be imposed without participation from middle managers. Participative management (referred to as theory Y by McGregor) is based on the philosophy that people like working and enjoy it as much as rest or play. This style relies on a sense of team spirit and involvement, and draws upon the higher level needs of job satisfaction (as expounded by Maslow). In this type of environment, participation of middle managers (and sometimes their staff) is considered the norm.

Participation can take many forms, from mere discussion to active setting of individual budgets. However, whichever form it takes, the member of middle management being asked to participate must believe that he can influence senior management by his involvement. If such influential power does not exist, the involvement is not real and is referred to as pseudo-participation which acts as a significant de-motivator since the middle manager is made aware that his views are of no interest to senior management. The real participation of middle management in the budget setting process, in theory motivates people to achieve targets, but where their performance is measured against such targets, it can influence the budget setting process by the introduction of budgetary slack and the encouragement of self-centred approaches leading to sub-optimisation and a lack of co-ordination.

Budgetary slack is the term used to describe the inclusion in a budget of excess resources/excessive costs over and above those genuinely believed to be required in order to perform the tasks efficiently. When this is done by a manager as part of his participation in the budget setting process, then if it is allowed to remain, it provides a safeguard for the manager if he is unable to achieve the real efficiency level inherent in the budget. The inclusion of such slack, however, invalidates not only the individual budget but the overall master budget of the organisation and may lead to incorrect strategic decisions.

Sub-optimisation is the term used to describe actions taken by organisational units which appear to be beneficial to the unit, but which are detrimental to the organisation as a whole. The value of an organisation is said to be greater than the sum of the values of its individual parts (synergy theory). However, personal performance evaluation of managers against their individual budgets may encourage them to take actions which are to the detriment of the organisation as a whole.

Co-ordination is the working together of two or more units for the benefit of the organisation and it should be actively encouraged by the budget setting process. Unfortunately, active middle management participation and their subsequent performance appraisal could lead to a dominance by one of the unit managers leading to a lack of co-ordination with the needs of other units to benefit the organisation as a whole.

Goal congruence is the term used to describe the equalisation of organisational objectives with the personal objectives of the middle manager. The participation of middle management in the budget setting process, in theory leads to the manager believing that the target is a personal one, the achievement of which thereby meets his personal objectives at the same time as his organisation's objectives.

An aspiration level is personal to the manager concerned. It represents the manager's opinion as to the target which he should be able to achieve. Successful budgeting requires the matching of individual aspiration levels to the level of efficiency demanded by the budget. A participative style of budget setting is more likely to achieve this than an authoritarian style, with the consequence that the target is more likely to be achieved.

The achievement of the target set out in the budget is more likely under a participative environment, because the manager accepts the target as a personal challenge which from the outset is believed to be achievable.

10 RESPONSIBILITY ACCOUNTING

Answer Plan

(a) Definition; control; responsibility of managers.

(b), (c) Type of maintenance; causal factor; agreed rates.

(a) (1) Responsibility accounting is a method of accounting which attributes costs and revenues to units of an organisation for which individual members of management are given responsibility.

(2) The manager concerned is considered to be able to control the activity of his unit and as a consequence may control the costs and revenues associated with those activities as a result of his decisions and actions. Only those costs and revenues deemed to be within the manager's area of control are reported to him.

(3) Managers are made responsible for the costs and revenues of a particular unit on the basis that he can control them. The accounting system is therefore designed to classify costs and revenues according to responsibility centre and report them to managers appropriately. The performance of the manager is then measured by comparing these costs and revenues against pre-determined agreed targets.

(b) The role of a maintenance department in such organisations is to provide services which can be classified into one of two types. One of these types is preventative maintenance. Preventative maintenance is planned and may be of a major or minor nature. The intention is to carry out such maintenance to reduce the risk of a need for ad-hoc or breakdown maintenance.

There are two aspects to preventative maintenance, the efficiency with which it is carried out, and the costs associated with any alteration to the planned timetable for its completion. The responsibility for the efficiency of the maintenance work lies with the manager of the maintenance cost centre, whereas the costs of idle time caused by alterations to planned timetables lies with the production manager who necessitated the change.

The responsibility for the costs of breakdown maintenance depends on the causal factor of the breakdown. If it were caused by the absence of or poor quality of preventative maintenance it is the responsibility of the maintenance department. However, if it is caused by misuse of the machinery by an operative, then it is the responsibility of production.

(c) (1) The accounting system must be designed in such a way as to separately identify the costs of preventative maintenance from the costs of breakdown maintenance.

(2) Within each of these two categories costs must be identified by their cause. This is achieved using the guidelines outlined in (b) above.

(3) Finally, the amounts to be charged from the maintenance cost centre to the other cost centres, where such a charge is appropriate, should be based on pre-determined agreed rates. This would be similar to a method of standard costing and would ensure that any inefficiencies in the performance of the tasks would not be transferred to the production department, even if that department caused the need for the maintenance to be carried out. Instead such inefficiencies would remain within the maintenance department.

11 RUBBLEFLINT

(a)

			Note
Chemical bearing rock (tonnes)		20,000	
Crushed rock for sale (tonnes)		12,000	1
Chemicals for separation (000 litres)		8,000	2
Chemical output for sale:	RBF1 (tonnes)	2,000	3
	RBF2 (tonnes)	4,666.67	3

Rubbleflint Ltd

Budgeted profit and loss statement for 4 week period

		£'000
Sales revenue		
RBF1 2,000 tonnes × £240		480
RBF2 4,666.67 tonnes × £120		560
Rock 12,000 tonnes × £40		480
		1,520
Costs:		
Chemical extraction		460
Crushing and water treatment		142
Chemical separation:	variable (8,000 × £12)	96
	fixed	4
		702

Production margin	818
Less administration/selling costs	650
Net profit	168

Notes:

(1) Crushed rock = 20,000 tonnes × 60% = 12,000 tonnes.

(2) Chemicals for separation = 20,000 tonnes × 40% x 1,000 litres = 8,000,000 litres.

(3) Chemical output = 8,000,000 litres/1,200 = 6,666.67 tonnes
RBF1 = 6,666.67 × 30% = 2,000 tonnes
RBF2 = 6,666.67 × 70% = 4,666.67 tonnes

(b) Costs up to the crushing and water treatment process are apportioned to joint products on a physical quantity of output basis. In the chemical separation process, unit costs for RBF1 and RBF2 are calculated after apportioning joint costs on a sales value basis. The normal losses in the chemical separation process are allowed for in the valuation of RBF1 and RBF2. Abnormal losses occur at the end of the chemical separation process and will be a weighted average of the value/tonne of RBF1 and RBF2.

(i) Crushing and water treatment: cost apportionment
Total cost = £460,000 + £142,000 = £602,000
Chemicals = 40% × £602,000 = £240,800
Rock = 60% × £602,000 = £361,200

(ii) Chemical separation: cost/tonne

	£
Total cost ex-crushing and water treatment	240,800
Chemical separation process costs	100,000
Total cost	340,800

	Sales revenue £	*Costs* £	*Quantity*	*Cost/tonne* £
RBF1	480,000	157,292	2,000	78.646
RBF2	560,000	183,508	4,666.67	39.323
	1,040,000	340,800	6,666.67	

Abnormal loss value per tonne = £340,800/6,666.67 = £51.12

(***Tutorial note:*** One might well argue that either RBFI is lost (value £78.646) or RBF2 is lost (value £39.323) or possibly both. Using this approach in part (c) avoids an awful lot of trouble.)

(c) **Chemical separation process account**

	£		*Quantity* (tonnes)	*Cost/tonne* £	£
Ex-crushing and water treatment		Normal loss	1,333.33		
(8m litres × £30.10/1,000)	240,800	RBF 1	2,000	78.646	157,292
Process cost	100,000	RBF 2	4,000	39.323	157,292
Product mix variance		Abnormal loss			
(200 tonnes × £39.323)	7,864	(yield variance)	666.67	51.12	34,080
	348,664		8,000.00		348,664

Note: The product mix and yield variances may also be calculated as follows:

		RBF1	*RBF2*	*Total*
1	Standard output expected (tonnes)	2,000	4,666.67	6,666.67
2	Actual output (tonnes) (in standard proportions)	1,800	4,200	6,000
3	Actual output (tonnes)	2,000	4,000	6,000
4	Standard cost/tonne	£78.646	£39.323	

	£	£	£
Yield variance (1 - 2) × 4	15,729 (A)	18,351 (A)	34,080 (A)
Mix variance (2 - 3) × 4	15,729 (F)	7,865 (A)	7,864 (F)

(***Tutorial note***: The above calculations give the same yield variance as the valuation of abnormal losses at the standard cost of £51.12 per tonne. However, the product mix variance is unnecessary if the abnormal loss of RBF2 is valued at £39.323 - although this is not what the examiner required, sadly.)

(d) Rubbleflint Ltd should use incremental costs and revenues in this evaluation. In this way we focus only on the additional cash flows which occur from the proposal.

Input is 8,000,000 litres.

	Tonnes
Expected yield per the original budget 8,000,000/1,200	6,666.67
Amended yield expected 8,000,000/1,100	7,272.73
Extra yield expected	606.06

Incremental revenue = 606.06 × £156	£94,545
Incremental costs:	£
Variable costs 8,000 × (£17 – £12)	40,000
Fixed costs £24,000 – £4,000	20,000
	60,000
Incremental profit	34,545

Note that the weighted average price per tonne = £240 × 0.3 + £120 × 0.7 = £156.

12 WYMA PLC

(a) Original standard data per unit:

	£	£
Selling price		80.00
Direct material cost 7 kg × £5	35.00	
Machine cost 0.3 hours × £32.43	9.73	44.73
Contribution		35.27

Note: machine cost per running hour = £30/0.925 = £32.43

Summary statement period 5

		£	£
Original budget contribution 48,000 × £35.27			1,693,000
Revision variances:	material usage	(84,700)	
	material price	(264,100)	
	machine efficiency	0	
	machine idle time	(15,200)	
	machine expenditure	47,400	
	sales price	(96,500)	(413,100)
Revised budget contribution			1,279,900
Sales volume variance			27,100
Revised standard contribution from sales achieved			1,307,000
Other variances:	sales price	(49,100)	
	material usage	(55,900)	
	material price	(93,100)	
	machine efficiency	30,500	
	machine idle time	(6,800)	
	machine expenditure	(8,500)	(182,900)
Actual contribution			£1,124,100

Note: ( ) indicates adverse variances.

(b) We must recalculate the revised unit standard data using the information available. This can be done by using the revision variances calculated in part (a) in conjunction with the original standard information given in the question.

Workings:

Material usage variance

= (original std quantity – revised std quantity) × budget units × original std price

We have -£84,700 = (7 - X) × 48,000 × £5

Solving gives X = 7.35 kilos (revised standard quantity)

Material price variance

= (original std price – revised std price) × budget units × revised std quantity/unit

We have -£264,100 = (£5 – £X) × 48,000 × 7.35

Solving gives X = £5.75 (revised standard price)

Machine time per unit remains unchanged at 0.3 hours.
(See nil revision variance in Table 1.)

Machine idle time variance

(original std idle time hours – revised std idle time hours) × original std cost per hour

We have -£15,200 = (1,168 – (14,400X/(100 – X)) × £30

Solving gives X = 10.4% (revised standard idle time)

Note: Original standard running hours for period 5 = 48,000 units × 0.3 hours = 14,400 hours. Original standard idle time = 14,400 × 0.075/(1 – 0.075) = 1,168 hours.

Machine expenditure variance

(original std cost per hour – revised std cost per hour) × revised gross hours

We have £47,400 = £30 – £X) × 16,071

Solving gives X = £27.05 (revised standard cost per hour)

Note: revised gross hours = 48,000 × 0.3/0.896 = 16,071 hours

Sales price variance

(original std price – original std price) × 48,000

We have -£96,500 = (X – 80) × 48,000

Solving we have X = £78 (revised standard selling price)

Revised standard contribution:

	£	£
Selling price		78.00
Direct material cost 7.35 kg × £5.75	42.26	
Machine cost 0.3 hours × £27.05/0.896	9.06	51.32
Contribution		£26.68

Note: A check with part (a) of the solution shows that the revised standard contribution per unit may be calculated in total as £1,279,900/48,000 = £26.66. The minor difference is due to rounding errors in the various calculations.

(c) The company is operating a standard cost system with planning and operational variance analysis. The summary statement (Table 1) shows the original budget contribution and revision variances for sales price, material and machine costs. These variances show the difference between ex ante and ex post standards at the original budgeted activity level. The revision variances are a measure of the extent to which it has been recognised that the original budget contribution has not been achieved because of permanent, non-controllable changes. Note that this has been a progressive feature, with an overall revision variance causing a fall in contribution of 9.0% in period 3, increasing to 14.6% in period 4 as the standard selling price is revised downwards, and increasing again to 24.4% in period 5. The period 5 movement in revised budget contribution is principally due to a substantial increase in standard material price. The standard revisions are an important part of the analysis as they show that either the original plans were over optimistic or that management have perhaps too readily lowered the achievement levels seen as the target for the company.

The sales volume variance indicates that the budgeted sales have not been achieved in total during periods 2 to 5. The question tells us that overall demand exceeds production capacity, yet Wyma plc have reduced the selling price. This may indicate that the company is having difficulty retaining market share, possibly due to other factors such as product reliability. The sales price reduction seems to have arrested the sales volume shortfall which has moved from a shortfall of budget contribution in period 2 to a gain of 1.6% in period 5. The sales volume variance is valued at revised standard contribution per unit which shows the opportunity cost of variations from budgeted sales. This is a useful measure as it approximates to the cash flow implications of changes in demand for the product.

The 'other variances' section of the trend statistics are the operational variances. These show the differences between the ex post standards and the actual results. Such variances should be able to be categorised as either controllable or random and non-recurring in nature. The trend in Wyma plc has been to 'slacken' standards when revisions have been made in periods 3 to 5, the exception being the machine cost per hour standard which was tightened in period 3. We would expect, therefore, that the adverse, operational variance percentages would reduce in size in periods 3 to 5. This has not occurred in some cases. This gives a focus for areas where worsening trends indicates that investigations should be expedited as a priority. For example, the material usage percentage has deteriorated from -1.1% to -3.3% from period 3 to period 5 despite the material usage standard having been revised in period 3 (see material usage revision variance of -5.0% in periods 3 to 5). The combined view of planning and operational variances is useful in showing an overall trend of movement from original (ex ante) standards to actual results. To obtain this pattern, the planning and operational variances percentages must be added together. For example, material price trend may be summarised as:

	Period 2	*Period 3*	*Period 4*	*Period 5*
Planning variances	0.00%	-6.3%	-6.3%	-15.6%
Operational variances	-5.6%	-10.0%	-12.0%	-5.5%
Total price variance	-5.6%	-16.3%	-18.3%	-21.1%

This shows an overall upward trend in material prices from the original standard of £5 per kilo.

13 ROCKALL GROUP

(a) **Rockpan division**

			£
Expected contribution (W1-3)			953,280
Less: Expected fixed cost (300,000 × 1.2)			(360,000)
Expected net profit			593,280
Sales volume variance (W4)			89,370 (F)
Sales price variance (W5)			115,500 (A)
			567,150
Cost variances:			
	F	*A*	
	£	£	
Direct material (W6)	114,240		
Direct labour (W7)	7,875		
Variable overhead (W8)		2,331	
Fixed overhead (W9)		8,880	
	122,115	11,211	110,904
Actual profit			£678,054

(b) Rockpan division's reduction in sales volume is less than that of the group, but it has not increased its prices to the same extent. This may be a deliberate policy but if it is the net effect has not been beneficial.

There has been an overall cost saving, particularly in the direct costs. It could be that the greater output level has given Rockpan better purchasing power than the other divisions which has resulted in lower prices being paid. Alternatively there may be greater efficiency of resource utilisation.

(c) The cost variances need to be analysed into their price and quantity components. This will enable variances to be reported to individual managers so that appropriate action can be taken.

WORKINGS

(W1)

Rockpan division volume in 19X0
= £2,640,000/£33 = 80,000 units

Expected volume for 19X3 = 80,000 × 80% = 64,000 units

Actual volume for 19X3 = £2,425,500/£34.65 = 70,000 units.

Volume exceeded target by 6,000 units.

(W2)

Target cost/selling price per unit for 19X3 is:

Selling price £33 + 10%	=	£36.30
Costs		
Direct material: (£960 × 1.24)/80,000	=	£14.88
Direct labour: (£360 × 1.15)/80,000	=	£5.175
Variable overhead: (£90 × 1.2)/80,000	=	£1.35
Contribution/unit	=	£14.895

(W3)

Expected contribution = 64,000 × £14.895 = £953,280

(W4)

6,000 units @ £14.895 = £89,370

(W5)

(£36.30 - £34.65) × 70,000 units = £115,500.

(W6)

(70,000 × £14.88) - £927,360 = £114,240 (F)

(W7)

(70,000 × £5.175) - £354,375 = £7,875 (F)

(W8)

(70,000 × £1.35) - £96,831 = £2,331 (A)

(W9)

£360,000 - £368,880 = £8,880 (A)

14 OPPORTUNITY COST

Opportunity may be defined as the best opportunity foregone by pursuing a given course of action. A possible problem is in the measurement of opportunity cost. It is not available in a normal accounting records system. To some extent it is a subjective measure which is constantly changing.

(a) *In standard costing.* Opportunity cost is a measure of the cost of the controllable part of operational variances, where a current efficient standard has been created which incorporates planning variances and those arising from permanent non-controllable operational factors. Opportunity cost may be seen as the contribution gain or loss arising from controllable variance factors such as marketing effort, efficiency or availability of labour or machine time.

Another illustration is the material price variance, which arises because of a management decision to use one type of material instead of another. Any adverse variance which occurs because of the material chosen is more expensive than the alternative is an opportunity cost of the decision.

A major problem in practice is the accurate analysis and identification of the variance elements which represent the opportunity cost in each case.

(b) *In transfer pricing.* Opportunity costs represents the contribution foregone by a division deciding to transfer goods or services to another division. It may vary from zero, where space capacity exists at the supplying division, to (selling price – variable cost) where the external sales are foregone. In order to achieve corporate profit maximisation, transfer prices should be set at marginal cost plus opportunity cost to the group. This may be stated as the general rule for transfer pricing whereby:

Transfer price = variable cost of goods transferred + opportunity cost to the group

This may lead to motivational problems, however, where performance measurement is affected by the transfer pricing method used. There is also the problem of the incompleteness of information as to the opportunity costs to the group of a transfer. This may detract from the use of this approach in practice.

(c) In accept/reject decisions, opportunity costs avoids the rejection of a contract on the grounds that a 'net loss' would result where conventional accounting matching of costs and revenues is applied. It recognises the sunk or unavoidable nature of many costs in the short term. For example, the original cost of material is irrelevant if the best alternative to using it on the contract is to sell it as scrap. There may even be a negative opportunity cost if by using the material on the contract the company is able to avoid disposal costs. The procedure should only be used for short-term decisions, given that opportunity cost is a subjective measure and may be subject to rapid change.

15 LATRO GROUP

(a) Consider the contribution per unit of fabric which will be earned by Latro Group from various uses/sources of fabric:

Product:	*Aye*	*Bee*	*Cee*	*External Sales (per unit of fabric)*
( ) = minus	£	£	£	£
Fabric sourcing by Numero Ltd:				
Selling price per product unit	42.00	62.00	56.00	
Less: Fabric cost (at £6.60)	(33.00)	(39.60)	(52.80)	
Conversion cost	(12.00)	(14.00)	(20.00)	
Contribution per product unit	(3.00)	8.40	(16.80)	
Contribution per fabric unit	(0.60)	1.40	(2.10)	n/a
Ranking		1		
Fabric sourcing by Exe Division:				
Selling price per product unit	42.00	62.00	56.00	9.00
Less: Fabric cost (at £4.00)	(20.00)	(24.00)	(32.00)	
Conversion cost	(12.00)	(14.00)	(20.00)	(4.00)
Contribution per product unit	10.00	24.00	4.00	5.00
Contribution per fabric unit	2.00	4.00	0.50	5.00
Ranking	3	2	4	1
Fabric sourcing by Wye Division:				
Selling price per product unit	42.00	62.00	56.00	10.00
Less: Fabric cost (at £4.80)	(24.00)	(28.80)	(38.40)	
Conversion cost	(12.00)	(14.00)	(20.00)	(4.80)

Contribution per product unit	6.00	19.20	(2.40)	
Contribution per fabric unit	1.20	3.20	(0.30)	5.20
Ranking	3	2		1

In order to maximise Latro Group contribution, the fabric available from each source should be transferred or sold in order to maximise contribution per fabric unit.

Using the ranking in the preceding calculations the Latro Group profit maximising strategy is:

		£
Sourcing from Numero Ltd:	To Division B 3,000 units × £1.40	4,200
Sourcing from Exe Division:	External sales 7,000 × £5.00	35,000
	To Division B 1,400 units × £4	5,600
Sourcing from Wye Division:	External sales 4,000 units × £5.20	20,800
	To Division B 2,000 units × £3.20	6,400
Total Latro Group contribution		72,000

This may also be expressed in terms of units of Bee and units of external fabric sales:

		£
External fabric sales:	from Exe Division 7,000 units × £5.00	35,000
	from Wye Division 4,000 units × £5.20	20,800
Sales of product Bee:	using external fabric 500 units × £8.40	4,200
	using Exe Division fabric 233.33 units × £24.00	5,600
	using Wye Division fabric 333.33 × £19.20	6,400
Total Latro Group contribution		72,000

(b) We see from the figures in (a) that external sales of fabric by Exe and Wye Divisions earn a greater contribution/unit than that earned by using the fabric to produce and sell Bee. In order to make 200 units of Aye and Cee, therefore, we should reduce sales of Bee in order to minimise the fall in Latro Group contribution.

200 units of Aye require 200 × 5 =	1,000 units of fabric
200 units of Cee require 200 × 8 =	1,600 units of fabric
Total	2,600 units of fabric

Hence the reduction in production and sales of Bee = 2,600/6 = 433.33 units.

The fall in Latro Group contribution may be calculated using any one of the fabric sourcing sets of contribution data from part (a) of the solution:

	Aye	*Bee*	*Cee*	*External*
Product change (units) ( ) = minus	200	(433.33)	200	
	£	£	£	£
Fabric sourcing by Numero Ltd:				
contribution/product unit	(3.00)	8.40	(16.80)	
group contribution gain/(loss)	(600)	(3,640)	(3,360)	(7,600)

or

Fabric sourcing by Exe Division:				
contribution/product unit	10.00	24.00	4.00	
group contribution gain/(loss)	2,000	(10,400)	800	(7,600)
or				
Fabric sourcing by Wye Division:				
contribution/product unit	6.00	19.20	(2.40)	
group contribution gain/(loss)	1,200	(8,320)	(480)	(7,600)

Hence the amended Latro Group contribution = £72,000 – £7,600 = £64,400

The particular sub-analysis of the £64,400 may be calculated in a number of ways depending upon which fabric sourcing is deemed to be diverted to Aye and Cee. For example, if we use the Numero Ltd sourcing we have:

		£
External fabric sales:	from Exe Division 7,000 units × £5.00	35,000
	from Wye Division 4,000 units × £5.20	20,800
Sales of product Bee:	using external fabric 66.67 units × £8.40	560
	using Exe Division fabric 233.33 units × £24.00	5,600
	using Wye Division fabric 333.33 × £19.20	6,400
Sales of product Aye using external fabric 200 × -£3.00		(600)
Sales of product Cee using external fabric 200 × -£16.80		(3,360)
Total Latro Group contribution		64,400

(c) The solutions in (a) and (b) require a central policy on transfer pricing and transfer destination or external sale of fabric. Such a policy requires that each division supplies information about its prices, costs and capacity opportunities. A model may then be constructed at group level and the profit maximising policy evaluated. This means that divisional autonomy is minimised.

If the divisions are given a high degree of autonomy, each will be attempting to maximise its own profit position without considering the possible impact of its actions on the overall position of Latro Group. Divisions Exe and Wye are likely to offer to transfer fabric at the external sales price available to them ie, £9 and £10 per unit respectively. At these prices even B Division would show a loss on its final product and may decide to limit its production/sales quantity to that which can be supplied by the purchase of fabric from the external company, Numero Ltd, at £6.60 per unit.

This would also reduce the production activity at Divisions Exe and Wye leaving spare capacity. It may be that Exe and Wye Divisions could increase external sales of fabric by offering the sales from spare capacity at a reduced price.

Divisions A and C may compete with Division B for the available supplies of fabric in order to maintain market share and capacity utilisation. Divisions A and C may be willing to operate at a loss in the short term. Such actions would reduce activity at Division B and would reduce Latro Group contribution in the short term.

9 NEW SYLLABUS EXAMINATIONS

JUNE 1994 QUESTIONS

16 (Question 1 of examination)

Section A – TWO questions ONLY to be attempted

A company extracts exhaust gases from process ovens as part of the manufacturing process. The exhaust gas extraction is implemented by machinery which cost £100,000 when bought five years ago. The machinery is being depreciated at 10% per annum. The extraction of the exhaust gases enhances production output by 10,000 units per annum. This production can be sold at £8 per unit and has variable costs of £3 per unit. The exhaust gas extraction machinery has directly attributable fixed operating costs of £16,000 per annum.

The company is considering the use of the exhaust gases for space heating. The existing space heating is provided by ducted hot air which is heated by equipment with running costs of £10,000 per annum. This equipment could be sold now for £20,000 but would incur dismantling costs of £3,000. If retained for one year the equipment could be sold for £18,000 with dismantling costs of £3,500.

The conversion to the use of the exhaust gases for space heating would involve the following:

(i) The removal of the existing gas extraction machinery. This could be implemented now at a dismantling cost of £5,000 with sale of the machinery for £40,000. Alternatively it could be sold in one year's time for £30,000 with dismantling costs of £5,500.

(ii) The leasing of alternative gas extraction equipment at a cost of £4,000 per annum with annual fixed running costs of £12,000.

(iii) The conversion would mean the loss of 30% of the production enhancement which the exhaust gas extraction provides for a period of one year only, until the new system is 'run-in'.

(iv) The company has a spare electric motor in store which could be sold to company X for £3,500 in one year's time. It could be fitted to the proposed leased gas extraction equipment in order to reduce the impact of the production losses during the running-in period. This course of action would reduce its sales value to company X in one year's time to £2,000 and would incur £2,500 of fitting and dismantling costs. It would, however, reduce the production enhancement loss from 30% to 10% during the coming year (year 1). This would not be relevant in year 2 because of an anticipated fall in the demand for the product.

The electric motor originally cost £5,000. If replaced today it would cost £8,000. It was purchased for another process which has now been discontinued. It could also be used in a cooling process for one year if modified at a cost of £1,000, instead of the company hiring cooling equipment at a cost of £3,000 per annum. Because of its modification, the electric motor would have to be disposed of in one year's time at a cost of £250.

Ignore the time value of money.

Required

(a) Prepare an analysis indicating all the options available for the use of the spare electric motor and the financial implications of each. State which option should be chosen on financial grounds. **(8 marks)**

(b) Prepare an analysis on an incremental opportunity cost basis in order to decide on financial grounds whether to convert immediately to the use of exhaust gases for space heating or to delay the conversion for one year.
(18 marks)

(c) Explain the steps in the construction and use of a spreadsheet model which will allow management to evaluate the financial impact of a change in one or more of the input variables on the decisions in (a) and (b) above.
(9 marks)
(Total 35 marks)

17 (Question 2 of examination)

Focusso plc makes and sells a single product. It has participated in an interfirm comparison scheme since 1 April 1991, at which time Comparito plc was identified as the most similar member company to Focusso plc with the same product, market share and cost and price structure.

Cost and revenue information for Focusso plc for the years to 31 March 1992, 1993 and 1994 is as follows:

	1992	*1992*	*1993*	*1994*
	Budget	*Actual*	*Actual*	*Actual*
	£'000	£'000	£'000	£'000
Sales revenue	1,200	1,320	1,461.6	1,625
Costs				
Direct material	480	565	512	590
Direct labour	120	136	152	171
Variable production overhead	240	253	292	330
Fixed production overhead	300	283	396	449
Selling price per unit	£150	£150	£157.50	£162.50

Stock levels remain unchanged throughout the three year period.

Focusso plc and Comparito plc both have indices of 100 for sales revenue and each element of cost in the budget for the year to 31 March 1992.

The actual indices for Comparito plc (all indices relative to the base year index of 100) for the years to 31 March 1992, 1993 and 1994 are as follows:

	1992	*1993*	*1994*
Sales revenue	106	102.9	98
Selling price	100	98	98
Costs			
Direct material	102	106	112.2
Direct labour	104	108	113
Variable production overhead	101	105	110
Fixed production overhead	100	104	108

Required

(a) Prepare a summary which shows the sales revenue index (analysed into volume and price indices) and cost indices for each element of cost for Focusso plc for each of the years to 31 March 1992, 1993 and 1994.
(9 marks)

(b) Compare the trend of sales and costs of Focusso plc over the years to 31 March 1992, 1993 and 1994 with that of Comparito plc and suggest possible reasons for the trend exhibited by Focusso plc.

You may assume that the impact of inflation on material, labour and overhead prices is approximately 5% in each year relative to the base year. Also, other changes in the Focusso plc indices are all due to positive business strategies aimed at longer term expansion and efficiency improvement. **(16 marks)**

(c) Prepare a forecast for the year to 31 March 1995 for Focusso plc which is presented to show its position relative to that forecast for Comparito plc using the following layout:

	£'000	£'000
Expected contribution for Comparito plc		X
Gain or loss for Focusso plc due to volume		X
		X
Gain or loss for Focusso plc due to		
Selling price	X	
Direct material cost	X	
Direct labour cost	X	
Variable production overhead cost	X	
		X
Expected contribution – Focusso plc		X
Less: Fixed production overhead cost		
Comparito plc	X	
Focusso plc (relative excess)	X	
		X
Expected profit – Focusso plc		X

The forecast indices for the year to 31 March 1995 (relative to the 1992 base of 100) are:

	Focusso plc	*Comparito plc*
Sales volume	135	105
Selling price	110	95
Costs		
Direct material	95	110
Direct labour	120	110
Variable production overhead	112	110
Fixed production overhead	152	110

(10 marks)
(Total 35 marks)

18 (Question 3 of examination)

Recyc plc is a company which reprocesses factory waste in order to extract good quality aluminium. Information concerning its operations is as follows:

(1) Recyc plc places an advance order each year for chemical X for use in the aluminium extraction process. It will enter into an advance contract for the coming year for chemical X at one of three levels – high, medium or low, which correspond to the requirements of a high, medium or low level of waste available for reprocessing.

(2) The level of waste available will not be known when the advance order for chemical X is entered into. A set of probabilities have been estimated by management as to the likelihood of the quantity of waste being at a high, medium or low level.

(3) Where the advance order entered into for chemical X is lower than that required for the level of waste for processing actually received, a discount from the original demand price is allowed by the supplier for the total quantity of chemical X actually required.

(4) Where the advance order entered into for chemical X is in excess of that required to satisfy the actual level of waste for reprocessing, a penalty payment in excess of the original demand price is payable for the total quantity of chemical X actually required.

A summary of the information relating to the above points is as follows:

			Chemical X costs per kg		
Level of reprocessing	*Waste available* '000 kg	*Probability*	*Advance order* £	*Conversion discount* £	*Conversion premium* £
High	50,000	0.30	1.00		
Medium	38,000	0.50	1.20		
Low	30,000	0.20	1.40		
Chemical X: order conversion:					
Low to medium				0.10	
Medium to high				0.10	
Low to high				0.15	
Medium to low					0.25
High to medium					0.25
High to low					0.60

Aluminium is sold at £0.65 per kg. Variable costs (excluding chemical X costs) are 70% of sales revenue.

Aluminium extracted from the waste is 15% of the waste input. Chemical X is added to the reprocessing at the rate of 1 kg per 100 kg of waste.

Required

(a) Prepare a summary which shows the budgeted contribution earned by Recyc plc for the coming year for each of nine possible outcomes. **(14 marks)**

(b) On the basis of maximising expected value, advise Recyc plc whether the advance order for chemical X should be at low, medium or high level. **(3 marks)**

(c) State the contribution for the coming year which corresponds to the use of (i) maximax, and (ii) maximin decision criteria, and comment on the risk preference of management which is indicated by each. **(6 marks)**

(d) Recyc plc are considering employing a consultant who will be able to say with certainty in advance of the placing of the order for chemical X, which level of waste will be available for reprocessing.

On the basis of expected value, determine the maximum sum which Recyc plc should be willing to pay the consultant for this information. **(6 marks)**

(e) Explain and comment on the steps involved in evaluating the purchase of imperfect information from the consultant in respect of the quantity of waste which will be available for reprocessing.

(6 marks)
(Total 35 marks)

Section B - TWO questions ONLY to be attempted

19 (Question 4 of examination)

Discuss the following statement giving examples to illustrate the meaning and relevance of each of points (a) and (b).

'A management accounting system may not realise its full potential because information is:

(a) insufficiently relevant **(9 marks)**
(b) subject to bias (ie. not neutral in nature).' **(6 marks)**
(Total 15 marks)

20 (Question 5 of examination)

In the operation of a standard costing system, variances may occur between the original standards for labour cost and the actual costs incurred. Such variances may be analysed into planning and operational categories.

(a) Explain the calculation and relevance of the range of variances which may appear in a summary profit statement where standard marginal costing with planning variances and operational variances is in operation, which stem from labour costs differing from the original standards. **(9 marks)**

(b) Suggest ways in which the variances may be useful to management for feedback and feedforward control purposes. **(6 marks)**
(Total 15 marks)

21 (Question 6 of examination)

Traditional budgeting systems are incremental in nature and tend to focus on cost centres. Activity based budgeting links strategic planning to overall performance measurement aiming at continuous improvement.

(a) Explain the weaknesses of an incremental budgeting system. **(5 marks)**

(b) Describe the main features of an activity based budgeting system and comment on the advantages claimed for its use. **(10 marks)**
(Total 15 marks)

EXAMINER'S COMMENTS

The overall performance indicated that there were some very well prepared candidates. However, many candidates were unable to marshall relevant data and discuss its use in control and decision making.

Question 1: tested candidates' ability to extract relevant information in order to decide on the choice and timing of a decision on the change of production equipment.

Many candidates need to improve their data presentation skills. Many candidates had only a superficial knowledge of spreadsheet models and in particular how these can help evaluate the impact of changes in one or more input variables.

Question 2: required candidates to prepare a series of revenue and cost indices for a company for a three year time period, and then implement an interfirm comparison over the period with a given set of indices for a similar company.

Many candidates failed to incorporate the relevant volume adjustment when preparing indices for variable items in part (a). Where this occurred, marks were awarded for relevant comment in part (b), using the indices calculated in (a). Where this occurred, marks were awarded for relevant comment in part (b), using the indices calculated in (a). Part (c) of the question required the preparation of a profit forecast for the coming year using a set of forecast indices. Once again, many candidates failed to incorporate the relevant volume adjustment into the calculations.

Question 3: tested candidates' ability to evaluate the financial impact of a range of outcomes of a production process where probabilities were assigned to key variables.

Many candidates were unable to interpret the range of chemical costs after taking into account discounts and premium adjustments to unit costs. Marks were awarded in parts (b) to (d) of the question for appropriate interpretation and comment, even where the figures in part (a) were incorrectly calculated. Few candidates were able to give a relevant explanation of the purchase of imperfect information in part (e).

Question 4: required candidates to discuss the impact of information relevance and bias on the ability of a management accounting system to achieve its full potential.

Many candidates tended to give a list of terms - timely, verifiability, reliability, etc, without focusing on the impact on aspects of the management accounting system. Many candidates had no idea of the ways in which bias in information could reduce the effectiveness of a management accounting system.

Question 5: required candidates to discuss the use of planning and operational variance analysis for labour costs.

This question was generally well answered, although some candidates did not focus on labour cost variance analysis.

Question 6: required candidates to explain the operation of incremental budgeting, activity based budgeting and comment on advantages which may be claimed for the use of activity based budgeting.

Many candidates wrote about activity based costing and the compilation of unit product costs rather than about activity based budgeting.

ANSWERS TO JUNE 1994 EXAMINATION

16 (Answer 1 of examination)

(a) Electric motor uses and cash flow impact of each use:

(i) **Use with exhaust gas extraction equipment**

	£
Production/sales enhancement 2,000 units × (£8 – £3) =	10,000
Less: Fitting and dismantling costs	(2,500)
Add: Sales value after one year	2,000
Net cash flow	£9,500

(ii) **Use in cooling process**

	£
Hire costs avoided	3,000
Less: Modification cost	(1,000)
Less: Disposal cost	(250)
Net cash flow	£1,750

(iii) **Hold in store and sell in one year for** £3,500

The company should use the motor in conjunction with the exhaust gases for space heating proposal during the coming year. The next best opportunity is to hold the motor in store for one year before sale rather than use it in the cooling process.

(b) Conversion to use of exhaust gases for space heating either now or in one year's time. The answer to part (a) of the question indicates that if conversion is implemented now, the spare electric motor should be used for the coming year to enhance production and then sold to company X after one year at the reduced price.

	Convert now £	*Convert in one year's time* £	*Net benefit/ (cost) of delay for one year* £
Cash inflows			
Production/sales enhancement (at £8)	72,000	80,000	8,000
Sales of space heating equipment (ducted air)	20,000	18,000	(2,000)
Gas extraction machine sale	40,000	30,000	(10,000)
Electric motor sale	2,000	3,500	1,500
	134,000	131,500	

Cash outflows			
Production/sales enhancement			
(VC at £3)	27,000	30,000	(3,000)
Exhaust gas extraction machine			
DAFC	16,000	(16,000)	
Dismantling cost	5,000	5,500	(500)
Space heating (ducted air)			
Running costs		10,000	(10,000)
Dismantling cost	3,000	3,500	(500)
Alternative exhaust gas extraction machinery			
Running cost	12,000		12,000
Leasing cost	4,000		4,000
Electric motor conversion cost	2,500		2,500
	53,500	65,000	
Net cash flow	80,500	66,500	
Net cost of delay for one year (£14,000)			(£14,000)

Note that the presentation format could vary from that shown above.

(c) The following steps should be implemented in the construction of the spreadsheet model:

(i) Identify all variables and create an input variable data section in the spreadsheet with one cell for each variable.

(ii) Create a work area in which intermediate steps in the model operation may be carried out. In this example it is necessary to evaluate the relative costs/benefits of the range of uses for the electric motor and decide which should be implemented on financial grounds (as per part (a) of the question).

(iii) Create an output section of the model, similar to the answer of part (b) of the question. Each value shown in the answer to part (b) will be the current value of a formula held in the cell memory using the relevant input variables.

The spreadsheet may then be used as a 'what if' analysis tool to evaluate the financial impact of changes in one or more of the input variables. Any combination of input variable values may be changed and the effect on the current net cost of delay in converting the space heating system may be monitored.

A one-way data table may be produced which will show the effect of a range of values of any one input variable on the net cost of delay. For example, values of production enhancement saving from 10% to 20% in bands of 1 %.

A two or three way data table may be produced, depending on the spreadsheet package in use, which will provide a matrix of solutions of net cost (or benefit) of delay from combinations of values of two or three key variables respectively.

(***Tutorial note:*** This is a commonly asked question, part (c), and you would be advised to study the words used by the examiner in his answer.)

17 (Answer 2 of examination)

(a) **Index summary – Focusso plc (all relative to 1992 budget of 100)**

	1992	*1993*	*1994*
Sales volume	110	116	125
Sales price	100	105	108.3
Costs			
Direct material	107	92	98.3
Direct labour	103	109.2	114
Production overhead			
Variable	95.8	104.9	110
Fixed	94.3	132	149.7

The sales volume for each year is calculated by dividing sales revenue by selling price. We have 1992 budget = 1,200,000/£150 = 8,000 units. Also 1993 actual = 1,461,600/£157.50 = 9,280 units. Hence the 1993 sales volume index is 9,280/8,000 = 1.16 (or 116 against a base of 100). The cost indices are calculated after adjusting the variable cost items to the 1992 budget activity level. For example the 1993 direct material index is calculated as (512/1.16)/480 = 0.92 (or 92 against a base of 100).

Note that the fixed production overhead cost indices do not require a volume adjustment. For example the 1994 index is 449/300 = 1.497 (or 149.7 against a base of 100).

(b)

	1992	*1993*	*1994*
Comparito plc sales volume index	106	105	100

The above indices are calculated as sales revenue index/selling price index. For example in 1993 102.9/98 = 1.05 (or 105 against a base of 100).

A summary of relevant points of comparison between Focusso plc and Comparito plc over the three years to 31 March 1992, 1993 and 1994 is as follows:

- Actual profits at Focusso plc for years 1992 to 1994 can be calculated as £83,000, £109,600 and £85,000 respectively.

- Market share has increased steadily to 25% above the 1992 planned level whereas Comparito plc demand has fallen back to the 1992 planned level after a 5–6% increase in 1992 and 1993.

- Focusso plc material cost index has fallen significantly in 1993 and 1994, whereas that of Comparito plc has increased at about the inflation rate. The Focusso plc material cost reduction may be due to using a more efficient processing procedure and employing higher grade workers who operate more efficiently with lower material wastage levels. To some extent the benefits gained in 1993 have been lost in 1994 (see indices of 92 and 98.3). This may require some investigation.

- Direct labour costs have increased to approximately the same extent in both companies. It is not known from the information available, however, whether Focusso plc have been using more expensive labour which has operated at an improved efficiency level thus assisting in providing increased capacity to facilitate improved market share.

- Variable production overhead cost indices for both companies have increased to 110% of the 1992 planned level.

- Fixed production overheads in Focusso plc have significantly outstripped those of Comparito plc. The overhead cost increases have occurred in conjunction with significant increases in sales (and hence production) at Focusso plc. The 1993 increase (index of 94.3 to 132) may be due to increased depreciation charges on new equipment purchased to increase production capacity. The 1994 increase (index of 132 to 149.7) may indicate the impact of a step function cost such as extra supervision costs as capacity utilisation expands to meet increased demand. The benefit of the step function in capacity may not have been translated fully into extra demand in 1994. It may be that demand in 1995 will enable the extra capacity to be fully utilised and to restore profit levels.

(**Note:** Credit will be given for alternative relevant comments.)

(c) **Forecast profit statement for the year to 31 March 1995 showing the Focusso plc forecast relative to that for Comparito plc**

	£'000	£'000
Expected contribution – Comparito plc (note 1)		226.80
Gain for Focusso plc due to volume (note 2)		64.80
		291.60
Gain or (loss) for Focusso plc due to		
Selling price (£1,200 × 1.35) × (1.10 – 0.95)	243.0	
Direct material (£480 × 1.35) × (0.95 – 1.10)	97.2	
Direct labour (£120 × 1.35) × (1.20 – 1.10)	(16.2)	
Variable prodn. o/h (£240 × 1.35) × (1.12 – 1.10)	(6.48)	
		317.52
Expected contribution – Focusso plc		609.12
Less: Fixed production overhead		
Comparito plc (£300 × 1.1)	330	
Focusso plc (relative excess)	126	
		456.00
Expected profit – Focusso plc		153.12

Notes

(1) **Comparito plc contribution**

	1992 plan £'000	*1995 indexed (no volume change)* £'000
Sales revenue	1,200 × 0.95	1,140
Variable costs	840 × 1.1	924
Contribution		216

Expected contribution 1995 = £216 × 1.05 = £226.8 (thousand).

(2) Focusso plc volume gain = £216 (1.35 – 1.05) = £64.8 (thousand).

(3) Focusso plc fixed production overhead forecast for the year to 31 March 1995 = £300 × 1.52 = £456 (thousand).

Hence excess over Comparito plc = £456 – 330 = £126 (thousand).

18 (Answer 3 of examination)

(a)

Advance order of chemical X	*Level of waste*	*Prob.*	*Contrib. (excl. X)* £'000	*Chemical X cost* £'000	*Net contrib.* £'000
High	High	0.30	1,462.5	500	962.5
	Medium	0.50	1,111.5	475	636.5
	Low	0.20	877.5	480	397.5
Medium	High	0.30	1,462.5	550	912.5
	Medium	0.50	1,111.5	456	655.5
	Low	0.20	877.5	435	442.5
Low	High	0.30	1,462.5	625	837.5
	Medium	0.50	1,111.5	494	617.5
	Low	0.20	877.5	420	457.5

Workings

(1)

	Waste available High	Medium	Low
Aluminium extracted (000 kg)	7,500	5,700	4,500
	£'000	£'000	£'000
Sales revenue (at £0.65 per kg)	4,875.0	3,705.0	2,925.0
Variable cost (at 70%)	3,412.5	2,593.5	2,047.5
Contribution	1,462.5	1,111.5	877.5

(2) **Examples of workings for chemical X cost**

- High advance level of order for chemical X and low actual requirement: The price of £1.00 is subject to a penalty of £0.60 per kg. The cost of chemical X is, therefore, 300,000 kg × £1.60 = £480,000.

- Low advance level of order for chemical X and medium actual requirement: The price is subject to a discount of £0.10 per kg. The cost of chemical X is, therefore, 380,000 × £1.30 = £494,000.

(b) The expected value (EV) contribution is calculated for each advance chemical order size by multiplying the contribution for each level of waste available by the probability of that level of waste occurring.

For example at high advance chemical X order:

EV = 962.5 × 0.30 + 636.5 × 0.50 + 397.5 × 0.20 = £686,500

Similarly:

Medium chemical X advance order:	EV = £690,000
Low chemical X advance order:	EV = £651,500

Hence the maximum expected value contribution = £690,000 when a medium advance order for chemical X is entered into.

(c) Maximax suggests that the decision maker should look for the largest possible profit from all the outcomes. In this case this is a high advance order of chemical X where there is a possibility of a contribution of £962,500. This indicates a risk seeking preference by management. Although it offers the possibility of the highest contribution, there is also a 20% likelihood that the worst outcome of £397,500 will occur. Maximin suggests that the decision maker should look for the strategy which maximises the minimum possible contribution. In this case this is a low advance order of chemical X where the lowest contribution is £457,500. This is better than the worst possible outcomes from high or medium advance orders of chemical X. This indicates a risk averse management posture.

(d) By using data from the solution to part (a), if the consultant tells the management of Recyc plc which level of waste will be available for reprocessing, they can choose the advance chemical X order strategy which will maximise contribution.

We have:

Consultant's advice	*Chemical X advance order*	*Contribution £'000*	*Prob.*	£'000
High waste	High	962.5	0.30	288.75
Medium waste	Medium	655.5	0.50	327.75
Low waste	Low	457.5	0.20	91.50
				708.00
EV without consultant's advice				690.00
Hence maximum payable to consultant				18.00

(e) Imperfect information acknowledges that the consultant's advice will not always be correct. Probabilities must be attached to the likelihood that the consultant will be correct or incorrect in his prediction. Such probabilities may be based on the level of success of the consultant in previous similar forecasts.

Posterior probabilities of a given waste level based on the combined effect of the original probabilities of waste available for processing and the probability of the actual waste level given a particular report (high, medium or low) from the consultant are then calculated.

These posterior probabilities measure the probability of a particular level of waste being available given a high, medium or low forecast.

The EV contribution is then calculated and hence the maximum sum payable to the consultant for his information.

It is argued that this procedure is more realistic than the assumption that the consultant will be able to predict the correct waste level with certainty. However it is necessary to estimate in advance the likelihood of the consultant being correct or incorrect in his forecast.

19 (Answer 4 of examination)

(a) Whether or not information is relevant and adequate for the purpose for which it is intended is the determining factor in its assisting the management accounting system to realise its full potential. A number of factors may be used to illustrate the impact of information on the effectiveness of the management accounting system. Examples are:

- Information should be both quantitative and qualitative. For example where a resource constraint exists, the contribution per unit of limiting factor may be used to determine the sequence in which the scarce resource should be allocated to products. It is also relevant, however, to take into account qualitative factors such as the effect of elimination of a product on quantitative grounds even though it is one for which an increasing market share is envisaged in future periods.
- Information should be classified in order to facilitate the implementation of relevant techniques eg. fixed/variable split to allow the use of contribution analysis.

- Information should facilitate comparison through time. For example, when examining the trend of costs it is important that information is available which enables price level changes to be allowed for in the comparison.

- The assessment of the relevance of information will depend on the purpose to which it is to be put. It may be necessary to have a material input standard per product unit specified to four decimal places, whereas a cash flow forecast may be sufficiently accurate if shown to the nearest thousand pounds.

- Information may be insufficiently relevant because it does not relate to the conditions which are likely to apply in the period in which it is being used. For example budgeted material prices and usage rates and labour rates of pay and efficiency levels may be unsuitable for use in preparing a price quotation for an order to be undertaken in six months time if the quotation is successful.

- The relevance of information may be affected by the management accounting methods in use. For example the comparison of ex-ante standards with actual costs instead of ex-post standards with actual costs.

(b) Neutrality of information implies that the information does not create bias in the management accounting system because of the nature of the information.

Much information will report only results against plan and will not measure the degree of effort expended by management. For example a variance report probably records the degree of failure to achieve a target rather than the degree of improvement from a previous actual position.

Information may be affected by events which occur elsewhere. For example idle time in one department may be caused by inefficiency in another department. If this fact is not included in the communication of the information, it is not being applied in neutral manner.

If information is neutral in nature it should not lead to opportunistic behaviour by management. For example a divisional manager may decide not to accept transfers of an intermediate product from another division because the transfer price will reduce the overall return on capital employed reported at his division. This action may not be in the interests of the achievement of corporate profit maximisation. A neutral transfer price will lead naturally to the decision being made being in the best interests of divisional and corporate goals.

(***Examiner's Note***: Relevant alternative illustrations will be accepted.)

(***Tutorial note***: 'Neutral' is not a term usually used to describe information. You need to study the examiner's understanding of the term neutral used in this context.)

20 (Answer 5 of examination)

(a) Where planning and operational variance analysis is in operation, it acknowledges the need to amend the original (ex-ante) standards to revised (ex-post) standards which incorporate any permanent changes in wages rates or labour efficiency.

In this way the comparison of ex-ante and ex-post standards measures the planning variances which are now deemed non-controllable. In a summary operating statement the valuation of such variances at the budgeted activity level measures the effect of changes in efficiency or rates of pay on budgeted contribution.

The ex-post standards are built into a revised standard contribution per product unit. In addition, the sales volume variance may be analysed to show the extent to which efficiency or idle time effects have gained or lost contribution, using the ex-post standards as the basis of the analysis.

The actual sales quantity multiplied by the revised standard contribution per unit gives the revised standard contribution valued using the ex-post standards.

The residual operational variances are calculated by comparing the ex-post standards with actual labour costs. The variances for wage rates, labour efficiency and idle time are those which are deemed controllable or random and non-recurring in nature.

(b) Feedback control involves the gathering of actual data and its comparison with control data, resulting in the measurement of deviations from the control data. The calculation of planning and operational variances provides feedback information at two levels. It measures the effect of the change from ex-ante to ex-post standards and also the differences between ex-post standards and actual cost. This gives management useful control information. It can focus on the operational variances where control action is likely to be effective and ignore the planning variances which are deemed non-controllable.

Feedforward control involves the prediction of outputs which are expected from a system at some future point in time. If the prediction differs from what is desired, actions are implemented in order to minimise the difference from the desired outcome.

As part of the forward planning process, ex-post standards may be used as the base. In addition, random, non-recurring aspects of the operational variances may be identified and eliminated from the forward planning. Plans can be formulated to eliminate part of current operational variances, particularly where this will help the achievement of a target profit level for the period under review.

21 (Answer 6 of examination)

(a) Incremental budgeting uses the previous year's budget as the starting point for the preparation of the next year's budget. It is assumed that the basic structure of the budget is acceptable and that adjustments will be made to allow for changes in volume, efficiency and price levels. The focus, therefore, tends to be on the existing use of resources rather than on identifying objectives and alternative strategies for the future budget period. It is argued that incremental budgeting does not question sufficiently the costs and benefits of operating a particular resource allocation structure.

Incremental budgeting may, therefore, be argued to have weaknesses in that:

- The resource allocation is not clearly linked to a strategic plan and the consideration of alternative strategies.
- There is a tendency to constrain new high priority activities.
- There is insufficient focus on efficiency and effectiveness and the alternative methods by which they may be achieved.
- It often leads to arbitrary cuts being made in order to meet overall financial targets.
- It tends not to lead to management commitment to the budget process.

(b) The main features and potential advantages of activity based budgeting are:

(i) The major focus is on strategically based resource allocation which aims at efficiency, effectiveness and continuous improvement. Features include:

  - Minimum and incremental levels are identified for each activity.
  - The probability of significant change from the present strategy is anticipated.
  - Key processes and constraints are identified and resource requirements quantified.
  - Efforts are made to identify critical success factors and the performance indicators which are most relevant for such factors.

(ii) Activities are seen as the key to effective planning and control.

(iii) It is argued that activities consume resources and that efforts should be focused on the control of the cause of costs not the point of incidence.

(iv) Costs are traced to activities with the creation of 'cost pools' which relate to an activity.

(v) Positive efforts are made to eliminate non-value added activities.

(vi) Focus is on total quality management with concentration on:

- Emphasis on process control through identification of cost drivers.
- The implementation of a 'right first time' philosophy aiming at zero defects.
- Measurement of total performance including cost, efficiency and effectiveness.
- Involvement of all members of the workforce.

DECEMBER 1994 QUESTIONS

Section A – TWO questions ONLY to be attempted

22 (Question 1 of examination)

Excel Ltd make and sell two products, VG4U and VG2. Both products are manufactured through two consecutive processes – making and packing. Raw material is input at the commencement of the making process. The following estimated information is available for the period ending 31 March 1995:

(i)

	Making £'000	*Packing* £'000
Conversion costs		
Variable	350	280
Fixed	210	140

40% of fixed costs are product specific, the remainder are company fixed costs. Fixed costs will remain unchanged throughout a wide activity range.

(ii) Product information:

	VG4U	*VG2*
Production time per unit		
Making (minutes)	5.25	5.25
Packing (minutes)	6	4
Production/sales (units)	5,000	3,000
Selling price per unit (£)	150	180
Direct material cost per unit (£)	30	30

(iii) Conversion costs are absorbed by products using estimated time based rates.

Required

(a) Using the above information:

(i) calculate unit costs for each product, analysed as relevant; **(10 marks)**

(ii) comment on a management suggestion that the production and sale of one of the products should not proceed in the period ending 31 March 1995. **(4 marks)**

(b) Additional information is gathered for the period ending 31 March 1995 as follows:

(i) The making process consists of two consecutive activities, moulding and trimming. The moulding variable conversion costs are incurred in proportion to the temperature required in the moulds. The variable trimming conversion costs are incurred in proportion to the consistency of the material when it emerges from the moulds. The variable packing process conversion costs are incurred in proportion to the time required for each product. Packing materials (which are part of the variable packing cost) requirement depends on the complexity of packing specified for each product.

(ii) The proportions of product specific conversion costs (variable and fixed) are analysed as follows:

Making process:	moulding (60%); trimming (40%)
Packing process:	conversion (70%); packing material (30%)

(iii) An investigation into the effect of the cost drivers on costs has indicated that the proportions in which the total product specific conversion costs are attributable to VG4U and VG2 are as follows:

	VG4U	*VG2*
Temperature (moulding)	2	1
Material consistency (trimming)	2	5
Time (packing)	3	2
Packing complexity	1	3

(iv) Company fixed costs are apportioned to products at an overall average rate per product unit based on the estimated figures.

Required

Calculate amended unit costs for each product where activity based costing is used and company fixed costs are apportioned as detailed above. **(12 marks)**

(c) Comment on the relevance of the amended unit costs in evaluating the management suggestion that one of the products be discontinued in the period ending 31 March 1995. **(4 marks)**

(d) Management wish to achieve an overall net profit margin of 15% on sales in the period ending 31 March 1995 in order to meet return on capital targets.

Required

Explain how target costing may be used in achieving the required return and suggest specific areas of investigation. **(5 marks)**

(Total 35 marks)

23 (Question 2 of examination)

Trenset plc has a semi-automated machine process in which a number of tasks are performed. A system of standard costing and budgetary control is in operation. The process is controlled by machine minders who are paid a fixed rate per hour of process time. The process has recently been reorganised as part of an ongoing total quality management programme in the company. The nature of the process is such that the machines incur variable costs even during non-productive (idle time) hours. Non-productive hours include time spent on the rework of products. *Note that gross machine hours = productive hours + non-productive (idle time) hours.*

The standard data for the machine process are as follows:

(i) Standard non-productive (idle time) hours as a percentage of gross machine hours is 10%.

(ii) Standard variable machine cost per gross hour is £270.

(iii) Standard output productivity is 100% ie, one standard hour of work is expected in each productive machine hour.

(iv) Machine costs are charged to production output at a rate per standard hour sufficient to absorb the cost of the standard level of non-productive time.

Actual data for the period August to November has been summarised as follows:

	August	*September*	*October*	*November*
Standard hours of output achieved	3,437	3,437	4,061	3,980
Machine hours (gross)	4,000	3,800	4,200	4,100
Non-productive machine hours	420	430	440	450
Variable machine costs (£'000)	1,100	1,070	1,247	1,218

Variance analysis

	£	£	£	£
Productivity	42,900 (A)	?	?	99,000 (F)
Excess idle time	6,000 (A)	?	?	12,000 (A)
Expenditure	20,000 (A)	?	?	111,000 (A)

Variance analysis (in % terms)

	%	%	%	%
Productivity	4.2 (A)	?	7.4 (F)	?
Excess idle time	5.0 (A)	?	4.8 (A)	?
Expenditure	1.9 (A)	?	10.0 (A)	?

Required

(a) Calculate the machine variances for productivity, excess idle time and expenditure for each of the months September and October. **(12 marks)**

(b) In order to highlight the trend of the variances in the August to November period, express each variance in percentage terms as follows:

Productivity variance: as a percentage of the standard cost of production achieved.

Excess idle time variance: as a percentage of the cost of expected idle time.

Expenditure variance: as a percentage of hours paid for at standard machine cost per hour.

(**Note:** The August and October calculations are given in the question.) **(6 marks)**

(c) Comment on the trend of the variances in the August to November period and possible inter-relationships, particularly in the context of the total quality management programme which is being implemented. **(8 marks)**

(d) Management are considering an investigation of the excess idle time variance during December. The decision whether to investigate will be made on the basis of the following estimated figures:

(i) The average excess idle time variance will be eliminated at the end of March as the existing total quality management programme takes effect. Until that time it is estimated that the excess idle time variance will continue to occur each month at a level equal to 75% of the November variance. The December idle time variance will remain unaffected irrespective of the action taken, and should not be included in your calculations.

(ii) The additional investigation will have an initial cost of £1,500 to determine whether the variance is controllable in the January to March period.

(iii) The cost of taking control action will be £7,000 per month which would eliminate the variance from January onwards if the variance responds to the planned control action. The variance may not respond to the control action and remain unchanged.

(iv) The probability that the variance is controllable in the January to March period is 0.4.

(v) The probability that the variance will respond to the proposed control action is 0.8.

Advise management of the expected net cost or benefit of the investigation proposal and comment on the reliability of the results obtained. Your answer should include a decision tree illustration of the situation.

(9 marks)
(Total: 35 marks)

24 (Question 3 of examination)

Bushworks Ltd convert synthetic slabs into components AX and BX for use in the car industry. Bushworks Ltd is planning a quality management programme at a cost of £250,000. The following information relates to the costs incurred by Bushworks Ltd both before and after the implementation of the quality management programme:

Synthetic slabs

Synthetic slabs cost £40 per hundred. On average 2.5% of synthetic slabs received are returned to the supplier as scrap because of deterioration in stores. The supplier allows a credit of £1 per hundred slabs for such returns. In addition, on receipt in stores, checks to ensure that the slabs received conform to specification costs £14,000 per annum.

A move to a just-in-time purchasing system will eliminate the holding of stocks of synthetic slabs. This has been negotiated with the supplier who will deliver slabs of guaranteed design specification for £44 per hundred units, eliminating all stockholding costs.

Curing/moulding process

The synthetic slabs are issued to a curing/moulding process which has variable conversion costs of £20 per hundred slabs input. This process produces sub-components A and B which have the same cost structure. Losses of 10% of input to the process because of incorrect temperature control during the process are sold as scrap at £5 per hundred units. The quality programme will rectify the temperature control problem thus reducing losses to 1 % of input to the process.

Finishing process

The finishing process has a bank of machines which perform additional operations on type A and B sub-components as required and converts them into final components AX and BX respectively. The variable conversion costs in the finishing process for AX and BX are £15 and £25 per hundred units respectively. At the end of the finishing process 15% of units are found to be defective. Defective units are sold for scrap at £10 per hundred units. The quality programme will convert the finishing process into two dedicated cells, one for each of component types AX and BX. The dedicated cell variable costs per hundred sub-components A and B processed will be £12 and £20 respectively. Defective units of components AX and BX are expected to fall to 2.5% of the input to each cell. Defective components will be sold as scrap as at present.

Finished goods

A finished goods stock of components AX and BX of 15,000 and 30,000 units respectively is held throughout the year in order to allow for customer demand fluctuations and free replacement of units returned by customers due to specification faults. Customer returns are currently 2.5% of components delivered to customers. Variable stock holding costs are £15 per thousand component units.

The proposed dedicated cell layout of the finishing process will eliminate the need to hold stocks of finished components, other than sufficient to allow for the free replacement of those found to be defective in customer hands. This stock level will be set at one month's free replacement to customers which is estimated at 500 and 1,000 units for types AX and BX respectively. Variable stockholding costs will remain at £15 per thousand component units.

Quantitative data

Some preliminary work has already been carried out in calculating the number of units of synthetic slabs, sub-components A and B and components AX and BX which will be required both before and after the implementation of the quality management programme, making use of the information in the question. Table 1 summarises the relevant figures.

Table 1

	Existing situation		Amended situation	
	Type A/AX (units)	Type B/BX (units)	Type A/AX (units)	Type B/BX (units)
Sales	800,000	1,200,000	800,000	1,200,000
Customer returns	20,000	30,000	6,000	12,000
Finished goods delivered	820,000	1,230,000	806,000	1,212,000
Finishing process losses	144,706	217,059	20,667	31,077
Input to finishing process	964,706	1,447,059	826,667	1,243,077
	2,411,765		2,069,744	
Curing/moulding losses	267,974		20,907	
Input to curing/moulding	2,679,739		2,090,651	
Stores losses	68,711		–	
Purchase of synthetic slabs	2,748,450		2,090,651	

Required

(a) Evaluate and present a statement showing the net financial benefit or loss per annum of implementing the quality management programme, using the information in the question and the data in Table 1.

(All relevant workings must be shown) **(27 marks)**

(b) Explain the meaning of the terms internal failure costs, external failure costs, appraisal costs and prevention costs giving examples of each. **(8 marks)**

(Total 35 marks)

Section B TWO questions ONLY to be attempted

25 (Question 4 of examination)

(a) The transfer pricing method used for the transfer of an intermediate product between two divisions in a group has been agreed at standard cost plus 30% profit mark-up. The transfer price may be altered after taking into consideration the planning and operational variance analysis at the transferor division.

Discuss the acceptability of this transfer pricing method to the transferor and transferee divisions. **(5 marks)**

(b) Division A has an external market for product X which fully utilises its production capacity.

Explain the circumstances in which division A should be willing to transfer product X to division B of the same group at a price which is less than the existing market price. **(5 marks)**

(c) An intermediate product which is converted in divisions L, M and N of a group is available in limited quantities from other divisions within the group and from an external source. The total available quantity of the intermediate product is insufficient to satisfy demand.

Explain the procedure which should lead to a transfer pricing and deployment policy resulting in group profit maximisation. **(5 marks)**

(Total 15 marks)

26 (Question 5 of examination)

(a) Explain the meaning and relevance of the term 'critical success factors' in a business, giving examples of such factors. **(6 marks)**

(b) If productivity is seen as a critical success factor in a manufacturing environment, suggest ways in which the management accountant should check that adequate control is being exercised over productivity measurement and over its use as a control mechanism.

(9 marks)
(Total 15 marks)

27 (Question 6 of examination)

'Endogenous and exogenous variables, policies, performance measures and intermediate variables are all relevant in model building for short-term decisions.'

Explain the meaning of each term in the above statement, giving examples in the context of multi-product production and sales in a company with limited production capacity. **(15 marks)**

EXAMINER'S COMMENTS

General comments

Questions 1 and 3 formed the basis of a pass for many candidates. Section A questions were generally well answered, although question 2 was answered by relatively few candidates. The answers to section B questions were poor. Candidates must answer the question set and not simply write down a series of general comments about the topic. The overall level of performance was encouraging and there were some very well prepared candidates.

Question 1: tested candidates ability to prepare unit product costs using volume related and activity based approaches to the charging of overhead costs. The question asked for comment on a management suggestion that one of the products be discontinued.

In this context, the relevant analysis would require the unitising of all fixed costs in order to show why the management suggestion had been made (ie, a perceived net loss being reported). Comment could then be made about the sunk nature of fixed costs. Candidates were given credit for acceptable comments and analysis. Many candidates were unable to explain the meaning and use of target costing.

Question 2: required candidates to calculate standard cost variances for two months and to express variances in percentage terms in order that a trend analysis could be commented on.

Many candidates did not attempt to comment on possible inter-relationships of variances or on the impact of the total quality programme on the variances.

Few candidates were able to support their answer with relevant calculations.

Question 3: required candidates to abstract relevant information from that given in the question in order to evaluate the financial cost or benefit of implementing a quality management programme.

Most candidates were able to abstract relevant quantitative information and express it in financial terms using the information given. Many answers did not achieve higher marks due to poor presentation.

Question 4: required candidates to explain or discuss the impact of specific circumstances on the acceptability/implementation of transfer pricing.

Many candidates gave simply a general exposition on transfer pricing methods in answer to each of parts (a) to (c). Few candidates even mentioned the relevance of planning and operational variances in (a) and few mentioned the use of an LP model in (c).

Question 5: tested candidates' understanding of critical success factors in business.

Most candidates simply listed some methods by which productivity may be measured, failing to note ways in which the management accountant should ensure that productivity measurement is being adequately controlled and effectively used as a control mechanism.

Question 6: tested candidates' ability to explain the meaning of various elements which are relevant in the structure of a model for short term decision making.

The question indicated that examples should be given in the context of a multi-product company with limited production capacity. Some candidates did not give examples and hence lost marks.

ANSWERS TO DECEMBER 1994 EXAMINATION

22 (Answer 1 of examination)

(a) (i) **Unit costs**

		VG4U	VG2
		£	£
Direct material		30.00	30.00
Variable conversion cost	– Making	43.75	43.75
	– Packing	40.00	26.67
		113.75	100.42
Product specific fixed costs			
Making		10.50	10.50
Packing		8.00	5.33
Total product specific cost		132.25	116.25
Company fixed cost			
Making		15.75	15.75
Packing		12.00	8.00
Total cost		160.00	140.00

Workings

Total estimated minutes

Making: 8,000 × 5.25 = 42,000
Packing: 5,000 × 6 + 3,000 × 4 = 42,000

Absorption rate per product unit (both products)

Making: Variable (£350,000/42,000) × 5.25 = £43.75
Fixed (£210,000/42,000) × 5.25 = £26.25

Note that fixed costs are 40% product specific and 60% company cost.

Packing cost per minute

Variable: £280,000/42,000 = £6.666
Fixed: £140,000/42,000 = £3.333

Unit costs are determined as cost per minute × minutes per unit.

eg, VG4U variable cost = £6.666 × 6 minutes = £40.00
VG2 fixed cost = £3.333 × 4 minutes = £13.33

Note that fixed costs are 40% product specific and 60% company cost.

(ii) The management suggestion is presumably based on the apparent net loss on each unit of VG4U when total cost is compared with selling price ie, £150 – £160 = £10 loss. This is incorrect in the short term in that VG4U is contributing £150 – £132.25 = £17.75 per unit to company fixed costs. Note that it is relevant to consider the product specific fixed costs as part of the relevant unit costs.

Discontinuing product VG4U would mean a fall in profit for the period to 31 March 1995 of £88,750 (£17.75 × 5,000 units) unless there is an alternative opportunity for the production capacity.

(b) Costs are charged to each activity in the estimated proportions and then to each product using the cost driver proportions given in the question.

		Total	*VG4U*	*VG2*
Product units			5,000	3,000
	(%)	£	£	£
Variable conversion cost				
Moulding (temperature)	(60)	210,000	140,000	70,000
Trimming (consistency)	(40)	140,000	40,000	100,000
Packing (time)	(70)	196,000	117,600	78,400
Packing material (complexity)	(30)	84,000	21,000	63,000
			318,600	311,400
Cost per product unit			63.72	103.80
Product specific fixed costs				
Moulding (60% × £84,000)		50,400	33,600	16,800
Trimming (40% × £84,000)		33,600	9,600	24,000
Packing (70% × £56,000)		39,200	23,520	15,680
Packing material (30% × £56,000)		16,800	4,200	12,600
			70,920	69,080
Cost per product unit			14.18	23.03

Company fixed costs = £210,000 + 140,000 – 70,920 – 69,080 = £210,000

Overall average cost per unit = £210,000/8,000 = £26.25

Hence amended unit costs are as follows:

	VG4U	*VG2*
	£	£
Direct material cost	30.00	30.00
Variable conversion costs	63.72	103.80
	93.72	133.80
Product specific fixed costs	14.18	23.03
	107.90	156.83
Company fixed cost	26.25	26.25
	134.15	183.08

(c) The total unit costs now show product VG2 as incurring a small loss of £3.08 per unit (£180 – £183.08). The relevant figure in the short term, however, is the product margin of £23.17 which is earned by VG2 (£180 – £156.83). Activity based costing gives unit product costs which have recognised the cost drivers which exist and which cause costs to occur. The ABC unit costs may be argued to be more accurate and hence provide a better measure of product unit margin and net profit for decision-making.

(d) When target costing is used it is necessary to focus effort on reducing costs for each product in order that the desired profit margin is achieved. The existing selling prices, costs and sales volume will result in an overall net profit of £70,000. This gives a net profit margin of 5.4% on sales. The required return is 15%. Given that the selling prices and sales quantities are to remain unchanged, costs must be squeezed if the required return is to be achieved.

Excel Ltd can examine the design specification for each product and the production methods in order to look for ways in which costs may be reduced without impairing the acceptability of the products to the customer.

Examples are:

- eliminate part of the material requirement
- use a cheaper material
- reduce the incidence of each of the cost drivers.

(Other examples could be given.)

23 (Answer 2 of examination)

(a) **Machine process variance calculations**

Note that standard charge rate per machine hour to allow for standard idle time = £270/0.9 = £300.

Productivity variance

= (Standard hours produced – Useful machine hours) × Standard rate per hour

Sept = [3,437 – (3,800 – 430)] × £300
= £20,100 (F)

Oct = [4,061 – (4,200 – 440)] × £300
= £90,300 (F)

Excess idle time variance

= (Expected idle time – Actual idle time) × Standard rate per hour

Sept = [(3,800 × 10%) – 430] × £300
= £15,000 (A)

Oct = [(4,200 × 10%) – 440] × £300
= £6,000(A)

Expenditure variance

= (Gross machine hours × Standard rate per hour) – Actual cost

Sept = (3,800 × £270) – £1,070,000
= £44,000 (A)

Oct = (4,200 × £270) – £1,247,000
= £113,000 (A)

(b)

		Aug	*Sept*	*Oct*	*Nov*
1.	Standard hours of production	3,437	3,437	4,061	3,980
2.	Gross machine hours	4,000	3,800	4,200	4,100
3.	Expected idle time hours (row 2 × 10%)	400	380	420	410
4.	Standard cost of production (row 1 × £300)	1,031,100	1,031,100	1,218,300	1,194,000
5.	Expected cost of idle time (row 3 × £300)	120,000	114,000	126,000	123,000
6.	Standard cost of machine time (row 2 × £270)	1,080,000	1,026,000	1,134,000	1,107,000

Variances [from question and answer (a)]:

7.	Productivity	(£)	(42,900)	20,100	90,300	99,000
8.	Excess idle time	(£)	(6,000)	(15,000)	(6,000)	(12,000)
9.	Expenditure	(£)	(20,000)	(44,000)	(113,000)	(111,000)

Variances (as percentages):

Productivity (row 7/row 4)	–4.2%	1.9%	7.4%	8.3%
Excess idle time (row 8/row 5)	–5.0%	–13.2%	–4.8%	–9.8%
Expenditure (row 9/row 6)	–1.9%	–4.3%	–10.0%	–10.0%

Note: In the above calculations, ( ) or – denotes adverse variances.

(Note that some of the above variance information was given in the question.)

(c) The variance trend for August to November may be summarised as follows:

- productivity has improved throughout the period
- excess idle time has fluctuated from month to month but has been adverse in all months
- expenditure has increased from August to October with the November variance being the same percentage (10%) as that in October.

Variance causes and interrelationships could be:

- Productivity in October and November shows a significant improvement which may have been achieved through increased expenditure on additional machine minders as indicated in the increased level of expenditure variance in October and November.
- The impact of the recent reorganisation of the machine process may have been under-estimated and a machine minder learning curve may have contributed to the productivity improvement.
- The fluctuating idle time may indicate that the 'right first time' philosophy of total quality management is not yet being achieved and varying levels of rework may be contributing to the idle time (non-productive time) reported.
- The improved productivity may be due, in part, to an improving impact of just-in-time procedures which ensure that input material of the required specification is available when required.

(Other relevant explanations would be accepted.)

(d) A decision tree representation may be shown as:

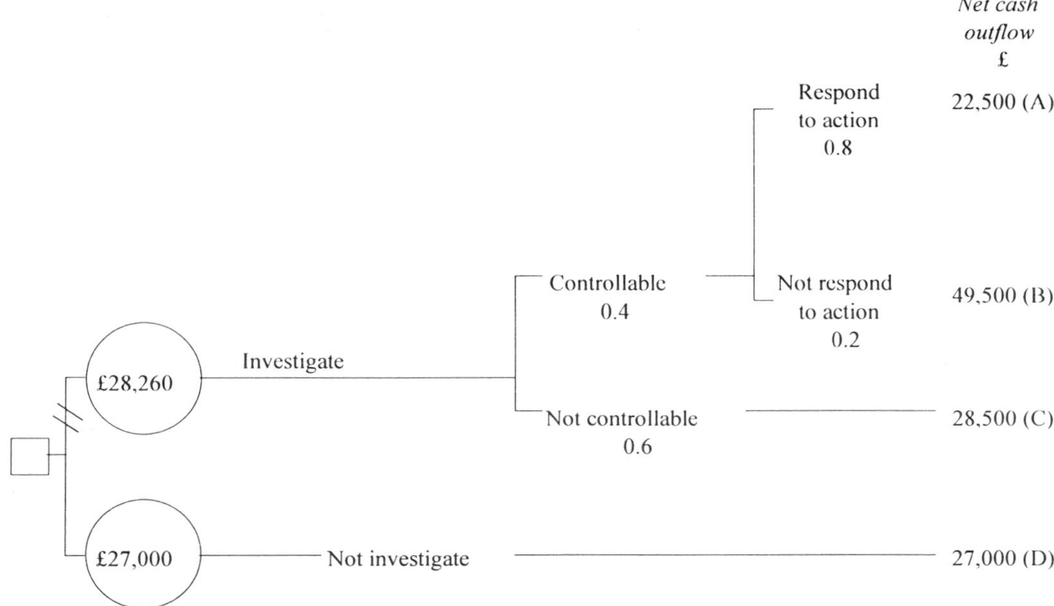

Workings for net cash outflows

	A £	*B* £	*C* £	*D* £
Initial investigation cost	1,500	1,500	1,500	–
Control action cost (£7,000 × 3)	21,000	21,000	–	–
Idle time variance cost				
If non-controllable (£12,000 × 75% × 3)	–	–	27,000	27,000
If controllable and responds	–	–	–	–
If controllable but does not respond	–	27,000	–	–
Total	22,500	49,500	28,500	27,000

The decision tree shows that the net cost over the January to March period of investigating the excess idle time variance is £1,260. It is better, therefore, not to investigate.

This could have been calculated in net terms as:

Benefits – Costs

= £9,000 × 3 × 0.32 – £1,500 – (3 × £7,000 × 0.4) = £8,640 – £1,500 – £8,400 = –£1,260

The reliability of the solution depends on the reliability of the data used.

- How accurate is the estimate of the excess idle time cost during the January to March period?
- What is the basis for the probabilities used? Are they based on historic observations which may not apply in the present TQM situation?
- How accurate are the estimates of the costs of control action and the variance saving which will result therefrom?

24 (Answer 3 of examination)

(a) **Financial (cost)/benefit of proposed changes**

	£
Elimination of synthetic slabs stock	
Stores losses 68,711 units × (£40 – 1)/100	26,797
Specification check	14,000
Savings on purchase quantity of synthetic slabs	
(2,748,450 – 2,090,651) × £40/100	263,120
Less: Increased price: 2,090,651 × £4/100	(83,626)
Curing/moulding process costs	
Variable cost reduction (2,679,739 – 2,090,651) × £20/100	117,818
Scrap sub-component sales forgone (267,974 – 20,907) × £5/100	(12,353)
Finishing process cost reduction	
Variable cost reduction (see note 1)	158,656
Scrap sales forgone (361,765 – 51,744) × £10/100	(31,002)
Finished goods stock	
Holding costs (45,000 – 1,500) × £15/1,000	653
	454,063
Less: Cost of quality management programme	250,000
Net (cost)/benefit of proposed changes	204,063

Note 1: Variable cost reduction

	£
Existing cost	
Type AX 964,706 × £15/100 =	144,706
Type BX 1,447,059 × £25/100 =	361,765
	506,471
Amended cost	
Type AX 826,667 × £12/100	(99,200)
Type BX 1,243,077 × £20/100	(248,615)
Net reduction in cost	158,656

(b) *Internal failure costs* occur when work fails to reach the design quality standards and the failure is detected before transfer to the customer. Examples include material losses in stores before issue, losses in a curing/moulding process and in a finishing process.

External failure costs occur when the product fails to reach design quality standards and failure is not detected until after transfer to the customer. An example is the free replacement of defective units returned by customers.

Appraisal costs are those associated with the evaluation of purchased material, processes and services to ensure conformance with the agreed specification. Examples include the inspection of synthetic slabs on receipt, the inspection of sub-components in curing/moulding and inspection of finished components.

Prevention costs are those associated with the implementation of a quality management programme. They are planned prior to the actual operation and are aimed at 'doing it right first time'. The total cost of the programme is estimated at £250,000 per year. Some of this will be spent on the improved temperature control in the curing/moulding. Expenditure on the alteration of the production cycle, such as the move to a JIT purchasing system and the conversion to a dedicated cell layout in finishing, will also help prevent quality losses.

(***Tutorial note:*** There is a minor inconsistency between the question and the answer. The benefit of reduced stores losses of slabs has been taken twice in (a). This would reduce the net benefit by 68,711 × (£40 ÷ 100) = £27,484 to £176,579).

25 (Answer 4 of examination)

(a) The use of a standard cost based transfer price is argued to be effective in that the transferor division is not allowed to pass on to the transferee division any inefficiencies in its operation. Such inefficiencies are left as adverse variances to be reported at the transferor division. The transferor division may be faced, however, with cost increases due to permanent and non-controllable changes from the original standards. For example, the acceptable level of material usage may have been underestimated or the wage rates finally negotiated with the employee representatives may have been understated. Such permanent changes may be reported as planning variances which may then be incorporated into a revised standard which reflects current efficient costs at the transferor division. In this way the transferor division is allowed to pass on such permanent cost changes to the transferee division. The residual variances are the operational variances which are still taken to be the responsibility of the transferor division and will be reported at that point. Operational variances will include items such as the cost of excess idle time due to poor production scheduling or increased material prices due to inefficient purchasing procedures.

(b) The normal criterion would be that division A should be able to charge division B with the market price of product X. The reasoning for this would be that the opportunity cost forgone by the group would be the contribution earned by division A from the external sale. Internal transfers between divisions in a group may not incur some costs which apply to external sales. For example the packing costs may be significantly reduced and transport may be arranged more cheaply on group vehicles. In this case the opportunity forgone by the group must be adjusted by the external costs which have been avoided. If division A transfers at a price which is reduced by the costs avoided, it will still report the same profit and its rate of return will be unaffected.

(c) Where there is a shortage of the intermediate product, a linear programming model can be formulated centrally which incorporates all relevant information about the selling prices and conversion costs of divisions L, M and N which are receiving it for conversion and sale, together with the external opportunities (if any) of the intermediate products. The solution to the linear programming model will then show to which divisions the available supplies of intermediate products should be directed in order to maximise group profit. The model will also show the shadow prices of the intermediate products which indicate the scarcity value of such products. The shadow price shows the extent to which profits can be increased if one additional unit of the scarce intermediate product is made available.

26 (Answer 5 of examination)

(a) Critical success factors are those areas of a business and its environment which are critical to the achievement of its goals and objectives. A company may, for example, express its main goal as being a world class business in its chosen areas of operation. Management should identify critical success factors since failure in any one such factor may prevent or inhibit the advancement of the company and the achievement of its goals. Lewis (1980) outlines as critical success factors – profitability, market position (ie, market share), productivity, product leadership, personnel development, employee attitudes, public responsibility, balance between short range and long range goals.

(Other relevant comment and examples would be accepted.)

(b) Where productivity is seen as a critical success factor it is necessary to maintain tight control over its measurement and interpretation. The main focus is likely to be on the results ie, the output measure and its use. The results may also be influenced, however, by control of the actions of those involved in tasks which influence the productivity measure.

Relevant checks that adequate control is being exercised over productivity measurement and use are:

- Is the productivity measurement congruent with the desired result? For example, a higher productivity measure may be obtained in one department which simply leads to higher levels of work in progress with consequent additional costs.

- Is the productivity measurement sufficiently accurate? It is important that the actual result is determined by and measured against well tested and agreed standards and not some crude measure. The productivity measure can only be used as a useful control base if it is an accurate measure of the desired goal or objective.

- Is the productivity measure objective and free from bias? For example, bias may occur where there is the capacity to make value judgements as to the inclusion of certain classes of idle time or rework in the productivity measure. Lack of control in this context could lead to action which will not result in a relevant strategy for the future. In addition, control must be implemented in order to ensure that the data is not manipulated in order to give measures which are acceptable to management, but which do not reflect what has actually occurred.

- Is the measure available at the appropriate time? If the productivity measure is to be used as a signal for control action it must be available quickly and at regular intervals. Where the technology permits, this could be available as part of an on-line information analysis in a computer integrated manufacturing system.

- Is the measure understandable? It is important that the users of the measure are conversant with its uses and limitations. The trend should be viewed as well as individual measures in order to monitor where an 'out of control' situation is indicated.

- Are the rewards (and punishments) associated with good (or bad) results significant and clearly defined? The behaviour of individuals in the provision of information and the acceptance of its use is likely to be influenced by the way in which the control process is implemented.

27 (Answer 6 of examination)

Endogenous variables are those which are under the control of the decision maker. They may also be called decision variables. The decision maker may be able to choose the price at which a product is sold and/or the amount to be spent on advertising. These variables are likely to influence demand for the product. Exogenous variables are those which are not controlled by the decision maker. They are external variables which are outside the decision maker's influence. For example, the price of raw materials may be determined by overall market forces with the decision maker unable to exert any influence on it.

Policies may exist which limit the decision-making process. For example, there may be an internal policy not to sub-contract production where company production capacity is a constraint. This may be because of concern about the quality of sub-contract work or its cost. There may be external constraints which limit the decision environment such as a ban on exporting certain products to specified countries. Again, there may be special packaging requirements for sales to specific destinations or product design specification constraints.

Performance measures are necessary in order that output from the model may be measured against the goals or objectives which the decision maker wishes to achieve. The goal may be to maximise profit in the short term, hence profit will be the performance measure. Alternatively it may be that maximising market share or ensuring a minimum market for all products is the first priority.

Intermediate variables occur where it is necessary to relate the endogenous and exogenous variables to the performance measure. An example would be the calculation of the contribution per unit of limiting factor in order to determine the ranking sequence in which products should be produced using the available production capacity, in order to achieve a profit maximising situation.

(Other examples would be accepted.)

JUNE 1995 QUESTIONS

Section A – TWO questions ONLY to be attempted

28 (Question 1 of examination)

Dry Dry Dry is a pop group which wishes to forecast the likely net profit or loss for a forthcoming tour. Appendix 1 shows a spreadsheet model of the likely financial implications of the tour. The variable data in rows 6 to 20 of the spreadsheet quantifies the current estimate of the financial implications of the tour as follows:

(i) Ticket sales are at a single selling price.

(ii) Merchandising sales are at a standard markup on cost.

(iii) A support band will pay a fee to be allowed to appear with Dry Dry Dry. The fee will be £10,000 where ticket sales are 25,000 tickets. The fee is **reduced** by 5% of the additional revenue from ticket sales in **excess** of 25,000 tickets or **increased** by 5% of the reduction in revenue from ticket sales **below** 25,000 tickets.

(iv) The promoter is paid a basic fee based on ticket sales of 30,000 tickets. This is **increased** by 10% of the additional revenue from ticket sales in **excess** of 30,000 tickets or **reduced** by 10% of the reduction in revenue from ticket sales **below** 30,000 units.

(v) The manager and agent are each paid on a commission only basis at a fixed percentage of ticket sales revenue.

(vi) Sundry fixed costs include transport, accommodation, lighting, etc.

The outline of the budgeted profit and loss statement is shown in rows 27 to 49 of Appendix 1.

Required

(a) Prepare the budgeted profit and loss statement for the Dry Dry Dry tour based on the input data in Appendix 1 showing all relevant workings. **(7 marks)**

(b) Explain the meaning of the information in the two-way data table shown in Appendix 1 and comment on the range of figures, including reference to your answer to part (a) of the question. **(6 marks)**

(c) Ticket sales quantity and commission and fee levels have been identified as the key variables. Probabilities have been estimated for the level at which the key variables (as shown in the data table) will occur. It has been assumed that all commission and fee levels will increase or decrease by the same percentage independently of the sales quantity. Additional relevant information is as follows:

Sales quantity (units)	*Probability*	*Commission/fee index*	*Probability*
24,000	0.25	1.2	0.2
36,000	0.60	1.0	0.7
40,000	0.15	0.9	0.1

(i) Prepare a summary which shows the range of possible net profit or loss outcomes, showing the combined probability of each outcome. **(8 marks)**

(ii) Calculate the expected value of net profit or loss, indicating how you have arrived at your answer. **(2 marks)**

(iii) Using your answer to (c)(i), calculate the cumulative probability of the net profit being not less than £100,000. **(2 marks)**

(d) Explain how the demand/price relationship could be incorporated into the model where it is estimated that an increase or decrease in price of £0.50 from the level in Appendix 1 will result in a decrease or increase respectively in forecast sales of 1,000 units. This rate of variation will apply for all levels of demand. In particular, state and illustrate the formula which would enable the ticket price to be calculated in the spreadsheet model in Appendix 1 for any ticket sales quantity and demand/price relationship. **(10 marks)**

(Total 35 marks)

29 (Question 2 of examination)

BS Ltd provides consultancy services to small and medium sized businesses. Three types of consultants are employed offering administrative, data processing and marketing advice respectively. The consultants work partly on the client's premises and partly in BS Ltd premises, where chargeable development work in relation to each client contract will be undertaken. Consultants spend some time negotiating with potential clients attempting to secure contracts from them. BS Ltd has recently implemented a policy change which allows for a number of follow-up (remedial) hours at the client's premises after completion of the contract in order to eliminate any problems which have arisen in the initial stages of operation of the system. Contract negotiation and remedial work hours are not charged directly to each client. BS Ltd carries out consultancy for new systems and also to offer advice on existing systems which a client may have introduced before BS Ltd became involved. BS Ltd has a policy of retaining its consultancy staff at a level of 60 consultants on an ongoing basis.

Additional information for the year ended 30 April 1995 is as follows:

(i) BS Ltd invoices clients at £75 per chargeable consultant hour.

(ii) Consultant salaries are budgeted at an average per consultant of £30,000 per annum. Actual salaries include a bonus for hours in excess of budget paid for at the budgeted average rate per hour.

(iii) Sundry operating costs (other than consultant salaries) were budgeted at £3,500,000. Actual was £4,100,000.

(iv) BS Ltd capital employed (start year) was £6,500,000.

(v) Table 1 shows an analysis of sundry budgeted and actual quantitative data.

Required

(a) (i) Prepare an analysis of actual consultancy hours for the year ended 30 April 1995 which shows the increase or decrease from the standard/allowed non-chargeable hours. This increase or decrease should be analysed to show the extent to which it may be shown to be attributable to a change from standard in:

(1) standard chargeable hours;
(2) remedial advice hours;
(3) contract negotiation hours;
(4) other non-chargeable hours. **(13 marks)**

(ii) Calculate the total value of each of (1) to (4) in (a)(i) above in terms of chargeable client income per hour. **(4 marks)**

(b) BS Ltd measure business performance in a number of ways. For each of the undernoted measures, comment on the performance of BS Ltd using quantitative data from the question and your answer to (a) to assist in illustrating your answer:

(i) Financial performance
(ii) Competitive performance
(iii) Quality of service

(iv) Flexibility
(v) Resource utilisation
(vi) Innovation.

(18 marks)
(Total 35 marks)

Table 1 for use with question 2

BS Ltd
Sundry statistics for year ended 30 April 1995

	Budget	*Actual*
Number of consultants		
Administration	30	23
Data processing	12	20
Marketing	18	17
Consultants hours analysis		
Contract negotiation hours	4,800	9,240
Remedial advice hours	2,400	7,920
Other non-chargeable hours	12,000	22,440
General development work hours (chargeable)	12,000	6,600
Customer premises contract hours	88,800	85,800
Gross hours	120,000	132,000
Chargeable hours analysis		
New systems	70%	60%
Existing systems advice	30%	40%
Number of clients enquiries received		
New systems	450	600
Existing systems advice	400	360
Number of client contracts worked on		
New systems	180	210
Existing systems advice	300	288
Number of client complaints	5	20
Contracts requiring remedial advice	48	75

30 (Question 3 of examination)

Milbao plc make and sell three types of electronic game for which the following budget/standard information and actual information is available for a four-week period:

Model	*Budget sales (units)*	*Standard unit data Selling price £*	*Variable cost £*	*Actual sales (units)*
Superb	30,000	100	40	36,000
Excellent	50,000	80	25	42,000
Good	20,000	70	22	18,000

Budgeted fixed costs are £2,500,000 for the four-week period. Budgeted fixed costs should be charged to product units at an overall budgeted average cost per unit where it is relevant to do so.

Required

(a) Calculate the sales volume variance for each model and in total for the four-week period where (i) turnover (ii) contribution and (iii) net profit is used as the variance valuation base.

(9 marks)

(b) Discuss the relative merits of each of the valuation bases of the sales volume variance calculated in (a) above.

(6 marks)

(c) Calculate the TOTAL sales quantity and sales mix variances for Milbao plc for the four-week period, using contribution as the valuation base. (Individual model variances are not required.) **(4 marks)**

(d) Comment on why the individual model variances for sales mix and sales quantity may provide misleading information to management. (No calculations are required.) **(4 marks)**

(e) The following additional information is available for the four-week period:

(1) The actual selling prices and variable costs of Milbao plc are 10% and 5% lower respectively, than the original budget/standard.

(2) General market prices have fallen by 6% from the original standard. Short-term strategy by Milbao plc accounts for the residual fall in selling price.

(3) 3% of the variable cost reduction from the original budget/standard is due to an over-estimation of a wage award, the remainder (ie, 2%) is due to short-term operational improvements.

(i) Prepare a summary for a four-week period for model 'Superb' ONLY, which reconciles original budget contribution with actual contribution where planning and operational variances are taken into consideration. **(8 marks)**

(ii) Comment on the usefulness to management of planning and operational variance analysis in feedback and feedforward control. **(4 marks)**

(Total 35 marks)

Section B – TWO questions ONLY to be attempted

31 (Question 4 of examination)

Explain how each of the undernoted quantitative ideas and techniques may improve the budgetary planning process, suggesting a specific aspect of budgetary planning in which each may be used:

(a) Learning curve
(b) Linear regression analysis
(c) Linear programming
(d) Economic order quantity
(e) Probability estimates.

(Note that detailed technical descriptions of each of (a) to (e) is NOT required.) **(15 marks)**

32 (Question 5 of examination)

Energy costs may include the following items in a company which manufactures and sells products:

- Maintaining a statutory temperature range in the workplace
- The operation of a specially humidified materials store
- Power costs per unit of output
- Power costs in the movement of raw materials and work in progress
- Losses from steam pipelines and steam valves
- Heat losses through windows

Explain how management may be assisted in the implementation of an energy cost reduction strategy through the application of (a) zero-base budgeting and (b) total quality management. Your answers to (a) and (b) should each refer to any THREE of the energy cost examples given in the question.

(15 marks)

33 (Question 6 of examination)

Lack of co-ordination between strategic planning and operational planning may result in *unrealistic plans, inconsistent goals, poor communication* and *inadequate performance measurement.*

(a) State key features or characteristics which should be incorporated in each of strategic planning and operational planning. **(7 marks)**

(b) Name and comment on examples of the cost implications of each of the factors shown in italics in the above statement which may occur from lack of relevant and appropriate operational planning. Your answer should be in the context of a strategic planning goal of sustaining competitive advantage at minimum cost through speedy delivery of quality products to customers. **(8 marks)**

(Total 15 marks)

APPENDIX 1 (for use with question 1)

	A	B	C	D	E	F	G
3	Budgeting/planning model						
4	Variable data input:						
5							
6	Ticket sales:	Quantity	36,000	Ticket price (£)	15		
7							
8	Merchandising:	Sales (£)	48,000	Markup (%)	50%		
9							
10	Support band:	Basic fee (£)	10,000	Adjustment (%)	5%	Trigger (quantity)	25,000
11							
12	Promoter:	Basic fee (£)	75,000	Adjustment (%)	10%	Trigger (quantity)	30,000
13							
14	Manager:	Commission (%)	20%				
15							
16	Agent:	Commission (%)	10%				
17							
18	Sundry fixed costs:	£	225,000				
19							
20				Commission and fee index		1.00	

APPENDIX 1 (for use with question 1 – continued)

	A	B	C	D	E	F
25	*Output*					
26					*Dry Dry Dry tour*	
27						
28					*Budgeted profit and loss statement*	
29				£		£
30	Revenue from ticket sales					540000
31						
32	Profit from merchandising					16000
33						
34	Support band fee (net)					1750
35						
36	**Total income**					557,750
37						
38						
39	Promoter fee (net)					
40						
41	Manager commission (net)					
42						
43	Agent commission (net)					
44						
45	Sundry fixed costs					
46						
47	**Total cost**					
48						
49	**Net profit or loss**					

APPENDIX 1 (for use with question 1 – continued)

	A	B	C	D	E	F	G	H
55			Two-way data table monitoring changes in net profit					
56			for a range of changes in ticket quantity and commission and fee levels					
57		**Note:**	**Support band and promoter BASIC fees are EXCLUDED from the indexing process**					
58						*Commission and fee index*		
59			+F49	0.8	0.9	1.0	1.1	1.2
60		Ticket	20,000	–31,000	–38,125	–45,250	–52,375	–59,500
61		sales	24,000	7,400	–2,425	–12,250	–22,075	–31,900
62		(units)	28,000	45,800	33,275	20,750	8,225	–4,300
63			32,000	84,200	68,975	53,750	38,525	23,300
64			36,000	122,600	104,675	86,750	68,825	50,900
65			40,000	161,000	140,375	119,750	99,125	78,500
66			44,000	199,400	176,075	152,750	129,425	106,100

ANSWERS TO JUNE 1995 EXAMINATION

28 (Answer 1 of examination)

Examiner's comments and marking guide

Question 1: tested candidates' ability to prepare output information from input variable data provided. In addition, it tested candidates' ability to comment on and abstract information from a spreadsheet datatable and use such information as part of a probability analysis exercise. It also tested candidates' understanding of demand/price relationships and their incorporation into the spreadsheet model of the situation.

Many candidates were unable to calculate the combined probabilities required in part (c). Some candidates attempted to calculate the net profit or loss for each outcome in (c) instead of simply extracting the relevant values from the datatable given in the question paper. A number of candidates were able to explain the formulation of the linear price/demand formula for use in the model, but many candidates were unable to cope with this requirement.

		Marks	
(a)	Revenue from ticket sales	0.5	
	Merchandising profit	1.0	
	Support band fee	2.0	
	Promoter fee	2.0	
	Manager commission	0.5	
	Agent commission	0.5	
	Sundry fixed cost	0.5	
		—	7
(b)	Basic explanation of data content	1	
	Profit per (a) referred to in data table	1	
	B/E position - comments	2	
	Worst outcome/best outcome situations	2	
	(other relevant comment accepted)	—	6
(c)	Combined probabilities	4	
	Net profit/loss values (from data table)	4	
		—	8
	EV calculation		2
	Cum prob of profit of £100,000 or more		2
(d)	Statement and explanation of price/demand formula	3	
	Derivation of specific formula using data in Appendix 1	4	
	Explanation of incorporation of formula for price into spreadsheet model as intermediate variable	3	
		—	10
			—
Total			35

Step by step answer plan

Step 1 Read the question again and make sure that you focus on precisely what is required. The question requires you to use data supplied in the spreadsheet (including datatable) in the appendix, and you should initially look carefully at this in conjunction with the question to work out the information you are being given.

Step 2 (a) You are given a format for the profit and loss within the spreadsheet, so follow that. Make sure you show all the workings, as asked - these can be shown on the face of the statement itself.

Step 3 (b) The information shown in the data table is not so obvious as that shown in the first part of the spreadsheet, so take time to ensure you understand it. The explanation is given to you in the heading to the table - the figures in the body of the table are the net profit/loss figures (not changes in profit as stated in the heading) resulting from different combinations of the two key variables referred to in the question - these form the column and row labels. The first figure to identify is the current net profit (as computed in (a)), corresponding to current ticket sales and commission/fee index given in the first part of the spreadsheet. To comment on the range of figures, you can first identify the highest and lowest profit levels; then it will be useful to comment on the points at which profits turn to losses, ie the break-even points.

Step 4 (c) Note that the main work you have to do here is the probability combinations - the profits/losses for all the expected combinations have already been done for you in the datatable discussed in (b). The probabilities for each sales level in combination with each fee index are multiplied together to get the overall probability of the particular combination (an application of the multiplication law of probability). The expected value is then obtained by multiplying each combined probability by the corresponding profit/loss taken from the datatable and the probability of profit being £100,000 or more can be obtained by adding together the probabilities corresponding to all profits over £100,000 (an application of the addition law)

Step 5 (d) The requirements here are to formulate the general and specific demand equation ("state"), show how it can be used to predict ticket price from quantity ("illustrate"), and explain how this can be incorporated into the spreadsheet as an intermediate variable.

Step 6 Now review your answer and ensure that it does precisely answer the question as set.

The examiner's answer

(a) Using the layout shown in Appendix 1, the forecast profit and loss statement will appear as follows:

Dry Dry Dry tour
Budgeted profit and loss statement

	£	£
Revenue from ticket sales		
36,000 × £15		540,000
Profit from merchandising		
48,000 × 0.50/1.50		16,000
Support band fee (net)		
10,000 + (25,000 – 36,000) × 0.05 × £15		1,750
Total income		557,750
Promoter fee (net)		
75,000 + (36,000 – 30,000) × 0.1 × £15	84,000	
Manager commission (net)		
£540,000 × 0.2	108,000	
Agent commission (net)		
£540,000 × 0.1	54,000	
Sundry fixed costs	225,000	
Total cost		471,000
Net profit or loss		86,750

(b) The two-way data table shows the net profit or loss for each of a range of combinations of ticket sales and commission/fee levels, using the variable data in the model.

- The existing situation is for ticket sales of 36,000 tickets and a commission/fee index level of 1.00. This may be read from the table to show a net profit of £86,750. Note that this corresponds to the answer calculated in part (a) of the question.

- The data table shows that the tour will break even at a ticket sales level between 24,000 and 28,000 tickets for all commission/fee levels except when commission/fee levels are 20% above the current level, when the break even sales will be between 28,000 and 32,000 tickets.

- The worst possible outcome in the range shown is a loss of £59,500 (top right). The best possible outcome in the range shown is a net profit of £199,400 (bottom left).
(TN1)

(c) (i) The range of possible outcomes using the probability estimates quoted are:

Sales (units)	*Prob.*	*Commission /fee index*	*Prob.*	*Combined prob.*	*Net profit /(loss) (£)*
24,000	0.25	1.2	0.2	0.050	(31,900)
		1.0	0.7	0.175	(12,250)
		0.9	0.1	0.025	(2,425)
36,000	0.60	1.2	0.2	0.120	50,900
		1.0	0.7	0.420	86,750
		0.9	0.1	0.060	104,675
40,000	0.15	1.2	0.2	0.030	78,500
		1.0	0.7	0.105	119,750
		0.9	0.1	0.015	140,375
				1.000	

(ii) For each row in the above table, multiply the combined probability by the net profit or loss and sum the answers.

The expected value profit is £62,058.50.

(iii) The cumulative probability of a net profit of not less than £100,000 occurring is 0.18. This is obtained from the table in part (i) above as 0.060 + 0.105 + 0.015 = 0.18.

(d) This monitors the relative change in demand for a given change in price. The price at any level of ticket sales may be expressed as the formula $P_Q = P_0 - aQ$

where
P_Q = price at ticket level Q
P_0 = price when ticket sales are zero
a = the rate of change of price per unit
Q = ticket sales level

The formula may be rearranged as $P_0 = P_Q + aQ$.

Using the data in Appendix 1 and the question we have:

$$\begin{aligned} P_0 &= P_Q + aQ \\ &= £15 + 0.0005 \times 36{,}000 \\ &= £33 \end{aligned}$$

The formula may thus be redefined as $P_Q = £33 - 0.0005Q$

For example at 28,000 tickets, $P_Q = 33 - 0.0005 \times 28{,}000 = £19$

The model may be amended by including the value for the rate of change per unit (a) as a variable data input item instead of the ticket price in cell E6. The formula for P_Q is then included in the model as an intermediate variable which will be recalculated for each value of ticket sales quantity (per cell C6). The intermediate variable value for ticket price will then be used in the relevant cell formulae in the output area of the model. The net profit will then be calculated using the ticket price together with the other variable data input as given.

Tutorial notes

1 As an example of how the figures have been derived, this figure shows the net profit from ticket sales of 20,000, and a commission/fee index of 0.8:

	£	£
Revenue (**20,000** × £15)		300,000
Profit from merchandising (as (a))		16,000
Support band fee (net)		
10,000 + (25,000 - **20,000**) × 0.05 × £15 × **0.8**		13,000
		329,000
Promoter fee (net)		
75,000 + (**20,000**-30,000) × 0.1 × £15 × **0.8**	63,000	
Manager commission (net) (300,000 × 0.2 × **0.8**)	48,000	
Agent commission (net) (300,000 × 0.1 × **0.8**)	24,000	
Sundry fixed costs	225,000	360,000
Net loss		**£(31,000)**

2 Most people will treat the general equation of a straight line demand curve as P = a – bQ, making subscripts unnecessary.

29 (Answer 2 of examination)

Examiner's comments and marking guide

Question 2: part (a) required candidates to prepare an analysis of chargeable and non-chargeable hours for a consultancy services business in order to show the quantity (hours) and value (in pounds) of each class of variance. Part (b) required comment on a range of performance measures relevant to the service business and to illustrate using data from a table of quantitative information provided in the question.

Most candidates failed to flex the budgeted hours analysis to the actual level of activity and hence obtained an inaccurate comparison. Some marks were awarded for relevant comparison and valuation of variances even where the appropriate flexing of the budget was not implemented.

Many answers to part (b) made little attempt to relate the comments to the question scenario and provided no reference to the quantitative measures provided in the question, eg, a high level of customer complaints as an indication of quality problems.

			Marks	
(a)	1.	Capacity gain over budget	4	
	2.	Excess remedial advice hours	3	
	3.	Excess contract negotiation hours	3	
	4.	Excess 'other' non-chargeable hours	3	
				13
(b)		Value of client income gains/losses (4 × 1)		4
(c)		Comments (on merit) (6 × 3)		18
Total				35

Step by step answer plan

Step 1 Read the question again and make sure that you focus on precisely what is required. Again, although the main body of the question is quite short, there is a lot of data in the table to assimilate. Have a careful look at this to ascertain what information you have been given.

Step 2 (a) Before you start your answer to (i), make sure you think about the layout - allow enough room to evaluate the hours as required in (ii). The requirement here is to compare the actual hours for each of the four categories given with the *standard hours for actual gross hours* ie against a *flexed* budget. The evaluation in (ii) shows the impact of excess non-chargeable hours on income - each extra non-chargeable hour spent means one less chargeable hour being available. However, this is partly mitigated by an increase in overall capacity (TN 1)

Step 3 (b) It is essential that you link your answer to the company and data used in the question. You should have learnt the general types of measures for each of the areas specified; jot these down then think how they could be applied to the data given for BS Ltd - in particular the data you haven't yet used, but also your answer to (a). Don't go overboard on any one area - there are equal marks for each.

Step 4 Now review your answer and ensure that it does precisely answer the question as set.

The examiner's answer

(a) (i) and (ii)

	Hours *Budget*	*Actual*	
Gross hours	120,000	132,000	
Non-chargeable hours			
Standard (16%)	(19,200)	(21,120)	
Excess		(18,480)	see analysis below
Chargeable hours	100,800	92,400	

	Hours *Standard*	*Actual*	*Variance*	*(ii) Client income gains/losses at £75/hour* £
Gross hours	132,000	132,000		
Non-chargeable hours				
Contract negot. (std. 4%)	5,280	9,240	(3,960)	(297,000)
Remedial advice (std. 2%)	2,640	7,920	(5,280)	(396,000)
Other (std. 10%)	13,200	22,440	(9,240)	(693,000)
Chargeable hours	110,880	92,400	(18,480)	
Budget chargeable hours	100,800			
Capacity gain over budget (TN 1)	**10,080**		10,080	756,000
Net fall in chargeable hours			**(8,400)**	**(630,000)**

Adverse variances in the workings are denoted as ( ).

(b) (i)

BS Ltd
Summary profit and loss account for the year ended 30 April 1995

	Budget £'000	*Actual* £'000
Revenue from client contracts (chargeable hours × £75)	7,560	6,930
Costs		
Consultant salaries (TN 2)	1,800	1,980
Sundry operating costs	3,500	4,100
	5,300	6,080
Net profit	2,260	850
Capital employed	6,500	6,500
Financial ratios		
Net profit: Turnover	29.9%	12.3%
Turnover: Capital employed	1.16 times	1.07 times
Net profit: Capital employed	34.8%	13.1%

The above figures show that BS Ltd has a poor *financial performance* during the year to 30 April 1995 compared to that budgeted. Client income is down and operating costs have increased. It would be useful, however, to have a more detailed analysis which attempts, where possible, to link the fall in profit to quality, flexibility, resource utilisation and innovation factors. In addition, it would be useful to have a longer term trend of financial results in order to see whether the current year figures are representative of a continuing decline or are due to specific short-term conditions.

The financial performance may be examined in more detail by establishing reasons for the fall in chargeable hours. The information in part (a) of the answer analyses the £630,000 fall in revenue and attempts to link it to specific factors such as increased time on remedial advice to clients.

(ii) *Competitiveness* may be measured in terms of market share or sales growth. BS Ltd turnover for the year to 30 April 1995 is lower than budgeted. The trend for the past five years may show a steady growth, however, indicating a high level of competitiveness in the longer term. The 1995 failure to achieve budgeted profit may be due to efforts to improve longer term competitiveness eg, through the retention of 60 consultants and the offer of 'free' remedial advice to clients.

Competitiveness may also be measured in terms of the relative success/failure in obtaining business from clients. Table 1 data shows that the budgeted uptake from client enquiries is 40% for new systems and 75% for existing systems advice. The actual percentages are 35% and 80% respectively. For new systems business the percentage has fallen, but the number of new systems worked on has increased from budget (210 from 180). For existing systems advice, although the percentage uptake is higher than budget, the total number of clients is down (288/300) on budget.

(iii) *Quality* is the totality of features of a service package which bear upon its ability to satisfy customer needs. Key quality factors must be identified and monitored in quantitative and/or qualitative ways. To some extent the increased level of remedial advice, an extra 5,280 hours compared to flexed budget, may indicate a quality problem. The question does indicate, however, that this is an innovation on the part of BS Ltd with a view to future demand improvement. The information in Table 1 indicates that client complaints were four times the budgeted level (20 compared with 5). Also, the number of clients requiring remedial advice was 75 compared to a budget level of 48. BS Ltd should investigate the reasons for the increases in order to identify and eliminate quality problems.

(iv) *Flexibility* may relate to the company being able to cope with flexibility of volume, delivery speed or job specification. We are told that BS Ltd retains 60 consultants in order that it has increased flexibility in meeting demand. The mix of consultants available will be another indicator of flexibility. Table 1 shows a change in mix from that budgeted which may indicate a high level of awareness of market changes and the need to provide for such changes. Delivery speed should be aided by the policy of retaining consultants and the mix of staff available. The ability to cope with a range of job specifications may be linked to the mix of consultants available. BS Ltd has moved to a work ratio of existing systems advice: new systems of 40%: 60% compared to a budget ratio of 30%: 70% which may indicate an ability to be flexible in response to market demands. Flexibility will be achieved at a cost. The analysis in part (a) of the answer shows the level of excess non-chargeable consultant hours. This may reflect the policy of retention of the consultancy team at 60 consultants.

(v) *Resource utilisation* may be measured in terms of output to input consultant hours. In the budget the hours charged to clients represents 84% of gross hours. The actual percentage for the year to 30 April 1995 was 70% of gross hours (92,400/132,000). There is a trade-off between resource utilisation, flexibility and innovation. The strategy implemented must be viewed not only in terms of the results for the current year, but also in terms of the likely impact on future levels of client demand. The increased level of remedial advice (6% of gross hours compared to 2% in the budget) may be viewed as a longer term investment.

(vi) *Innovation* should be viewed in terms of its impact on financial performance, competitiveness, quality, flexibility and resource utilisation in both the short and long term. BS Ltd has an innovative feature in allowing 'free' remedial advice after the completion of a contract. In the short term this is adversely affecting financial performance. The answer to part (a) of the question shows that remedial advice hours are 5,280 hours in excess of the standard allowance of 2% of gross hours. This may have resulted in loss of fee income from contracts forgone. The excess hours may also indicate that the **process** of remedial advice needs to be reviewed. It may be necessary to limit the level of such advice on any one contract. This sort of decision is very much a value judgement which must balance potential future benefits against current financial costs.

Did you answer the question?

Note that the examiner addresses each area by first giving a brief explanation of the aspect being measured - one sentence. He then immediately gets down to specifics relating to BS Ltd, drawing on the data supplied and the analysis computed in (a).

Tutorial notes

1 In order to reconcile the budgeted revenue (from chargeable hours) to the actual revenue, two basic differences need to be recognised. First, given the actual level of hours worked (132,000), the proportion of chargeable to non-chargeable is lower than expected; secondly, the overall capacity of hours available is higher than expected. This is summarised as follows

		hours	£'000	*Variance*
Actual revenue		92,400	6,930	
	Loss due to excess non-chargeable hours			**(1,386)**
Standard revenue		110,880	8,316	
(132,000 × 84%)	**Gain from increase in capacity**			**756**
Budgeted revenue		100,800	7,560	
(120,000 × 84% hours)				
Total variance		**(8,400)**		**(630)**

2 Consultant salaries:

Budget :	basic	(30 + 12 + 18) × £30,000 =	£1.80m
			£m
Actual :	basic	(23 + 20+17) × £30,000 =	1.80
	bonus	(10% increase in hours) 10% × £1.8m =	0.18
			£1.98m

30 (Answer 3 of examination)

Examiner's comments and marking guide

Question 3: tested candidates' ability to calculate and comment on sales variance analysis, together with the use of planning and operational variances as a planning and control aid.

Most candidates made a good attempt at parts (a) to (c) of the question. Part (d) asked for comments on the relevance of individual model variances for sales mix and sales quantity. The use of the weighted average approach was noted at the November 1994 Teachers' Conference as being non-examinable, following the abandonment of this method in the 8th edition of Horngren/Foster. Candidates were given credit for any relevant comment in part (d).

In part (e) many candidates were unable to use the information provided in order to prepare the summary statement illustrating the planning and operational variance analysis.

				Marks	
(a)	Calculations:	turnover basis		3	
		contribution basis		3	
		net profit basis		3	
				—	9
(b)	Discussion (on merit)				6
(c)	Calculations:	sales quantity var		2	
		sales mix var		2	
				—	4
(d)	Comments (on merit)				4
(e)	(i)	Original budget contribution		1	
		Revision variances:	selling price	1	
			variable cost	1	
		Sales volume variance		1	
		Residual variances:	selling price	1	
			variable cost	1	
		Overall presentation and sub-totals		2	
				—	8
	(ii)	Comments (on merit) -	re feedback	2	
		-	re feedforward	2	
				—	4
Total					35

Step by step answer plan

Step 1 Read the question again and make sure that you focus on precisely what is required. It is a variance analysis question, with an emphasis on sales variances, and incorporating planning and operational variances.

Step 2 (a) (b) These parts contrast the various ways of evaluating the effects of changes in sales volumes (individually, for each model) - in terms of revenue or margin (marginal/absorption). The basic variance can be calculated in terms of units first, then multiplied by each of the valuation bases in turn. Your discussion must highlight relative merits of each - you are not being asked to say which is best.

Step 3 (c) Having looked at individual volume variances for each product, you are now asked to consider the sales overall, and compute mix and quantity variances. Even though you are told that individual model variances are not required, if you are used to computing the total figures via a split between models, that is fine. The key extra piece of information you need is the contribution from actual total sales quantity in standard mix.

Step 4 (d) You may or may not have actual figures for individual model mix/quantity variances from (c). It doesn't matter, these figures are not actually required. As the examiner says, you do not need to refer to particular ways of valuing the individual variances - just comment upon the general information that may be conveyed by splitting the variance up.

Step 5 (e) You are now given information that allows the computation of a revised (ex-ante) standard as well as actual contribution per unit. This allows a planning and operational variance analysis to be carried out in reconciling budget contribution with actual. The basic approach is to start with (original) budgeted contribution, then use planning variances to adjust this to revised budgeted contribution, showing separately the effects of the change in selling price and variable cost per unit (using the originally budgeted volume, as this has not been revised). The remaining difference is due to operational factors, and normal variance analysis is carried out, with the revised figures used in place of the original.

The linking of planning and operational variances with feedback and feedforward control is popular with the examiner and requires a clear but precise explanation for four marks here.

Step 6 Now review your answer and ensure that it does precisely answer the question as set.

The examiner's answer

(a)

	Superb	*Excellent*	*Good*	*Total*
1. Budget sales (units)	30,000	50,000	20,000	100,000
2. Actual sales (units) in std. proportions	28,800	48,000	19,200	96,000
3. Actual sales (units)	36,000	42,000	18,000	96,000
Standard unit valuations:				
4. Selling price (£)	100	80	70	
5. Contribution (£)	60	55	48	
6. Profit (£)	35	30	23	
Sales volume variance				
On turnover basis (1 – 3) × 4 (£)	600,000(F)	640,000(A)	140,000(A)	180,000(A)
On contribution basis (1 – 3) × 5 (£)	360,000(F)	440,000(A)	96,000(A)	176,000(A)
On profit basis (1 – 3) × 6 (£)	210,000(F)	240,000(A)	46,000(A)	76,000(A)

Note: fixed cost per unit = £2,500,000/100,000 units = £25

Note: the presentation style used equates increased sales from budget as negative or favourable variances (as opposed to increased costs which are negative or adverse variances).

(***Tutorial note:*** You should think about variances; don't blindly follow formulae).

(b) The choice of turnover, contribution or net profit as the valuation basis for the sales volume variance will be affected by a number of factors:

– The way in which the information is presented to management will affect the choice of valuation base eg, whether a standard absorption or standard marginal cost system is in operation.

– In some circumstances management may prefer to think in terms of market share expressed as turnover and will wish to monitor changes in sales using turnover as the measure.

– It may be argued that as an aid to decision-making the valuation base chosen should be that which most closely approximates to cash flows. The turnover basis ignores the impact of variable costs and overstates the impact of any variance. The net profit basis includes a deduction for fixed costs. This means that the cash flow impact is understated, since fixed costs are sunk and will remain unaffected by volume changes. The contribution basis is the closest approximation to the cash flow effect of a change in sales units.

(c) The quantity and mix variances may be calculated using the information in (a) above as follows:

	Superb	*Excellent*	*Good*	*Total*
Variance	£	£	£	£
Sales quantity (1 – 2) × 5	72,000(A)	110,000(A)	38,400(A)	220,400(A)
Sales mix (2 – 3) × 5	432,000(F)	330,000(A)	57,600(A)	44,400(F)

Note that only the *total* variances for quantity and mix are required. The variances could have been calculated as follows:

Sales quantity variance

= Total volume change × Standard weighted average contribution per unit
= 4,000 units × £55.10
= £220,400(A)

Sales mix variance = Volume variance – Quantity variance
= £176,000(A) – £220,400(A)
= £44,400 (F)

(d) The individual model variances for quantity and mix were calculated in (c) above using individual model contribution per unit as the valuation base. The calculations could have been implemented using the budgeted weighted average contribution as the valuation base (as shown in Horngren/Foster *Cost accounting – a managerial emphasis*). This approach gives the same ***total*** quantity and mix variances but different model variances.

It is argued that the weighted average approach gives a more consistent set of signals to management. For example where the product mix is such that less of a product earning a contribution per unit which is lower than the budgeted weighted average is sold, the mix variance reported will be *favourable.* This indicates a relative swing towards more profitable product(s).

This will be true in Milbao plc where the budgeted weighted average contribution of £55.10 per unit is greater than that of the Excellent and Good products which are £55 and £48 respectively.

*(**Note:*** You are NOT asked to demonstrate the variance calculation.)

A further twist in this discussion is that in the eighth edition of Horngren/Foster (1994), the authors have abandoned the weighted average approach.

Did you answer the question?

Note that the 'weighted average' valuation method is not actually examinable, so there is no need to comment on this: 'candidates were given credit for any relevant comment'. For example, if it is assumed that the individual variances will be valued at individual model contributions per unit, then any product for which the sales are proportionately lower than expected will show an adverse mix variance. But if these sales were replaced by more sales of a profitable product, the overall effect will actually be favourable.

(***Tutorial note:*** The problem of which method to use (weighted average or not) is avoided if you don't waste time splitting mix variances; unfortunately, examiners regularly ask for this to be done.)

(e) (i) Using the information given:

	Original standard	*Revised standard*	*Actual*
	£	£	£
Selling price	100	94.00	90
Variable cost	40	38.80	38
Contribution/unit	60	55.20	52

Summary statement – Model 'Superb' for four-week period

	£	£
Original budget contribution (30,000 × £60)		1,800,000
Revision variances (planning)		
Selling price 30,000 × £6	180,000(A)	
Variable cost 30,000 × £1.20	36,000 (F)	
		144,000(A)
Revised budget contribution (30,000 × £55.2)		1,656,000
Sales volume variance (6,000 × £55.2)		331,200(F)
Revised standard contribution		1,987,200
Residual variances (operational)		
Selling price 36,000 × £4	144,000(A)	
Variable cost 36,000 × £0.8	28,800 (F)	
		115,200(A)
Actual contribution (36,000 × £52)		1,872,000

(ii) Planning and operational variance analysis assists management in both feedback and feedforward control. The isolation of the planning variances which are deemed to be permanent and non-controllable, leaves management free to focus on the operational variances. This feedback information can then be analysed to determine which of the operational variances are controllable and which are not. Efforts can then be concentrated on examination of the controllable variances and determining the cost/benefit of their investigation.

The isolation of the planning and operational variances also assists in forward planning. Future plans may be quantified using revised standards as the starting point, together with whatever proportion of the operational variances it is hoped will be eliminated.

31 (Answer 4 of examination)

Examiner's comments and marking guide

Question 4: required candidates to explain how each of a number of quantitative applications may improve the budgetary planning process, giving a specific aspect of budgetary planning in which each may be used.

Many candidates gave a partial technical explanation of each technique with no reference to its specific use in some aspect of budgetary planning.

	Marks
Relevance to budgetary planning	2
Specific applications in budgetary planning	1
	3
For each of (a) to (e) 5 × 3	15

Step by step answer plan

Step 1 Read the question again and make sure that you focus on precisely what is required. For each idea/technique given an explanation of how it might improve the budgetary process, *with* a specific planning example is required.

Step 2 Whilst a technical description is specifically *not* required, some general explanation of the general principles will usually be a good way to start your answer. Then think of how it fits into the overall budgetary process, and give a brief example of a specific item within the budget to which it may be applied.

Step 3 Now review your answer and ensure that it does precisely answer the question as set.

Items not required by the examiner for this question

- detailed technical descriptions of the techniques

The examiner's answer

(a) *Learning curve theory* recognises that where fairly repetitive tasks are being undertaken by employees, the time taken to perform the task will be affected by a learning curve until a steady state performance level is reached. Failure to recognise the learning effect may result in incorrect labour costs both in the annual budget and periodic budgets. Recognition of the relevant learning curve is important when setting budgets for labour. The learning curve effect will affect, for example, the accuracy of the cash budget and the planning for short-term overdraft facilities as required.

(b) *Linear regression analysis* enables the line of best fit through a series of points to be formulated and the degree of correlation between variables to be calculated. The regression line may be used in budgetary planning in sales forecasting and in the analysis of costs into fixed and variable components. Where alternative approaches such as the high-low method or the visual inspection scatter graph are used, the straight-line equation formulated is likely to be less accurate, leading to inaccurate budgetary planning information.

(c) *Linear programming* allows a model to be prepared which expresses the objective of the model (eg, maximising of contribution) as a linear relationship subject to a set of constraints (eg, limited availability of machine time). A two dimensional model may be solved graphically. For a multi-dimensional situation a computer software package is likely to be used into which relevant data are input and from which a print-out of results may be obtained. A linear programming model may be used in the budgetary planning process, for example, in determining the product mix which should be chosen in order to maximise profit where there is a limited availability of materials, machine time, product sales, etc.

(d) *Economic order quantity* is that which will result in the total of stock ordering and holding costs being minimised. This information is useful for planning for efficient stock control from a financial viewpoint. The size of the purchase order quantity will influence the budgets for material stock levels and for the costs of ordering and holding stock. For example, the EOQ will determine the number of orders to be placed each year and holding costs such as those for space, supervision and insurance.

(e) *Probability estimates* are useful when reviewing a range of possible levels at which budgets may be set. When reviewing alternative budgetary planning scenarios it will be useful to evaluate at least the best, worst and most likely outcomes for each scenario. The use of probability estimates will assist in the comparison between alternative plans. The expected value profit of alternative plans may be calculated and the plan with the highest expected value profit may be chosen. In addition, the probability estimate attached to each outcome of a plan may be used in comparing and evaluating the relative risk attached to each. For example the plan with the highest expected value profit may also have the highest probability of a loss making outcome.

Did you answer the question?

Note how little of the examiner's answers is spent on describing the technique/idea itself - just enough to give a general idea of the type of situation it is designed to assist with. He then switches to the specific are of budgetary planning, as required.

32 (Answer 5 of examination)

Examiner's comments and marking guide

Question 5: required candidates to explain how the application of (a) Zero Base Budgeting (ZBB) and (b) Total Quality Management (TQM) could assist in the implementation of an energy cost reduction strategy.

Many candidates were unable to provide a brief explanation of ZBB and TQM as a basis of their answer and few referred in a meaningful way to the energy related illustrations provided in the question. This did not require any specialist knowledge but did require the candidate to link the examples to the application of each technique. For example the application of a just-in-time approach to the production cycle as part of a TQM programme would assist in reducing the energy required to provide a humidified store.

	Marks	
ZBB - brief background + discussion as cost reduction aid	5	
- specific reference to energy cost examples in Q (any three)	3	
TQM - brief background + discussion as cost reduction aid	4	
- specific reference to energy cost examples in Q (any three)	3	
Total		15

Step by step answer plan

Step 1 Read the question again and make sure that you focus on precisely what is required. The aim is energy cost reduction, the means are ZBB and TQM, for each of which the particular target areas are three of the six given.

Step 2 For each method, start with a brief description of its principles and features. Then turn to the cost reduction aspects - how this can be tackled generally, and then as specifically applied to three of the examples given.

Step 3 Now review your answer and ensure that it does precisely answer the question as set.

Items not required by the examiner for this question

- lengthy discussions of the general advantages and disadvantages of ZBB and TQM

The examiner's answer

Incremental budgeting uses the previous year's budget as its base. The assumption is made that the budget model will remain in force and that the next year's budget will be prepared by adjusting the existing budget to allow for changes in activity, price levels and efficiency. This procedure is unlikely to assist in an energy cost reduction strategy since it will not examine in a critical way the activities which cause energy costs to occur.

Zero-base budgeting requires that all expenditure is justified. A series of decision packages is created for each department or segment of the business. The packages must be ranked and must compete with each other for a share of available financial resources. In creating the series of decision packages, consideration must be given to the relevant costs of each package.

The organisation is committed to expenditure on some costs. An example in the question is the energy cost of maintaining a statutory minimum temperature or the operation of the specially humidified material store. Zero-base budgeting can, however, facilitate examination of ways of reducing the cost of providing such requirements.

Some costs will vary according to activity level. Power costs per unit of output will vary with production level. Power costs in the movement of raw materials and work in progress are driven by the degree of movement which is required. Zero-base budgeting will assist in focusing on such costs and on ways in which they may be reduced.

In some circumstances, management judgement may be applied in the level and direction of expenditure where resources are limited. The energy losses from steam pipelines and steam valves may be reduced through the insulation of the steam pipes to reduce heat loss and through increased maintenance of the valves to reduce steam losses. Such proposals will incur costs and a cost/benefit analysis must be carried out in order to determine the net cost saving (if any) from procedures to reduce energy costs.

Total quality management is a business philosophy which has a number of features including:

- an environment of zero defects at minimum cost
- awareness by all employees of ways of minimising the cost at which products of agreed design specification reach the customer
- the elimination of waste of all types
- it embraces all aspects of the operation of the business
- it recognises the need to minimise non-value added activities.

In the context of energy costs, total quality management principles may be applied to the energy cost examples given in the question.

- Can the minimum temperature be maintained in a more cost effective way?
- Would a just-in-time delivery system of materials be cheaper than operating the humidified store?
- Can power costs per unit of output be reduced by the elimination of the need for re-work and minimising defective units?
- Movement of materials is a non-value added activity. Can such movements be reduced, hence reducing energy costs of movement?
- Losses from steam pipelines and valves and heat losses from windows are waste which can be eliminated after considering the cost/benefit implications of actions to eliminate such losses.

Did you answer the question?

Note that the examiner has used more than the three required examples for each method for your information. Don't do more than asked - marks will only be given for the first three considered (which won't necessarily be the best!)

33 (Answer 6 of examination)

Examiner's comments and marking guide

Question 6: required candidates to state key features of strategic planning and operational planning. In particular, in the context of ways in which lack of co-ordination of strategic and operational planning could lead to a range of problems with cost implications. Candidates were asked to frame their answers in the context of a strategic planning goal of sustaining competitive advantage at minimum cost through speedy delivery of quality products to customers.

All relevant explanations of, and distinctions between, strategic and operational planning were accepted in answer to part (a). In part (b) few candidates were able to provide relevant examples of problems arising from lack of co-ordination of strategic and operational planning. For example an operational decision to increase stock levels to ensure speedy delivery would see increasing stock levels as a 'good' performance measure. This ignores the strategic aims of quality products at minimum cost which would require other performance measures such as level of customer complaints, returned goods, etc.

		Marks	
(a)	Definitions and key elements (on merit)	7	
(b)	Relevant illustrations and cost implications for each (4 × 2)	8	
Total			15

Step by step answer plan

Step 1 Read the question again and make sure that you focus on precisely what is required. The subject matter is the comparison and co-ordination between strategic and operational planning. Your starting point then will be to have a think about these two areas and jot down a few key aspects of each to get them clarified in your mind before meeting the specific requirements of the question.

Step 2 (a) This is a requirement that could be approached in a number of ways - by reference to specific areas of business, with particular examples, or a more general answer highlighting the difference in perspective/time-scale/ implementation.

Step 3 (b) You have to read this requirement very carefully to ensure that you meet it precisely . You are asked to comment on particular *cost* implications of *given factors* that may arise through inappropriate *operational* planning. The context is the strategic goal of *speedy* delivery of *quality* goods at *minimum cost.* Try to think of specific examples of operational plans taking one or more of these aims in isolation from the others, and the possible cost implications .

Step 4 Now review your answer and ensure that it does precisely answer the question as set.

The examiner's answer

(a) Strategic planning requires an understanding of the long-term goals or objectives of an organisation. For example, the organisation long-term goals may be expressed as. 'To sustain our competitive advantage with minimum operating costs compatible with delivering a quality product/service to our customers and seeking continuous performance improvement'. Strategic planning should include in its key features and characteristics that it should:

- Agree and communicate to all concerned, the chosen business direction embracing the principles of its main goals.

- Involve management in the development of plans.

- Be action oriented and seek to 'manage change'.
- Require commitment from all parties.

Operational planning involves a set of plans to combat problems and set in motion actions to implement the strategic plan.

Operation planning requires:

- The formulation of action plans.
- Consideration of organisational structure change to facilitate the implementing of plans.
- The creation of financial plans/budgets.

(b) The strategic planning goal of speedy delivery of quality products to customers at minimum cost may not be achieved because of:

Unrealistic plans: The operational plan may call for a build up of finished goods stock in order to ensure availability of products for early delivery to customers in response to demand. This may incur additional costs because of lack of finished goods or through the need to write-off obsolete stock where customer demand patterns change quickly.

Inconsistent goals: The operational plan may require extra inspection points in order to ensure that only quality products reach the customer. This may be successful but would incur additional costs which would be inconsistent with the strategic planning goal of minimum cost.

Poor communication: The overall strategic planning goals are likely to include the need to be action oriented and seek to manage change. Lack of communication between strategic planners and operational planners is likely to lead to the operational plan of stock build-up rather than a move to a just-in-time production system geared to be responsive to changing customer demand patterns. Excess costs such as the write-off of obsolete stock is, therefore, likely to occur.

Inadequate performance measurement: Increasing stock levels may be seen as a 'good' performance indicator where the operational planning decision is to build up stocks to allow speedy delivery to customers. Increased stock levels do not measure factors such as the level of customer complaints through the delivery of faulty products and the need to supply replacements free of charge. Such replacements are a substantial additional cost to the company.

Coordinated strategic planning and operational planning should ensure that the objectives of the strategic plan can be achieved in the most efficient and effective way through the operational plans which are instituted. This should eliminate excess costs such as those illustrated above.

Did you answer the question?

Note here that the examiner has used the same example - that of inappropriate stock build up - to illustrate most of the factors in the question; however care has been taken to show how it can be specifically (and differently) related to each factor, particularly in terms of the additional costs that may be incurred.

DECEMBER 1995 QUESTIONS

Section A – TWO questions ONLY to be attempted

34 (Question 1 of examination)

A nursing home has a maximum capacity of 80 beds. Budgeted information for the year ended 31 December 1995 is as follows:

(i) Budgeted costs for the year assuming 100% capacity utilisation are as follows:

	£	
Administration	92,000	(100% fixed)
Catering	164,000	(70% variable, 30% fixed)
Cleaning	32,000	(20% variable, 80% fixed)
Laundry	80,000	(100% variable)
Medical supervision	260,000	(30% variable, 70% fixed)
Sundry overheads	100,000	(25% variable, 75% fixed)

(ii) Variable costs vary in proportion to the number of beds occupied.

(iii) Fixed costs are incurred equally in each of four quarters of the year.

(iv) The budgeted charge at which residents are invoiced is £30 per day. Each quarter is treated as 90 days for invoicing purposes.

(v) The budgeted occupancy rate is 90% for the year to 31 December 1995.

Actual information for the **quarter** ended 30 June 1995 is as follows:

(i) Actual costs incurred for the quarter are:

	Variable £	*Fixed* £
Administration		22,000
Catering	27,500	12,400
Cleaning	1,525	6,200
Laundry	19,380	
Medical supervision	18,525	43,600
Sundry overheads	6,000	18,000

(ii) Average occupancy during the quarter was 76 beds per day.

(iii) Fee income from residents during the quarter was increased by short-term residents who agreed to pay a premium rate of £35 per day and who were invoiced in total for 700 bed days.

A number of permanent changes were acknowledged at the start of the quarter ended 30 June 1995 which would affect the budgeted costs:

(1) A rearrangement of the administrative staff requirement reduces salaries by £2,000 per quarter.

(2) Catering variable costs will be increased by 3% because of food price increases.

(3) Cleaning fixed costs will increase by £240 per quarter in order to comply with new legislation.

(4) Laundry costs will be reduced by 5% as the result of a policy of contracting-out the laundry service.

(5) Medical supervision variable costs will be reduced by 5% through the rationalisation of drug requirements.

(6) Sundry overhead fixed costs will be reduced by £5,000 per quarter through a rationalisation of the night duty staff requirement.

A summary operating statement for the **quarter** ended 30 June 1995 which recognises planning and operational variances is presented as follows:

	£	£	£
Original budgeted contribution			125,955
Revision variances			1,003 (F)
Revised budget contribution			126,958
Less: Fixed costs (total)			
Original budget		105,950	
Revision variance		6,760 (F)	
			99,190
Revised budget profit			27,768
Occupancy variance (contribution gain or loss)			7,053 (F)
Other variances	*Variable*	*Fixed*	
Residents' fees	3,500 (F)		
Cost variances (total)	1,741 (A)	3,010(A)	
	1,759 (F)	3,010 (A)	1,251 (A)
Actual net profit			33,570

Note: (F) = favourable (A) = adverse

Required

(a) Using the information in the question, prepare detailed workings to show how each of the figures in the operating statement for the quarter ended 30 June 1995 have been calculated.

(22 marks)

(b) Estimate the occupancy rate (%) for the **six months** ending 31 December 1995 which will result in a net profit of £65,000 for the six month period if the actual cost and revenue statistics are as per those applicable in quarter 2 other than:

(i) Operational variances for costs are reduced to 40% of the rate at which they were incurred in quarter 2.

(ii) Fee income premium for short stay residents will boost overall fees by 5% of the budget bed day fee.

(7 marks)

(c) Explain to the nursing home owners the ways in which the planning and operational variance model enhances their ability to implement feedback and feedforward control.

(No quantitative data required.)

(6 marks)
(Total 35 marks)

35 (Question 2 of examination)

Sapu plc make and sell a number of products. Products A and B are products for which market prices are available at which Sapu plc can obtain a share of the market as detailed below. Estimated data for the forthcoming period is as follows:

(i) Product data

	Product A	*Product B*	*Other products*
Production/sales (units)	5,000	10,000	40,000
	£'000	£'000	£'000
Total direct material cost	80	300	2,020
Total direct labour cost	40	100	660

(ii) Variable overhead cost is £1,500,000 of which 40% is related to the acquisition, storage and use of direct materials and 60% is related to the control and use of direct labour.

(iii) It is current practice in Sapu plc to absorb variable overhead cost into product units using overall company wide percentages on direct material cost and direct labour cost as the absorption bases.

(iv) Market prices for Products A and B are £75 and £95 per unit respectively.

(v) Sapu plc require a minimum estimated contribution: sales ratio of 40% before proceeding with the production/sale of any product.

Required

(a) Prepare estimated unit product costs for Product A and Product B where variable overhead is charged to product units as follows:

(i) Using the existing absorption basis as detailed above. **(6 marks)**

(ii) Using an activity based costing approach where cost drivers have been estimated for material and labour related overhead costs as follows:

	Product A	*Product B*	*Other products*
Direct material related overheads – cost driver is material bulk. The bulk proportions per unit are:	4	1	1.5
Direct labour related overheads – cost driver is number of labour operations (not directly time related). Labour operations per product unit	6	1	2

(10 marks)

(b) Prepare an analysis of the decision strategy which Sapu plc may implement with regard to the production and sale of Products A and B. Use unit costs as calculated in (a)(i) and (a)(ii) together with other information given in the question in your analysis. Your answer should include relevant calculations and discussion and be prepared in a form suitable for presentation to management. **(10 marks)**

(c) Explain how Sapu plc could make use of target costing in conjunction with activity based costing with respect to Products A and B. **(6 marks)**

(d) If spare production capacity exists in Sapu plc, comment on the relevance of the present decision criterion of a minimum Contribution: Sales ratio of 40%. **(3 marks)**

(Total 35 marks)

36 (Question 3 of examination)

A company is considering the improvement of the lighting system in one of its offices. The following information is available.

(i) The building will be sold in three years time. It is proposed that the existing lighting be replaced by either large or small 'task-focused' lighting units at a cost of £750 per unit for small units and £1,250 per unit for large units. The total requirement will be for 80 small units or 50 large units. All purchases will be paid for immediately (year 0).

(ii) The quantity of electricity used will be reduced from that of the existing lighting system by 40% if small units are introduced, and by 30% if large units are introduced. The electricity cost allocated to the office in the year prior to purchase (year 0) is £50,000 for the existing lighting system. This includes a £10,000 share of standing charges paid by the company and the balance at a constant cost per unit of electricity used.

(iii) The existing lighting system has maintenance costs of £12,000 per annum in the year prior to purchase (year 0). This includes a £5,000 share of the salary of an electrician who will be retained by the company whether or not he undertakes this work. The balance is for spare parts. Most of the spare parts are purchased as required but £1,000 worth per annum are taken from stock purchased some time ago. The spare parts stock is sufficient to last for a further two years (at £1,000 per annum). Such spare parts would currently (year 0) cost 30% more to purchase than the original purchase price. Existing stocks could not be sold or used elsewhere if not used for lighting maintenance.

(iv) The new lighting system (large or small units) will have maintenance costs of £5,000 in year 1 (at year 1 prices) which will include a £3,000 share of the salary of the electrician currently used for lighting maintenance. The remaining cost is for spare parts which will be specially purchased. The quantity of spare parts required will increase by 25% in year 2 and by a further 10% of the year 2 level in year 3.

(v) It is estimated that the task-focused lighting (large or small units) will increase the saleable value of the building by £15,000 at the end of year 3 with the cash flow relating to the sale taking place at the end of year 4.

(vi) It is estimated that all costs will increase because of price level changes according to the following index table (all indices expressed in terms of a year 0 index of 100).

Year	*0*	*1*	*2*	*3*
Index	100	105	110	115

(Ignore taxation.)

Required

(a) Determine whether it is financially worthwhile to introduce either of the task-focused lighting systems on 1 January year 1 where the cost of capital is 10%.

Your answer should include all relevant working calculations and should give reasons for the exclusion of any of the above data from the decision model. **(22 marks)**

(b) Calculate the level of estimated increase in the saleable value of the building at which the company would be indifferent on financial grounds to a change from the existing lighting to the task focused (small) lighting units, given that all other variables remain as in part (a). **(3 marks)**

(c) Give two examples of additional variables which may be relevant to the lighting decision process and suggest the possible types of quantifiable impacts of each. **(4 marks)**

(d) Explain ways in which a spreadsheet representation of the decision model would enable uncertainty to be allowed for in the calculations. **(6 marks)**
(Total 35 marks)

Section B – TWO questions ONLY to be attempted

37 (Question 4 of examination)

(i) Costs may be classified in a number of ways including classification by behaviour, by function, by expense type, by controllability and by relevance.

(ii) Management accounting should assist in *each* of the planning, control and decision making processes in an organisation.

Discuss the ways in which relationships between statements (i) and (ii) are relevant in the design of an effective management accounting system.

(15 marks)

38 (Question 5 of examination)

The acceptability of an investment proposal at a division within a vertically integrated group may be affected by the financial performance measure used and the accounting procedures in operation within the group.

Expand on this statement incorporating the following terms into your discussion.

(i) Return on investment
(ii) Residual income
(iii) Transfer pricing
(iv) Annuity depreciation
(v) Net present value.

(15 marks)

39 (Question 6 of examination)

Expand on the role of the management accountant in each of cost control and cost reduction, incorporating a comparison of the two into your discussion. Your answer should include definitions, objectives and areas of focus, techniques which may be used and personnel involvement in each of cost control and cost reduction; consideration should be given to the role of total quality management and alternative approaches to budgeting in the provision of effective information for cost control and cost reduction.

(15 marks)

ANSWERS TO DECEMBER 1995 EXAMINATION

34 (Answer 1 of examination)

Examiner's comments and marking guide

Question 1: tested candidates' ability to analyse input data in order to explain the steps in the compilation of an operating statement containing planning and operational variances. It also tested candidates' ability to use variance information in a forward planning role and to comment on the use of variances in planning and control.

While most candidates were able to explain the compilation of the variances in part (a), few were able to use the additional information in order to implement the forward planning calculations. In part (c) some candidates did not write about the relevance of the variance analysis in the context of the nursing home.

		Marks	*Marks*	*Marks*
(a)	Original budget contribution:			
	- revenue element	1		
	- variable cost **	3	4	
	Revision variance variable (3 × 1)		3	
	Fixed cost budget:			
	- original **	1		
	- revision variance (3 × 1)	3	4	
	Occupancy variance		3	
	Other variances:			
	- resident fees		2	
	- cost variances (variable)		4	
	- cost variances (fixed)		2	
				22
	** marks per workings table in answer for each expense type: 6 × 0.5 = 3, plus fixed cost per quarter = 1			
(b)	Contribution required for six months		3	
	Est. contribution per bed day		2	
	Bed days required		1	
	Occupancy rate required		1	
	(allow up to 3 marks for method)			7
(c)	Feedback control enhancement (on merit)		3	
	Feedforward control enhancement (on merit)		3	6
Total				35

Step by step answer plan

Step 1 Read the question again and make sure that you focus on precisely what is required. It requires calculations to prove figures in a given operating statement, that incorporates planning and operational variances, for a service business.

Step 2 (a) Here is a variance analysis question with a difference - you know what the answers are supposed to be! This can be reassuring (if your answers agree) or off-putting (if they don't). In the latter case, don't spend hours on one figure trying to get it right, and run out of time to try the other, possibly easier, calculations.

The first thing to do is to sort out the data. The statement is prepared for a quarter, on a marginal cost basis, starting with a budgeted contribution that will be based on a 90% occupancy rate, and includes revision (planning variances). The starting point, then is the original quarterly budget. As well as accounting for the different time-scale, variable costs (only) have to additionally be flexed to the budgeted occupancy rate (TN 1). The budgeted quarterly fee income can then be brought in to get original budgeted contribution (and you also have the original budget fixed costs)

Step 3 Next on the statement are the revision variances, brought about by the permanent changes. These only affect costs, and can be shown as adjustments against the quarterly budgeted costs obtained in Step 2. Applying the variable cost revisions gives the revised budgeted contribution; the revisions to fixed costs are brought in further down, to get to revised budget profit.

Step 4 Now you get onto the operational variances - the differences between the revised budget profit and actual profit. The first change to account for is the occupancy rate - from 90% (budget) to 95% (actual), valued at revised standard contribution (this is equivalent to the sales volume variance). The remaining variances are computed along normal lines.

Step 5 (b) Here, you are working back from a target net profit to determine how many bed-days need to be sold - this uses basic CVP analysis, for which you need expected fixed costs for the period and contribution per bed-day. If you recognise this as being the approach needed in your answer, you will get some credit, even if you don't get all the figures right.

Step 6 (c) The link between planning and operational variances and feedback/forward control is popular with the examiner (see June 1995 Q3) and it is well worth ensuring you understand it. Always try to illustrate your answer with data from the question.

Step 7 Now review your answer and ensure that it does precisely answer the question as set.

The examiner's answer

(a) **Cost analysis workings**

	Annual budget (at 100% capacity)		*Quarterly budget (at 90% capacity)*		*Revision variance changes to budget*	
	Fixed £	*Variable* £	*Fixed* £	*Variable* £	*Fixed* £	*Variable* £
Administration	92,000				2,000	
Catering	49,200	114,800		25,830		–775
Cleaning	25,600	6,400		1,440	–240	
Laundry		80,000		18,000		900
Medical	182,000	78,000		17,550		878
Sundry	75,000	25,000		5,625	5,000	
	423,800	304,200	105,950	68,445	6,760	1,003

Examiner's notes

(1) Quarterly fixed cost = £423,800/4 = £105,950
(2) In revision changes a minus sign (–) signals an increase in cost

(See also Tutorial note)

The above workings show the values for the revision variances, fixed and variable, together with the budgeted fixed and variable costs.

Original budget for the quarter:

	£
Resident fee income = 90 days × 80 beds × 90% × £30 =	194,400
Less: Variable cost (as above)	68,445
Original budgeted contribution	£125,955

Occupancy variance calculations:

Revised budget variable cost at 90% capacity = £68,445 – 1,003 = £67,442

Revised budgeted contribution = £194,400 – £67,442 = £126,958

Occupancy in bed days per quarter:

Budget = 90 × 80 × 0.9 = 6,480 bed days

Actual = 90 × 80 × 0.95 = 6,840 bed days

Revised standard contribution per bed day = £126,958/6,480 = £19.5923

Occupancy variance = (6,840 – 6,480) × £19.5923 = £7,053 (F)

Operational variances:

Variable cost = Flexed revised budget – Actual cost = £71,189* – 72,930 = £1,741 (A)

Fixed cost = £99,190 – 102,200 = £3,010 (A)

Fee income premium = 700 bed days × £5 = £3,500 (F)

* Variable cost budget adjusted to actual activity = £67,442 × 0.95/0.90 = £71,189

(b)

	£
Actual fixed costs for quarter 2	102,200
Operational variance saving: 60% × £3,010	1,806
Revised fixed cost per quarter	100,394
Revised fixed cost for six months (× 2)	200,788
Net profit required for six months	65,000
Contribution required for six months	265,788

Expected contribution per bed day for the six months to 31 December may be calculated as:

	£
Revised standard contribution (per above)	19.5923
Add: Fee income increase 5% × £30	1.5000
Less: Residual operational variances (£1,741 × 0.4)/6,840) (adverse)	–0.1018
Estimated actual contribution per bed day	£20.9905

Hence bed days of occupancy for the six months to 31 December:

£265,788/£20.9905 = 12,662

Now 100% capacity for six months = 80 × 180 = 14,400 bed days

Hence occupancy rate required to give a net profit of £65,000:

(12,662/14,400) × 100 = 87.93%

(c) Feedback control occurs when planned results are compared with actual results and the differences are noted and investigated. Planning and operational variance analysis enhances this process by segregating those variances which are deemed permanent changes to the original plan and hence non-controllable items. Planning variances are built into revised (ex-post) standards. The revised standards are compared with actual results to give a set of operational variances which should be the focus of any investigation and corrective action. This process is illustrated in the calculations in part (a) of the question. Feedforward control is where the desired outcome is compared with that which is estimated will occur if the current plan is implemented. Where any deviation exists between the desired outcome and the current plan, corrective action may be implemented in order to achieve the desired outcome. In part (b) of the question, we see that an occupancy rate of 87.93% with a 60% reduction in operational variance levels from those applicable in quarter 2 will enable a net profit of £65,000 to be achieved in the six months to 31 December. If the current plan had been for an occupancy rate of (say) 85% the desired profit would not have been achieved and an amendment to approximately 88% would have rectified the problem.

Tutorial notes

1 Annual 100% budget variable catering cost = £164,000 x 70% = £114,800
Quarterly 90% budget variable catering cost = £114,800 /4 x 90% = £25,830

All others are calculated in a similar way

35 (Answer 2 of examination)

Examiner's comments and marking guide

Question 2: part (a) required candidates to prepare estimated unit costs using traditional volume related overhead absorption bases and also using an activity based approach. Part (b) required candidates to prepare a report which analysed ways in which the decision strategy on the production and sale of products would alter depending on the overhead absorption approach used. Part (c) required the explanation of why the use of target costing plus activity based costing was relevant in respect of the products under review. Part (d) required comment on the impact of spare production capacity on the decision making process.

Many candidates were unable to apply the cost driver information in a correct manner. Surprisingly, a large number of candidates were unable to correctly calculate unit product costs where the volume related absorption bases were used. The report in part (b) was generally well prepared, with analysis and comment on the contribution: sales ratio for each product under each basis of overhead absorption. In part (c) many candidates were unaware of the meaning of target costing. In addition, comments on activity based costing were often unrelated to the situation in the question. In part (d) a significant minority were unable to make relevant comment on the impact of spare production capacity on the decision process in the company.

			Marks	*Marks*
(a)	(i)	Product costs for A and B:		
		- direct material (2 × 0.5)	1	
		- direct labour (2 × 0.50)	1	
		- variable overhead:		
		- material related (2 × 1)	2	
		- labour related (2 × 1)	2	
			—	6

(ii)	Product costs for A and B:		
	- direct material (2 × 0.5)	1	
	- direct labour (2 × 0.5)	1	
	- variable overhead:		
	- material bulk factor (2 × 2)	4	
	- number of labour ops (2 × 2)	4	10
(b)	Calculation of CS ratio for A and B using:		
	- existing unit costs (2 × 1)	2	
	- amended unit costs (2 × 1)	2	
	Comments on CS ratio for A and B relative to 40% minimum required:		
	- existing costs	2	
	- amended costs	2	
	Overall presentation and analysis	2	
			10
(c)	Target costing features:		
	- market identified for A and B at specific prices	2	
	- how to squeeze costs of A to achieve target contribution	2	
	- further squeeze of costs of B to ensure CS ratio maintained (marks on merit)	2	
			6
(d)	Relevance of marginal cost where spare exists	2	
	Impact in longer term	1	
			3
Total			35

Step by step answer plan

Step 1 Read the question again and make sure that you focus on precisely what is required. This question involves elements of variable (note) overhead absorption, ABC, decision making and target costing.

Step 2 (a) Your first step is to split the overhead costs between material and labour related elements. When calculating the traditional absorption bases, note that "company wide" percentages are used; these are therefore calculated by reference to total relevant overhead costs as a percentage of total related material/labour cost - not just for the two products being considered. Once these percentages have been determined, they can be applied to the two particular products (using total or unit costs) to determine the total unit product costs.

When applying the ABC approach, note that the weightings (cost drivers) given are per unit. Before calculating the overall cost per cost driver, these need to be applied to the budgeted number of units for all products.

Step 3 (b) The answer to this part should be in report format, for which marks will be given (or lost). "Prepare an analysis of the decision strategy" may make it sound more complex than it is. The question tells you that a minimum CS ratio needs to be reached before a product is launched - thus all you are required to do is to determine the CS ratio for each product using both methods of overhead absorption. Note that as this is a report to management, you need to show a full statement of unit costs, rather than simply referring to your answers in (a) . The discussion and presentation elements of this part carry 6 of the 10 marks, so don't stint on them!

Step 4 (c) To answer this sensibly, you need to have a basic awareness of the principles of target costing. It is a topic that comes up quite regularly in exam questions, so make sure you are familiar with it. Once again, the golden rule (even if you are only talking about the ABC aspects) is to relate your points to the particular circumstances/data in the question.

Step 5 (d) You should appreciate the change in perspective that comes with spare capacity - normal margins are no longer necessarily relevant, and basic "relevant costing" principles apply.

Step 6 Now review your answer and ensure that it does precisely answer the question as set.

The examiner's answer

(a) (i) **Workings**

Material related overhead cost = 40% × £1,500,000 = £600,000

Overhead absorption rate =
(£600,000/£2,400,000) × 100/1 = 25% on direct material cost

Labour related overhead cost = 60% × £1,500,000 = £900,000

Overhead absorption rate =
(£900,000/£800,000) × 100/1 = 112.5% on direct labour cost

Using the overhead absorption rates calculated above and average direct material and direct labour costs from the data in the question we have:

	Unit costs	
	Product A	*Product B*
	£	£
Direct material cost	16	30
Direct labour cost	8	10
	24	40
Variable overhead		
Material related at 25%	4	7.5
Labour related at 112.5%	9	11.25
Total variable cost	37	58.75

(ii) **Workings**

Material related overhead has bulk as the cost driver.

Total bulk factor = (5,000 × 4) + (10,000 × 1) + (40,000 × 1.5) = 90,000

Material related overhead per unit of bulk = £600,000/90,000 = £6.67

Hence overhead cost per product unit:

Product A = £6.67 × 4 = £26.67
Product B = £6.67 × 1 = £6.67

Labour related overhead has the number of labour operations as the cost driver.

Total labour operations = (5,000 × 6) + (10,000 × 1) + (40,000 × 2) = 120,000

Labour related overhead per labour operation = £900,000/120,000 = £7.50

Hence overhead cost per product unit:

Product A = £7.50 × 6 = £45
Product B = £7.50 × 1 = £7.50

The amended unit product costs may now be shown as:

	Product A	*Product B*
	£	£
Direct material cost	16	30
Direct labour cost	8	10
	24	40
Variable overhead:		
Material related	26.67	6.67
Labour related	45.00	7.50
Total variable cost	95.67	54.17

(b) From: Management accountant

To: Management team

Subject: Production/sales strategy for Products A and B

The unit market prices for Products A and B are £75 and £95 respectively. At these prices we can obtain market share of 5,000 units of A and 10,000 units of B in the forthcoming period. The unit product cost and contribution information may be calculated using our existing basis for the absorption of variable overhead cost by product units or by using an ABC approach which recognises the cost drivers which cause costs to occur.

Unit product information is as follows:

	Product A		*Product B*	
	Existing approach	*ABC approach*	*Existing approach*	*ABC approach*
	£	£	£	£
Direct material cost	16	16	30	30
Direct labour cost	8	8	10	10
	24	24	40	40
Variable overhead cost				
Material related	4	26.67	7.50	6.67
Labour related	9	45.00	11.25	7.50
Total variable cost	37	95.67	58.75	54.17
Contribution	38	(20.67)	36.25	40.83
Selling price	75	75.00	95.00	95.00
Contribution: sales (%)	50.7%	–ve	38.2%	43.0%

Based on the company policy of a minimum contribution: sales ratio of 40% before proceeding with the sale of any product, our current product costing procedure would confirm the production and sale of Product A with a CS ratio of 50.7%, but would reject Product B with a CS ratio of 38.2%.

The amended product costs using the ABC approach which recognises the cost drivers for overhead cost will reverse our decision. Product A would now be rejected with a negative CS ratio whereas Product B would be acceptable with a CS ratio of 43%. The ABC based calculations recognise the relatively high cost driver levels for Product A and I would recommend that we use the ABC calculations as the basis for our decision strategy and produce and sell Product B.

(c) The environment in which Sapu plc finds itself is suited to the application of target costing.

- A market has been identified at specific selling prices for each of Products A and B.

- Product A does not conform to the company's required minimum CS ratio of 40%. Ways must be found to reduce costs considerably for this product if the 40% CS ratio target is to be achieved. The high cost driver incidence in both material bulk and labour operations provide targets where a considerable reduction in unit overhead cost could be achieved. It may also be possible to reduce the incidence of direct material cost and direct labour cost through, for example, design specification changes.

- Whilst Product B achieves the minimum target CS ratio of 40%, the company may wish to seek further cost reductions in order to ensure that future price increases do not reduce the CS ratio below 40%.

Did you answer the question?

Note how closely the examiner's comments are related to the particular circumstances of Sapu plc and its products, and uses information previously derived to support the discussion.

(d) Where spare production capacity exists, any contribution to fixed costs will provide a net cash inflow to the company. Hence any selling price in excess of variable cost will be acceptable on financial grounds in the short term so long as no alternative opportunity exists for the capacity.

The company may not wish to pursue a marginal cost pricing policy for products which utilise spare capacity if it feels that this action is likely to affect future orders from customers for other products where the 40% CS ratio criterion is being applied.

36 (Answer 3 of examination)

Examiner's comments and marking guide

Question 3: part (a) required candidates to evaluate the financial viability of installing one of two new lighting systems. In addition, in part (b) candidates were required to determine the level of residual value of the building at which the company would be indifferent to change to a new lighting system where all other variables remained as given. Candidates were also required to suggest additional variables relevant to the decision (part (c)) and to explain the use of a spreadsheet representation of the model to enable uncertainty to be allowed for (part (d)).

The presentation of answers to part (a) was generally poor. The method by which price level adjustments and relevant costs had been used in the analysis was poorly documented. Many candidates did not attempt to discount the cash flows in order to arrive at an NPV figure. This question highlighted the lack of expertise of many candidates in information analysis and presentation. Few candidates were able to formulate a correct procedure for the sensitivity problem in part (b). Most candidates suggested additional variables in part (c) but many were of dubious relevance. In part (d) many answers simply gave an outline description of a spreadsheet without focusing on its use in allowing for uncertainty.

			Marks	*Marks*
(a)	Existing cash flows:			
	- relevant maint cost	Yr 1	2	
		Yr 2	1	
		Yr 3	2	
	- relevant elec cost	Yr 1	1	
		Yr 2	0.5	
		Yr 3	0.5	
	Task focused cash flow:			
	- relevant maint. (small and large)			
		Yr 1 (2 × 1)	2	

	Yr 2 (2 × 1)	2	
	Yr 3 (2 × 1)	2	
	- relevant electricity (Years 1 - 3)		
	- small - factor by 0.6 (3 × 0.5)	1.5	
	- large - factor by 0.7 (3 × 0.5)	1.5	
	Capital investment (small and large) (2 × 0.5)	1	
	Building value enhancement (2 × 0.5)	1	
	Net benefit/loss from change in lighting		
	plus DCF - small	2	
	- large	2	
	(note that this is simply an arithmetic aspect of the exercise)		22
	All the above marks assume clear working calculations and reasons for inclusion/exclusion of data.		
(b)	Method (on merit)		3
(c)	Two variables and quantitative impact (2 × 2)		4
(d)	Spreadsheet use (on merit)		6
Total			35

Step by step answer plan

Step 1 Read the question again and make sure that you focus on precisely what is required. It concerns a choice between two investment options. The requirement for an NPV approach is indicated by the presence of a cost of capital. You should also note that adjustments for inflation will be required.

Step 2 (a) The key here is clear presentation - you have a lot of data to organise and process, and you must ensure the examiner can see your route through. A tabular approach, with both options in one table, is the most efficient, but it must be kept clear. Any workings should be put in separate notes (cross-referenced) , as should the required explanations for omitted data.

For each option, you need to determine the future incremental cash flows (costs) that result from taking that option in comparison with keeping things as they are, working systematically through the information in the question. In this example, where some of the existing cash flows need to determined before the changes can be determined, it is perhaps clearest and less prone to error to specifically show existing cash flows, new cash flows (for each option) and thus incremental flows (representing cost savings after the initial investment) These can be done as workings or as part of the tabular answer. Don't forget to come to a (written) conclusion!

Step 3 (b) This is a sensitivity analysis exercise. Currently the small lighting units option is favoured over keeping status quo, as it has a positive NPV of cost savings. Contributing to this positive NPV is the PV of the increase in saleable value of the building. If this were to reduce, so would the NPV, until it reaches zero (by which time the PV of the value increase must have dropped by the whole NPV). At this point the company would be financially indifferent about going ahead with the new lighting.

Step 4 (c) These examples must be quite specific (and relevant to the given situation) to get marks

Step 5 (d) The greatest benefit of a spreadsheet based model is that it can be used to rapidly assess the effects of changes in underlying values and parameters used in the computation - ie where there is uncertainty about the actual values that will arise. This is the main aspect that must be brought out in your answer.

Step 6 Now review your answer and ensure that it does precisely answer the question as set.

Items not required by the examiner for this question

- general descriptions of spreadsheets without reference to their use with uncertainty

The examiner's answer

(a)

Year	Description	*Discount factor at 10%*	*Existing lighting cash flow (a)*	*Task-focused (small)* Cash flow (b)	*Net flow (b – a)*	*DCF*	*Task-focused (large)* Cash flow (c)	*Net flow (c – a)*	*DCF*
			£	£	£	£	£	£	£
0	Capital investment	1.000		(60,000)	(60,000)	(60,000)	(62,500)	(62,500)	(62,500)
1	Electricity cost	0.909	(42,000)	(25,200)	16,800	15,271	(29,400)	12,600	11,453
	Maintenance cost		(6,300)	(2,000)	4,300	3,909	(2,000)	4,300	3,909
2	Electricity cost	0.826	(44,000)	(26,400)	17,600	14,538	(30,800)	13,200	10,903
	Maintenance cost		(6,600)	(2,619)	3,981	3,288	(2,619)	3,981	3,288
3	Electricity cost	0.751	(46,000)	(27,600)	18,400	13,818	(32,200)	13,800	10,364
	Maintenance cost		(8,395)	(3,012)	5,383	4,043	(3,012)	5,383	4,043
4	Increase in value	0.683		15,000	15,000	10,245	15,000	15,000	10,245
	NPV					5,112			(8,295)

Note: ( ) = minus or negative values

Examiner's working notes

(1) The figures in the above table take into account the reduction in the quantity of electricity required if small or large task-focused units are used (ie, 40% and 30% respectively). (TN 1)

(2) The cash flows for each of years 1 to 3 have been adjusted for price level changes using the indices given in the question.

(3) The electrician salary is ignored in all calculations since it is a company sunk cost which will remain whatever decision is taken.

(4) The spare parts stock has no alternative use and hence it has nil opportunity cost.

(5) The maintenance cost for specially purchased spares for the existing system will be:

Year 1 £12,000 – 5,000 – 1,000 = £6,000 × 1.05 = £6,300

Year 2 £6,000 (as for year 1) × 1.10 = £6,600

Year 3 The stock of spare parts is exhausted and this quantity (£1,000 at original stock cost) will be specially purchased at a cost (year 0 prices) of 30% more than the original purchase price. The total cost for year 3 will be:

	£
£6,000 × 1.15	6,900
£1,000 × 1.30 × 1.15	1,495
	£8,395

(6) The maintenance cost for the new lighting systems may be calculated as:

Year 1: £5,000 – £3,000 = £2,000
Year 2: £2,000 × 1.25 × 1.10/1.05 = £2,619
Year 3: £2,000 × 1.25 × 1.10 × 1.15/1.05 = £3,012

(7) The increase in saleable value of the office because of the installation of the new lighting of £15,000 is shown as a cash inflow in year 4 when the cash flow in respect of sale is expected to take place.

The net change in cash flows arising from the installation of either the large or small task-focused lighting units are calculated and discounted at the cost of capital rate of 10%. This shows a positive NPV of £5,112 for the small task-focused units indicating that it is financially worthwhile to change. A negative NPV of £8,295 is shown where a change to the large task-focused units is considered indicating that this option is not financially worthwhile.

(b) The indifference point for the company is where the NPV is zero. This will occur where:

Saleable value increase from the new lighting = (£10,245 – 5,112)/0.683 = £7,515

(c) Examples of additional variables and their possible quantitative impact are:

- Effect on employee efficiency. The new lighting may improve the rate and quality of work. It may also allow a reduction in the total number of staff required because of increased efficiency.

- Employee job satisfaction. The new lighting may improve job satisfaction leading to reduced absenteeism and reduced labour turnover. Absenteeism and labour turnover are cost drivers and any reduction in their incidence will reduce total cost.

- Reduction in errors caused by the poor lighting eg, in design drawings or job specifications sent to customers. Such errors could lead to loss of business in the future.

Did you answer the question?

Note you were only required to give two examples - the examiner has given an additional one for information only

(d) The decision model output is represented by the working tabulation in part (a) of the answer. A spreadsheet representation of the model would allow variable input data to be segregated and the output statement to be formulated using cell formulae for the relevant combinations of input variable data. Uncertainty could then be allowed for in a number of ways.

- One variable: A one way data table could be constructed showing the NPV values for a range of values of, for example, the cost of capital percentage.

- Two variables: A two way data table could be prepared showing the range of NPV values for any combination of two variables such as percentage reduction in electricity usage and maintenance cost estimate for the new systems in year 1.

- A range of variables: A What-if analysis could be carried out by changing any combination of input variables and monitoring the effect on NPV.

- Probabilities could also be attached to a range of values for key variables and best, worst and most likely EV outcomes calculated.

Tutorial notes

1 The share of the electricity standing charges is ignored, as this does not represent an incremental cash flow. The existing year 1 variable electricity charges thus £(50,000 - 10,000) = £40,000 x 1.05 = £42,000. This is reduced by 40% for the small lights (to 60% x £42,000 = £25,200); and by 30% for the large lights, (to 70% × £42,000 = £29,400).

2 A presentation of the NPV calculation which shows time (0 to 4) across the page - as a cash budget - for each system (large and small) is preferable to that shown here.

37 (Answer 4 of examination)

Examiner's comments and marking guide

Question 4: required candidates to relate a number of cost classification bases to the implementation of planning, control and decision aspects of a management accounting system.

Many candidates gave definitions of cost classifications and of planning, control and decision making. They did not indicate, however, the relationship between particular cost classification bases and each of planning, control and decision making.

	Marks
Cost classifications explanation and	
- link to planning (5 × 1)	5
- link to control (5 × 1)	5
- link to decision-making (5 × 1)	5
Total	15

Step by step answer plan

Step 1 Read the question again and make sure that you focus on precisely what is required. It is the *relationships* between the two statements that are most important, not the individual statements in isolation.

Step 2 You must ensure that the structure of your answer shows that you are relating the two statements. The best approach is probably to take each of the management accounting processes in turn, give a brief explanation of its aims, and then show how the various cost classification methods can be used to assist in meeting those aims.

Step 3 Now review your answer and ensure that it does precisely answer the question as set.

The examiner's answer

The major focus of management accounting in the planning process is likely to be in the preparation of the master budget, incorporating relevant functional budgets, as quantification of the business plan. The plan finally implemented is likely to be the result of an evaluation of the financial implications of a range of short-term strategies taking into account factors such as limited resource constraints and choice of product mix. The range of cost classification bases given in the question are relevant in the budgeting and planning process as follows:

- *By behaviour:* in that a fixed/variable analysis will enable plans for a range of activity levels to be prepared and compared.

- *By function:* in that the master budget will be supported by a budget for each function.

- *By expense type:* in that a definition of each expense type will assist in a consistent approach to the planning estimates using previous plans and actual data as starting points.

- *By controllability:* in that areas which are deemed controllable may be the focus of greater planning effort with regard to price and performance levels which should be incorporated into the plan.

- *By relevance:* in that when planning the use of limited resources contribution per unit of limiting factor is a relevant measure, whereas committed fixed costs should be ignored.

The control process involves the comparison of actual data with the plan, the measurement of variances and the instigation of necessary remedial action. The cost classification bases are important in achieving an effective control mechanism.

- *By behaviour:* for control purposes the planned data should be flexed to actual activity (using a fixed/variable classification) in order to provide a meaningful comparison and variance analysis.

- *By function:* this will assist in ensuring that control is related to the management member responsible for each business function.

- *By expense type:* this will assist in ensuring that like items of expense are compared with each other on a consistent basis.

- *By controllability:* in order that effort is focused on variances over which it is anticipated control can be exercised.

- *By relevance:* in order that items over which no control can be exercised are not seen as a focus of the control process although they will be relevant to some extent for future planning purposes.

The decision-making process will operate in many different situations, each of which will use different cost classifications, such as:

Whether to close a department or discontinue a product.
Calculation of break-even point activity.
Whether to further process a product before sale.

Cost classification bases are relevant in such decision-making situations.

- *By behaviour:* a fixed/variable analysis is relevant in the calculation of break-even point activity.

- *By function and expense type:* both are relevant in determining whether to further process a product. Which are the incremental costs of the further process? This is more readily estimated where function and expense types are clearly classified.

- *By controllability:* sunk costs which cannot be avoided are irrelevant for decision-making.

- *By relevance:* short-term decision-making focuses on incremental and opportunity costs and ignores sunk costs and unavoidable costs.

If the management accounting system is to provide effective information analysis, it is important that a consistent approach is taken when classifying costs in order that planning, control and decision-making may be implemented in a relevant manner.

Did you answer the question?

Note that the examiner has structured his answer to discuss how the two statements can be linked in the design of an effective system.

(Other relevant discussion and illustration of the statements in the question would be accepted.)

38 (Answer 5 of examination)

Examiner's comments and marking guide

Question 5: required candidates to discuss ways in which alternative financial performance measures for an investment proposal at a division may be affected by the basis on which the performance measures are calculated.

The question required linkages, such as, between the use of annuity depreciation and the equalisation of residual income reporting over the life of a proposal or the impact of transfer prices on the cost and revenue components of profit and hence on the reporting of ROI or RI. Many candidates simply wrote a general explanation of the meaning of each of the terms given in the question and did not attempt to show how the terms were interrelated.

	Marks
For each of terms (i) to (v)	
- definition, discussion on use as a performance measure and impact on decision-making re - an investment proposal (5 × 3)	15

Step by step answer plan

Step 1 Read the question again and make sure that you focus on precisely what is required. A discussion of divisional investment appraisal was required, incorporating five related terms given. Some relationships between the terms should have been established in a good answer

Step 2 First look at the five terms. Three of them are potential investment appraisal measures (ROI, RI and NPV); the remaining two affect the figures that may be incorporated into those measures. Accounting procedures can affect all items. The best approach, then, is to discuss the three performance measures in terms of how they may affect divisional management investment decisions, potential problems that may arise, and specifically how the transfer pricing and (annuity) depreciation can affect them. Bring in accounting procedures wherever appropriate.

Step 3 Now review your answer and ensure that it does precisely answer the question as set.

Items not required by the examiner for this question

- isolated explanations of the five given terms without any interrelation

The examiner's answer

An investment proposal may be evaluated in a number of ways. The data given in the question includes return on investment (ROI), residual income (RI) and net present value (NPV) which are three examples of performance measure which may be used. A problem may exist in that there may not be compatibility of the accept/reject signal given to management by each method. This problem may be due to the effect of the investment proposal on the overall performance of the division and from a group/corporate viewpoint.

The accounting procedures used within the group may affect the performance measures. Consider each of ROI, RI and NPV. Return on investment (ROI) = net profit/capital employed.

- Both the numerator and denominator may be affected by the accounting procedures used in the group.

- Transfer pricing policy will affect the net profit reported on transferred goods, both into and out of the division. Where, for example, part of a proposal involves the transfer of components from another division, the transfer price allowed will affect net profit reported at the receiving division.

- The depreciation method used will affect both the net profit reported and the asset base used in calculating ROI.

- An investment proposal may provide a return in excess of cost of capital but reduce the overall ROI at the division. Divisional management may reject the proposal where ROI is the performance measure used.

Residual income (RI) = Net profit – (Imputed interest on capital employed).

- Residual income will suffer from the problems associated with transfer pricing, depreciation method and asset base which applied to ROI.

- It is argued that it does at least measure the excess of profit over the cost of capital and as such is an absolute measure of net benefit to the organisation. This is in contrast to ROI where an investment proposal could provide a return in excess of the minimum required (as reflected by the cost of capital rate) but result in a decrease in the overall ROI reported, hence leading to rejection.

- Where RI is used as the performance measure, a positive RI will be viewed as a net benefit and lead to acceptance of the proposal.

Net present value (NPV) is the value of the estimated cash flow streams for the proposal discounted at the cost of capital rate less the initial investment sum. A positive NPV indicates that the proposal will provide a return in excess of the cost of capital. NPV has advantages over ROI and RI.

- It focuses on cash flows and should therefore, incorporate transfer prices at opportunity cost to the group and ignore depreciation, hence avoiding potential measurement problems.

- It includes cash flows over the life of the proposal and is not, therefore, susceptible to the criticism of ROI and RI that they may be viewed in the short term with fortuitous results depending on the pattern of estimated cash flows.

Did you answer the question?

Note that although the examiner has gone through each of the performance measures separately, he has brought in the effects of transfer pricing and depreciation policies on those measures. He now goes on to link the three measures in terms of possible conflict of decisions, and to specifically discuss the use of annuity depreciation in this context. In this way he has integrated the five terms in the question within a coherent discussion of investment appraisal, rather than simply going through them in isolation.

A major problem is the lack of compatibility of signal to management from ROI, RI and NPV for any one investment proposal. A number of points may be raised to illustrate this problem. Consider a proposal where a constant cash flow stream each year is expected.

- Where straight-line depreciation is used, early years may show a low ROI and negative RI even though the overall NPV is positive. This could lead to rejection by divisional management unless NPV was being used.

- The use of the annuity depreciation method will help to make the measures compatible. An annual equivalent cash flow (AECF) to give a return equal to the cost of capital is calculated (initial investment/discount factor). Then, annuity depreciation = AECF minus imputed interest on capital employed. Imputed interest and hence annuity depreciation are recalculated each year.

This approach gives ROI and RI figures from year 1 onwards which are compatible with the NPV measure. It avoids, therefore, the potential problem of divisional management taking a short-term view and rejecting a proposal because of short-term ROI or RI deficiencies.

Where the cash flow stream varies from year to year, the annuity depreciation approach does not overcome the problem of incompatibility of signals from ROI, RI and NPV, and an alternative approach (not discussed here) would be required.

The above discussion considers ways in which the accept/reject signals from ROI, RI and NPV could be made compatible. In order to achieve compatibility, however, would require the use of accounting procedures which are unlikely to be used as part of the financial accounting system used for the preparation of published accounting statements. In addition, the problems of risk and uncertainty associated with the estimated financial data for a proposal are likely to lead on many occasions to the use of the payback or discounted payback period approach as the basis for determining the acceptability of an investment proposal.

39 (Answer 6 of examination)

Examiner's comments and marking guide

Question 6: required candidates to compare and contrast the role of management accounting in cost reduction and cost control. The question specified a number of specific areas which should be incorporated into the comparison.

Many candidates simply gave explanations of some of the terms with no attempt to contrast cost control and cost reduction.

A favourite answer was to write solely about total quality management. Few answers attempted to discuss the differing ways in which personnel at all levels may be involved in cost control and cost reduction.

	Marks
Definitions	2
Objectives and focus	3
Techniques - including current innovations	6
Personnel involvement	4
Total	15

(answers may interlink the various aspects of the discussion and marks may be allotted accordingly)

Step by step answer plan

Step 1 Read the question again and make sure that you focus on precisely what is required. Within a composite requirement like this, you should go through it carefully, underlining the separate parts. Then think how you can incorporate them all into a structured answer, using an outline answer plan.

Step 2 The starting point will be the two terms themselves - define them, outline their objectives and how they differ in terms of their areas of focus. This will act as a comparison, and covers the first part of the requirement.

Step 3 You then need to turn to the general context of the question - that of the role of the management accountant - and think about the techniques he/she may employ and the involvement of other personnel. The last part of the requirement gives a clue here, mentioning TQM and alternative methods of budgeting, and you should concentrate your discussion around these ideas.

Step 4 Now review your answer and ensure that it does precisely answer the question as set.

Items not required by the examiner for this question

- isolated explanation so the terms given with no attempt to link them within the areas of cost control and reduction
- a detailed discussion of TQM to the exclusion of everything else

The examiner's answer

Cost control may be defined as 'the systematic appraisal of results to ensure that actual and planned operations coincide or if there are any deviations that corrective action is taken'. Cost reduction may be defined as 'seeking permanent reductions in cost without impairing the acceptability of the product or service to the customer through unit cost reduction at a given activity and through unit cost reduction through increased productivity'.

It may be argued that cost control is a more passive exercise, where the main objective is checking whether actual results conform with the plan or budget. The control process may be detailed in that it focuses on individual business functions and cost classifications, but the control function is satisfied if variances from plan are small.

Cost reduction may be seen as a more active exercise which focuses on seeking permanent reductions in cost. It does not consider that the existing business model is acceptable without change.

Did you answer the question?

These three paragraphs answer the first part of the requirement - as well as defining cost reduction and control, by discussing the objectives and areas of importance, it also gives a clear comparison of the two.

The main management accounting technique used in the control of costs is budgeting and budgetary control. Where a system of incremental budgeting is applied, the previous budget and actual data are used as the base from which the current budget is prepared. Allowances are made to allow for inflation and anticipated changes in efficiency and activity. It is assumed, however, that the existing budget model is still relevant.

Budgeting can be made more likely to foster an environment of cost reduction where a zero-based approach is used. Zero-based budgeting requires that all expenditure is justified. A series of decision packages is created for each department or segment of the business. The packages must be ranked and compete with each other for a share of available financial resources. This approach requires managers to justify expenditure at all stages and does not assume that previous budget allowances should be continued.

The extent to which employees are involved in the budget setting and control process is the subject of constant debate. It may be argued that employee involvement tends to be pseudo rather than real. The process may appear to incorporate input from employees at various levels in the organisation, but the final decisions tend to be implemented on a top down basis. Employee involvement in the cost reduction process would traditionally have taken the form of worker suggestion schemes for method changes, possibly in return for a bonus where the suggested change brought about cost reductions.

Current focus is on the application of total quality management allied to activity based budgeting. The major focus of activity based budgeting is on strategically based resource allocation which aims at efficiency, effectiveness and continuous improvement. The focus is on minimum and incremental levels for each activity and the probability of significant change from existing strategy is anticipated. The identification of resource requirements for incremental levels of each activity will help in achieving cost reduction.

Total quality management seeks to control and reduce costs with concentration on:

- emphasis on process control through identification of cost drivers;
- the implementation of a 'right first time' philosophy aiming at zero defects;
- measurement of total performance including cost, efficiency and effectiveness.

A key feature of ABB and TQM is that all members of the workforce should be involved in a real and meaningful way. For example, the operation of so called 'quality circles'. This is where employees are given the opportunity to discuss ways of improving the methods by which their part of the business process is implemented.

Did you answer the question?

The remaining parts of the lengthy requirement have now been answered, including the ways in which personnel may be involved at various levels, an important part of the question (carrying four of the 15 marks)

JUNE 1996 QUESTIONS

Section A - TWO questions ONLY to be attempted

40 (Question 1 of examination)

Leano plc is investigating the financial viability of a new product X. Product X is a short life product for which a market has been identified at an agreed design specification. It is not yet clear whether the market life of the product will be six months or 12 months.

The following estimated information is available in respect of product X:

(i) Sales should be 10,000 units per month in batches of 100 units on a just-in-time production basis. An average selling price of £1,200 per batch of 100 units is expected for a six month life cycle and £1,050 per batch of 100 units for a 12 month life cycle.

(ii) An 80% learning curve will apply in months 1 to 7 (inclusive), after which a steady state production time requirement will apply, with labour time per batch stabilising at that of the final batch in month 7. Reductions in the labour requirement will be achieved through natural labour turnover. The labour requirement for the first batch in month 1 will be 500 hours at £5 per hour.

(iii) Variable overhead is estimated at £2 per labour hour.

(iv) Direct material input will be £500 per batch of product X for the first 200 batches. The next 200 batches are expected to cost 90% of the initial batch cost. All batches thereafter will cost 90% of the batch cost for each of the second 200 batches.

(v) Product X will incur directly attributable fixed costs of £15,000 per month.

(vi) The initial investment for the new product will be £75,000 with no residual value irrespective of the life of the product.

A target cash inflow required over the life of the product must be sufficient to provide for:

(a) the initial investment plus 33 ⅓% thereof for a six month life cycle, or

(b) the initial investment plus 50% thereof for a 12 month life cycle.

Note: learning curve formula:

$$y = ax^b$$

where
- y = average cost per batch
- a = cost of initial batch
- x = total number of batches
- b = learning factor (= –0.3219 for 80% learning rate)

Required

(a) Prepare detailed calculations to show whether product X will provide the target cash inflow over six months and/or 12 months. **(17 marks)**

(b) Calculate the initial batch labour hours at which the cash inflow achieved will be exactly equal to the target figure where a six month life cycle applies. It has been determined that the maximum labour and variable overhead cost at which the target return will be achieved is £259,000. All other variables remain as in part (a). **(6 marks)**

(c) Prepare a report to management which:

(i) explains why the product X proposal is an example of a target costing/pricing situation; **(3 marks)**

(ii) suggests specific actions which may be considered to improve the return on investment where a six month product cycle is forecast; **(6 marks)**

(iii) comments on possible factors which could reduce the rate of return and which must, therefore, be avoided. **(3 marks)**

(Total 35 marks)

41 (Question 2 of examination)

Easterpark Division is considering an investment opportunity to which the following information relates:

(i) Initial investment of £6,000,000 with a project life of five years and nil residual value. Straight-line depreciation is used.

(ii) The project will provide 4,800 hours of process time per annum, the chargeable proportion of which will have a likely contribution of £500 per chargeable hour.

(iii) The required return (cost of capital) is estimated at 10%. *Ignore taxation.*

(iv) Tables 1 and 2 are part of the output of a spreadsheet model using the variable input data provided in the question.

Required:

(a) Discuss the acceptability of the proposal using the data in the question and Tables 1 and 2. You should take into account the range of performance measures available and the likelihood that management will tend to take a short-term view because of a group policy of rapid management turnover at each division as part of a career development programme. **(10 marks)**

(b) (i) Calculate and present the year 1 and year 2 figures from Table 1 where annuity depreciation is used, based on a cost of capital of 10%. **(8 marks)**

(ii) Comment on the acceptability of the revised figures produced in (b) (i) and their impact on management decision-making in relation to the investment proposal. **(4 marks)**

(c) Explain (with relevant calculations) the approximate relationship between the residual incomes over the five-year period and net present value of the investment stated in Table 1. **(3 marks)**

(d) (i) The proportion of process time able to be converted into chargeable output will be linked to a decision on annual maintenance expenditure. The incremental and total annual maintenance cost and the incremental percentage of process time which will be available as chargeable where such maintenance is implemented is as follows:

Maintenance level	*Chargeable proportion of process time* %	*Incremental cost* £	*Total cost* £
1	77.5	260,000	260,000
2	8.0	100,000	360,000
3	2.5	80,000	440,000

All three levels of maintenance cost are currently implemented in the evaluation of the proposal in Tables 1 and 2.

Determine whether implementing maintenance at level 1 only OR at level 1 plus level 2 only, will improve the profitability of the proposal per annum when the contribution is £500 per chargeable hour.
(4 marks)

(ii) Explain the process of introducing a zero-based budgeting exercise at Easterpark Division and how such an exercise could affect the implementation of the decision in (d) (i) above.

(6 marks)
(Total 35 marks)

Table 1

Financial evaluation of the investment where straight-line depreciation is in use

	year 1	year 2	year 3	year 4	year 5
Investment (WDV at beginning of year)	£ 6,000,000	£ 4,800,000	£ 3,600,000	£ 2,400,000	£ 1,200,000
Contribution	2,112,000	2,112,000	2,112,000	2,112,000	2,112,000
Less maintenance cost	440,000	440,000	440,000	440,000	440,000
Net margin	1,672,000	1,672,000	1,672,000	1,672,000	1,672,000
Less depreciation	1,200,000	1,200,000	1,200,000	1,200,000	1,200,000
Net profit	472,000	472,000	472,000	472,000	472,000
Less imputed interest at 10%	600,000	480,000	360,000	240,000	120,000
Residual income	-128,000	-8,000	112,000	232,000	352,000
Return on investment %	7.9%	9.8%	13.1%	19.7%	39.3%
NPV of investment (£) at 10%	338,552				

Table 2

	Year 1 values for various performance measures where straight-line depreciation is in use			*Over 5 year life*
Contribution per hour £	Net profit £	Residual income £	ROI	NPV £
450	260,800	-339,200	4.3%	-462,107
460	303,040	-296,960	5.1%	-301,975
470	345,280	-254,720	5.8%	-141,844
480	387,520	-212,480	6.5%	18,288
490	429,760	-170,240	7.2%	178,420
500	472,000	-128,000	7.9%	338,552
510	514,240	-85,760	8.6%	498,684
520	556,480	-43,520	9.3%	658,816
530	598,720	-1,280	10.0%	818,948
540	640,960	40,960	10.7%	979,079
550	683,200	83,200	11.4%	1,139,211

42 (Question 3 of examination)

EVCO plc produces and sells a single product by passing a single raw material through three consecutive production processes - making, converting and finishing. A system of standard process costing is in operation for which the following information is available for the period ended 30 April 1996:

(i) Stocks are held at constant levels at the beginning and end of the period as follows: raw material(4,000 kg at £0.75 per kg); WIP - converting (500 units); WIP - finishing (500 units); finished goods (500 units).

(ii) Process accounts are debited with the actual costs incurred for the period.

(iii) All losses and transfers between processes or into finished goods are valued at standard cost at their stage of completion. Such unit standard costs may be determined from the information in Table A.

(iv) WIP in converting and finishing is held at the beginning of each process.

(v) The units transferred into finished goods will eventually comprise free replacements to customers, finished goods stock losses and the balance as net sales to customers.

Table B shows the summary profit and loss account for the period ended 30 April 1996 showing budget and actual analysis of gross profit/(loss).

Information relevant to the profit and loss account is as follows:

(i) Free replacements to customers and finished goods stock losses are valued at standard cost per unit.

(ii) The price reduction penalty is allowable on goods delivered late to customers at 5% of the normal selling price of £30 per unit.

EVCO plc presently relies on the variances (£) reported in its standard process system as its main source of control information.

Required

(a) Prepare accounts for the period ended 30 April 1996 using 'backflush accounting' instead of the present system. The accounts required are (i) raw materials and in-process account (ii) finished goods stock account. **(10 marks)**

(b) Discuss the merits of the use of the backflush accounting procedure in EVCO plc as in (a) above. **(5 marks)**

(c) Prepare a report for the period ended 30 April 1996 to the management team of EVCO plc which:

(i) details the factors which have contributed to the poor performance of EVCO plc **(6 marks)**

(ii) expresses budget and actual levels (units and percentage) for each of the following as examples of non-financial indicators of performance:

- free replacements to customers (compared to units delivered)
- late deliveries to customers (against net sales units)
- finished goods stock losses (compared to stock level) **(6 marks)**

(Show all relevant workings)

(iii) suggests features of a total quality programme which should help EVCO plc to overcome the present poor level of performance. **(8 marks)**

(Total 35 marks)

Table A

EVCO plc: Standard process accounts for the period ended 30 April 1996

	Making process		Converting process		Finishing process	
	Product units	£	Product units	£	Product units	£
DR						
WIP b/f			500	7,909	500	10,054
Transfers from previous process			6,800	107,563	6,025	121,156
Raw material cost	8,000	96,000				
Conversion costs		18,800		30,100		14,390
	8,000	114,800	7,300	145,572	6,525	145,600
CR						
Normal losses	800		504		298	
Transfers to next process	6,800	107,563	6,025	121,156	5,365	124,655
WIP damage (written off)			75	1,186	60	1,207
Abnormal process losses	400	6,327	196	3,934	302	6,822
Residual variance		910		11,387		2,862
WIP, c/f			500	7,909	500	10,054
	8,000	114,800	7,300	145,572	6,525	145,600

Table B

EVCO plc: Summary profit and loss account for the period ended 30 April 1996

	Actual		Budget	
	£	£	£	£
Sales revenue		145,050		150,000
Less standard cost of sales		112,341		116,175
Standard contribution		32,709		33,825
Less:				
WIP damage losses	2,393		1,437	
Finished goods losses	697		232	
Abnormal losses	17,083			
Residual process variances	15,159			
Free replacements to customers	11,617		4,832	
Price reduction penalty	1,160		750	
Raw material stock damage losses	240		120	
		48,349		7,371
Gross profit/(loss)		(15,640)		26,454

Section B - TWO questions ONLY to be attempted

43 (Question 4 of examination)

A bank has a section of its business which has two functions:

(1) answering credit control queries from customers both by telephone and in writing;

(2) investment business queries involving responding by telephone and in writing about surrender values, assignment of policies and maturity value quotations.

The staff are arranged in four workgroups, one for each of four geographical areas. Each workgroup consists of 30 employees plus supervisor. Each employee is expected to answer telephone enquiries and a proportion of written enquiries for both credit control and investment business.

Flexi-time working is allowed and considerable overtime is paid in addition to a basic salary payment. There is a high backlog of written enquiries and customers have been complaining about poor telephone response times and quality of response. High staff turnover exists and staff morale is low.

As management accountant you are part of a team required to investigate and report on performance measurement and effectiveness of operations.

Required

(a) Explain, giving examples of their incidence in the provision of the above services, any THREE of the following.

(i) intangibility
(ii) heterogeneity
(iii) simultaneity
(iv) perishability **(8 marks)**

(b) Suggest a possible reorganisation of the workforce into a team or 'cell' structure and discuss the advantages which such a system may have over the existing situation. **(7 marks)**

(Total 15 marks)

44 (Question 5 of examination)

(a) 'It may be argued that in a total quality environment, variance analysis from a standard costing system is redundant.'

Discuss the validity of this statement. **(8 marks)**

(b) Using labour cost as the focus, discuss the differences in the measurement of labour efficiency/effectiveness where (i) total quality management techniques and (ii) standard cost variance analysis are implemented. **(7 marks)**

(Total 15 marks)

45 (Question 6 of examination)

Istana Division is part of the Marmaris Group. Istana Division produces a single product for which it has an external market which utilises 80% of its production capacity.

Taman Division, which is also part of the Marmaris Group, requires units of the product available from Istana Division as input to a product which will be sold outside of the group. Taman Division's requirements are equal to 40% of Istana Division's production capacity.

Taman Division has a potential source of supply from outside the Marmaris Group. This outside supplier can supply 75% of Taman Division's requirement. The outside source may wish to quote a higher price if Taman Division only intends to take up part of its product availability.

Required

Discuss aspects of transfer pricing principles and information availability which will affect the likely achievement of group profit maximisation from the sourcing decisions made by Taman Division in the above situation. **(15 marks)**

ANSWERS TO JUNE 1996 EXAMINATION

40 (Answer 1 of examination)

Examiner's comments and marking guide

Question 1: tested candidates' ability to analyse input data in order to determine whether a new product would achieve a target level of return over its life cycle and to determine the initial batch time allowance at which a specified target return would be achieved. The question also required the preparation of a report relating to the situation provided.

A number of candidates were unable to apply the learning curve formula (which was provided in the question). There was some evidence of candidates not having a calculator with the required function keys. Care was taken in the marking process to ensure that marginal pass/fail candidates were not disadvantaged. Many candidates were unable to calculate the correct raw material cost for the second 6 month period. The report section of the question was generally well answered.

		Marks	*Marks*
(a)	Sales 2 × 0.5	1	
	Direct material 2 × 1	2	
	Direct labour - first six months	4	
	- second six months	6	
	Variable overhead 2 × 0.5	1	
	DAFC 2 × 0.5	1	
	Target return 2 × 0.5	1	
	Decision	1	
		—	17
(b)	Method (on merit)	2	
	Correct figures	4	
		—	6
(c)	Target costing/pricing explanation	3	
	Specific action to improve	6	
	Problems to be avoided	3	
	(allow up to 2 marks for presentation)	—	12
			—
Total			35
			—

Step by step answer plan

Step 1 Read the question again and make sure that you focus on precisely what is required. It is essentially a short term costing/cash flow exercise, incorporating learning effects and target costing, followed by a report.

Step 2 (a) You are required to calculate the net cash flows arising from the production over both a six month and a twelve month period. Set up a proforma statement to start, with columns for the two periods, and narrative relating to the different categories cash flows discussed in (i) to (v) of the question.

Step 3 Now work through each of these paragraphs, slotting in the resulting cash flows as you go, cross-referencing to working where necessary. If you have problems with the learning curve calculations because of a lack of appropriate buttons on your calculator (or lack of expertise in their use) then be warned, but, if unable to calculate a figure, make an apporpriate rough estimate.

Step 4 (b) This is an exercise in working backwards through your previous learning curve calculations, and again necessitates accurate use of the power button on your calculator (though note there are 2 marks for method, even if you can't get to the figures, so its worth showing what you'd *like* to do even if you aren't able to!)

Step 5 (c) Up to two marks are given for presentation, so use a suitable format ; the structure is dictated by the requirements.

Step 6 Now review your answer and ensure that it does precisely answer the question as set.

The examiner's answer

(a)

	6 month	*12 month*
Sales units	60,000	120,000
	£	£
Sales revenue (1)	720,000	1,260,000
Costs:		
Direct material (2)	271,000	514,000
Direct labour (3)	191,340	315,423
Variable overhead (4)	76,536	126,169
DAFC	90,000	180,000
	628,876	1,135,592
Net cash inflow	91,124	124,408

Required cash inflow for target return:		
£75,000 + 33.33%	£100,000	
£75,000 + 50%		£112,500

The target return will be achieved over a 12 month life cycle.

Working notes:

(1) Sales for six months and 12 months are at £1,200 and £1,050 per batch of 100 units respectively.

(2) Direct material:

	£
batches	
200 × £500	100,000
200 × £450	90,000
200 × £405	81,000
for six months	271,000
600 × £405	243,000
for 12 months	514,000

(3) Direct labour:

For first six months:

$$y = ax^b$$
$$= 2{,}500 \times 600^{-0.3219}$$
$$= £318.90$$

Hence total cost = £318.90 × 600 batches = £191,340

For seven months: $y = ax^b$
$= 2,500 \times 700^{-0.3219}$
$= £303.461$

Hence total cost = £303.461 × 700 batches = £212,423

All batches after the first 700 will have the labour cost of the 700th batch.

For 699 batches: $y = ax^b$
$= 2,500 \times 699^{-0.3219}$
$= £303.601$

Hence total cost = £303.601 × 699 batches = £212,217

Cost of 700th batch = £212,423 – £212,217 = £206

Total cost for 12 months = £212,423 + (£206 × 500) = £315,423

(4) Variable overhead is £2 per hour ie, 40% of direct labour.

(b) Variable overhead is dependent on labour cost.

To achieve the target return of £100,000 in the six months, labour and overhead must be reduced by the current shortfall of £8,876.

Maximum labour and overhead = £259,000
let y = average labour cost per batch of product
We require 1.4 × 600 × y = £259,000
Solving y = £308.333
Now learning curve is $y = ax^b$

Substituting $308.33 = a \times 600^{-0.3219}$
$a = £2,417$ (approx)

Hence initial batch labour hours = £2,417/£5 = 483.4 hours (approx)

(c)

Leona plc
Report on new product proposal

(i) The proposal for the new short life product X is an example of target costing/pricing in that the cycle is such that:

- the market has been identified in terms of quantity and price
- the required rate of return over the life of the product has been set
- the need to ensure that costs can be restructured in order to provide the required return over six months has been evaluated.

(ii) A number of specific actions may be considered in order to improve the return on investment:

- reduce the initial labour cost per batch by examination of the production process with a view to the elimination of unnecessary operations.
- improve the learning curve rate, possibly by additional training or change in the method of production
- reduce the material losses in the early batches prior to the steady state being reached
- examine the variable overhead element which is being absorbed per labour hour. Is labour hours the sole and/or most relevant cost driver?
- investigate whether the £15,000 per month of DAFC contains any non-value added overheads which may be eliminated
- investigate whether any of the DAFC may be sourced more cheaply.

(iii) All of the above must be considered taking into account the need to provide a product of the agreed design specification and performance, otherwise free replacement of faulty units to the customer and/or warranty claims may reduce the return from the product.

A person
Management Accountant
June 1996

41 (Answer 2 of examination)

Examiner's comments and marking guide

Question 2: part (a) required candidates to discuss the acceptability of an investment opportunity making reference to data provided in the question. Parts (b) and (c) required a recalculation of the data provided for residual income and return on investment using annuity depreciation and to comment on the acceptability of the revised figures. Part (d) required an analysis of the incremental gain or loss where maintenance was implemented at one of three levels and comment on the relevance of zero base budgeting in this exercise.

Many candidates failed to achieve full marks in part (a) through not commenting on the effect of contribution per hour on the viability of the proposal. In part (b) many candidates calculated the correct annual equivalent value of the initial investment but did not split this into depreciation and interest elements. Alternative presentation approaches were accepted in part (c). Part (d) was generally well answered other than a lack of specific reference to the maintenance cost situation in the ZBB decision.

			Marks	*Marks*
(a)	Table 1 comments:			
	ROI and RI short term		3	
	ROI and RI long term		1	
	NPV		2	
	Table 2 comments:			
	For change in contribution/hour			
	impact on ROI, RI, NPV (on merit)		4	
			—	10
(b)	(i)	Annual equivalent cash flow	2	
		Imputed interest 2 × 0.5	1	
		Depreciation 2 × 1	2	
		Overall layout (incl profit, RI)	2	
		ROI 2 × 0.5	1	
			—	8
	(ii)	Comments on merit		4
(c)	Calculation and comment			3
(d)	(i)	Increase loss - level 1	2	
		Increase profit - level 2	2	
			—	4
	(ii)	ZBB explained (on merit)	4	
		Eastpark comment	2	
			—	6
				—
Total				35
				—

Step by step answer plan

Step 1 Read the question again and make sure that you focus on precisely what is required. It examines the topic of divisional investment evaluation and the possible effects on managerial decision-making of various measures. It requires a working knowledge of annuity depreciation and the relationship between RI and NPV - whether to choose this question will be dictated by your confidence in these areas.

Step 2 (a) At this stage, you don't need to worry about where the figures have come from, just what they are showing. Table 1 shows the standard position of an investment that is acceptable in the long term in danger of being rejected by management with a short-term view. However, the question asks you to also comment on Table 2 - the effects of changing contribution per hour on the various measures. Don't potentially lose 40% of the marks by ignoring this.

Step 3 (b) Don't forget that the annual equivalent to the initial investment accounts for both the imputed interest (for RI) as well as the annuity depreciation. This separation is important for the purposes of the ROI computation, that uses profit after the depreciation element only (which also determines the investment WDV). Don't forget the commentary.

Step 4 (c) Your answer should include both computations that illustrate the relationship, and a brief written explanation.

Step 5 (d) (i) the only elements affected by the level of maintenance are the contribution (dependent upon chargeable hours) and the maintenance cost. Thus you should assess the effects of the changes from one level to the next on the net margin (which will be the same each year). You can do this on an incremental basis (as in this answer) or simply compute the net margin at each of the three cumulative levels.

Step 6 (d) (ii) Introduce your answer by outlining the ZBB process/principles, then relate to Easterpark, particularly in respect of the maintenance levels.

Step 7 Now review your answer and ensure that it does precisely answer the question as set.

The examiner's answer

(a) A range of financial performance measures are available for the Easterpark investment opportunity. Return on investment (ROI) and residual income (RI) may be viewed in the short or longer term. Where a short-term view is taken, as may be by Easterpark management, ROI (7.9%) is less than the cost of capital (10%) in year 1 and again in year 2 (9.8%). Similarly, RI in year 1 is negative (-£128,000) and again in year 2 (-£8,000). Both of these measures will lead to the rejection of the proposal on financial grounds where a short-term view is taken in the decision process. In the longer term both ROI and RI are acceptable.

Table 1 shows that on a discounted cash flow basis over the life of the proposal a positive NPV of £338,552 is reported which would make it viable where the cost of capital is 10%.

Table 2 shows the impact of change in the contribution per hour on the interpretation of each performance measure for year 1 (or for NPV). The proposal is still financially viable where NPV is used even if contribution falls to £480 per hour.

In the short term residual income would only indicate acceptance of the proposal where contribution per hour was £540 or more. Return on investment (based on year 1) would indicate acceptance where contribution per hour was £530 or more.

(b) (i)

Using annuity depreciation:	*Year 1*	*Year 2*
	£	£
Investment (WDV at beginning of year)	6,000,000	5,017,304
Contribution	2,112,000	2,112,000
Less: maintenance cost	440,000	440,000
Net margin	1,672,000	1,672,000
Less: depreciation	982,696	1,080,966
Net profit	689,304	591,034

Less: imputed interest	600,000	501,730
Residual income	89,304	89,304
Return on investment %	11.5%	11.8%

Working notes:

Required annual equivalent cash inflow = £6,000,000/3.791 = £1,582,696
For year 1: imputed interest = 10% × £6,000,000 = £600,000
depreciation = £1,582,696 – £600,000 = £982,696
For year 2: investment WDV = £6,000,000 – £982,696 = £5,017,304
imputed interest = 10% × £5,017,304 = £501,730
depreciation = £1,582,696 – £501,730 = £1,080,966

(ii) The use of annuity depreciation for the calculation of ROI and RI will make the proposal acceptable even in the short term where these measures are used. RI is equalised at £89,304 in each year. ROI is now in excess of the required return of 10% even in year 1, due to the adjusted depreciation charge.

A problem with the use of annuity depreciation in the calculations is that it is unlikely to be used in practice as part of the financial reporting system.

(c) The discounted value of the residual income = NPV.

Year	*RI* £	*DCF factor*	*Discounted cash flow* £
1	-128,000	0.909	-116,352
2	-8,000	0.826	-6,608
3	112,000	0.751	84,112
4	232,000	0.683	158,456
5	352,000	0.621	218,592
	NPV		338,200

This differs slightly from the NPV shown in Table 1 (£338,552) because of a slight difference in the Annuity Table and Present Value Table values used when discounting the cash flows.

This confirms that the residual income value is the excess cash inflow available over that required to provide a return equivalent to the cost of capital.

(***Tutorial note:*** Clearly this neat trick will not work if the method of depreciation is changed.)

(d) (i) Incremental hours at level 2 = 4,800 × 8% = 384 hours
Incremental hours at level 3 = 4,800 × 2.5% = 120 hours
Now incremental gain/(loss) = incremental contribution - incremental cost
At level 2 = (384 × £500) - £100,000 = £92,000
At level 3 = (120 × £500) - £80,000 = (£20,000)

This means that incorporating maintenance at level 1 only will result in a net fall in profit of £72,000 from the present level. Incorporating maintenance at level 1 + level 2 will result in a net increase in profit of £20,000 over the present level.

(ii) The principles and steps in introducing zero-base budgeting may be summarised as:

- it rejects the idea that the current model/strategy is the best
- it requires incremental packages of activity for each function - such as maintenance - to be evaluated
- it is up to the function manager to put the best possible case for each incremental package
- each function will then compete with others for a share of available budget funds.

The final decision may rely on the strength of argument put by the maintenance manager.

For Easterpark Division, maintenance is possibly one of a number of services competing for funds. The maintenance manager may lose out on level 2 even though it will add to company profitability. This would make the proposal less attractive in financial terms.

Alternatively the manager may be able to argue the case for the inclusion of level 3 even though it would result in an incremental loss of £20,000, if he can convince management of intangible benefits such as long-term ability to sustain market share.

Did you answer the question?

The reference to the maintenance decision in the context of ZBB is an essential part of this answer.

42 (Answer 3 of examination)

Examiner's comments and marking guide

Question 3: part (a) required candidates to convert a set of standard process accounts provided in the question into a format where backflush accounting was in operation. Part (b) required a discussion of the merits of a backflush accounting format. Part (c) required the preparation of a report which specified factors contributing to the poor performance of the company by analysing financial data provided; calculation of a number of non-financial indicators of performance and suggestion of how a total quality programme could help overcome poor performance.

There was evidence that candidates at some centres had made use of illustrative material in the *Students' Newsletter* in order to improve their knowledge of this topic. A sympathetic view was taken in the marking of part (a) which was essentially a consolidation of data provided in Table A in the question. The report required in part (c) provided many candidates with the platform from which to obtain a pass in this question. Many candidates could have improved their performance through a better analysis of the non-financial indicators of performance and a greater attempt to relate the quality improvement comments to the situation in the question.

			Marks	*Marks*
(a)	Input and output items in material and in-process account and finished goods account (10 × 1)			10
(b)	Backflush accounting principles compared to EVCO now		3	
	Short time cycle		1	
	Low stock and WIP levels		1	
			—	5
(c)	(i)	Poor performance factors (6 × 1)	6	
	(ii)	Percentage indicators (6 × 1)	6	
	(iii)	TQM features including use to EVCO (4 × 2)	8	
			—	20
				—
Total				35
				—

Step by step answer plan

Step 1 Read the question again and make sure that you focus on precisely what is required. The subject matter is drawn from the "modern developments" part of the syllabus, and requires a working knowledge of backflush accounting and an appreciation of the features of TQM

Step 2 (a) Backflush accounting removes the need for separate raw materials and process accounts - the materials and in-process account (MIPA) carries all the relevant cost information in one account. Thus you need to pick up all information concerning opening stocks and process inputs from Table A and debit the MIPA; it will be credited with all closing stocks and transfers to finished goods. The balancing figure represents "residual variances" (TN 1) the finished good account is mainly written up from the P&L.

Step 3 (b) You should be familiar with the claimed for merits for backflush accounting, the main one being simplicity and thus cost efficiency. This can (and should) be clearly illustrated in your answer by reference to your answer to (a) compared with Table A .

Step 4 (c) If you struggled a bit with the technicalities of backflush accounting, this report offers a reprieve, as it has more general requirements. Use a report format, and structure its contents around the requirements. In (i), try to identify as many contributory factors as possible; (ii) requires some explanation of how unit figures have been derived form the monetary data in Table B, and (iii) needs a general framework of the aims of TQM in improving performance, along with specific reference to EVCO.

Step 5 Now review your answer and ensure that it does precisely answer the question as set.

The examiner's answer

(a)

Materials and in-process account

	£		£
Material and in-process stock b/f	20,963	To finished goods (at standard)	124,655
Variable costs:		Residual variances (TN1)	34,635
Material cost	96,000	Material and in-process stock c/f	20,963
Conversion cost	63,290		
	180,253		180,253

Finished goods account

	£		£
Finished goods stock b/f	11,618	To cost of sales (P/L)	112,341
Ex-materials and in-process account	124,655	Free replacements (P/L)	11,617
		Stock losses written off (P/L)	697
		Finished goods stock c/f	11,618
	136,273		136,273

Working notes:

(1) Material and in-process stock = 4,000kg × £0.75 + £7,909 + £10,054 = £20,963
(2) Conversion cost = £18,800 + £30,100 + £14,390 = £63,290
(3) Residual variances:

	£	
Residual variance	15,159	(For all processes)
Abnormal process losses	17,083	(For all processes)

WIP damage written off	2,393	(For all processes)
	34,635	

(4) Finished goods stock = 500 units × £23.235 = £11,618
Note that unit cost may be obtained from Table 1 as £124,655/5,365 = £23.235

(5) Other values are taken directly from Tables 1 and 2

(b) The accounting system currently in use by EVCO plc records quantities and values in each of making, converting and finishing processes. This system records the inputs to each process, the transfers from one process to another, normal and abnormal losses and residual variances.

The use of 'backflush accounting' focuses on the output and then works backwards when allocating costs between cost of goods sold (or finished goods) and stock valuations. Backflush accounting will be seen as relevant where the overall process cycle time is short and levels of materials and WIP are low. Such conditions are likely to occur where a just-in-time approach to production and sales is in force. EVCO plc currently has a policy of holding constant levels of stocks and WIP. It also uses the standard process costing variance analysis as its control mechanism. A move to a backflush accounting system would require alternative performance indicators for the various aspects of production and sale, such as a set of non-financial indicators.

The backflush accounting system simplifies the accounting records by avoiding the need to trace the movement of materials and WIP through the production processes.

(c)

EVCO plc

Report to management team

Subject: performance measurement

(i) The accounting information for the period ended 30 April 1996 highlights a number of major problems as follows:

- deteriorating profit levels with an actual loss of £15,640 instead of a budget profit of £26,454
- reduction in sales volume of approximately 3.5%
- high levels of process losses as indicated by high abnormal losses written off
- high levels of losses to raw materials, WIP and finished goods
- high levels of residual process variances which probably indicate poor levels of productivity and high idle time
- likely customer dissatisfaction through high replacement of faulty units and late deliveries.

(ii) Customer dissatisfaction may be due to high levels of faulty goods and late deliveries which may be worsened by losses of finished goods before delivery. The following budget and actual figures apply:

	Budget	*Actual*
Free replacement (as percentage of sales delivered)	208/5208 = 4%	500/5335 = 9.4%
Late deliveries (as percentage of net sales)	500/5000 = 10%	773/4835 = 16%
Finished goods stock losses (as percentage of stock)	10/500 = 2%	30/500 = 6%

(*Note:* the units in the above calculations are obtained from Table B values (£) using £23.235 as unit valuation and a price penalty reduction value of £1.50 per unit as appropriate.

eg, Actual finished goods losses = £697/23.235 = 30 units
Budget late deliveries = £750/1.50 = 500 units).

(iii) A total quality management programme should help overcome the range of problems which currently exist. Total quality management should, for example, aim at:

- an environment of zero defects at minimum cost eg, to overcome process losses
- delivery of a quality product to customers thus eliminating free replacements
- reduction in cycle times and the elimination of non-value added activities thus reducing stock levels/losses and avoiding late deliveries
- improved awareness of all personnel of the need for a 'quality culture' in the company in order to improve performance at all levels.

Did you answer the question?

Note that the examiner has related his general comments about the principles of TQM to the specific circumstances of EVCO.

I shall be pleased to supply any further information on request.

A Person
Management Accountant
June 1996

Tutorial notes

1 The residual variances figure in what is usually called a Raw and in Progress account represents the balancing figure on the account, and incorporates losses and damage costs separately identified in Table A:

		£
WIP damage	(1,186 + 1,207)	2,393
Abnormal process losses	(6,327 + 3,934 + 6,822)	17,083
Residual variance	(910 + 11,387 + 2,862)	15,159
		34,635

(There is no need to prove this, however)

43 (Answer 4 of examination)

Examiner's comments and marking guide

Question 4: required candidates to explain the relevance of features such as intangibility in the provision of a service, using a bank scenario provided in the question as the area of focus. In addition, candidates were required to suggest a possible reorganisation of the workforce and the advantages which should result from this.

This was the least popular question in Section B of the paper and was generally poorly answered. Considerable latitude was given in the marking process in determining acceptable explanations of features such as intangibility and also on possible reorganisation of the workforce.

The current list of recommended articles from the *Students' Newsletter* contains reference to the focus of this question and to additional relevant reading.

		Marks	Marks
(a)	Terms explained 3 × 1	3	
	Examples 3 × 1	3	
	Plus floating marks on merit for good quality answers	2	
		—	8
(b)	Problems identified	3	
	Advantages of team grouping	4	
		—	7
			—
Total			15
			—

Step by step answer plan

Step 1 Read the question again and make sure that you focus on precisely what is required. We are considering performance measurement and work organisation in a service business.

Step 2 (a) First note that only three of terms need explanation. These four terms are used by the examiner in the distinction of the characteristics of service products from those manufactured; however even if you have not specifically studied them, a reasonable common sense interpretation would have been awarded some marks. As usual, take care to illustrate your explanations with examples from the business given.

Step 3 (b) The best approach here would be to first identify the existing problems and then think how some sort of cell structure may improve matters. Make sure that you specify the composition and segregation of the teams in your new system before discussing the advantages .

Step 4 Now review your answer and ensure that it does precisely answer the question as set.

The examiner's answer

(a) **Intangibility:** in a service business it is less likely that there will be a single measurable output object. In the bank example, the helpfulness of employees or the speed of response to enquiries may influence the customer perception of the output quality and quantity.

Heterogeneity: the standard of performance in providing the service may vary. This is particularly so where there is a high labour input as in the bank example. It may be difficult to compare the performance of employees through time or with each other. Efforts should be made to specify a standard of performance which should be aimed for in both tangible and intangible aspects of the service. For example reply to written queries within 48 hours or telephone call-back within one hour for awkward telephone queries.

Simultaneity: this refers to the production and consumption of a service being at the same time. There is no opportunity to check it before delivery to the customer. In the bank example this applies to the telephone queries. Responses to written queries could be checked, however, before being sent out.

Perishability: services cannot be stored. This causes problems where there is a fluctuation in demand. A surge in telephone enquiries may swamp the system. A surge in written queries could probably be overcome through overtime working of the employment of temporary staff.

Did you answer the question?

Note how the examiner has illustrated each service characteristic with an example from the question. Also note that only three of these were required.

(b) The existing system appears to have a number of problems:

- poor telephone response time and quality of response
- high backlog of written queries
- high staff turnover and low morale
- high level of overtime working.

The bank will wish to ensure that 'value for money' is being achieved in the delivery of the service to customers. Failure to respond in a timely and efficient manner is likely to lead to loss of existing customers and potential new customers.

The present work distribution into geographical area groups where each employee is expected to answer telephone queries and undertake written work on any topic is unlikely to produce a quality system.

Did you answer the question?
When asked to design and discuss the advantages of a new scheme, it is always useful to start by highlighting the problems of the old.

It would be more appropriate to have teams of employees with each team responsible for a particular type of enquiry. Each team would be responsible for telephone and written responses in a specific area eg, maturity value quotations. This should be effective in a range of ways including:

- team resources can be directed to telephone or written queries according to demand fluctuations
- team ethos can be cultivated in order to increase pride in work and to help achieve an overall high level of performance
- overtime requirements should be reduced through better work organisation
- staff turnover and associated costs should be reduced through the improved quality of work environment and team support
- customers should receive a quicker and more effective response to queries which should help the corporate image of the bank and its ability to retain or increase its market share.

44 (Answer 5 of examination)

Examiner's comments and marking guide

Question 5: required candidates to discuss the relevance of standard cost variance analysis in a total quality environment with specific reference to the measurement of labour efficiency/effectiveness.

Many candidates listed features of a total quality management system with little attempt at highlighting specific differences in philosophy from that of a standard cost environment. Some candidates did focus on the wider view of labour effectiveness measures claimed for a total quality system.

		Marks	*Marks*
(a)	General comments	2	
	Specific TQM v Standards differences (any 3) 3×2	6	
		—	8
(b)	Std costing - efficiency linked to output, etc	3	
	TQM - effectiveness, failure costs, etc	4	
	(overall allow marks on merit)	—	7
			—
Total			15
			—

Step by step answer plan

Step 1 Read the question again and make sure that you focus on precisely what is required. It looks at the possible redundancy of traditional standard costing in the more modern TQM environment. Careful thought as to whether you can really integrate the two should be made before choosing this question.

Step 2 (a) The best way to structure your answer is to outline the features of one of the systems, then show how the other either complements these or is incompatible with them. What you mustn't do is simply describe each of them separately and hope that the examiner can see the differences!

Step 3 (b) The key point here is the difference in scope of the measures used in the two environments - standard costing being the narrower, more volume/task related of the two.

Step 4 Now review your answer and ensure that it does precisely answer the question as set.

The examiner's answer

(a) Standard costing involves the setting of standards at agreed levels of price and performance and the measurement of actual events against such standards in order to monitor performance. The variance analysis will measure changes in performance and price for sales, material, labour and overhead. A basic assumption is that the standards will apply over a time period during which they provide a suitable base against which to measure actual events.

A total quality environment adopts a different philosophy:

- it aims towards an environment of zero defects at minimum cost. This conflicts with the idea of standard costs which, for example, accept that a planned level of yield loss has been built into material standards

- it aims towards the elimination of waste, where waste is defined as anything other than the minimum essential amount of equipment, materials, space and worker time. Standard costs may be set at currently attainable levels of performance which build in an accepted allowance for 'waste'

- it aims at continuous improvement. The focus is on performance measures which illustrate a continuous trend of improvement rather than a 'steady state' standard performance which is accepted for a specific period

- it is an overall philosophy requiring awareness by all personnel of the quality requirements in providing the customer with products of agreed design specification. Standard costing tends to place control of each variance type with specific members of management and workforce. This view may cause conflicting decisions as to the best strategy for improvement.

Did you answer the question?

You must make a clear attempt at a comparison between the two philosophies, rather than simply listing their separate features.

(b) Standard costing will measure labour efficiency in terms of the ratio of output achieved: standard input. This measure focuses on quantity and does not address other issues of effectiveness. Effectiveness in a total quality context implies high quality with a focus on value added activities and essential support activities. Efficiency (in terms of output) may be achieved at a cost. In a total quality context such costs may be measured as internal or external failure costs which will not be identified in the standard cost variance measure.

In a standard cost system, individual labour task situations are used as a basis for efficiency measurement. In a total quality environment it is more likely that labour will be viewed in multi-task teams who are responsible for the completion of a part of the production cycle. The team effectiveness is viewed in terms of measures other than output, including incidence of rework, defect levels at a subsequent stage in production, defects reported by the customer.

45 (Answer 6 of examination)

Examiner's comments and marking guide

Question 6: required candidates to discuss the transfer pricing principles which would affect the achievement of group profit maximisation in a specific situation provided in the question.

Many candidates wrote about transfer pricing methods in general terms and either failed to relate to the specific situation in the question or only provided a brief reference to the situation. In addition, many candidates failed to provide a sufficiently broad analysis of the range of transfer pricing methods which could be related to the scenario provided in the question.

		Marks	*Marks*
(a)	General rule principles	3	
	Different views of Istana/Taman situation (4 × 3)	12	
		—	15
			—
Total			15
			—

Step by step answer plan

Step 1 Read the question again and make sure that you focus on precisely what is required. It is a discursive question on transfer pricing, as usual within the context of a specific set-up.

Step 2 A good starting point is discussion of the "general rule" of transfer pricing, and how its proper application will rely on accurate information availability. You then need to consider the given situation in two parts - where transfers are at the expense of outside sales, and where they are made from spare capacity. You should make some attempt at analysis of the percentages given to ascertain the exact position as regards the extent of outside supplier's involvement and influence.

Step 3 Now review your answer and ensure that it does precisely answer the question as set.

The examiner's answer

If group profit maximisation is to result from decisions made using transfer prices, the transfer prices should be set using the 'general rule' that transfer price = marginal cost + opportunity cost to the group. The information flow between divisions which will enable the general rule principle to be applied may be affected by the degree of autonomy that each division is allowed. Divisional autonomy implies that the management at each division is allowed to operate in an independent manner free from directives from group management. In this situation, divisional management are likely to operate at arms' length and simply quote the best price which they think the market will bear.

Did you answer the question?

This general 'setting the scene' introductory paragraph allows the examiner to bring in the "information availability" aspect of the requirement. He then goes on to consider how the general rule may be applied in the specific circumstances outlined.

The Istana Division - Taman Division situation may be studied from a number of viewpoints:

(i) Where Istana Division has an external market for its product (80% of its capacity), the transfer price should be set at market price in order to comply with the general rule. In this way any external supply available to Taman Division at less than the market price of Istana Division's product will increase group profit.

(ii) It may be that there are some costs associated with external sales which are not incurred on inter-divisional business. For example less packaging may be required and delivery costs may be reduced. In such a situation, Istana Division should quote an adjusted market price which excludes the costs not relevant to inter-divisional business. In this way Istana Division will earn the same profit as it would from external sales and Taman Division will reject external supplier quotes which are in excess of the adjusted market price quoted by Istana Division.

(iii) Istana Division has 20% spare capacity for which, it appears, no external market exists. It should offer to transfer output from the 20% spare capacity to Taman Division at marginal cost on the basis that zero opportunity cost to the group exists for this capacity. In this way Taman Division will reject any external supplier quotes in excess of the marginal cost of Istana Division.

(iv) We are told that the external supplier can supply 75% of Taman Division's requirement. This is equivalent to 30% of the capacity of Istana Division. Remember that Istana Division has 20% spare capacity, which means that the residual 10% which the external supplier could provide represents external sales of Istana Division. It will be useful for Istana Division to indicate the quantities which it is willing to supply at different prices viz., 20% capacity at marginal cost and 10% capacity at adjusted market price. In this way Taman Division can evaluate the offer from the external source taking into account the possibility that the external source may require a higher price for a part order.

DECEMBER 1996 QUESTIONS

Section A - TWO questions ONLY to be attempted

46 (Question 1 of examination)

Tritex plc produces a number of products which pass through three consecutive processes - Making, Converting and Finishing - before sale to customers.

Until recently, Tritex plc has prepared standard product costs per unit for each product using (a) control standards and (b) current standards. Appendix 1 shows extracts from these standards for Product A. These standards plus a detailed variance analysis have been the main focus of control information. The control standards are based on industry average performance and the current standards are based on the level of performance which it is anticipated should be attainable using last year's actual performance as the starting point.

The control and current standard product costs per unit incorporate the following specifications:

(a) Process losses (%) are expressed as a percentage of input to each process.
(b) Material requirement is based on the input to the Making process.
(c) Labour requirement is based on the total hours per unit of output from a process.
(d) Variable overhead is absorbed on the basis of net processing hours (ie, excluding idle time) per unit of output from a process.
(e) Variable overhead is absorbed into all products using an average rate per net processing hour.
(f) Work-in-progress is 100% complete at the end of each process.

Tritex plc has produced amended unit standard process costs which incorporate Activity Based Costing (ABC) and the planned effects of a Total Quality Management (TQM) programme. Appendix 1 shows an extract of such a standard cost for product A.

The ABC/TQM standard costs incorporate the following in their specification:

(a) Zero idle time allowance for labour. Employees will carry out some rework, material handling and maintenance not previously included in the standard labour cost.

(b) The cost driver for all variable overhead in the Making process is the number of steam operations per product unit and overhead is absorbed on this basis. For product A this should result in an overhead cost reduction of 30% per product unit from the control standard cost. Any residual difference is due to improved work practices.

Required

(a) Prepare workings which show the calculation of the appropriate values in the cells marked (?) in the Current Standard Cost for product A in Appendix 1. **(6 marks)**

(b) As a benchmarking exercise, discuss the differences between the control standard and current standards for product A (per Appendix 1), highlighting possible reasons for such differences. **(9 marks)**

(c) Use the ABC/TQM standard for product A together with information provided in the question to indicate specific ways in which Tritex plc is proposing to implement a total quality philosophy. Your answer should include discursive and quantitative elements. **(12 marks)**

(d) Standard costing and variance analysis provides some control information. Adoption of a total quality philosophy will require additional information from the control system. Identify and comment on the additional information which may be provided where a total quality philosophy is adopted.

(8 marks)
(Total: 35 marks)

Appendix to Question 1

Extracts from standard product cost per unit - Product A for each of Current Standard, Control Standard, ABC/TQM Standard

	Losses	*Product Units*	*sqm/unit hours/unit steam ops/unit (see note 1)*	*rate/sqm rate/hour rate/ steam op*	*Cost*	*WIP value per unit*
	%			£	£	£
Current Standard Cost						
Making Process (input)	9.0%	?				
Raw material			6.720	0.85	?	
Labour			0.142	4.75	?	
Overheads			0.125	7.00	?	
sub-total making					?	?
Converting Process (input)	13.0%	?				
Finishing Process (input)	7.0%	?				
Control Standard Cost						
Making Process (input)	5.0%	1.2312				
Raw material			6.000	0.80	5.910	
Labour			0.108	5.00	0.632	
Overheads			0.100	6.32	0.739	
sub-total making					7.281	6.225
Converting Process (input)	10.0%	1.1696				
Finishing Process (input)	5.0%	1.0526				
ABC/TQM Standard Cost						
Making Process (input)	1.0%	1.0465				
Raw material			6.000	0.90	5.651	
Labour			0.095	6.00	0.591	
Overheads			1.000	0.36	0.373	
sub-total making					6.615	6.385
Converting Process (input)	2.5%	1.0360				
Finishing Process (input)	1.0%	1.0101				

Note 1: The charge basis per unit for material, labour and overhead (and corresponding cost per unit) will be one of the above. The specific basis (and cost) which will apply for a particular expense type may vary for each of current, control and ABC/TQM standards. The information provided in the question gives the details from which you can determine the relevant basis in each case.

47 (Question 2 of examination)

A holiday resort operates a clifftop cable car to transport tourists to and from the beach during the holiday season.

During the 1996 season the following operating information applied:

(i) Average variable cost per single cable car journey was £10.

(ii) Total fixed cost for the season was £48,000.

(iii) The fare structure incorporates a return fare which gives a 10% saving as compared to paying for two single journeys. The fares per single journey were as follows: Adult £1.00; Juvenile £0.60; Senior Citizen £0.50.

(iv) The cable car has a maximum capacity of 30 passengers per journey. It operated for 100 journeys per day on each of 120 days during 1996.

(v) Total passenger journeys represented 60% capacity utilisation per journey. The capacity utilised comprised 50% adult, 30% juvenile and 20% senior citizen journeys. For all passenger categories, 75% of the tickets sold were for single journey fares and the remainder for return fares.

(vi) Advertising revenue from displays in the cable car totalled £20,000. This is a fixed annual sum from contracts which will apply each season up to and including 1998.

It is anticipated that costs will increase by 5% due to inflation during the 1997 season and that fares will also increase by 5% from the 1996 levels. While the fare increase has been agreed and cannot be altered, it is possible that the inflation effect on costs may differ from the forecast rate of 5%.

Required

(a) Prepare a statement showing the budgeted net profit or loss for the 1997 season where capacity utilisation per journey and passenger mix is expected to be the same as in 1996, but the number of cable car journeys per day will be increased to 120 journeys, with the same length of operating season. (All relevant workings must be shown). **(7 marks)**

(b) Explain the meaning of the information in the two-way data table shown in Appendix 2 which has been extracted from a spreadsheet model of the situation and comment on the range of values including reference to your answer to part (a). **(6 marks)**

(c) Capacity utilisation and the rate of inflation have been identified as key variables for 1997. Probabilities have been estimated for the level at which the key variables will occur. Capacity utilisation and inflation are independent of each other. The estimates are as follows:

Capacity utilisation	*Probability*		*Inflation*	*Probability*
%			%	
80	0.15		2	0.2
60	0.60		5	0.5
40	0.25		8	0.3

(i) Prepare a summary which shows the range of possible net profit or loss outcomes, showing the combined probability of each outcome, using Appendix 2 as appropriate. **(8 marks)**

(ii) Calculate the expected value of net profit or loss, indicating how you arrived at your answer. **(2 marks)**

(iii) Using your answer to c(i), calculate the cumulative probability of the net profit being greater than £30,000. **(2 marks)**

(d) Calculate the percentage of maximum capacity at which the cable car will breakeven during 1997 where the variables are as used in the calculations in (a), except that an amended inflation rate has resulted in total costs of £205,440. **(6 marks)**

(e) Explain ways in which a spreadsheet model could be used to calculate the effect of EACH of the following variable data changes on profit for 1997 where all other variables remain unchanged:

(i) Changes in passenger mix
(ii) Changes in the overall fare increase between 1% and 10% in steps of 1%. (No calculations required). **(4 marks)**

(Total: 35 marks)

Appendix 2

Two-way data table monitoring changes in net profit for a range of levels of capacity utilisation and inflation.

		Capacity utilisation (%)				
		20%	40%	60%	80%	100%
	1%	-104,927	-35,935	33,058	102,050	171,043
	2%	-106,847	-37,855	31,138	100,130	169,123
	3%	-108,767	-39,775	29,218	98,210	167,203
	4%	-110,687	-41,695	27,298	96,290	165,283
	5%	-112,607	-43,615	25,378	94,370	163,363
Inflation (%)	6%	-114,527	-45,535	23,458	92,450	161,443
	7%	-116,447	-47,455	21,538	90,530	159,523
	8%	-118,367	-49,375	19,618	88,610	157,603
	9%	-120,287	-51,295	17,698	86,690	155,683
	10%	-122,207	-53,215	15,778	84,770	153,763

48 (Question 3 of examination)

The budget for the Production, Planning and Development Department of Obba plc is currently prepared as part of a traditional budgetary planning and control system. The analysis of costs by expense type for the period ended 30 November 1996 where this system is in use is as follows:

Expense type	*Budget* %	*Actual* %
Salaries	60	63
Supplies	6	5
Travel cost	12	12
Technology cost	10	7
Occupancy cost	12	13

The total budget and actual costs for the department for the period ended 30 November 1996 are £1,000,000 and £1,060,000 respectively.

The company now feels that an Activity Based Budgeting approach should be used. A number of activities have been identified for the Production, Planning and Development Department. An investigation has indicated that total budget and actual costs should be attributed to the activities on the following basis:

Activities:		*Budget* %	*Actual* %
1.	Routing/scheduling - new products	20	16
2.	Routing/scheduling - existing products	40	34
3.	Remedial re-routing/scheduling	5	12
4.	Special studies - specific orders	10	8
5.	Training	10	15
6.	Management & administration	15	15

Required

(a) (i) Prepare TWO budget control statements for the Production Planning and Development Department for the period ended 30 November 1996 which compare budget with actual cost and show variances using:

- a traditional expense based analysis and
- an activity based analysis. **(6 marks)**

(ii) Identify and comment on FOUR advantages claimed for the use of Activity Based Budgeting over traditional budgeting using the Production Planning and Development example to illustrate your answer. **(12 marks)**

(iii) Comment on the use of the information provided in the activity based statement which you prepared in (i) in activity based performance measurement and suggest additional information which would assist in such performance measurement. **(8 marks)**

(b) Other activities have been identified and the budget quantified for the three months ended 31 March 1997 as follows:

Activities	*Cost Driver Unit basis*	*Units of Cost Driver*	*Cost*
			£000
Product design	design hours	8,000	2,000 (see note 1)
Purchasing	purchase orders	4,000	200
Production	machine hours	12,000	1,500 (see note 2)
Packing	volume (cu.m.)	20,000	400
Distribution	weight (kg)	120,000	600

Note 1: this includes all design costs for new products released this period.

Note 2: this includes a depreciation provision of £300,000 of which £8,000 applies to 3 months depreciation on a straight line basis for a new product (NPD). The remainder applies to other products.

New product NPD is included in the above budget. The following additional information applies to NPD:

(i) Estimated total output over the product life cycle: 5,000 units (4 years life cycle).
(ii) Product design requirement: 400 design hours
(iii) Output in quarter ended 31 March 1997: 250 units
(iv) Equivalent batch size per purchase order: 50 units
(v) Other product unit data: production time 0.75 machine hours; volume 0.4 cu metres; weight 3 kg.

Required:

Prepare a unit overhead cost for product NPD using an activity based approach which includes an appropriate share of life cycle costs using the information provided in (b) above. **(9 marks)**
(Total: 35 marks)

Section B - TWO questions ONLY to be attempted

49 (Question 4 of examination)

Performance in education or training institutions may be viewed in the context of the performance of the institution and the performance of staff.

(a) Briefly discuss each of FIVE performance measures, including financial and non-financial measures, which may be used. **(10 marks)**

(b) Discuss the motivational factors likely to influence the level of performance of staff and suggest ways in which efforts may be made to quantify such factors. **(5 marks)**
(Total: 15 marks)

50 (Question 5 of examination)

Strategic decisions may involve dealing with steady, increased or decreased demand for any particular product or its discontinuance.

(a) 'Alternative valuation bases and relevant costs may be used for the valuation of units of a product'. Discuss this statement in the context of decision making for:

(i) disposal of existing product units no longer required
(ii) replacement of product units to meet current demand
(iii) increase in the level of product units as demand increases
(iv) decrease in the level of product units as demand falls. **(10 marks)**

(b) Discuss how the timescale of the decision may affect the treatment of each of committed costs and discretionary costs in decision making. **(5 marks)**

(Total: 15 marks)

51 (Question 6 of examination)

(a) Spiro Division is part of a vertically integrated group of divisions all located in one country. All divisions sell externally and also transfer goods to other divisions within the group. Spiro Division performance is measured using profit before tax as a performance measure.

(i) Prepare an outline statement which shows the costs and revenue elements which should be included in the calculation of divisional profit before tax. **(4 marks)**

(ii) The degree of autonomy which is allowed to divisions may affect the absolute value of profit reported. Discuss this statement in relation to Spiro Division. **(6 marks)**

(b) Discuss the pricing basis on which divisions should offer to transfer goods in order that corporate profit maximising decisions should take place. **(5 marks)**

(Total: 15 marks)

ANSWERS TO DECEMBER 1996 EXAMINATION

46 (Answer 1 of examination)

Examiner's comments and marking guide

Question 1: this question tested candidates' ability to implement relevant calculations in the preparation a standard process unit cost. It also required candidates to compare and contrast control, current and TQM standards. Finally, it required candidates to identify additional information which may be required where a total quality philosophy is adopted.

Many candidates were unable to implement the relevant calculations in order to prepare the standard process cost information. This was disappointing, since an article in the *Students' Newsletter* has incorporated calculations of a similar nature. Many of the answers comparing the alternative standard costs did not attempt to quantify the differences despite this being specifically asked for in part (c).

		Marks	
(a)	Input to each process (3 × 0.5)	1.5	
	Raw material cost	1	
	Labour cost	1	
	Overhead cost	1	
	WIP per unit	1.5	6
(b)	Current vs control standard		
	process losses and reasons	2	
	material input and reasons	2	
	net labour hours and reasons	2	
	labour idle time and reasons	2	
	overheads and reasons	2	max 9
	(1 mark for identification/quantification and 1 mark for reasons)		
(c)	ABC/TQM standard -		
	identification AND comment in TQM		
	context in relation to:		
	process losses	3	
	material		3
	labour	3	
	overhead	3	12
(d)	Comments and examples on range of additional		
	control information (on merit)		8
Total			35

Step by step answer plan

Step 1 Read the question again and make sure that you focus on precisely what is required. It considers various ways and environments in which cost standards may be set, in the context of a series of manufacturing processes.

Step 2 (a) Take a little time to study the Appendix. It gives a means of computing the standard cost per finished making process *output* unit under the various types of standard. There are losses, so to get one unit of *output*, more than one unit of *input* will be needed. The first three boxes are completed by working back from one unit of output from the finishing process through to the initial input that will be required to the making process (TN 1) Once these units have been established, the costs can be applied to get the individual and overall cost of the WIP unit

Step 3 (b) When comparing the current and control standards, go through each aspect of the cost you are given in the Appendix (including loss rates) and where the difference is significant, state the difference between the figures on an absolute or relative basis - ie *use* the data you are given, instead of simply saying one is higher or lower in vague terms. Then try to think why this difference may have arisen.

Step 4 (c) This involves a similar comparison of the elements of the unit cost as in (b), but this time you need to relate the differences specifically to the introduction of ABC and TQM.

Step 5 (d) Standard costing is quite limited in the control information it supplies. TQM involves a much wider interpretation of desirable performance, including non-financial aspects. Once you have thought of a few of these, the additional information required will become apparent.

Step 6 Now review your answer and ensure that it does precisely answer the question as set.

The examiner's answer

(a)

(TN 1) Input to Finishing	= 1/0.93	=	1.0753
Input to Converting	= 1.0753/0.87	=	1.2360
Input to Making	= 1.2360/0.91	=	1.3582

		£
Raw material cost (based on input)		
= 1.3582 × 6.72 × 0.85	=	7.758
Labour cost (based on output)		
= 1.236 × 0.142 × 4.75	=	0.834
Overhead cost (based on output)		
= 1.236 × 0.125 × 7.00	=	1.082
Sub-total Making	=	£9.674

Work-in-progress per unit = £9.674/1.236 = £7.827. (TN 1)

(b) A number of differences may be noted when comparing the control standard and current standard costs for product A:

(i) Process losses (%) are considerably higher in the current standard. This may be due to factors such as lack of training of employees, poor machine performance, lack of motivation, sacrifice of quality for speed of throughput.

(ii) The current standard specification includes 12% more material (sqm.) which has a price per sqm. which is 5p above the control standard. The extra material may be due to product specification differences which may indicate the need for a design review by Tritex. The price difference could indicate better quality material but could also indicate a less efficient purchasing function.

(iii) Net labour hours per unit (0.125 to 0.100 hours) are 25% greater in the current standard. In addition, idle time is greater. For the current standard idle time is 12% of input labour as compared with 8% in the control standard. Labour rate of pay per hour in the current standard is 25p lower than in the control standard. The greater operating time and higher idle time may be due in part to a less skilled grade of labour being used. Operating time may be higher because of lack of training, poor motivation, poor machine performance. Idle time may be higher because of expected levels of machine breakdown and poor production flow (eg, waiting for raw materials).

(iv) Overheads are incurred at a higher rate per hour in the current standard (£7 to £6.32). This may be due to the efficiency with which overhead items are sourced externally or provided internally (e.g. maintenance), and/or due to the price at which they are obtained. In addition, the overheads are absorbed on the basis of processing time which is higher per unit in the current standard. It may be that processing time is not the relevant cost driver for such overheads.

Did you answer the question?

The examiner wants to see that you are really looking at the data he has provided, and understand it, so quote/manipulate the figures within your answer wherever appropriate.

(c) Total quality management embraces continuous improvement aiming at features such as zero defects at minimum cost, supply of quality products at the agreed design specification on a right-first-time basis, elimination of waste, elimination of non-value added activities.

The ABC/TQM standard cost for product A shows:

(i) A low level of process losses. This indicates a move towards the zero defects aim of TQM.

(ii) Raw material input is 6sqm. per unit which is the same as the control standard. The price per sqm. is £0.90 which is higher than the control standard (£0.80). This may indicate a better quality material in order to provide the design specification required by customers. It may also indicate the cost of a just-in-time purchasing agreement which supplies materials of an agreed specification when required, thus reducing, for example, stock holding costs and returns of defective products from customers.

(iii) The overall labour time per unit has fallen by approximately 12% from the control standard (0.108 to 0.095 hours).

Labour cost now has zero idle time allowance and employees are expected to carry out some re-work, material handling and maintenance tasks. This indicates a TQM policy of having a highly skilled, well motivated, multi-task workforce who will embrace the zero defect, right-first-time philosophy. It will also help to reduce waste and non-value added activities. This labour environment seems to be achieved by paying premium rates of pay (£6 per hour) for highly skilled, well motivated employees.

(iv) Overhead costs are being absorbed on the basis of steam operations per product unit which has been recognised as the cost driver rather than an average rate per operating hour. This appears to indicate that product A was being overcharged with overhead cost under the old system. The comparative rates per unit of product are:

Control standard = 0.1 × £6.32	=	£0.632
ABC/TQM standard = 1 × 0.36	=	0.360
Total saving	=	£0.272

We are told that the reduction due to the recognition of the change in cost driver to steam operations per unit is 30% × £0.632 = £0.190. The residual saving of £0.082 (£0.272 - 0.90) is due to improved work practices as part of the TQM programme.

Did you answer the question?

Again, note the quite detailed use of the data from the Appendix (this time specifically required by the question)

(d) The standard cost and variance analysis control system provides some information such as relative levels of process losses (yield variances) and efficiency and expenditure variances. There are, however, a number of additional features which a TQM environment linked to the use of non-financial indicators will require:

(i) TQM aims at continuous improvement. The focus should be on performance measures which illustrate a continuous trend rather than a 'steady state' standard performance which is accepted for a specific period.

(ii) Many measures are not highlighted by the standard cost/variance system. Additional quantitative measures may be kept to monitor:

- customer dissatisfaction (eg, level of replacements of faulty goods, number of late deliveries)
- high levels of stock losses (raw material, WIP, finished goods)
- market share (is this growing, shrinking, changing?)
- levels of non-value added activities (eg, re-work, material handling)

(iii) Increased focus may be placed on attempts to measure and value internal and external failure cost, appraisal costs and prevention costs in the operation of a TQM programme.

(Marks will be awarded for alternative relevant comments in parts (b) to (d)).

Tutorial notes

1 A diagrammatic representation:

Input ⟶	MAKING ⟶		CONVERTING ⟶		FINISHING ⟶	OUTPUT
1.3582 units		*1.236 units*		*1.0753 units*		*1 unit*
	loss 9%				loss 7%	

The cost of the 1.236 units of output from the making process are ascertained by applying material unit cost to the 1.3582 units of input, and the labour and overhead rates to the 1.236 units of output, as indicated by the question. The total cost is then converted to a cost per *unit* of output from the making process.

47 (Answer 2 of examination)

Examiner's comments and marking guide

Question 2: tested candidates' ability to prepare a budgeted profit and loss account. It also required candidates to explain the meaning of the information in a two way datatable provided in the question. Part (c) required the use of this information and probability estimates to prepare a range of profit and loss outcomes and associated combined probabilities and hence calculate the expected value profit. Part (d) required the calculation of the break-even capacity for the situation. Part (e) required comment on the use of spreadsheets in testing the sensitivity of the model to changes in variables.

This question was generally well answered. In part (d) many candidates were unable to use the appropriate procedure for the calculation of the break-even capacity.

		Marks	
(a)	Fare revenue:		
	use of correct journeys	1	
	use of correct percentages	0.5	
	use of correct prices	3	
	Advertising revenue	0.5	
	Variable cost	1	
	Fixed cost	0.5	
	Overall presentation and totals	0.5	7

(b)	Comments on data table and information (on merit)			6
(c)	(i) Combined probability schedule		4	
	Profit or loss schedule		4	
				8
	(ii) EV profit			2
	(iii) Cumulative probability of Profit greater than £30,000			2
(d)	For method (on merit) up to		3	
	Correct figures		3	
				6
(e)	Spreadsheet use (on merit) (2 × 2)			4
Total				35

Step by step answer plan

Step 1 Read the question again and make sure that you focus on precisely what is required. Very similar to the Dunburgh Bus Company (June 1995), it involves the use of spreadsheet modelling and probability distributions to assess the effect of changes in key estimates in decision making.

Step 2 (a) Set out a proforma statement to identify the information required. You will need to do some computations, mainly for the revenue, and these can be done on the statement (if simple) or in separate, cross-referenced, workings.

Step 3 (b) The figures in the body of the data-table are the net profit/loss figures resulting from different combinations of the two key variables referred to in (c) of the question - these form the column and row labels. The first figure to identify is the current net profit (as computed in (a)), corresponding to current inflation rate (5%) and capacity utilisation (60%). To comment on the range of figures, you can first identify the highest and lowest profit levels; then it will be useful to comment on the points at which profits turn to losses, ie the break-even points.

Step 4 (c) Note that the main work you have to do here is the probability combinations - the profits/losses for all the expected combinations have already been done for you in the data-table discussed in (b). The probabilities for each capacity utilisation rate in combination with each inflation rate are multiplied together to get the overall probability of the particular combination (an application of the multiplication law of probability). The expected value is then obtained by multiplying each combined probability by the corresponding profit/loss taken from the data-table and the probability of profit being greater than £30,000 can be obtained by adding together the probabilities corresponding to all profits of £30,000 or more (an application of the addition law)

Step 5 (d) Whilst it would be possible to use the standard computation for break-even here (costs/contribution per unit), care is needed as the variable costs relate to cable-car journeys, whilst revenues accrue on passenger journeys. There is also a complex fare structure to incorporate. So go back to basics: break-even is where total revenue - total costs. Putting in what is known in this equation will allow computation of the unknown - breakeven fare revenue. Comparison of this with the current revenue at 60% capacity will indicate the breakeven capacity . Other valid approaches would, of course, be equally acceptable (although they may be more time consuming)

Step 6 The use of a spreadsheet for "what if" problems is one of its main features and you should describe the application of this to the problems given. Where a series of progressive changes in one or two variables are being evaluated, a data table can be incorporated.

Step 7 Now review your answer and ensure that it does precisely answer the question as set.

The examiner's answer

(a) Workings:

Passenger journeys for 1997:

Maximum 120 × 120 × 30	=	432,000	
Planned 120 × 120 × 30 × 60%	=	259,200	
Single fare 259,200 × 75%	=	194,400	
Return fare 259,200 × 25%	=	64,800	(single journeys)

Inflation adjusted fares for 1997 per single journey equivalent:

	Single (£)	*Return (£)*
Adult	1.05	0.945
Juvenile	0.63	0.567
Senior Citizen	0.525	0.4725

Note: single fares are 1996 fares increased by 5%. Return fare equivalent includes 10% reduction eg, £1.05 × 90% = £0.945.

Budgeted Profit and Loss Statement 1997

			£	£
Revenue from fares				
Single	: Adult	194,400 × 50% × £1.05	102,060	
	: Juvenile	194,400 × 30% × £0.63	36,742	
	: Senior Citizen	194,400 × 20% × £0.525	20,412	
Return	: Adult	64,800 × 50% × £0.945	30,618	
	: Juvenile	64,800 × 30% × £0.567	11,022	
	: Senior Citizen	64,800 × 20% × £0.4725	6,124	
				206,978
Advertising revenue				20,000
Total Income				226,978
Less:				
Variable cost		120 × 120 × £10 × 1.05	151,200	
Fixed cost		£48,000 × 1.05	50,400	
				201,600
Net profit or loss				25,378

(All figures to nearest £)

(b) The two-way data table shows the net profit or loss for each of a range of combinations of capacity utilisation and inflation levels, using the variable data in a spreadsheet model of the situation.

The existing situation is for 60% capacity utilisation and an inflation effect of 5% on costs. Note that this gives a net profit of £25,378 as calculated in part (a) above.

The data table shows the best possible outcome as a profit of £171,043 at 100% capacity at 1% inflation. The worst possible outcome is a loss of £122,207 at 20% capacity and 10% inflation.

The data table indicates that breakeven point is between 40% and 60% capacity utilisation. The figures indicate that breakeven is likely to be at approximately 50% capacity utilisation at low inflation, moving towards 60% capacity utilisation at high levels of inflation.

(c) (i) The range of possible outcomes using the probability estimates quoted and values from Appendix 2 are:

Capacity Utilisation %	*Prob*	*Inflation* %	*Prob*	*Combined Prob*	*Net profit /loss* £
80	0.15	2	0.2	0.03	100,130
		5	0.5	0.075	94,370
		8	0.3	0.045	88,610
60	0.6	2	0.2	0.12	31,138
		5	0.5	0.30	25,378
		8	0.3	0.18	19,618
40	0.25	2	0.2	0.05	-37,855
		5	0.5	0.125	-43,615
		8	0.3	0.075	-49,375
				1.000	

(ii) For each row in the above table, multiply the combined probability by the net profit or loss and sum the answers. The expected value of net profit is £17,902.55.

(iii) The combined probability of a net profit of more than £30,000 is 0.03 + 0.075 + 0.045 + 0.12 = 0.27.

(d) For breakeven point total revenue = total cost
Total cost remains fixed for the number of journeys as does advertising revenue.

Total fares revenue changes as capacity utilisation changes.
At breakeven point we require total fares revenue = total cost minus advertising revenue = £205,440 – £20,000 = £185,440.

From part (a), revenue from fares at 60% capacity = £206,978
For breakeven, capacity utilisation = 185,440/206,978 = 89.6% of the budgeted level of 60% ie, 89.6% × 60% = 53.8% of maximum capacity.

Did you answer the question?

This shows how a seemingly complex problem can be made relatively easy if you go back to basics rather than trying to apply standard formulae to a non-standard situation. As the structure of the fare revenue (in terms of single/return, age mix) remains the same the only cause of a change in total revenue is activity level - in this case, utilisation.

OR an alternative approach is as follows:

let N = number of passenger journeys at breakeven Hence 0.75N = single journeys and 0.25N = return journeys. Using the mix of adult/juvenile/senior citizen journeys of 50%/30%/20%, the total number of journeys may be expressed as:

	Single	*Return*
Adult	0.375N	0.125N
Juvenile	0.225N	0.075N
Senior Citizen	0.15N	0.05N

eg, adult single = 0.75N × 0.5 = 0.375N

Using the 1997 fares as calculated in (a) we can express total revenue in terms of N and equate this to total cost less advertising revenue for breakeven point. 0.375N × 1.05 + 0.225N × 0.63 + 0.15N × 0.525 + 0.125N × 0.945 + 0.075N × 0.567 + 0.05N × 0.4725 = 205,440 - 20,000
Solving gives N = 232,228 journeys. Maximum journeys = 432,000 (as calculated in (a))
Hence percentage capacity utilisation at breakeven = 232,228/432,000 = 53.8%.

(e) The spreadsheet may be used as a 'what-if' analysis tool by changing the values of any one or more variables on a one-off basis and noting the effect on profit or loss.

The passenger mix could be changed to (say) adult/juvenile/senior citizen of 40%/40%/20% and the amended net profit noted where all other variables remain unchanged. A similar procedure could be applied by changing the fare prices by (say) 3% and noting the amended profit.

The use of data tables will enable a range of changes in one or more variables to be monitored and summarised. A one-way data table could be prepared which would show the net profit or loss for fare increases of 1% to 10% in 1% steps.

48 (Answer 3 of examination)

Examiner's comments and marking guide

Question 3: Part (a) of this question tested candidates' knowledge of activity based budgeting through the preparation of a simple activity based budget (ABB) statement, the identification and comment on advantages claimed for ABB, comment on the information provided in the ABB statement and suggestion of additional information which would assist in performance measurement in the situation provided. Part (b) required the preparation of a unit cost for a product using an activity based cost approach on a life cycle basis.

A number of candidates did not show variances in the budget statements despite this being specifically stipulated in the question. Many candidates wrote about activity based costing (ABC) as if they were discussing activity based budgeting (ABB). In part (b) a significant number of candidates were unable to implement all of part of the calculations required in the preparation of the unit cost.

			Marks	
(a)	(i)	Operating statements:		
		traditional basis	2	
		ABB basis	4	
				6
(ii)	Advantages and discussion (4 × 3)			12
(iii)	Activity change + comments		2	
	Cost analysis by expense			
	Type for each activity		2	
	Cost driver info		2	
	Root causes of cost drivers		2	
	(allow marks on merit for other relevant comment)			
				8
(b)	ABC unit cost:			
	Product design		2	
	Purchasing		2	
	Production		1	
	Depreciation		2	
	Packing		1	
	Distribution		1	
				9
Total				35

Step by step answer plan

Step 1 Read the question again and make sure that you focus on precisely what is required. It principally considers the application of activity based *budgeting* (ABB) to an overhead department of a company. It also brings in the basic concept of life cycle costing

Step 2 (a) (i) The preparation of the statements is simply a matter of applying the given percentages to the total budget/actual costs as appropriate. Note that it is a control statement, and therefore will include variances as requested.

Step 3 (ii)/(iii) Take care to write about ABB rather than the perhaps more familiar ABC - they are, of course, linked, but are at different stages of the budgeting/costing process. For each of the four advantages you are required to discuss, you must relate your points back to the given example wherever possible. When discussing the use of the ABB control statement in performance measurement, fist run through each activity's result, paying attention to the nature of the activity - primary, secondary, value / non-value adding, etc. Then think about the underlying factors that may be causing these results, which should give you some ideas for the further information you need.

Step 4 (b) For each overhead unit cost you need two elements - the usage rate of the cost driver and the cost per cost driver unit. The latter can be derived directly from the table given. The usage rate is derived by spreading the total usage over the entire life cycle of the product over the total output (thus, for example, the product design costs are not just borne by the units produced in the first quarter).

Step 5 Now review your answer and ensure that it does precisely answer the question as set.

Items not required by the examiner for this question:

- Discussion of the advantages of ABC

The examiner's answer

(a) (i)

Production Planning and Development
Operating Statement for period ended 30 November 1996
(Traditional Expense based Analysis)

Expense	*Budget* £'000	*Actual* £'000	*Variance* £'000
Salaries	600	667.8	67.8(A)
Supplies	60	53.0	7.0(F)
Travel cost	120	127.2	7.2(A)
Technology cost	100	74.2	25.8(F)
Occupancy cost	120	137.8	17.8(A)
Total	1,000	1,060.0	60.0(A)

Production Planning and Development
Operating Statement for period ended 30 November 1996
(Activity based Analysis)

Activity	*Budget* £'000	*Actual* £'000	*Variance* £'000
Routing/scheduling - new products	200	169.6	30.4(F)
Routing/scheduling - existing products	400	360.4	39.6(F)
Remedial re-routing/scheduling	50	127.2	77.2(A)

Special studies - specific orders	100	84.8	15.2(F)
Training	100	159.0	59.0(A)
Management and Administration	150	159.0	9.0(A)
Total	1,000	1,060.0	60.0(A)

Note: (A) = adverse (F) = favourable

(ii) Advantages claimed for the use of activity based budgeting include:

- Resource allocation is linked to a strategic plan for the future, prepared after considering alternative strategies.

  Traditional budgets tend to focus on resources and inputs rather than on objectives and alternatives. In the question, the traditional budget focuses on overall expenditure on resources such as salaries and the overall expenditure variance.

- New high priority activities are encouraged rather than focusing on the existing planning model. Activity based budgeting focuses on activities. This allows the identification of the cost of each activity eg, Special studies. It facilitates focus on control of the resources required to provide the activity. It will also help where financial constraints exist in that activities may be ranked and their importance considered, rather than arbitrary cuts being made in areas such as production planning and development.

- There is more focus on efficiency and effectiveness and the alternative methods by which they may be achieved. Activity based budgeting assists in the operation of a total quality philosophy. Focus within individual activities can be on areas such as waste reduction, inefficiency removal, innovation in methods.

- It avoids arbitrary cuts in specific budget areas in order to meet overall financial targets. Activities 1, 2 and 4 in the budget in (i) are primary activities which add value to products. Activity 3 (remedial re-scheduling) is a non-value added activity which should be eliminated. Activities 5 and 6 (Training and Management) are secondary activities which support the primary activities. Efforts should be made to ensure that their objectives are achieved in an efficient manner at minimum cost.

- It tends to lead to increased management commitment to the budget process. This should be achieved since the activity analysis enables management to focus on the objectives of each activity. Identification of primary, secondary and non-value added activities should also help in motivating management in activity planning and control.

Did you answer the question?

Note that ABB is basically concerned with the identification of costs with activities, and the use of this information in planning and decision making, than with detailed product costing that is the domain of ABC. The examiner has given five advantages here for your information - only four were required. Note that most points have been illustrated with reference to the department in the question.

(iii) In assessing the performance of an activity we must measure its cost and the quality of its provision.

Did you answer the question?

This is a crucial point, and one that you should always bear in mind under the "modern management philosophy". Quality must be considered alongside cost - and control statements showing cost variances will thus only give part of the performance story.

The statement in (i) shows the budget v actual cost comparison for each activity. This indicates that cost has fallen in all three primary activities - development of routing, existing routing and special studies. Remedial re-routing is double the budget level which must be investigated since it is a non value added activity. Training cost has increased by 50% from budget. This may be related to the high level of remedial re-routing where staff under training have not been performing efficiently.

For each activity it is also possible to prepare a cost analysis which compares budget v actual resources for salaries, etc in a similar way to the overall traditional budget statement given in the question. This will enable investigation of factors such as why salary costs for the activity exceed budget by £X'000 or why supplies are below budget by £Y'000.

The cost information does not specify the cost driver for each activity and the budget v actual comparison of these. For example staff hours is likely to be the cost driver for an activity such as routing/scheduling whereas for training the cost driver may be number of staff trained. It is also necessary to determine the efficient cost driver level e.g. staff hours per individual route development for a new product. How does this compare with the actual staff hours per individual route development? Again, a comparison of budget cost versus actual cost per staff member trained will give an indication of efficiency of provision of the activity.

A further aspect of performance measurement is to determine the 'root cause' of each cost driver. For example the staff hours required per route designed may be linked to the level of technology and software systems used. The root cause of employee training may be high labour turnover due to poor career prospects or a stressful work environment. It is important that such root causes are identified, since continuous improvement of the provision of an activity will only be achieved through improvement in the factors which influence its incidence.

(b) Calculate the cost per unit of cost driver for each activity. For example for purchasing, rate per purchase order = £200,000/4,000 = £50. Additional workings are detailed as required for individual activities.

Activity based overhead cost per unit of product NPD

		£
Product design (note 1)	0.08 hours × £250	20
Purchasing (note 2)	0.02 orders × £50	1
Production (note 3)	0.75 machine hours × £100	75
Depreciation (note 4)		25.60
Packing	0.4 cu.metres × £20	8
Distribution	3kg × £5	15
Total		144.60

Note 1: design hours per unit over product life = 400/5,000 = 0.08 hours.

Note 2: purchase orders per unit = 1/50 = 0.02 orders.

Note 3: machine costs (excluding depreciation) = £1,500,000 - £300,000 = £1,200,000
cost per machine hour = £1,200,000/12,000 = £100

Note 4: asset cost over life of product
= £8,000 × 4 quarters × 4 years = £128,000 (TN 1)
depreciation per product unit = £128,000/5,000 = £25.60.

Tutorial notes

1 The depreciation has to be separated out as it is not driven by machine hours, but by time.

49 (Answer 4 of examination)

Examiner's comments and marking guide

Question 4: required candidates to discuss performance measures which may be used in the context of education or training institutions. It also required discussion of the motivational factors likely to influence staff in such institutions and to comment on ways in which efforts could be made to quantify such factors.

Considerable latitude was allowed in the marking process as to the type of institution referred to. Many candidates did not refer to performance measures by type, such as quality and flexibility, but marks were awarded where illustrations of such measures were provided. In part (b) many candidates did not attempt to suggest ways in which to quantify factors likely to influence the performance of staff.

This question was attempted by a majority of candidates and was generally well answered.

		Marks
(a)	Performance measures and comment (5 × 2)	10
(b)	Discussion (on merit)	5
Total		15

Step by step answer plan

Step 1 Read the question again and make sure that you focus on precisely what is required. It concerns performance measurement in a particular service industry - education and training. As the examiner indicates in his comments, you could have framed your answer in the context of any such institution - presumably one of which you have had direct experience!

Step 2 (a) In order to achieve some sort of coherence to your answer, you need to think about the particular desirable attributes of an education or training institution, and then think about how these may be measured. The categorisation used in the answer is commonly used for service businesses, and gives a useful framework for your answer. However, credit will be given for any five relevant measures, whether or not they are categorised in this way.

Step 3 (b) Here you have to first of all think what will motivate a teacher/lecturer/trainer to give a good performance (which will not just include performance in the classroom) - both financial and on a "higher needs" level. In other words what will make him "feel good" about his job, and thus (presumably) improve performance? Then consider how the institution's management may be able to measure the extent to which these "feel good" factors are present.

Step 4 Now review your answer and ensure that it does precisely answer the question as set.

The examiner's answer

The answer to this question could be framed in the context of one of a range of education or training institutions. The answer which follows is written with reference to a possible set of circumstances for a UK university. Answers framed in the context of another type of institution would be equally acceptable.

(a) Performance measurement requires confirmation that the mission statement of the institution is being implemented on a continuing basis. Performance measures which may be used include financial performance, competitiveness, quality of service, flexibility, resource utilisation and innovation.

Financial performance: the key measure will be cost per graduate. This can be monitored through time to see if real savings are being achieved and also measured against competing institutions.

Competitive performance: this will be measured in terms of the student population attracted to the institution. The growth rate may be measured in total and by course. In addition, the 'hit rate' i.e. the ratio of uptake to applications may be monitored by course.

Quality of service: this is a contentious issue which will include the quality of academic input, academic environment and ancillary support services such as student accommodation, health and financial advice. Quality may be measured in terms of throughput rate i.e. percentage of students who obtain a qualification and the proportion of honours to ordinary graduates. It may also be measured through student responses to questionnaires on issues such as tutoring, handout material and advice from staff. Measurement of quality may also be attempted through staff review programmes and internal reviews of the effectiveness of committee structures in the institution.

Flexibility: this may be measured in terms of modes of learning environment on offer including full-time, part-time and distance learning study. A further measure of flexibility is the availability of intermediate entry and exit points to courses in order to allow for variations in qualifications held by students on entry and to ensure that an intermediate exit qualification is available for students who do not perform to their expectations or who leave for financial or personal reasons.

Resource utilisation: the main resources are staff and accommodation. A key performance measure is the student: staff ratio. This may be measured for each course, department or faculty and monitored against targets and through time. The percentage fill of accommodation is another useful resource measure.

Innovation: examples may include the type of course provided, such as moves into new and topical course areas such as a degree in environmental accounting. Innovation may also be measured by the type of learning environment. For example, a multi-mode approach may be offered where students can study partly by distance learning and partly by attendance at classes. Innovation in teaching and learning methods may include the use of interactive multi-media material.

(Other relevant points would be accepted.)

Did you answer the question?

Note that the examiner has discussed many more than the required five measures under these headings, for your information. The use of these headings ensures that you consider all areas of the business, and should mean that you bring in measures for both the staff and the institution itself, and financial and non-financial - besides, the examiner is very keen on these headings. If you are short of ideas, think of your own experiences of such institutions, and the aspects that made you feel you were getting a good (or not so good) service!

(b) Agency theory sees the employee as the agent for a task where the outcome will depend on the effort put into the task by the employee. Expectancy theory states that the individual chooses his/her actions based on valence and expectancy. Valence may be intrinsic, such as a feeling of competence, or extrinsic such as the level of bonus, promotion, attendance at conferences. Expectancy is derived from the perceived probabilities that such rewards will follow from a given set of actions. This will apply to academic staff in the same way as in any other work environment.

Performance may also be affected by the attitudes of staff summarised in terms such as 'pride in work' or 'professional attitude'. Behaviouralists will also argue that positions on Maslow's hierarchy of human needs will influence the attitude of staff to work. Consider the higher level needs of belonging, esteem and self-actualisation. In the academic context, the lecturer may belong to a group of peers with similar academic goals; gain esteem from the achievement of goals such as the publication of research papers; gain self actualisation through being a main contributor in new course design or innovative teaching methods.

The measurement of performance may be viewed in a number of ways including:

(i) The number of papers published in research journals.
(ii) Pass rates in courses in which the staff member is involved.
(iii) Staff review procedures by peers or immediate superiors.
(iv) Results of responses to student questionnaires on various aspects of staff performance and attitude.

(Other relevant points would be accepted).

50 (Answer 5 of examination)

Examiner's comments and marking guide

Question 5: required candidates to discuss the relevant valuation basis for units of a product in the context of a number of decision making situations. It also required discussion of the effect of timescale on the treatment of discretionary and committed costs in decision making.

The standard of answer to this question was generally poor. Many candidates were unable to identify costs which were relevant to each of the decision situations provided. Some candidates answered in the context of product prices rather than costs. In part (b) many candidates gave basic definitions of discretionary and committed costs but were unable to explain the relevance of timescale of decision making in each case.

		Marks
(a)	Discussion and relevant costs (4 × 2.5)	10
(b)	Relevant comments and examples including timescale (2 × 2.5)	5
Total		15

Step by step answer plan

Step 1 Read the question again and make sure that you focus on precisely what is required. It concerns relevant costs, but it takes a couple of minutes to spot what it's about.

Step 2 (a) It is important that you think carefully about what is being asked here to avoid going off on the wrong track. You are considering how product units should be valued (ie *costed*) for *decision making* - this is not referring to selling prices, or valuation for reporting purposes. For each of the decision situations described, think what the true cost is to the business of going ahead.

Step 3 (b) Whilst it will help your answer to give a brief definition/explanation of the two types of cost, this is not the main point. You must consider how timescale of a decision will affect the categorisation of costs under these headings.

Step 4 Now review your answer and ensure that it does precisely answer the question as set.

The examiner's answer

(a) (i) Disposal of existing product units which are no longer required means that the price at which the product could be sold in the past is no longer relevant. Historical costs are irrelevant in the circumstances. The important measure is the net realisable value of the units. The calculation of net realisable value will depend on the circumstances of disposal. It may be that the units can be sold for alternative use after further work has been carried out on them. The relevant costs are those directly associated with the alteration for sale. It may be that the units can only be sold as scrap after incurring disposal costs such as transport or break-up costs. This could leave a negative net realisable value where additional costs exceed scrap revenue.

(ii) When units are being replaced to meet current demand, replacement cost is the relevant value for decision making purposes. This may be the same as the current valuation on a full cost basis including direct costs plus an absorbed share of indirect costs. It may be, however, that replacement costs will rise eg, because of increases in the price of inputs or the need for the replacement of assets used in the production process. In this situation it may also be relevant to know the cost of external sourcing as the replacement basis, in order that a make or buy decision can be made.

(iii) A decision relating to the impact of an increase in output level should only include incremental or additional costs caused directly by the increase in output. Existing fixed costs which will now support the larger total output should be ignored. However, any new or 'incremental' fixed costs should be included. Variable costs may also fall where the increased activity level results in economies of scale such as better purchasing agreements with suppliers or lower machine costs through increased efficiency of operation at higher activity levels.

It may be that the expanded activity level will require the acquisition of additional resources eg, additional machinery or factory space or the payment of a salary to additional supervisors. In this way the additional contribution, if any, to be obtained from the increased output may be calculated.

(iv) Where the level of activity is to fall, any decision should only take into account those costs which will change as a result of the decision. These are avoidable costs which must be distinguished from committed or sunk costs. As demand falls, some fixed costs may be avoidable eg, salary of a supervisor no longer required, while others will remain e.g. occupancy costs of production space. There may be a negative aspect to avoidable costs in that some variable costs may increase because of the lower level of activity eg, higher purchasing costs and machine operating costs.

Did you answer the question?

This question requires some thought to get onto the right lines. On the whole, it is talking about the principles of marginal or relevant costing in decision making, and how those are applied to the four situations given. Note that whilst one may tend to think "fixed costs are irrelevant in decision making" this is not always the case - in (ii), for example, we are basically considering whether to continue production or not; all associated production overheads are thus relevant and included in product valuations.

(b) Committed costs are viewed as those which must be incurred irrespective of the decision taken. Timescale is important in such a classification. It is a well known view in Economics that 'in the very long run, all costs are variable while in the very short run all costs are fixed'. An example would be the leasing costs for a building. If a lease is renewable each year, this is quite different when cost classification is being made, from a lease to which the company is committed for 20 years. For a short term decision relating to (say) a three year period, the long-term lease is a committed cost which should be excluded, whereas the short-term lease is incremental each year and should be included.

Discretionary costs are those in which management judgement is an important factor. The decision maker has discretion as to whether it is relevant and necessary to incur such costs. Examples may be as divergent as expenditure on research and development, staff training or operation of a management accounting function. For short-term decision making it may be argued that such costs are not directly relevant to a particular project eg, should we undertake a one-off contract. For longer term decisions, however, the discretionary nature of such costs is reduced. In order to maintain market share and develop new materials, research and development expenditure is vital. Staff training is required to ensure continuing high quality input in the provision of goods and services to customers. The management accounting function is (we hope!) of value in assisting management in planning, control and decision making.

51 (Answer 6 of examination)

Examiner's comments and marking guide

Question 6: required candidates to prepare an outline statement showing the costs and revenue elements required in the calculation of divisional profit or loss. It also required comment on the effect of the degree of autonomy allowed to a division on the level of profit reported. Finally, candidates were required to discuss the transfer pricing basis which should lead to corporate profit maximising decisions.

The general standard of answer to this question was poor. This was disappointing given the range of questions which have been asked in this topic area in previous examination diets.

Many candidates did not even attempt to distinguish between internal/external costs and revenues or divisional specific information in the outline statement. Comments on the effect of autonomy on profit levels were generally incomplete. In part (b) a large number of candidates simply listed a number of possible transfer pricing methods and made no attempt to comment on the application of a general rule which might lead to corporate profit maximising decisions.

			Marks	
(a)	(i)	Statement construction (on merit)		4
	(ii)	Discussion of autonomy on:		
		External sales/internal transfer mix	1.5	
		Transfer price impact:		
		- on revenue	1.5	
		- on input costs	1.5	
		Cost levels	1.5	
				6
(b)	'General rule' philosophy		2	
	Relevant examples		3	
				5
Total				15

Step by step answer plan

Step 1 Read the question again and make sure that you focus on precisely what is required. It examines the are of divisional performance measurement, focused on profitability, and includes discussion of transfer pricing setting.

Step 2 (a) (i) When planning your statement you need to think about how it may be used. It is likely that it will be used for performance measurement of both the division and its management. this requires categorisation of items under as controllable (for managerial evaluation), traceable (ie divisional specific) , head office allocated, etc. It will also be useful to distinguish internal and external activities (which was indicated in the question).

Step 3 (ii) You need to remember the context of this question to get the main points out in this part - you are considering a division that trades both internally and externally. The extent to which the divisional manger has control over the levels and prices of these trades (in particular internal sales, which are far more controllable, given the opportunity) will undoubtedly affect his reported profit. Other general points on how costs may be influenced are also relevant.

Step 4 (b) You must be sure to answer this part in the context of corporate profit maximising - ie define, discuss and illustrate the "general rule" of transfer pricing.

Step 5 Now review your answer and ensure that it does precisely answer the question as set.

The examiner's answer

(a) (i) A summary of the calculation of divisional profit may be shown as:

	£
Sales to outside customers	XXXX
Inter-divisional sales	XXXX
	XXXX
Less:	
Variable costs of goods sold	(XXXX)

Variable divisional expenses	(XXXX)
Controllable contribution	XXXX
Less: Controllable divisional fixed costs	(XXXX)
Controllable profit before tax	XXXX
Less: Head Office costs	(XXXX)
Net profit before tax	XXXX

(ii) The degree of autonomy allowed to a division will affect the extent to which divisional management can control various aspects of income and expenditure. A number of illustrations of this are as follows:

- The ratio of internal transfers to other divisions to external sales may be determined to a greater extent by divisional management where an increased level of autonomy is given. Where internal transfers take place at a lower price than external sales, an increased proportion of transfers will result in a decreased profit reported at the division.

- The degree of autonomy will also affect the transfer price policy of each division. Where a fully directed central pricing policy is applied, the transfer price may be as low as marginal cost where spare capacity exists at the transferring division. This will reduce the profit reported at Spiro Division for goods which it is transferring out to other divisions. Conversely it will increase its reported profit for goods which are transferred in from other divisions for further processing before sale.

- Where complete autonomy is given to divisions, Spiro Division may increase its reported profit by purchasing a component from an outside source at a price which is lower than the lowest internal transfer price available. This will increase its absolute reported profit but may not be in the best interests of the group if spare capacity exists at one or more of the supplying divisions within the group.

- The level of costs incurred and hence profit reported at Spiro Division may be affected by the degree of autonomy allowed. It may be that some costs are reduced through local purchasing agreements which embrace a just-in-time policy not available if head office arranged purchasing on a group basis (or vice-versa).

- The degree of autonomy will influence the extent to which some functions are centralised and charged to Spiro Division from head office on some apportioned basis. The level of such charges and the basis of apportionment used will affect the absolute profit reported at Spiro Division.

Did you answer the question?

Note how the examiner has put the emphasis in his answer on the internal trading aspects, being particularly pertinent to the Spiro Division. If you're not quite sure what is expected, always look at the overall context of the question, including later requirement, to get some hints.

(Other examples would be accepted).

(b) In order that corporate profit maximising decisions take place it is desirable that management at divisions are able to make decisions which take into account all relevant internal and external circumstances.

The 'general rule' of transfer pricing states that transfer prices should be set at marginal (variable) cost plus opportunity cost to the group. Where the general rule is correctly applied, any decision made with regard to internal transfer versus external sale or internal purchase versus external sourcing should lead naturally to the best decision from the corporate viewpoint on financial grounds.

For example, consider where division A can sell component X externally at £15 (variable cost £8) and has no spare capacity and division B can purchase component X externally at £12. Division B should purchase externally and division A should sell externally in order that corporate profit is maximised. If division A transfers to division B in this situation, a contribution of £7 is being forgone by the group on each unit of external sale (the opportunity cost to the group).

Consider, however, where division A has spare capacity with which to provide units of component X for division B. In this situation there is no opportunity forgone by internal transfer and the transfer price should be set at £8 (ie, variable cost). In this situation division B will purchase from division A rather than buy externally at £12 and group profit will be improved.

Did you answer the question?

The question asks for "the pricing basis". Note how the examiner has not gone into all the individual transfer pricing methods (market based, cost plus, dual price etc), but has centred his discussion around the "general rule" for profit maximisation. In different circumstances, this may lead to a cost based or market price based price being used. A discussion of the use of marginal cost and marginal revenue should have earned high marks, although the examiner has shown little interest in this in a transfer pricing context.

(Other examples would be accepted).

JUNE 1997 QUESTIONS

Section A - TWO questions ONLY to be attempted

52 (Question 1 of examination)

(a) A production department produces metal 'base plates' for electronic circuits by cutting, drilling and finishing metal sheets which are received from suppliers.

Budget and actual cost data for the production department for the period ended 31 May 1997 is as follows:

	Budget	*Actual*
	£	£
Machine minder labour cost	10,000	11,000
Power cost	20,000	16,500
Indirect material cost	4,000	4,300
Maintenance cost	6,000	5,800
Depreciation charge	8,000	8,000
Occupancy cost	12,000	12,000
Gross machine hours	5,000	4,250
Non-productive (idle time) hours	1,000	950
Output achieved (standard hours)		3,795

Notes:

(1) Gross machine hours = productive hours + idle time hours.

(2) One standard hour of work = expected output in one productive machine hour.

(3) Machine minder labour cost is treated as an overhead cost.

Required:

(i) Calculate, in terms of standard hours of gain or loss, measures of the change from budget for EACH of efficiency, idle time, capacity utilisation and production volume.

(6 marks)

(ii) Comment on possible dysfunctional consequences of the use of the measures calculated in (i). Comment also on possible alternative relevant aspects of performance on which to focus.

(6 marks)

(iii) Calculate the total cost variance for the department where costs are absorbed at a predetermined rate per standard hour. Identify the additional information necessary to enable a more detailed set of standard cost variances to be prepared.

(4 marks)

(b) The production department above is made up of a number of activities which have been identified as cutting, drilling, finishing, remedial processing and production reporting. The total flexed budgeted cost for each activity is expressed as a percentage of the original total budgeted cost of the production department.

The flexed budget percentages and the actual costs of the activities for the period ended 31 May 1997 are as follows:

	Actual cost £	*Flexed budget* *% (see note 1)*
Cutting	18,500	30
Drilling	11,200	20
Finishing	18,800	35
Remedial processing	6,400	10
Production reporting	2,700	5

Note 1: the total flexed budget is £54,000. The percentages for each activity have been arrived at after taking into account the fixed/variable nature of the original budget data.

Required:

(i) Prepare a summary statement for the production department for the period ended 31 May 1997 which compares budget and actual costs where an activity based budgeting approach is in use.

(5 marks)

(ii) Categorise each activity as primary, secondary, value added or non-value added. Give reasons for your choice of categories.

(8 marks)

(iii) Discuss ways in which improved effectiveness of operation of the production department may be achieved by focusing on the 'root causes' of the cost driver for an activity.

Include comment on the cutting and drilling activities in order to illustrate your answer.

(6 marks)
(Total: 35 marks)

53 (Question 2 of examination)

The Alphab Group has five divisions A, B, C, D and E. Group management wish to increase overall group production capacity per year by up to 30,000 hours. Part of the strategy will be to require that the minimum increase at any one division must be equal to 5% of its current capacity. The maximum funds available for the expansion programme are £3,000,000.

Additional information relating to each division is as follows:

Division	*Existing capacity (hours)*	*Investment cost per hour* £	*Average contribution per hour* £
A	20,000	90	12.50
B	40,000	75	9.50
C	24,000	100	11
D	50,000	120	8
E	12,000	200	14

A linear programme of the plan has been prepared in order to determine the strategy which will maximise additional contribution per annum and to provide additional decision-making information. Appendix 2.1 shows a print-out of the LP model of the situation.

Required:

(a) Formulate the mathematical model from which the input to the LP programme would be obtained.

(6 marks)

(b) Use the linear programme solution in Appendix 2.1 in order to answer the following:

(i) State the maximum additional contribution from the expansion strategy and the distribution of the extra capacity between the divisions. **(3 marks)**

(ii) Explain the cost to the company of providing the minimum 5% increase in capacity at each division. **(3 marks)**

(iii) Explain the effect on contribution of the limits placed on capacity and investment. **(2 marks)**

(iv) Explain the sensitivity of the plan to changes in contribution per hour. **(4 marks)**

(v) Group management decide to relax the 30,000 hours capacity constraint. All other parameters of the model remain unchanged. Determine the change in strategy which will then maximise the increase in group contribution. You should calculate the increase in contribution which this change in strategy will provide. **(6 marks)**

(vi) Group management wish to decrease the level of investment while leaving all other parameters of the model (as per Appendix 2.1) unchanged.

Determine and quantify the change in strategy which is required indicating the fall in contribution which will occur. **(6 marks)**

(c) Explain the limitations of the use of linear programming for planning purposes. **(5 marks)**

(Total: 35 marks)

Appendix 2.1

Divisional investment evaluation
Optimal solution - detailed report

Variable		*Value*
1	DIV A	22,090.91
2	DIV B	2,000.00
3	DIV C	1,200.00
4	DIV D	2,500.00
5	DIV E	2,209.09

	Constraint	*Type*	*RHS*	*Slack*	*Shadow price*
1	Max Hours	<=	30,000.00	0.00	11.2727
2	DIV A	>=	1,000.00	21,090.91	0.0000
3	DIV B	>=	2,000.00	0.00	-2.7955
4	DIV C	>=	1,200.00	0.00	-1.6364
5	DIV D	>=	2,500.00	0.00	-4.9091
6	DIV E	>=	600.00	1,609.09	0.0000
7	Max Funds	<=	3,000,000.00	0.00	0.0136

Objective function value = 359,263.6

Sensitivity analysis of objective function coefficients

	Variable	*Current coefficient*	*Allowable minimum*	*Allowable maximum*
1	DIV A	12.50	10.7000	14.0000
2	DIV B	9.50	- Infinity	12.2955
3	DIV C	11.00	- Infinity	12.6364
4	DIV D	8.00	- Infinity	12.9091
5	DIV E	14.00	12.5000	27.7778

Sensitivity analysis of right-hand side values

	Constraint		Type	Current value	Allowable minimum	Allowable maximum
1	Max	Hours	<=	30,000.00	18,400.00	31,966.67
2		DIV A	>=	1,000.00	- Infinity	22,090.91
3		DIV B	>=	2,000.00	0.00	20,560.00
4		DIV C	>=	1,200.00	0.00	18,900.00
5		DIV D	>=	2,500.00	0.00	8,400.00
6		DIV E	>=	600.00	- Infinity	2,209.09
7	Max	Funds	<=	3,000,000.00	2,823,000.00	5,320,000.00

Note: RHS = Right-hand side

54 (Question 3 of examination)

Scotia Health Consultants Ltd provides advice to clients in medical, dietary and fitness matters by offering consultation with specialist staff.

The budget information for the year ended 31 May 1997 is as follows:

(i) Quantitative data as per Appendix 3.1.

(ii) Clients are charged a fee per consultation at the rate of: medical £75; dietary £50 and fitness £50.

(iii) Health foods are recommended and provided only to dietary clients at an average cost to the company of £10 per consultation. Clients are charged for such health foods at cost plus 100% mark-up.

(iv) Each customer enquiry incurs a variable cost of £3, whether or not it is converted into a consultation.

(v) Consultants are EACH paid a fixed annual salary as follows: medical £40,000; dietary £28,000; fitness £25,000.

(vi) Sundry other fixed cost: £300,000.

Actual results for the year to 31 May 1997 incorporate the following additional information:

(i) Quantitative data as per Appendix 3.1.

(ii) A reduction of 10% in health food costs to the company per consultation was achieved through a rationalisation of the range of foods made available.

(iii) Medical salary costs were altered through dispensing with the services of two full-time consultants and sub-contracting outside specialists as required. A total of 1,900 consultations were sub-contracted to outside specialists who were paid £50 per consultation.

(iv) Fitness costs were increased by £80,000 through the hire of equipment to allow sophisticated cardio-vascular testing of clients.

(v) New computer software has been installed to provide detailed records and scheduling of all client enquiries and consultations. This software has an annual operating cost (including depreciation) of £50,000.

Required:

(a) Prepare a statement showing the financial results for the year to 31 May 1997 in tabular format. This should show:

(i) the budget and actual gross margin for each type of consultation and for the company

(ii) the actual net profit for the company

(iii) the budget and actual margin (£) per consultation for each type of consultation.

(Expenditure for each expense heading should be shown in (i) and (ii) as relevant).

(15 marks)

(b) Suggest ways in which each of the undernoted performance measures (1 to 5) could be used to supplement the financial results calculated in (a). You should include relevant quantitative analysis from Appendix 3.1 for each performance measure:

1. Competitiveness; 2. Flexibility; 3. Resource utilisation; 4. Quality; 5. Innovation.

(20 marks)
(Total: 35 marks)

Appendix 3.1

For use with question 3

Statistics relating to the year ended 31 May 1997

	Budget	*Actual*
Total client enquiries:		
- new business	50,000	80,000
- repeat business	30,000	20,000
Number of client consultations:		
- new business	15,000	20,000
- repeat business	12,000	10,000
Mix of client consultations:		
- medical	6,000	5,500 (note 1)
- dietary	12,000	10,000
- fitness	9,000	14,500
Number of consultants employed:		
- medical	6	4 (note 1)
- dietary	12	12
- fitness	9	12
Number of client complaints:	270	600

Note 1: Client consultations INCLUDES those carried out by outside specialists. There are now 4 full-time consultants carrying out the remainder of client consultations.

55 (Question 4 of examination)

Negoto plc are about to enter into negotiations to attempt to obtain an order for a specific job. The work will be implemented in Negoto plc's factory and then delivered to the customer. The work will be carried out in the preparation and assembly departments. The following pricing information has been made available for use in the negotiations:

Job estimate:

	£
Direct material cost	100,000
Direct labour cost (assembly dept)	20,000
Prime cost	120,000
Add: 80% of prime cost to absorb overheads	96,000
Total cost	216,000
Profit mark-up	54,000
Quotation price	270,000

Notes:

(i) The preparation department is semi-automated and comprises a number of separate tasks. Machine labour cost is considered part of overhead cost. It is estimated that the job will require a total of 400 machine hours of work.

(ii) The assembly department is labour intensive and 2,000 hours at £10 per hour have been estimated as the charge to this job.

Required:

Discuss ways in which the management accounting system should verify and improve on the above information. The changes should allow Negoto plc to negotiate with the prospective customer using pricing information which is more accurate and more flexible than that shown in the original job estimate.

(15 marks)

56 (Question 5 of examination)

(a) Discuss the use of the following as aids to EACH of planning and control:

(i) rolling budgets
(ii) flexible budgets
(iii) planning and operational variances.

(9 marks)

(b) Discuss the extent to which the incidence of budgetary slack is likely to be affected by the use of each of the techniques listed in (a).

(6 marks)
(Total: 15 marks)

57 (Question 6 of examination)

Strategic management accounting may help decision-making through the use of *committed*, *discretionary* and *engineered* cost classifications.

Required:

(a) Explain the meaning of the terms shown in italics in the above statement.

(6 marks)

(b) With reference to the above statement discuss the classification and use of information in each of the following situations:

(i) A company intends to manufacture goods under licence on payment of a royalty of £10 per unit. The royalty agreement also requires the payment of a fee of £10,000 per year irrespective of the number of units produced. The basic agreement is for a five year period and early exit from the agreement would incur a penalty lump-sum payment of £30,000.

(ii) An open cast mining venture incurs variable costs of £50 per tonne of output. It currently spends £100,000 per year on advertising to maintain its market share. It is estimated that a further £20,000 per year would be required to increase its market share by 10%. Management have been considering closure of the mine because of low profit levels. The lease of the site is fixed for a five year period at a cost of £375,000. The mining company are required to pay for the lease at the rate of £75,000 per year. Early closure of the mine would mean payment of the outstanding portion of the lease.

(iii) Distribo Ltd sells and distributes short-life fresh food products to retailers. The current distribution cost is 10% of selling price per unit. An additional investment of £100,000 per annum in computer software for distribution planning should help to increase the speed of distribution to retailers. It should also help expand the level of sales to retailers. The software would require additional computer staff. The current salary bill of £140,000 would be increased by 15% as a result.

(9 marks)
(Total: 15 marks)

ANSWERS TO JUNE 1997 EXAMINATION

52 (Answer 1 of examination)

Examiner's comments and marking guide

Question 1: Part (a) tested candidates' ability to calculate variations from standards valued in terms of standard hours. It also required comment on possible dysfunctional consequences of such measures. Finally it required comment on additional information necessary to enable a set of standard cost variances to be prepared. Part (b) required candidates to prepare an ABB (activity based budget) statement and to categorise each activity as primary, value-added, etc. Finally it required comment on the relevance of focusing on the root causes of the cost driver for an activity.

Part (a) of this question was extremely poorly answered. Most candidates were unable to implement the relevant calculations. Few candidates were able to explain possible dysfunctional aspects of such measures. Some candidates were able to calculate the total cost variance (£) but many were unable to cite the fixed/variable split of costs as necessary for a detailed variance analysis.

Part (b) was generally well answered. Some candidates had difficulty in commenting on the relevance of identifying the root causes of cost drivers.

			Marks	*Marks*	*Marks*
(a)	(i)	Calculation of each measure (4 × 1.5)		6	
	(ii)	Comment on each measure (4 × 1.5)		6	
	(iii)	Correct calculation	2		
		Comment (on merit)	2		
				4	
					16
(b)	(i)	Flexed budget	2		
		Actual costs	1		
		Variances	1		
		Overall presentation	1		
				5	
	(ii)	Correct categories (5 × 1)	5		
		Relevant reasons (on merit)	3		
				8	
	(iii)	General comment on root causes	2		
		Examples for cutting and drilling (2 × 2)	4		
				6	19
Total					35

Step by step answer plan

Step 1 Read the question again and make sure that you focus on precisely what is required. It is a standard costing question, incorporating activity based budgeting and value analysis.

Step 2 (a) (i) You need to view the standard hour variances as a composite package to ensure you don't double count or omit some hours in your analysis. The overall variance is that of production volume; the efficiency, idle time and capacity utilisation are deemed to be sub-variances. The capacity utilisation "flexes" the budget to actual gross hours; the idle time and efficiency variances are thus extracted by comparison with a flexed budget (TN 1).

Step 3 (ii) Possible dysfunctional consequences can be identified by thinking - what action might be taken to improve the variances? Will this necessarily be a good thing? What other aspect(s) of performance may this conflict with? This last point leads onto the second part of the requirement.

Step 4 (iii) This total cost variance is calculated like any other - comparison of actual cost (for actual production) against the standard cost for actual production. Production here is measured in standard (productive) hours, and thus a standard cost per productive hour needs to be computed from the original budget. To analyse this variance further, you need to know how much of the cost would be expected to vary with productive hours and how much is fixed (and thus may be contributing to over/under absorption)

Step 5 (b) (i) (ii) The first computation needed is the split of the flexed budgeted total cost between activities using the percentages given; these are then compared with the actual activity costs to give total activity cost variances. Ensure you give clear reasons for your choice of categorisation of activities.

Step 6 (iii) Do not spend too much time on generalities before looking specifically at the cutting and drilling activities - it is likely to become too "waffly".

Step 7 Now review your answer and ensure that it does precisely answer the question as set.

The examiner's answer

(a) (i) (TN 1)

		Standard hours
Budget output = (5,000 - 1,000)	=	4,000
Actual output achieved	=	3,795
Loss due to production volume	=	(205)

Also: *Standard hours*

Gain due to efficiency
= Standard hours of output achieved - expected output
= 3,795 - (4,250 - 950) = 495

Loss due to capacity utilisation
= expected productive hours - budget productive hours
= (4,250 × 80%) - 4,000 = (600)

Loss due to excess idle time
= expected idle time - actual idle time
= (4,250 × 20%) - 950 = (100)

Net loss due to production volume = (205)

(ii) An efficiency gain measure focuses on output: input. This may lead to an emphasis on quantity rather than quality. It could also lead to the passing of faulty goods to the customer with subsequent problems such as free replacement, free back up service or loss of future business.

An adverse capacity measure will tend to imply a need to increase capacity utilisation eg, in order to avoid under-absorption of fixed costs. Such thinking could lead to a build up of stocks of finished goods which will incur holding costs and may be difficult to sell in a changing market. It may be considered more appropriate to focus on achieving quality output in response to customer requirements on a just-in-time basis.

An excess idle time measure may seem to be legitimising the idle time in the budget. It may be argued that more effort should be put into greater flexibility in the use of time with a substantial reduction (if not elimination) of idle time. This strategy could be aided by focusing on more flexible production systems.

Output volume focuses on volume achieved. It is affected by the other measures discussed. It may be more appropriate to focus on measures such as percentage of on-time deliveries to customers.

(iii) Standard absorption rate per productive machine hour
= budget cost/budget productive hours
= £60,000/4,000
= £15

Total cost variance
= costs absorbed in production achieved - actual cost
= (3,795 × £15) - £57,600
= £675 (adverse)

In order that a more detailed analysis may be achieved, it is necessary that costs are classified into fixed and variable components. In this way a flexed budget can be prepared and the valuation of variances for efficiency, idle time, capacity and expenditure can be implemented. The sum of such variances will be the £675(A) cost variance calculated above.

(b) (i)

Production department

Summary operating statement for the period ended 31 May 1997

Activity	*Flexed budget* £	*Actual* £	*Variance* £
Cutting	16,200	18,500	2,300 (A)
Drilling	10,800	11,200	400 (A)
Finishing	18,900	18,800	100 (F)
Remedial processing	5,400	6,400	1,000 (A)
Production reporting	2,700	2,700	Nil
Total	54,000	57,600	3,600 (A)

(ii) **Cutting, drilling** and **finishing** are primary activities which are contributing directly to the production of the base plates. They are also value added in nature in that they add features for which the customer is presumably willing to pay.

Remedial processing is a secondary and non-value added activity which should not occur in a total quality environment where a right-first-time philosophy is in force. The fact that there is a budget level of this activity indicates that the company acknowledges that it is not yet able to guarantee a defect free production cycle.

Production reporting is a secondary activity which supports the operational aspects of the department. It is non-value added in nature in that it does not add attributes for which the customer will be willing to pay.

(iii) The root cause is the factor or factors which cause the cost driver of an activity to occur at its current level. If we wish to reduce the incidence of a cost driver or to improve the efficiency with which it is implemented, we must focus on the root causes(s) of the activity.

If we consider the activities in the question, possible examples could be as follows:

Cutting: This may have the number of cuts as the cost driver. What is the root cause of the need for cuts? It may be that the root cause is the size and shape of the blank metal sheets from which the base plates are produced. For example 1m × 2m rectangular sheets rather than 0.5m × 0.5m square sheets may be purchased from the supplier. The larger sheets will require more cutting before the base plates are produced. The root cause may also be linked to the production method in use. For example, could sheets be 'stacked' so that (say) 10 sheets are cut at once rather than singly?

Drilling: The root cause of the requirement for the number of holes to be drilled may be the product design specification. Is it possible that the design specification could be changed without impairing the acceptability of the product to the customer? A change in the design specification could possibly lead to a reduction in the number of holes required from 10 to 4 holes thus reducing the cost driver incidence by 60%.

(Other relevant examples and comment would be accepted.)

(TN 1)

Did you answer the question?

The examiner is looking for tangible evidence of understanding of the principles of activity based management here, by asking for specific comment on these two activities. It will not be sufficient to talk in general terms about assessing the cost efficiency of cost drivers, etc, without giving actual examples such as these cited by the examiner.

Tutorial notes

1 The variances could be extracted on a "line by line" basis as follows:

		Standard hours	*Var*
Budget output for budget gross hours		4,000	
	capacity		*600A*
Std output for std productive hours (for actual gross hours) (4,250 × 80%)		3,400	
	idle time		*100A*
Std output for actual productive hours ((4250 -950)		3,300	
	efficiency		*495F*
Actual output for actual productive hours		3,795	
	production volume		*205A*

2 The (excess) idle time variance could be regarded as part of the capacity variance (one reason for the adverse capacity) and calculated in the conventional way by comparing budgeted productive hours, 4,000, and actual productive hours, (4,250 – 950 = 3,300). The resulting variance is 700 hours.

53 (Answer 2 of examination)

Examiner's comments and marking guide

Question 2: required candidates to use data provided in order to formulate the mathematical model from which a LP (linear programming) programme would be obtained. Candidates were then required to answer a series of questions related to the interpretation of a computer print-out of the optimal solution of the LP model. Candidates were finally required to explain possible limitations to the use of LP for planning purposes.

This question was generally well answered by the minority, of candidates who attempted it. Parts (b) (v) and (vi) were poorly answered. They required determination and quantification of changes in strategy which would maximise group contribution where a specific constraint (eg hours capacity) was relaxed.

			Marks	*Marks*	*Marks*
(a)	(i)	Objective function		1.5	
		Capacity constraint		1.5	
		Funds constraint		1.5	
		Divisional minima		1.5	
				—	6
(b)	(i)	Extra contribution	1		
		Distribution of capacity	2		
			—	3	
	(ii)	Shadow price explanation (on merit)		3	
	(iii)	Shadow price comment (2 × 1)		2	
	(iv)	Examples of increase/decrease (on merit)		4	
	(v)	Transfer of investment from E to A	4		
		Calculation of contribution increase	2		
			—	6	
	(vi)	Allowable decrease in investment	1		
		Transfer of capacity from E to A	3		
		Calculation of fall in contribution	2		
			—	6	
				—	24
(c)		Limitations of LP (on merit)			5
					—
Total					35
					—

Step by step answer plan

Step 1 Read the question again and make sure that you focus on precisely what is required. This is a linear programming problem that involves more than two variables, and thus needs solution by simplex. This is given in the Appendix, using the Examiner's customary simplex computer package. Provided you have a good understanding of terms such as "slack", "shadow price" and "sensitivity analysis" you will be able to work out the relevance of the information you are being given.

Step 2 (a) This is the basic set-up of a LP problem - define variables, state objective and constraints in terms of the variables. The constraints are dictated by the production capacity, funds available and minimum divisional capacity increases.

Step 3 (b) The first part of the appendix gives details of the position at the optimal solution, which gives the information required for answering (i) to (iii). Looking at the distribution of additional capacity between divisions, you can see that only divisions A and E are allocated above their minimum - so it likely that if some or all of the minimum constraints on divisions B, C and D were lifted, a greater contribution could be earned. This is supported by the negative shadow prices associated with these constraints. The positive shadow prices for the total capacity increase and funds constraints indicate the effects of increasing these limits on contribution.

Step 4 The second part of the appendix gives the ranges within which each divisions hourly contribution can vary before the optimal solution changes, as required for (iv).

Step 5 In (v), one of the critical constraints is removed, and the problem reverts to a single limiting factor situation, which can be solved from the basic information given in the main part of the question (TN 2 and 3). Note, however, that overall effect in terms of extra hours allocated and extra contribution earned can be derived from the Appendix, even if you can't work out how this is actually to be achieved.

Step 6 The reduction of the funds availability will have an immediate effect on the maximum contribution earnable. The shadow price of funds given in the second table of the Appendix will only apply down to the allowable minimum funds level, given in the last table. You therefore assume this is point to which management will move. Again, the overall effect of this move (in terms of reduction in total investment and drop in contribution) can be readily assessed from the Appendix tables, and statement of these will earn half marks. To get full marks, you need to show how this is achieved in terms of shifting investment from E to A.

Step 7 This part should be a welcome relief, but note that the emphasis of the requirement is on the limitations for planning purposes, so ensure you explain the relevance of all your points to that aspect.

Step 8 Now review your answer and ensure that it does precisely answer the question as set.

The examiner's answer

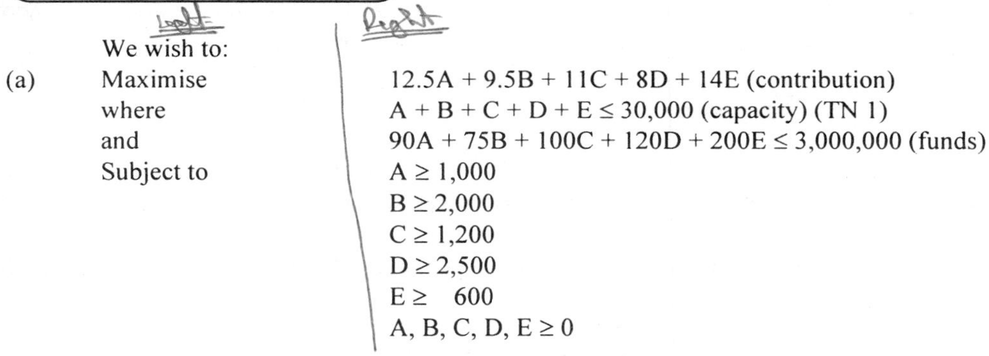

We wish to:

(a) Maximise $12.5A + 9.5B + 11C + 8D + 14E$ (contribution)

where $A + B + C + D + E \leq 30{,}000$ (capacity) (TN 1)

and $90A + 75B + 100C + 120D + 200E \leq 3{,}000{,}000$ (funds)

Subject to
$A \geq 1{,}000$
$B \geq 2{,}000$
$C \geq 1{,}200$
$D \geq 2{,}500$
$E \geq 600$
$A, B, C, D, E \geq 0$

Examiner's note: the minimum capacity requirements for each division are 5% of current capacity. For example for division A = 20,000 × 5% = 1,000 hours.

(***Tutorial note:*** Since A ≥ 1,000, B ≥ 2,000 etc, the need to state that A ≥ 0, is removed. What is important is to explain what A, B, C etc represent. A is the extra hours to be worked in division A, etc. Clearly it would have been more appropriate to use lower case letters for variables to distinguish them from the divisions.)

(b) (i) The objective function shows that the maximum contribution from the additional 30,000 hours within the overall budget of £3,000,000 is £359,263.60.

The maximum contribution is achieved where the investment provides additional hours in each division as follows:

Division	*Hours*
A	22,090.9
B	2,000
C	1,200
D	2,500
E	2,209.1
Total	30,000

Note that only divisions A and E have been allocated more hours than the minimum required.

(ii) The shadow prices indicate the opportunity cost of the constraints. For divisions B, C and D the shadow prices measure the cost per hour of choosing to provide the minimum quantity according to group strategy. For example for division D the cost is a loss of contribution of £4.91 per hour. There are no net opportunity costs for divisions A and E.

(iii) For the hours and investment constraints the shadow prices indicate the extra contribution which would be available for each extra hour of machine time (£11.27) or additional £ of investment (1.36p).

(iv) The contribution coefficient table shows the sensitivity of the plan to changes in the contribution per hour. For example, decreases in contribution would have no effect on the planned allocation in respect of divisions B, C and D.

For division A contribution would have to rise above £14 per hour or fall below £10.70 per hour for a change in the planned allocation between divisions to occur. For division E corresponding contributions per hour of £27.78 and £12.50 respectively would apply.

(v) If the group relaxes the 30,000 hours capacity constraint, additional contribution could be earned. This could be achieved by transferring investment from division E to division A. (TN 2)

We could transfer 1,609.1 hours from division E. This would leave the minimum requirement of 600 hours in division E. The investment released from division E (at £200 per hour) is £200 × 1,609.1 = £321,820. This investment will provide 3,575.77 hours in division A (£321,820/£90) where investment is required at £90 per hour.

Note that the net additional hours = 3,575.77 – 1,609.1 = 1,966.67 hours. This is the allowable maximum (in excess of 30,000) shown in the sensitivity of RHS values table in Appendix 2.1.

The additional contribution is extra hours × shadow price per hour = 1,966.67 × £11.2727 = £22,170 (TN 3).

(vi) The allowable minimum funds per Appendix 2.1 is £2,823,000. This is a fall of £177,000 from the current level. The fall in contribution is fall in investment (£) × shadow price per £ = 177,000 × 1.36p = £2,407.

This strategy may be implemented by reducing the hours in division E from 2,209.1 to the allowable minimum of 600 hours. This will release 1,609.1 hours to division A. (TN 2) This will reduce the investment in division E by 1,609.1 hours × £200 = £321,820. The additional investment required in division A will be 1,609.1 × £90 = £144,820. The net reduction in investment = £321,820 – £144,820 = £177,000 (as indicated above).

(c) Linear programming has a number of features which limit its usefulness for planning purposes.

- It is assumed that all the variables are infinitely divisible which undermines the credibility of the solution. For example in the Alphab situation, 2,209.091 hours are allocated to division E.

- All relevant relationships are assumed to be linear in nature. For example the model does not allow for economies of scale or diminishing marginal returns.

- The model does not allow for uncertainty, hence all relationships must be stated with certainty and without the incorporation of probability distributions.

- The model is only as accurate as its formulation. For example, all possible uses of scarce resources must have been identified and incorporated into the model.

Tutorial notes

1 Note here that the variables A, B etc are defined as the *additional* capacity to be allocated to divisions A, B, etc

2 If the capacity constraint is relaxed, then the key constraint now is funds. We wish to maximise the contribution generated from the cash available, and the divisions can be ranked by contribution earned per £ invested:

A: £12.50/£90 = 0.14

B:	£9.50/£75 = 0.13	
C:	£11/£100 = 0.11	
D:	£8/£120 = 0.07	
E:	£14/£200 = 0.07	

Thus as much as possible of the investment should be allocated to A, subject to the minimum capacity constraints.

This rationale can also be used to determine the optimum strategy in (vi), where funds are being restricted within the capacity constraint. A greater loss of contribution will result from £1 of investment taken away from A than from E

3 Alternatively, the extra contribution can be calculated as :

		£
Extra hours of A:	3,575.77 x £12.50	44,697
Fewer hours of E:	1,609.1 x £14	(22,527)
		22,170

54 (Answer 3 of examination)

Examiner's comments and marking guide

Question 3: Part (a) tested candidates ability to prepare a statement of financial results detailing information for each of three services offered to clients by a firm of health consultants. Part (b) required candidates to comment on the use of each of five performance measures incorporating relevant quantitative analysis from an Appendix of statistics provided in the question.

Part (a) was generally well answered. In many cases the presentation of answer was poor. many candidates did not attempt to calculate the contribution per consultation for each service and hence lost marks. In part (b) many candidates did not attempt to use data from the Appendix provided. This was specifically asked for in the question. In addition, many candidates did not refer to other data provided in the question eg, the view of the cardiovascular testing equipment as an example of innovation.

		Marks	*Marks*
(a)	Original budget:		
	Client fees	1	
	Healthfood contribution	1	
	Salaries	1	
	Profit margin for each type of consultation	0.5	
	Variances:		
	Fee income	1	
	Healthfood contribution loss	1	
	Salary change	1	
	Fitness equipment	1	
	Actual gross margin by type of consultation	0.5	
	General company costs:		
	Enquiry costs	1	
	General fixed costs	0.5	
	Software systems costs	0.5	
	Margin per consultation:		
	- budget (3 × 0.5)	1.5	
	- actual (3 × 0.5)	1.5	
	Overall presentation	2	
			15

(b)	For each performance measure - comment and relevant quantitative data (on merit) (5 × 4 marks)	20
Total		35

Step by step answer plan

Step 1 Read the question again and make sure that you focus on precisely what is required. It examines the area of performance evaluation, as applied to a service business.

Step 2 (a) Before you pick up your calculator, think about the layout of your statement, and draft a pro-forma. Note that whilst budget and actual gross margins are required for each consultancy and the company, net profit is required on actual terms for the company only. Perhaps the most efficient approach is to start with a full analysis of budget gross margin, then adjust these figures with variances to get to actual gross margins; actual company costs can then be taken off company gross margin to get to actual net profit. Other layouts would, of course, be acceptable, but make sure you don't waste time computing figures that are not specifically required eg budget net profit, or split of company costs between consultancies. Finally, don't forget the margins per consultation for each type, as requested.

Step 3 (b) It is essential here that you use information (including non-quantitative) and data from the question and appendix as the main content of your answer here.

Step 4 Now review your answer and ensure that it does precisely answer the question as set.

The examiner's answer

(a)

Scotia Health Consultants Ltd

Operating statement for the year ended 31 May 1997

	Medical £'000	*Dietary* £'000	*Fitness* £'000	*Total* £'000
Budget:				
Client fees	450.0	600.0	450.0	1,500.0
Healthfood mark-up (cost × 100%)		120.0		120.0
Salaries	(240.0)	(336.0)	(225.0)	(801.0)
Budget gross margin	210.0	384.0	225.0	819.0
Variances:				
Fee income gain/(loss)	(37.5)	(100.0)	275.0	137.5
Healthfood mark-up loss		(30.0)		(30.0)
Salaries increase (TN 1)	(15.0)		(75.0)	(90.0)
Extra fitness equipment			(80.0)	(80.0)
Actual gross margin	157.5	254.0	345.0	756.5
Less: company costs:				
Enquiry costs - budget				(240.0)
- variance				(60.0)
General fixed costs				(300.0)
Software systems cost				(50.0)
Actual net profit				106.5

Budget margin per consultation (£)	35.00	32.00	25.00
Actual margin per consultation (£)	28.64	25.40	23.79
(See Tutorial note)			

(b) **Competitiveness** may be measured in terms of the relative success/failure in obtaining business from enquiries from customers. The percentages are as follows:

	Budget	*Actual*
Uptake from enquiries:		
new business	30%	25%
repeat business	40%	50%

Repeat business suggests customer loyalty. The new business figures are disappointing, being below the budgeted level of uptake.

In absolute terms, however, new business is 5,000 consultations ABOVE budget whereas repeat business is 2,000 consultations BELOW budget.

There are variations within the types of consultation. Medical and dietary are DOWN on budget by approximately 8% and 16% respectively. Fitness is UP on budget by approximately 60%.

Flexibility may relate to the company being able to cope with flexibility of volume, delivery speed and job specification. Examples of each may be taken from the information in Appendix 3.1.

Additional fitness staff have been employed to cope with the extra volume of clients in this area of business.

Medical staff levels have been reorganised to include the use of external specialists. This provides flexibility where the type of advice required (the job specification) is wider than expected and may improve delivery speed in arranging a consultation more quickly for a client.

Dietary staff numbers are unchanged even though the number of consultations has fallen by 16% from budget. This may indicate a lack of flexibility. It may be argued that the fall in consultations would warrant a reduction in consultant numbers from 12 to 11. This could cause future flexibility problems, however, if there was an upturn in this aspect of the business.

Resource utilisation measures the ratio of output achieved from input resources. In this case the average consultations per consultant may be used as a guide.

	Average consultations per consultant		
	Budget	*Actual*	*Rise(+) or fall(–)*
Medical (full-time only)	1,000	900	–10%
Dietary	1,000	833	–16.7%
Fitness	1,000	1,208	+20.8%

These figures show that:

(1) Medical consultants are being under-utilised. Could this be due to a lack of administrative control? Are too many cases being referred to the outside specialists? This may, however, be viewed as a consequence of flexibility - in the use of specialists as required.

(2) Dietary consultants are being under-utilised. Perhaps there should be a reduction in the number of consultants from 12 to 11 as suggested above.

(3) Fitness consultants are carrying out considerably more consultations (+20.8%) than budgeted. There are potential problems if the quality is decreasing. Overall complaints from clients are up by 120%. How many relate to fitness clients?

It may be, however, that the new cardio-vascular testing equipment is helping both throughput rates and the overall level of business from fitness clients.

Quality of service is the totality of features and characteristics of the service package that bear upon its ability to satisfy client needs. Flexibility and innovation in service provision may be key quality factors.

The high level of complaints from clients (up from 1% to 2% of all clients) indicates quality problems which should be investigated.

Quality of service may be improving. For example the new cardio-vascular testing equipment may be attracting extra clients because of the quality of information which it provides. Quality may also be aided through better management of client appointments and records following the introduction of the new software systems.

Innovation may be viewed in terms of the performance of a specific innovation. For example, whether the new computer software improved the quality of appointment scheduling and hence resource utilisation; improved competitiveness in following up enquiries and hence financial performance; improved flexibility in allowing better forward planning of consultant/client matching.

Innovation may also be viewed in terms of the effectiveness of the process itself. Are staff adequately trained in its use? Does the new software provide the data analysis which is required?

(See Tutorial note)

Did you answer the question?

Note how *specific* the examiner's answer is to the business being considered. You must make as much use as you can of the information given in your answer, and you are specifically asked to carry out quantitative analysis from the appendix. Think about non-quantitative factors too; it is likely that you have had some personal experience of at least one of these types of service, which should help with ideas for innovation and quality of service.

Tutorial notes

1 Salary increases are computed as follows:

		£
Medical:	Employed consultants saving (2 @ £40,000)	80,000
	Sub-contracted fees (1,900hrs @ £50)	(95,000)
Net increase		£15,000
Fitness:	3 extra consultants at £25,000	£75,000

2 If no information is given eg, about actual expenses, just guess or pick any suitable number and bash on. A very wide range of presentations are possible.

3 Don't be put off by the fact that the items listed as (1 - 5) in part (b) are not actually performance measures. Write something intelligent about each aspect of performance, supply your own measures and make suitable reference to Appendix 3.1 as suggested. You may produce other, better, measures.

55 (Answer 4 of examination)

Examiner's comments and marking guide

Question 4: required candidates to discuss ways in which the management accounting system should verify and improve on existing information provided in the question in relation to a quotation price for a prospective order.

Most candidates answered this question in a very narrow way. Many answers only commented on overhead cost absorption. Many candidates were only able to suggest that an ABC system would solve all problems. Answers should have included a broad based discussion of all costs and profit mark-up aspects of the quotation. Answers should also have commented on possible ways in which additional information could be obtained and verified.

	Marks
Guide to marking:	
- general comment on need for (i) price to provide ROI and (ii) minimum price	2
- general comment on additional information	2
Specific comments on:	
direct material cost	2
direct labour cost	2
other job specific costs	2
overhead absorption	3
profit mark-up	2
Total	15

Step by step answer plan

Step 1 Read the question again and make sure that you focus on precisely what is required. You are being asked to consider the adequacy of the information provided by the accounting system in a job quotation for negotiation purposes.

Step 2 You first need to discuss the basic principles of costing information for negotiation pricing. As well as knowing the price you would like to achieve, you need to know how low you are able to go without it resulting in an actual cash loss. This will immediately identify a general lack of detail in the information given. You then need to consider *each* element of the quotation, expanding on the specific information improvements required, and how the management accounting system can contribute to this.

Step 3 Now review your answer and ensure that it does precisely answer the question as set.

Items not required by the examiner for this question

- detailed discussion of overhead absorption methods to the exclusion of other aspects of quotation

The examiner's answer

The pricing information is to be used in negotiations for the specific job. The information required will range from:

(i) A quotation price which includes a relevant share of company costs plus a profit element which provides an acceptable contribution to company ROI, to

(ii) a minimum price which comprises the incremental costs which will be incurred in providing the job to the customer. This will be particularly relevant where spare production capacity exists and any price above the minimum cost will provide a contribution to company fixed costs.

Negoto plc may then negotiate according to the circumstances which prevail in terms of the degree of competition envisaged and/or the availability of spare production capacity.

The existing information is inadequate in a number of ways:

(i) It does not distinguish between variable and fixed costs.

(ii) It does not identify job specific fixed costs.

(iii) It does not indicate that consideration has been given to the cost driers which are relevant in charging overhead costs to the job

(iv) It does not indicate the rationale for the profit mark-up which has been used.

Did you answer the question?

Note the well defined structure of this answer - an introduction as to the general information requirements for a price negotiation exercise, followed by an overview of the failings of the information provided. The examiner then goes on to apply these principles to each individual element of the quotation, without narrowing his view just to one area (eg overheads).

The accuracy and relevance of each element of the quotation price may be considered separately:

Direct material cost: What is the basis for the charge of £100,000? Has a bill of material been prepared from the job specification? Have stock items been valued at replacement cost rather than on a FIFO basis? It may be that some items will be old stock which have scrap value as their opportunity cost when setting a minimum price for the job.

Direct labour cost: How has the 2,000 hours in assembly been estimated? Does this represent the time taken for similar jobs? Does the wage rate include any expected overtime premium or special allowances? It will be relevant to determine whether any of the labour cost is a company fixed cost through a policy of retention of skilled workers. Any such committed fixed costs should be excluded from a minimum price.

Overhead cost: It is necessary to determine whether labour hours and machine hours are the relevant cost drivers for preparation and assembly respectively. For example it may be that the preparation department should be split into a number of activities. A cost pool and cost driver would be identified for each activity. The cost drivers may be argued to provide a more accurate basis for the absorption of costs by the job. This also provides the opportunity for value added and non-value added activities to be recognised with a view to altering the proposed production method to eliminate non-value added areas.

In addition, the fixed/variable nature of the overhead costs should be determined to allow a minimum cost to be prepared.

It is also relevant to determine whether there are any job specific costs which may be identified. For example there may be special design drawing costs or special machine tooling costs which can be identified. There may be specific aspects of administration, selling and distribution costs which can be identified with the job. For example it may be that an outside haulage company is used for distribution and a specific estimate of this cost can be obtained. In this way the incremental costs for use in a minimum price can be determined.

Efforts may be made to absorb a share of administration/selling cost eg, as a percentage of production cost. This percentage could be obtained from the overall budget of Negoto plc. It may be argued that this is unlikely to be an accurate estimate.

An alternative would be to inflate the profit mark-up percentage to represent the return required to allow for administration/selling costs and profit.

Profit: The profit mark-up used in the quotation provided is 25% on total cost (ie, 20% margin on selling price). Negoto plc should determine the overall target relationship between capital employed/sales revenue/profit. It may be that 20% margin on selling price for this job reflects the degree of competition normally expected for this type of work.

The above analysis should provide the necessary information from which a quotation price on a full cost plus profit basis and a minimum price based on incremental costs may be prepared.

56 (Answer 5 of examination)

Examiner's comments and marking guide

Question 5: required candidates to discuss the use of rolling budgets, flexible budgets and planning and operational variances in each of planning and control. It also required comment on the extent to which budgetary slack is likely to be affected by the use of each technique.

Most candidates were able to make a reasonable attempt at answering this question. It was disappointing to find that many candidates were unable to describe the operation of rolling budgets or flexible budgeting. Many of the answers gave very superficial comments on the impact of each technique on the incidence of budgetary slack.

		Marks	*Marks*
(a)	For each technique - description	1	
	use in planning	1	
	use in control	1	
		3	
	(3 × 3 marks)		9
(b)	Budgetary slack defined	1.5	
	Comment re - each technique (3 × 1.5)	4.5	
			6
Total			15

Step by step answer plan

Step 1 Read the question again and make sure that you focus on precisely what is required. The subject matter is techniques that may be used in planning and control, and their possible effect on the incidence of budgetary slack.

Step 2 (a) For each technique, first give a brief explanation of how it works. Then consider how it can help in *both* planning and control areas.

Step 3 (b) Again, start with an explanation of budgetary slack. Then ask yourself, for each technique, is the use of this technique likely to increase or decrease the chances of budgetary slack occurring? There is not be a definitive answer - the examiner is looking for you to recognise and adequately explain the possible effects.

Step 4 Now review your answer and ensure that it does precisely answer the question as set.

The examiner's answer

(a) A **rolling budget** may be defined as a budget continuously updated at the end of each control period (eg, quarter). At the end of each period a comparison is made between the actual results and the original budget. Where circumstances are felt to have changed on a permanent basis, the budget for the remaining quarters is revised to reflect the new conditions expected. A budget for an additional quarter is also prepared hence reinstating an annual forecast from the present time period forward. It may be argued that this approach assists planning in that budgets are more realistic and achievable since they are continuously revised. It may also result in more realistic planning by management who recognise that rolling budgets will allow for contingency and innovation in the planning process. Rolling budgets should also provide a more relevant control base against which to monitor actual results on an ongoing basis. This should allow more meaningful feedback control information and provide more appropriate feedforward control.

A **flexible budget** is one which recognises the distinction between fixed, variable and semi-variable costs. In this way it may be prepared to show the planned results at each of a number of activity levels. This may be a useful planning tool, for example, in recognising and highlighting where step function costs will have a significant impact on the plan. Step function changes may result in a fall in the level of profit forecast which will not be compensated for until activity rises to a higher level.

A flexible budget is useful as a control aid. Where actual results are at an activity level which differs from the original budget, the budget may be adjusted or 'flexed' to show the allowed figures for the level of activity which actually occurred. This means that the planned versus actual comparison and the resulting variances provide more meaningful control information.

Planning and operational variances occur where it is recognised that some aspects of the original plan should be permanently changed because of changes in the environment in which the business operates. Original (ex-ante) standards will have been used in preparing the original plan. A set of revised (ex-post) standards may be prepared which incorporate any permanent changes to the original plan. For example the method of manufacture may have been altered hence permanently changing the machine time requirement per product unit.

The planning and operational variances are a relevant control aid. The difference between the original and revised plan may be reported as a set of planning variances which it is now accepted are permanent and non-controllable. Focus may then be concentrated on the difference between the revised plan and actual results. This provides a set of operational variances over which it is expected some control may be exercised.

Planning and operational variances may be used in forward planning. Forward plans may use the revised standards as a starting point. Further adjustment may be made to such plans for whatever proportion of any adverse operational variances it is estimated can be eliminated, together with the cost of such elimination.

Did you answer the question?

Note that the examiner has started his discussion for each technique with an explanation of what it is/how it is implemented. He then turns to consider its roles, first in planning, and then in control. Even where a technique has a more obvious application in one of the areas over the other, you must try to consider each separately.

(b) **Budgetary slack** may result from the process whereby managers bargain for a share of available resources. The slack represents a reduction in efficiency due to the budget request for a resource being greater than necessary. This phenomenon may be linked to the performance measurement system in force. This may put pressure on managers to provide themselves with a 'safety valve' or 'cushion' to ensure that approved targets will be met.

Rolling budgets may reduce the incidence of budgetary slack. Managers may recognise that rolling budgets provide the facility for continuous updating of benchmarks. This may reduce the feeling of the need to build in slack to the original budget. On the other hand, it may encourage budgetary slack in that the continuous improvement impact of the rolling budget may be seen as an additional short-term threat.

Flexible budgets are prepared at the planning and control stage based on an agreed set of planning standards. The use of flexible budgets should not, therefore, in themselves cause budgetary slack to be built into the planning and control system. It may be argued that the incidence of budgetary slack would be unaffected whether a fixed or flexible budgeting system was in operation.

Planning and operational variances involve the creation of revised standards which will incorporate agreed permanent changes (whether favourable or unfavourable). This situation should act against the incidence of budgetary slack when original standards are set. It may be argued that pressure to justify changes as permanent changes to be built into revised standards will lead to the revised standards containing an element of budgetary slack.

(Other relevant discussion and comment would be accepted.)

Did you answer the question?

Note that the examiner doesn't come up with one "right" answer. Don't be afraid of discussing seemingly conflicting effects - provided you explain them adequately, and show their relevance to the question of budgetary slack, you will get credit.

57 (Answer 6 of examination)

Examiner's comments and marking guide

Question 6: tested candidates' knowledge of the meaning of committed, discretionary and engineered costs. It also required candidates to identify such costs in each of three situations provided in the question and to comment on their use.

The standard of answer to this question was generally satisfactory. A number of candidates were unable to explain the use of engineered costs. Many candidates gave correct examples of each cost category but did not attempt to comment on their use in decision making.

		Marks
(a)	Each cost classification (3 × 2)	6
(b)	For each situation - example and comment on each of the three cost classifications (3 × 3 marks)	9
Total		15

Step by step answer plan

Step 1 Read the question again and make sure that you focus on precisely what is required. It concerns the classifications of costs in relation to decision-making.

Step 2 (a) When defining the three cost terms, you can illustrate your answer with simple examples, but make sure you do give a general definition as well.

Step 3 (b) Read this requirement carefully - "...discuss the *classification* and *use...*". Make sure that each of these aspects is addressed in your discussion of each situation.

Step 4 Now review your answer and ensure that it does precisely answer the question as set.

The examiner's answer

(a) Strategic management accounting should be an aid to decision-making and not to historical reporting systems. The accounting system must produce relevant information for decision-making and not raw financial data which requires processing and interpretation by its recipients.

The analysis of costs into committed, discretionary and engineered classifications will assist in the strategic decision process.

A committed cost is one which will be incurred irrespective of the course of action chosen.

A discretionary cost is one which will be incurred only if a particular course of action is chosen. It is incremental in nature.

An engineered cost has an input to output relationship which is relatively predictable. For any given level of input resources the output cost may be calculated.

(b) (i) The basic royalty payment of £10 per unit is an engineered cost. The more units produced the higher the royalty payment. The annual royalty fee of £10,000 is a committed cost. It is payable irrespective of the level of output which is decided on. It is relevant, for example, when considering the break-even quantity of the product involved. The penalty lump-sum payment of £30,000 is a discretionary cost. If the decision strategy is to cease production of the product, the penalty fee is payable. This could mean that it will be in the company's interest to continue producing and selling units at a loss since the early exit fee would increase the level of loss incurred.

(ii) The variable cost of £50 per tonne is an engineered cost. The £100,000 advertising fee is a committed cost required to maintain the current market share. The additional advertising expenditure of £20,000 is a discretionary cost. It would only be incurred on financial grounds if the strategy to increase market share by 10% would result in incremental contribution in excess of £20,000.

The lease of the site of £375,000 over the five year period is a committed cost. Although it is payable at the rate of £75,000 per year, a strategy of early closure of the mine would require the payment of the outstanding portion of the lease. In this case the time scale of any closure strategy would be important since the balance of the £375,000 would be payable. For example closure at the end of year 2 would mean an exit cost of £225,000 ie, the outstanding portion of the lease. This could present cash flow problems for the company in the short term.

(iii) The distribution cost of 10% of selling price is an engineered cost. The additional investment of £100,000 per annum on computer software is a discretionary cost. The current salary bill of £140,000 is a committed cost whereas the 15% increase proposed in conjunction with the software investment is a discretionary cost. The discretionary costs are relevant when determining the financial viability of the strategy. Extra sales would have to give a contribution equal to the software investment plus extra salaries before a break-even situation would exist.

Did you answer the question?

Note that the examiner has first gone through each cost involved in the situation and classified them, with explanation. he has then gone on to consider how they may be used in the required decision making. You must read the requirement carefully to ensure you pick up all aspects that are required (and to which marks will be allocated).

DECEMBER 1997 QUESTIONS

Section A – TWO questions ONLY to be attempted

58 (Question 1 of examination)

Quarefel plc is considering entering the market for a single product which has an estimated life cycle of three years. The following information has been gathered:

(i) The total market size is estimated as: Year 1: 800,000 units; Year 2: 1,200,000 units; Year 3: 600,000 units.

(ii) Quarefel plc intends to use a flexible manufacturing system which will be able to produce up to 200,000 units per year. The equipment will cost £2,000,000 (payable year 0) and will have an estimated residual value of £400,000 (receivable at the end of year 4).

(iii) An advertising campaign will be implemented by Quarefel plc on the following basis:Year 0: £1,200,000; Year 1: £1,000,000; Year 2: £800,000.

(iv) Quarefel plc has estimated its sales (Q) in '000 units and selling price per unit (P) for each year over the life of the product. This may be expressed in terms of the price/demand function P= 70 – 0·15Q.

(v) The year 1 market share is crucial. Annual sales units for Quarefel plc for years 2 and 3 are expected to increase or decrease from the year 1 level achieved in proportion to the change in the size of the overall market from one year to the next, in so far as the production capacity of Quarefel plc will allow. The prices set by Quarefel plc in each of years 2 and 3 will be set in accordance with the price/demand function estimate detailed in (iv) above.

(vi) Variable cost is estimated at £25 per product unit.

(vii) Fixed costs directly attributable to the product (other than advertising) are estimated at £600,000 per year for each of years 1 to 3.

(viii) Quarefel plc has an estimated cost of capital of 12% for this type of proposal.

Ignore taxation and inflation.

Required:

(a) Using the above information, calculate the net present value (NPV) and internal rate of return (IRR) of the proposal where a year 1 launch price of £60 per unit is used. (All working calculations must be shown). **(12 marks)**

(b) Explain how the use of target costing would assist in the achievement of the required return where a year 1 launch price of £60 is used. **(8 marks)**

(c) Discuss the relationship between the NPV and the IRR of the new product proposal referring to the summary information provided below. Your answer should include a suitable graphical representation of NPV and IRR for each of year 1 launch prices of £45 and £65.

NPV and IRR for a range of year 1 prices where other variables are as given in the question:

Year 1 selling price/unit (£)		35	45	55	65
NPV	*(£000)*	395·1	1,585·6	1,313·1	–2,478·3
IRR	*(%)*	17·3	36·2	32·2	–27·8

NPV and IRR for a range of values of discount rates where year 1 price is £60 per unit and other variables are as given in the question:

Discount rate		9%	11%	13%	15%
NPV	*(£000)*	157·0	– 44·9	–169·0	–285·4
IRR	*(%)*	10·3	10·3	10·3	10·3

(9 marks)

(d) Quarefel plc wishes to consider the optimum sales volume for each of years 1 to 3 where the restrictions of a year 1 price of £60 per unit and the linking of market share in years 2 and 3 to that obtained in year 1 are removed.

Calculate the strategy (units and selling price) for each of years 1 to 3 which will maximise the return achievable over the life of the product.

(6 marks)

(Total: 35 marks)

59 (Question 2 of examination)

An organisation has two divisions A and B which make sole use of the output of a service division which provides printing and stationery services. Estimated information for the divisions for the year ending 31 December 1997 is as follows:

(i)

	Division A	*Division B*	*Service Division*
	£m	£m	£m
Capital employed	40	25	14
Profit (before service division costs)	10	8	
Total costs:			7

(ii) each division has a 15% target return on capital employed.

(iii) an activity based costing study has revealed the following additional analysis for the service division:

Service provided to:	*Cost driver*	*Division* A	*Division* B	*Service cost* £m
Sales	No. of customers	10,000	5,000	1·8
Advertising	No. of product types	8	12	2·4
Production	No. of batches	60,000	60,000	0·8
Administration	No. of employees	800	200	2·0

(iv) Management at each division has determined independently that the stationery and print service could be obtained from external suppliers for a fee per annum of £2m and £4·5m for division A and division B respectively.

Required:

(a) Prepare a summary which shows the return on capital employed reported at each of divisions A, B and the service division for EACH of the following transfer price bases from the service division:

(i) total cost on 50/50 basis

(ii) total cost on 50/50 basis plus profit mark-up of 30%

(iii) total cost using an activity based cost approach

(iv) external supplier prices.

(14 marks)

(b) Discuss the acceptability of each of the charge bases in (a) to the management at each division and to the organisation as a whole.

(6 marks)

(c) The service division is located in premises for which the lease expires on 31 December 2001. Central management have negotiated with a single external supplier of stationery and print services. Additional information is available as follows:

1. The external supplier contract fee will be £5m for each of the first two years. Fees will then rise by 10% above the 1998 level. Fees will also increase in proportion to any change of level of service required but will not allow any fee reduction where demand for the service falls.
2. The service division annual costs of £7m are analysed as follows:

	£m
variable cost	4·2
fixed cost (depreciation)	0·6
fixed cost (lease of premises)	1·2
fixed cost (others)	1·0

3. 75% of leasing costs to the end of the contract must be paid in the event of early exit from the contract.
4. Fixed assets could be sold for £0·5m at 31 December 1997 with nil residual value at 31 December 2001.
5. Other fixed costs will increase or decrease by a step function of 10% where the service division activity increases or decreases by more than 10% respectively.
6. The probabilities of the level of service provision required during the four years to 31 December 2001 have been estimated as:

Current (1997) level	0·5
Increase of 20%	0·2
Decrease of 20%	0·3

Ignore taxation and the time value of money.

You are required to:

(i) Determine whether the optimum strategy on financial grounds is closure of the service division on 31 December 1997 or 31 December 2001. Your answer should include expected value information and should comment on how the level of service activity may influence the decision. **(10 marks)**

(ii) Suggest additional financial and non-financial factors which could influence the decision strategy. **(5 marks)**

(Total: 35 marks)

60 (Question 3 of examination)

(a) Inex Ltd make and sell product X to which the following standard information applies:

(i) Raw material is purchased at £5 per square metre on a just-in-time basis. The purchasing manager has the responsibility for the sourcing of raw material.

(ii) Each unit of product X requires 3 square metres of raw material.

(iii) Product X is manufactured in a conversion process in which the variable conversion cost per product unit of output is estimated at £12·50 (0·5 hours at £25 per hour). The conversion process manager is deemed responsible for material usage and conversion process efficiency and expenditure variances.

The actual events for the period ending 30 November 1997, which may be considered as representative of future periods, are as follows:

(i) 17,000 square metres of raw material purchased at £4·50 per square metre is used to produce 5,000 units of product X. The purchasing manager has made the decision to buy from a cheaper source.

(ii) 2,800 hours of conversion process time at a variable cost of £20 per hour is used to achieve the output of 5,000 units of product X. A change in the processing method was implemented at the start of the period.

Production capacity is available in order to produce in excess of 5,000 units of product X if required.

Required:

(i) Calculate standard cost variances for material usage and price and for conversion process efficiency and expenditure for the period ended 30 November 1997. **(4 marks)**

(ii) Suggest, giving your reasons, whether decisions should be based on:

1. the variances over which EACH manager has control or

2. the effect of EACH of material cost variance and conversion cost variance. **(4 marks)**

(b) It has been established that the reasons for the variances for the period ended 30 November 1997 are as follows:

1. 80% of extra material used is due to purchasing from the cheaper source. The balance of extra material usage is due to the amended processing method which was introduced.
2. 60% of the extra hours used is due to the amended processing method. The balance of extra hours is due to the change to a cheaper material source.

Required:

Prepare a schedule of costs for the FOUR alternative strategies which incorporate different combinations of existing and amended material sources and conversion process methods and hence determine the profit maximising strategy.

(6 marks)

(c) Using the period ended 30 November 1997 as representative of future periods, additional information relating to a future period is as follows:

1. Product X is sold at £50 per unit to two customers A and B who require 2,700 and 1,800 units respectively.
2. Replacement units of product X are supplied to customers for units found to be defective on arrival at the customer premises. Such units are supplied without further charge to the customer (referred to below as 'free replacements'). The level of such replacements is likely to be affected in the future by the changes (as relevant) to material source and conversion method implemented during the period to 30 November 1997.

   Estimates of free replacements per period are as follows:

	Customer A	Customer B
Existing free replacements (units)	300	200
Future extra free replacements		
due to the implementation of:		
cheaper material source	50	60
alternative conversion method	180	80

Free replacements are incurred in proportion to the units delivered to customers.

3. Other relevant customer specific costs are estimated as:

	Customer A	*Customer B*
Distribution cost per unit delivered	£2·50	£5·00
Rebates to customers (% of gross sales)	2%	5%
Customer specific after sales service:		
costs per unit of sale	£4	£2

Required:

(i) Calculate the estimated customer specific contribution, in total and per product unit, for the period where a strategy of using the original material source and the amended conversion method is adopted. This strategy would result in production variable cost per unit of product X of £26.12 **(9 marks)**

(ii) Future production constraints may limit thė total units produced to 4,000 units of product X per period. Determine the profit maximising sales (units) strategy to customers A and B where all other variables per unit will remain unchanged. **(4 marks)**

Required:

(d) Prepare a report which discusses ways in which the alternative decision-making focus in each of sections (a), (b) and (c) of the question has contributed to a change in decision-making strategy by the company. **(8 marks)**

(Total: 35 marks)

Section B – TWO questions ONLY to be attempted

61 (Question 4 of examination)

(a) Given a focus on continuous improvement, discuss the advantages and disadvantages of standards and variances as forward planning tools. **(10 marks)**

(b) Discuss ways in which focus on the minimisation of adverse material price variances may have a dysfunctional impact on the control process. **(5 marks)**

(Total: 15 marks)

62 (Question 5 of examination)

Discuss the factors which should be considered when preparing and agreeing the manufacturing cost per product unit in a processing industry.

Your answer should include, but not be limited to, factors such as:

- the monetary value attached to elements of cost for single or joint products
- the impact on such valuations of the introduction of just-in-time procedures, total quality programmes and the application of backflush accounting. **(15 marks)**

63 (Question 6 of examination)

It may be argued that budgeting may be linked to planning and control because either

(a) The method of budgeting chosen as part of an accounting information system determines the range and relevance of planning and control information which is available, or

(b) The planning and control information deemed necessary and desirable determines the method of budgeting which is implemented.

Required:

Choose FOUR alternative budgeting techniques and discuss ways in which EACH technique provides the planning and control information deemed necessary by management.

Your answer should include reference to the issue of the direction of causality as illustrated in statements (a) and (b) above. **(15 marks)**

ANSWERS TO DECEMBER 1997 EXAMINATION

58 (Answer 1 of examination)

Examiner's comments and marking guide

Question 1. Part (a) tested candidates' ability to implement relevant calculations in determining the NPV and IRR of a proposal to market a short life product over a life cycle of three years. This included calculations involving price/demand relationships. Part (b) required explanation of how the use of target costing would assist in the achievement of the desired rate of return. Part (c) required discussion and graphical illustration of NPV and IRR data relating to the product which were provided. Finally, part (d) required calculation of the optimum price/demand strategy over the life of the product where the restrictions on price and demand included in part (a) were removed.
In part (a) many candidates could have gained extra marks by correctly calculating the price/demand information for the product for each of years 1 to 3. In part (b) many candidates did not discuss the application of target costing e.g. through value engineering. In part (c) many candidates were unable to prepare relevant graphs to illustrate the relationship between NPV and IRR. In part (d) answers which applied either calculus or tabulation of data were accepted. Many candidates omitted the marginal cost of £25 per unit from their calculations and hence did not gain full marks. Many candidates gave good answers to part (a) and then failed to achieve many marks in sections (b) to (d).

			Marks
(a)	capital and residual value (2 × 0.5)	1	
	advertising	1	
	correct prices and VC. calcualtion		
	(years 1 – 3) (3 × 1)	3	
	quantity (year 1)	1	
	quantity (years 2 and 3) (2 × 0.5)	1	
	revenue	0.5	
	DAFC	0.5	
	calculation of NPV	2	
	calcualtion of IRR	2	12
(b)	Comment on:		
	target costing principles	2	
	existing problem	1	
	design versus control focus, value engineering		
	supplier links, total quality, etc (on merit)	5	8
(c)	graphical representaiton (on merit)	4	
	comment on NPV/IRR links (on merit)	5	9
(d)	correct approach (on merit)	3	
	correct price and units	3	6
Total			35

Step by step answer plan

Step 1 Read the question again and make sure that you focus on precisely what is required. Parts (a), (c) and (d) are computational, while part (b) requires a discussion.

Step 2 For part (a), set out the usual proforma for calculating the NPV of a project with a life of three years, with columns for the flows arising from Time 0 to Time 4. Use the discount rate of 12% provided.

Step 3 Use linear interpolation to estimate the IRR, by calculating the NPV using any other discount rate. Incidentally, part (c) tells you the answer is 10.3%, so be delighted if you get this answer to part (a).

Step 4 Target costing enables costs to be designed-out prior to starting production in order to meet required cost levels. Take the opportunity to suggest quality initiatives to reduce costs.

Step 5 Part (c) requires you to draw a graph and then interpret it.

Step 6 Part (d) can best be approached by remembering that returns are maximised at the point where MR = MC.

Step 7 Now review your answer and ensure that it does precisely answer the question as set.

The examiner's answer

(a) Working notes:
The price/demand function for each year is P = 70 – 0·15Q
Where P = £60 in year 1 we have: 60 = 70 – 0·15Q
Hence Q = 66,667 units
The selling price per unit for years 2 and 3 will be linked to the estimated demand (as a proportion of the overall market).
Market size change: year 1 to year 2 : +50%
: year 2 to year 3 : –50%

For Quarefel plc we have:
Estimated sales (units) year 1 (as above) 66,667 units
year 2 66,667 × 1.5 = 100,000 units
year 3 100,000 × 0.5 = 50,000 units
Estimated selling prices: year 2: P = 70 – 0.15 (100) = £55
year 3: P = 70 – 0.15 (50) = £62.5

Cash flow analysis

	Year 0	*Year 1*	*Year 2*	*Year 3*	*Year 4*
Estimated sales (units)		66,667	100,000	50,000	
Estimated selling price/unit (£)		60	55	62.5	
	£000	£000	£000	£000	£000
Capital cost/residual value	–2,000·00				400·00
Advertising cost	–1,200·00	–1,000·00	–800·00		
Sales revenue		4,000·02	5,500·00	3,125·00	
Variable costs (at £25 per unit)		–1,666·68	–2,500·00	–1,250·00	
Directly attributable FC		–600·00	–600·00	–600·00	
Net cash flow	–3,200·00	733·34	1,600·00	1,275·00	400·00
Discount factor at 12%	1	0·893	0·797	0·712	0·636
Discounted cash flow	–3,200·00	654·88	1,275·20	907·80	254·40
Hence NPV =	–107·72				
Additional workings to allow calculation of IRR:					
Discount factor at 10%	1	0·909	0·826	0·751	0·683
Discounted cash flow	–3,200·000	666·61	1,321·60	957·53	273·20
Hence NPV =	18·94				

By linear interpolation IRR $= 10\% + 2\% (18{\cdot}94/(18{\cdot}94 + 107{\cdot}72))$
$= 10{\cdot}3\%$

(b) Where a launch price of £60 is used, variable cost is £25 per unit and other directly attributable costs are as given in the question, the NPV is negative. This indicates that the cost of capital criterion has not been achieved.

If the market share has been accurately forecast at appropriate selling prices in years 1 to 3, costs must be reduced from the current forecast level if the proposal is to be viable where the cost of capital is 12%.

Target costing will involve comparison of the current forecast cost levels with a target level which must be achieved. Any gap between the current estimate and the target cost must be closed. The process of eliminating the difference between the current forecast and target costs is more likely to be achievable at the design stage.

It is easier to 'design-out' cost prior to production than to'control-out' cost during the production phase. A number of techniques may be used to assist in the achievement of the target cost.

A value engineering exercise may be carried out in order to evaluate necessary features of the product such as quantity and quality of materials and components and the conversion processes required to achieve the desired quality of the finished article. This exercise will involve discussions between members of various disciplines within Quarefel plc such as design, production, maintenance. It will also involve discussions with suppliers of materials and components and with customers about the required design and tolerance features of the product.

Total quality techniques such as the use of quality circles may be used to look for ways of reducing the cost of the product. A quality circle may take the form of meetings of a work team responsible for some aspect of the product in order that they may discuss ways of improving the implementation of their work. This may, for example, involve the identification of non-value added activities which should be eliminated.

A focus on value added and non-value added activities will allow focus on the identification of cost drivers and their root causes, in order to allow reduction in the incidence and cost of such cost drivers.
(Other relevant points would be accepted.)

(c)

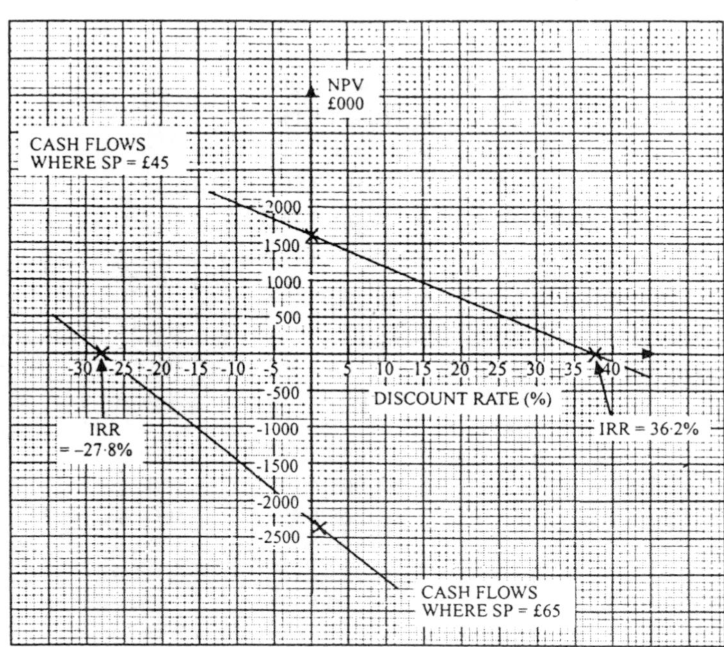

The above diagram shows the IRR for a given cash flow stream occurs where NPV = 0. For a launch price of £65, IRR = –27·8% and NPV= –£2,478,300 where cost of capital rate is 12%. For a launch price of £45, the different cash flow stream gives an IRR of 36·2% and NPV of £1,585,600 where the cost of capital is 12%. The IRR is a single point on the graph of each cash flow stream. The NPV of the cash flow stream will vary according to the cost of capital rate at which the cash flows are discounted. The second table of data in the question shows that for a launch price of £60 per unit in year 1, NPV varies with cost of capital (from £157,000 to –£285,400). The IRR for the cash flow stream is shown as a constant figure of 10·3%

(d) For profit maximisation we wish to produce and sell to the point where marginal revenue = marginal cost.
The price function is P = 70 – 0·15Q
The revenue function is R = 70Q – 0·15Q2
Differentiating with respect to Q we obtain the marginal revenue function:
MR = 70 – 0·3Q.
Now marginal cost MC = 25
For profit maximising sales volume let MR = MC
70 – 0·3Q = 25
Hence Q = 150,000 units and P = 70 – 0·15(150) = £47·50
This price and demand would then apply for each of years 1 to 3.

59 (Answer 2 of examination)

Examiner's comments and marking guide

Question 2. In part (a), candidates were required to calculate the return on capital employed for each of two divisions A and B and for a service division which provided printing and other services to A and B where each of four possible charge bases for the service was applied. Part (b) required discussion of the acceptability of the charge bases to the management at each division and to the organisation as a whole. Part (c) involved a decision making exercise about whether to outsource the service and close the service division. Candidates were also required to provide examples of additional information that would help in this decision. This question was generally well answered and formed the foundation for many candidates for the achievement of a pass in this paper. In part (a) candidates failed to pick up marks by not showing the ROCE for the service division. In part (c) the presentation of many answers was poor and difficult to follow. Many candidates did not show figures for an increase or decrease of 20% in activity from the current level as required. In addition, the application of probabilities in order to obtain expected value figures was often either ignored or incorrectly applied.

			Marks
(a)	calculation of ROCE for each division:		
	cost on 50/50 basis	3	
	cost on 50/50 basis plus profit	3	
	cost on ABC basis	5	
	external supplier price basis	3	14
(b)	comments on each of the four bases (on merit) (4 × 1.5)		6
(c)	external fees (3 × 0.5)	1.5	
	variable cost (3 × 0.5)	1.5	
	depreciation	0.5	
	leasing cost (6 × 0.25)	1.5	
	other cost	1	
	overall layout and net flows	1	
	expected value calcualtion (2 × 0.5)	1	
	comments	2	10
(d)	additional factors (on merit)		5
Total			35

Step by step answer plan

Step 1 Read the question again and make sure that you focus on precisely what is required.

Step 2 Head up columns for division A, division B and the service division, so that each of the ROCE figures required in part (a) can quickly be derived.

Step 3 For part (b), go through each of the four charge bases in turn, and discuss whether they are likely to be acceptable to the divisions and to the organisation as a whole.

Step 4 Part (c)(i) is a conventional expected value problem. Calculate the EV of closure in 1997 and in 2001, and select the alternative with the lower expected cost. Part (ii) calls for additional factors to take into account. With 5 marks available, make sure that you note down at least 5 separate points.

Step 5 Now review your answer and ensure that it does precisely answer the question as set.

The examiner's answer

(a)

		Division A	Division B	Service division
		£m	£m	£m
Capital employed		40	25	14
(i)	Total cost on 50/50 basis:			
	Profit (before service charges)	10	8	
	Service division charge	3·5	3·5	
	Net profit	6·5	4·5	nil
	Return on capital employed	16·3%	18·0%	nil
(ii)	Total cost on 50/50 basis plus 30% profit:			
	Profit (before service charges)	10	8	
	Service division charge	4·55	4·55	
	Net profit	5·45	3·45	2·1
	Return on capital employed	13·6%	13·8%	15·0%
(iii)	Total cost on ABC basis:			
	Profit (before service charges)	10	8	
	Service division charge	4·16	2·84	
	Net profit	5·84	5·16	nil
	Return on capital employed	14·6%	20·6%	nil
(iv)	External supplier prices:			
	Profit (before service charges)	10	8	
	Service division charge	2·00	4·50	
	Net profit	8·00	3·50	–0·5
	Return on capital employed	20·0%	14·0%	–3·6%

Working notes:

1. Where the service division charges out total cost plus 30% profit mark-up we have:

	£m
total cost	7·0
profit mark-up	2·1
charge out	9·1

Hence charge to each division is £9·1/2 = £4·55.

2. Where activity based costs are used when charging out the service division costs we have:

Service type	Cost driver	Service costs	Division A	Division B
		£m	£m	£m
Sales	customers	1·8	1·20	0·60
Advertising	product types	2·4	0·96	1·44
Production	batches	0·8	0·40	0·40

Administration	employees	2·0	1.60	0·40
Total			4·16	2·84

3. Total external sales value of the service is £6·5m. Where this is used as the charge-out from the service division, it will report a net loss of £0·5m.

(b) The required return on capital employed for each division is 15%. Division A will achieve this return where a 50/50 cost basis or an external supplier price basis is used. It will not find the 50/50 cost plus profit mark-up or the ABC bases acceptable. Division B will achieve the required 15% return where the 50/50 cost basis or the ABC basis is used. It will not find the 50/50 cost plus profit mark-up or the external supplier price acceptable.

The service division will only find the 50/50 cost plus profit mark-up basis acceptable. This enables it to record a return of 15%. It will be unhappy with the cost based approaches which result in it reporting a nil return on capital employed. It is unlikely to find the external price basis acceptable since this results in it recording a negative return on capital employed of 3·6%

The organisation requires the charge basis to provide a stimulus for improvement in performance at each division.

Division A is likely to seek to reduce its requirement for the stationery and print service where an ABC cost basis is used for transfers. This will make this approach appealing to the organisation. Division B, however, records its highest return (20·6%) where the ABC approach is used and is unlikely to attempt to economise on its use of the service.

The external supplier price basis provides the organisation with an external benchmark. This shows that the service division must attempt to reduce its costs below the current £7m. It also suggests a problem with the structure of the service division in that its ABC costs to divisions A and B are radically different from the corresponding external quotes. We have:

	Division A	Division B
	£m	£m
Internal (ABC) costs	4·16	2·84
External price quotations	2·00	4·50
Net internal (cost)/benefit	(2·16)	1·76

This may stimulate action to re-appraise the methods used by the service division.

The organisation is unlikely to find the 50/50 cost based methods acceptable. The arbitrary nature of the cost apportionment and of the mark-up to the service division will not provide any stimulus for change at each division.

(c) (i)

	Closure 1997			*Closure 2001*		
Activity	*+20%*	*current*	*–20%*	*+20%*	*current*	*–20%*
	£m	£m	£m	£m	£m	£m
External fees	25·20	21·00	21·00			
Variable cost				20·16	16·80	13·44
Fixed cost:						
sale of assets	(0·50)	(0·50)	(0·50)			
lease	3·60	3·60	3·60	4·80	4·80	4·80
others				4·40	4·00	3·60
Net flow	28·30	24·10	24·10	29·36	25·60	21·84
Probability	0·22	0·52	0·32	0·22	0·52	0·32
Expected value		£24·94m			£25·224m	

Where the high or existing activity levels are used as the decision base, the decision on financial grounds will be to close the service division now (1997). Where the low activity level is used the decision will be to retain the service division until 2001. An expected value approach would indicate that the service division should be closed now (1997).

(ii) Other financial and non-financial factors which could influence the decision are:

- possibility of revenue from external use of the service division premises if it is closed now.
- other relevant costs of closure such as redundancy costs.
- ability to request change in the specification of external service mix during the period of the contract without price penalties
- acceptability of the quality of the external service through time
- reliability of the external provider. Its economic viability
- the loss of expertise for internal provision at a future date if things go wrong with the external supply.

(Other relevant points would be accepted.)

Did you answer the question?

The examiner asks for both financial and non-financial factors, and there are 5 marks available. Make sure that you have made enough separate points to attract all 5 marks.

60 (Answer 3 of examination

Examiner's comments and marking guide

Question 3. This question tested candidates' ability to implement calculations for a number of related situations and to discuss the alternative decision making focus of such information. In part (a) candidates were required to calculate standard cost variances for material and conversion costs and to suggest whether decision making should be based on areas controllable by individual managers or on the effect of each of material cost and conversion cost variance. Part (b) required the preparation of a schedule of costs in order to determine which of four alternative strategies involving change in material quality purchased and/or change in processing method would lead to profit maximisation. Part (c) focused on customer specific cost analysis and its use in decision making. Part (d) required the preparation of a report which discussed the contribution of the information provided in each of sections (a) to (c) to a change in decision making strategy by the company.

In part (a) many candidates were unable to calculate the standard cost variances. In addition, many candidates simply attempted to provide reasons for the occurrence of individual variances and not the best grouping for decision making as asked. In part (b) many candidates were unable to calculate the relevant material and conversion costs for each of the alternative strategies. Marks were given where unit rather than total figures were used. In part (c) the most common faults were (i) the use of incorrect free replacement quantities for each customer and (ii) the use of incorrect quantities for the calculation of total contribution (£) for each customer. Marks were awarded for correct procedures even where incorrect quantities were used. Poor presentation was a major problem in answers provided. Many candidates did not make any attempt, or made a very poor attempt, at the preparation of a report in section (d). This meant failure to gain a significant number of marks.

				Marks
(a)	(i)	variance calcualtions (4 × 1)		4
	(ii)	comments (2 × 2)		4
(b)		correct material and conversion cost for each alternative (8 × 0.75)		6
(c)	(i)	Units delivered to A/B (2 × 1)	2	
		production/dist. cost per unit (2 × 0.5)	1	
		other costs per unit (2 × 0.5)	1	
		sales revenue A/B (2 × 0.5)	1	
		production/dist. cost total (2 × 0.5)	1	
		other cost total (2 × 0.5)	1	
		customer contribution (2 × 0.5)	1	
		overall presentaiton	1	9

	(ii)	contribution/unit (2 × 0.5)	1	
		sales (units) to A	1	
		sales (units) to B	2	4
(d)		standard cost variance focus	2·5	
		use of extra info. on sourcing/method	2·5	
		customer specific info.	3	8
Total				35

Step by step answer plan

Step 1 Read the question again and make sure that you focus on precisely what is required. This is a question on variance analysis which is usually a fairly popular topic with students.

Step 2 Part (a) involves the calculation of standard cost variances. Think of how each manager of the company would react to the variances reported.

Step 3 To save time in part (b), you could lay out your answer in a columnar fashion, with each of the four strategies in a separate column. Looking ahead to part (c), we are expecting in part (b) to recommend a strategy of using the original material source and the amended conversion method.

Step 4 Again in part (c), you could save time by laying out your answer in a columnar form, with separate columns for Customer A and Customer B.

Step 5 Write the report required for part (d). Make sure that you answer in report format, with an introduction, body and conclusions clearly laid out.

Step 6 Now review your answer and ensure that it does precisely answer the question as set.

The examiner's answer

(a) (i)

Material price variance	= AQ × (SP – AP)
	= 17,000 × (5 – 4.50) = £8,500(F)
Material usage variance	= (SQ – AQ) × SP
	= ((5,000 × 3) – 17,000) × 5 = £10,000(A)
Conversion efficiency variance	= (SHP – AH) × SR
	= ((0.5 × 5,000) – 2,800) × 25 = £7,500(A)
Conversion expenditure variance	= (SR – AR) × AH
	= (25 – 20) × 2,800 = £14,000(F)

Note: AQ = actual quantity; SQ = standard quantity; SP = standard price; AP = actual price; SHP = standard hours produced; AH = actual hours; SR = standard rate; AR = actual rate.

(ii) 1. The purchase manager will be likely to wish to continue to source the raw material from the cheaper supplier where the material price variance is his performance benchmark. The conversion manager has a net adverse variance of £3,500 when the material usage and conversion efficiency and expenditure variances are added together (£10,000(A) + £7,500(A) + £14,000(F)). A likely strategy will be an emphasis on improvement in the effectiveness of the conversion process, possibly at some additional expenditure, in order to reduce the level of excess material usage.

2. The net effect of the material variances is an adverse material cost variance of £8,500(F) + £10,000(A) = £1,500(A). This could lead to moves to reduce material usage, possibly by using a more expensive material. It would be hoped that this could then result in a net favourable material cost variance.

In the conversion process the net variance is a favourable cost variance of £7,500(A) + £14,000(F) = £6,500(F). It is likely to be felt that this should not be jeopardised through additional expenditure on improvement in processing method.

(b) Alternative strategies of material sources and conversion methods

	Existing material Existing method	*Amended material Existing method*	*Existing material Amended method*	*Amended material Amended method*
	£	£	£	£
Material:				
15,000 × £5	75,000			
16,600 × £4.50		74,700		
15,400 × £5			77,000	
17,000 × £4.50				76,500
Conversion cost:				
2,500 × £25	62,500			
2,620 × £25		65,500		
2,680 × £20			53,600	
2,800 × £20				56,000
Total cost	137,500	140,200	130,600	132,500

Examples of workings:
Material for amended material and existing method:
15,000 + (80% of 2,000) = 16,600 sq.m.
Conversion hours for existing material and amended method:
2,500 + (60% of 300) = 2,680 hours.

The profit maximising strategy is to use the existing material source and the amended conversion process method. This will give a total material and conversion cost of £130,600.

(c) (i) Strategy of using existing material and amended conversion method

Unit data:	*Customer A*	*Customer B*
	£	£
Production cost (given)	26·12	26·12
Distribution cost (given)	2·50	5·00
(1)	28·62	31·12
Units delivered to customers (2)	3,180	2,080
Other costs:	£	£
Rebates to customers	1·00	2·50
Service back-up	4·00	2·00
(3)	5·00	4·50
Units of sale to customers (4)	2,700	1,800
Total estimates for the future period:	£	£
Sales revenue (4) × £50	135,000	90,000
Less: production/distribfution cost (1 × 2)	(91,012)	(64,730)
Less: other costs (3 × 4)	(13,500)	(8,100)
Customer contribution (5)	30,488	17,170

(ii) Inex Ltd will sell 2,700 units of product X to customer A. The balance of production capacity will be used to allow sales to customer B.
Production capacity required for customer A = 3,180 units
Production capacity available for customer B = 4,000 – 3,180

Production capacity available for customer B = 820 units.
Units available for sale to customer B = available production capacity less free replacement units.
Existing replacements (% of units delivered) = 200/2,000 = 10%
Additional replacements (% of units delivered) = 80/2,080 = 3.85%
Maximum sales possible to customer B = 820 × 90% 96.15% = 709 units

(d) To: Inex Ltd management
From: A N Accountant
Subject: Information analysis and decision-making strategey

Decision-making strategy will be affected by the degree of information available and the extent to which the decision-maker has access to such information. Inex Ltd has to formulate a strategy for production and sale of product X. This strategy should take into account the likely effect of changes in the sourcing of raw materials and changes in the method of production in the conversion process. In addition, it should take into account customer specific information where total demand cannot be satisfied because of production capacity constraints. In part (a) the focus is solely on standard cost variances. The way in which the variance information was linked to a decision-maker influenced the likely strategy to be pursued. For example, the assumption that the purchasing manager focused only on the material price variance could lead to a continuation of the purchase of cheaper material. This may not be the strategy which will provide overall benefit. As shown in part (a), the use of a more expensive material may lead to a reduction in excess material usage with a net beneficial impact on costs.

In part (b) additional information is available about the estimated impact of cheaper sourcing of material and the amended processing method on costs. The schedule of estimated cost for each combination, e.g. amended conversion method and original material source, enables the cost minimising strategy to be calculated.

In part (c) additional information is supplied about free replacements to customers and costs relating to distribution, rebates and after sales for specific customers. This information enables customer specific contribution per unit to be calculated. In part (c) this is used to determine the profit maximising sales strategy where production capacity is less than demand. The information may also be used to allow comparison of specific items between customers. For example why is the amended conversion method expected to cause greater additional free replacements to customer A than to customer B (180/3,180 = 5.7% versus 80/2,080 = 3.8%)? Again, do the high distribution costs per unit for customer B indicate that there should be a reappraisal of the high rebate percentage (customer B 5%; customer A 2%)?

The deliberations in the question assume that the figures for the period provided are representative of those for future periods. It is important that any strategy changes should be based on trends and projections and/or specific known changes for future periods.

Did you answer the question?

Although the wording of part (d) may seem hard to understand, there are 8 marks available so you have to have a go. As long as you write a report covering the topic required, you are bound to pick up some marks.

61 (Answer 4 of examination)

Examiner's comments and marking guide

Question 4. This question required candidates to discuss the advantages and disadvantages of using standards and variances where a continuous improvement focus exists in an organisation. In addition, candidates were required to suggest possible dysfunctional impacts of focusing on the minimisation of an adverse material price variance.

Many candidates prepared a basic discussion of the arguments for and against the use of standards and variances. Most candidates made little reference to the impact of a continuous improvement focus on the argument. This was a key aspect of the question to which a number of marks were allotted. In part (b) many candidates mentioned only the relationship between quality and price and ignored a number of other factors on which comments were required for full marks.

			Marks
(a)	arguments for standards	5	
	arguments for actual data	5	10
	(minimum of 3 points for each – on merit)		
(b)	minimum of three points (on merit)		5
Total			15

Step by step answer plan

Step 1 Read the question again and make sure that you focus on precisely what is required.

Step 2 Part (a) concerns an environment striving for continuous improvement. The idea is that it might be more appropriate to try and improve the current actual performance month-by-month rather than using predetermined standards. With 10 marks available, you must try and list out 5 advantages and 5 disadvantages to gain full marks.

Step 3 Similarly, you must make 5 separate points in part (b). Saying that cheap goods are likely to be of low quality is fine for one mark, but you have to then make four further points.

Step 4 Now review your answer and ensure that it does precisely answer the question as set.

The examiner's answer

(a) The information used for forward planning should reflect the efficient conditions likely to exist during the period for which the plan will apply. Planning will be more difficult where a high degree of change is envisaged in areas such as mix of business activities or methods of manufacture or service provision.

Arguments which may be given for the use of standards and variances include:

- standards may be viewed as a measure of current best practice to which the plan should aim
- standards should provide 'building blocks' which may be used in the preparation and evaluation of plans for new products or activities.
- standards may be set at the long run 'ideal' level of performance or at a short term 'currently attainable' level. This should help improve the flexibility of the planning process.
- variances may be split into planning and operational sub-sets and into controllable and non-controllable elements. Non-controllable planning variances may be built into revised standards for use in planning. An estimate of possible improvements to eliminate adverse operational variances and the likely cost and timescale of such improvements will assist the planning process.
- current actual performance data may contain short term non-recurring inefficiencies or gains which should be excluded from any planning data.

A number of points may be raised suggesting the use of current actual performance data rather than standards:

- the business environment and markets may be subject to considerable change which would mitigate against the continued use of standards which relate to outdated conditions
- current management thinking would be towards the use of a total quality philosophy which has continuous improvement as the planning goal. Improvement from the current performance level would be built into the planning process in a move towards a zero defect, right first time situation.
- standards may be argued to lead to a continuation of existing methods and stifle moves towards new strategies and methods. In this situation the forward plan would tend to be an extension of the current situation.

- standards may be argued to foster a functional planning philosophy which is not in tune with the seeking of overall improvement when forward planning is being implemented. For example target costing may be used in conjunction with value engineering in planning for new products and markets. These techniques require a more integrated approach with inputs from various disciplines into the plan at an early stage.

The debate may include arguments for and against the use of both standards and current actual data as the starting point in the planning process. The weight of argument is likely to depend on the type of business situation and the preferences (and prejudices) of those responsible for the management of the planning process.

(Other relevant points would be accepted.)

Did you answer the question?

Was your answer to part (a) based on a focus on continuing improvement? General comments about whether standards are a good or bad tool are not required. The question is set on a specific type of environment.

(b) The basic assumption in variance analysis and control is that minimisation of adverse variances will move events closer to the planned level of performance. In the case of the material price variance the purchasing manager would pursue a strategy of obtaining materials from a supplier(s) who will continue to offer the standard price. This strategy may be flawed for a number of reasons:

- it will not lead to loyalty to suppliers. In a total quality environment, links with suppliers to discuss the features of materials and components which are required are an important part of the control process
- it could lead to the purchase of inferior quality materials resulting in adverse material usage variances which outweigh any price savings
- undue focus on price may lead to quality problems leading to returns of products from customers and free replacements and compensation claims
- focus on price may lead to bulk purchases in order to obtain high price discounts. This could lead to high storage costs and problems of obsolescence
- it could lead to insufficient emphasis on features of supply such as on-time delivery. This could lead to production delays and the additional costs which would follow.
(Other relevant points would be accepted.)

62 (Answer 5 of examination)

Examiner's comments and marking guide

Question 5. This question required candidates to discuss factors to be considered in the preparation and agreement of the manufacturing cost per unit in a processing industry. The question suggested that the impact of factors such as joint products, JIT, total quality programmes and backflush accounting should be incorporated into the answer.

Answers to this question were of a very poor standard. Many candidates did not answer in the context of a processing industry situation. This showed poor exam technique in not reading what the question actually asked. In addition, many candidates wrote about the meaning of features such as JIT and TQM without attempting to relate their answer to the impact of such techniques on unit cost in a processing industry.

	Marks
comments on materials and recycling, WIP and backflush a/c, normal loses, conversion cost, standard or actual basis (all on merit) (5 × 3)	15

Step by step answer plan

Step 1 Read the question again and make sure that you focus on precisely what is required. This question is based in a processing industry.

Step 2 Imagine yourself as an accountant in a processing industry; raw materials, labour and overheads are input into a number of processes in turn, with the output from one process becoming the input of the next process. In some processes, joint products and by products may emerge.

Step 3 Now that you are in the right context for the question, plan the points that you will make. Write in short paragraphs for each point, including at least every topic referred to in the question, but adding others to earn the full 15 marks.

Step 4 Now review your answer and ensure that it does precisely answer the question as set.

The examiner's answer

In a processing industry raw materials may be passed through a number of processes in which the materials are converted into one or more finished products. Factors which should be considered in the preparation of agreed manufacturing costs per product unit will include:

- are materials added only at the initial process or also at intermediate processes? In what proportions will the materials be required? The proportions of materials may be detailed in a technical specification which should be adhered to in order that the finished product will conform to customer specification requirements

- materials must be sourced to meet the material specification. The price of such materials may be affected by the purchasing policy in force. It may be that a just-in-time system is in operation for which suppliers are compensated by a slightly increased price

- it may be that some work in progress is re-cycled for use as part of the input material in subsequent batches. This assumes a level of process losses which is deemed an acceptable part of efficient operation. Where this occurs it is necessary to determine the basis on which such re-cycled material will be charged. This should be at its opportunity cost which may vary from its sales value as scrap to a negative value where disposal costs are avoided.

- the level of normal losses in each process must be agreed. This information will enable the input to each process to be determined such that one unit of finished product is finally obtained. It may be argued that the concept of normal losses is incompatible with a total quality environment. It is likely, however, that some residual level of normal loss may occur e.g. due to moisture loss, which must be allowed for.

- the basis of charging for conversion cost (labour and overhead) must be agreed. This may be implemented using a single volume related cost driver in each process e.g. machine hours. It may also be argued, however, that an activity based system should be applied which determines activities and their cost drivers and charges conversion cost accordingly. As a prerequisite to the agreement of such charges, a study should be carried out to determine value added and non-value added activities. Efforts should be made to eliminate non-value added activities and to reduce the incidence of the cost drivers for value added activities consistent with the achievement of the required product design specification.

- will the unit cost be based on actual or standard specifications and costs? It may be argued that the trend of actual costs through time, coupled with a series of non-financial performance indicators will be of more benefit than a standard unit cost from which a variance (£) analysis is determined. The use of standard costs may be seen as useful in order to supply the valuation of work in progress at intermediate stages in the production cycle. Where a just-in-time system is in operation, however, with fast throughput rates and minimum work in progress, it may be decided that a backflush accounting system should be applied. This would minimise the need for intermediate work in progress valuations by using a combined materials and in process account with an estimation of the residual value of any small quantities of material and work in progress which existed

- where two or more joint products emerge from a process, the basis of cost apportionment should be agreed. This may be implemented in a number of ways including physical quantity, sales value at separation point or sales value after further processing. This procedure is only really of relevance for stock valuation purposes. Where a backflush accounting system is in operation, as outlined above, the relevance of such valuation is minimised.

(Other relevant points would be accepted.)

Did you answer the question?

Notice how every point made in the exminer's answer is specific to a process costing environment. General comments on quality and backflushing will not earn you any marks; they have to be relevant to a processing industry.

63 (Answer 6 of examination)

Examiner's comments and marking guide

Question 6. This question required candidates to discuss the provision of planning and control information by each of four budgeting techniques. The question also required discussion of the issue of causality. The question stated the problem of "does the technique used cause the planning and control style used OR does the planning and control style required by management determine the technique which is applied."

The aspect of causality was totally ignored by most candidates. Most candidates were able to name four alternative approaches to budgeting. Many candidates did not discuss in any meaningful way the possible planning AND control merits of each approach.

		Marks
four budgeting techniques named (4 × 1)	4	
comments on desirable/available information and link to each method (4 × 3)	12	15 (max)

Step by step answer plan

Step 1 Read the question again and make sure that you focus on precisely what is required. You are invited to think of four alternative budgeting techniques: fixed budgeting, flexible budgeting, incremental budgeting, ZBB and ABB come to mind, so choose four of them.

Step 2 The question does not invite you to discuss these topics in general. You are being asked:
(i) does the technique satisfy management's information needs? and
(ii) does the budgeting technique determine the information management is given, or does the information management require determine the budgeting technique adopted?

Step 3 For each of the four chosen techniques in turn, address the issues raised in step 2.

Step 4 Now review your answer and ensure that it does precisely answer the question as set.

The examiner's answer

The statements raise the issue of direction of causality – what causes what? Is it the case that where a particular budgeting system is in operation it will determine the planning and control information which is perceived by management as desirable? Alternatively is it more likely that planning and control information requirements which are desirable will be determined by management and the budgeting system will be designed in order to provide such information?

The problem may be explored in the context of budgeting techniques such as fixed budgeting, flexible budgeting, incremental budgeting, zero-base budgeting and activity based budgeting.

Fixed budgeting assumes that a single activity level will apply. Planning information is restricted to a single set of data although uncertainty could be allowed for by producing a number of scenarios. This could provide for high, low and most likely outcomes or for the attachment of subjective probabilities to the alternatives and the calculation of an expected value outcome. This type of budgeting could demotivate management if they are being measured against unrealistic targets.

It may be deemed necessary to have budgets available at the planning stage for a range of activity levels and to allow comparison with actual data at the control stage on a relevant basis. This requirement could be achieved by implementing a Flexible budgeting system as part of the accounting information system.

The budgeting system should provide for planned changes in price and performance levels. Where incremental budgeting is in operation a number of features will apply:

- it assumes that the existing planning model is still relevant

- it focuses on current resources used and changes to such resources. The budget for the following time period will be prepared by adding incremental percentages to the existing model to allow for planned changes in activity, prices and efficiency of operation

- the budget process is likely to be departmental/segmental in nature.

An incremental budgeting system is therefore deficient in that it does not clearly link resource allocation to a strategic plan for the future. It will tend to constrain new, high priority activities through its focus on the existing planning model. It may lead to arbitrary cuts in specific budget areas in order to meet overall financial targets.

Where management are able to express in advance specific planning and control features which are not provided by an incremental budgeting system, a more relevant alternative method of budgeting may be chosen and implemented. Zero-base budgeting removes the implied right of existing activities to receive a continued allocation of resources. It shifts the burden of proof to the manager of an activity or department to justify all expenditure. Zero-base budgeting is of particular use in planning and controlling expenditure in discretionary areas where there is competition for a share of a limited amount of funds. The process involves estimating costs and benefits for each 'package' in each department or activity. A ranking process will then be applied which determines the packages to which funds will be allocated.

The budgeting systems considered so far are principally functionally based and are likely to reinforce functional prejudice which does not have the best interests of the business as a first priority. It may be argued that Activity based budgeting will improve the range and volume of information. The introduction of such a system should lead to a new planning and control perspective being accepted by management. ABB focuses on the allocation of resources to activities where efficiency, effectiveness and continuous improvement are pursued as part of a total quality philosophy.

The use of ABB will focus on the provision of information relating to factors such as:

- activities – are they value added or non-value added in nature?

- cost drivers which determine the level of resource for each activity. How can the incidence of a cost driver be reduced? Is it possible to provide information which will help highlight the relationship between a cost driver and its root cause? Can the quality of performance of an activity be measured in terms of 'how well' it is being delivered? For example what percentage of the routing of products is achieved without bottlenecks? Is 85% good? To answer this question the trends must be monitored through time. In this way the planning and control requirements are determining the information which the budgeting system should produce.

  (Alternative relevant comment and discussion would be accepted.)

Did you answer the question?

The examiner's answer does not contain a detailed description of each budgeting technique. This was not asked for in the question, and you have wasted valuable time if you have contained a paragraph explaining each technique in your answer. Concentrate only on answering the question as set.

JUNE 1998 QUESTIONS

Section A – TWO questions ONLY to be attempted

64 (Question 1 of examination)

Stow Health Centre specialises in the provision of sports/exercise and medical/dietary advice to clients. The service is provided on a residential basis and clients stay for whatever number of days suits their needs.

Budgeted estimates for the year ending 30 June 1999 are as follows:

(i) The maximum capacity of the centre is 50 clients per day for 350 days in the year.

(ii) Clients will be invoiced at a fee per day. The budgeted occupancy level will vary with the client fee level per day and is estimated at different percentages of maximum capacity as follows:

Client fee per day	*Occupancy level*	*Occupancy as percentage of maximum capacity*
£180	High	90%
£200	Most likely	75%
£220	Low	60%

(iii) Variable costs are also estimated at one of three levels per client day. The high, most likely and low levels per client day are £95, £85 and £70 respectively.

The range of cost levels reflect only the possible effect of the purchase prices of goods and services.

Required:

(a) Prepare a summary which shows the budgeted contribution earned by Stow Health Centre for the year ended 30 June 1999 for each of nine possible outcomes. **(6 marks)**

(b) State the client fee strategy for the year to 30 June 1999 which will result from the use of each of the following decision rules:
(i) *maximax*; (ii) *maximin*; (iii) *minimax* regret.

Your answer should explain the basis of operation of each rule. Use the information from your answer to (a) as relevant and show any additional working calculations as necessary. **(9 marks)**

(c) The probabilities of variable cost levels occurring at the high, most likely and low levels provided in the question are estimated as 0·1, 0·6 and 0·3 respectively.

Using the information available, determine the client fee strategy which will be chosen where maximisation of expected value of contribution is used as the decision basis. **(5 marks)**

(d) The calculations in (a) to (c) concern contribution levels which may occur given the existing budget.

Stow Health Centre has also budgeted for fixed costs of £1,200,000 for the year to 30 June 1999.

Discuss ways in which Stow Health Centre may instigate changes, in ways other than through the client fee rate, which may influence client demand, cost levels and profit.

Your answer should include comment on the existing budget and should incorporate illustrations which relate to each of four additional performance measurement areas appropriate to the changes you discuss.

(15 marks)
(35 marks)

65 (Question 2 of examination)

The activity matrix in Figure 2.1 shows the budget for the sales order department of Cognet plc. Relevant information with regard to the operation of the sales order department is as follows:

(i) A team of staff deals with existing customers in respect of problems with orders or with prospective customers enquiring about potential orders.

(ii) The processing of orders requires communication with the production and despatch functions of the company.

(iii) The nature of the business is such that there is some despatching of part-orders to customers which helps reduce stock holding costs and helps customers in their work flow management.

(iv) Sales literature is sent out to existing and prospective customers by means of a monthly mailshot.

Cognet plc has decided to acquire additional computer software with internet links in order to improve the effectiveness of the sales order department. The cost to the company of this initiative is estimated at £230,000 p.a.

It is estimated that there will be the following cost and volume changes to activities in the sales order department:

1. Reduction in overall salaries by 10% per annum, applied to the existing salary apportionments.
2. Reduction of 60% in the stores/supplies cost in the sales literature activity only.
3. £20,000 of the computer software cost will be allocated to the sales literature activity. The balance will be shared by the other activities in proportion to their existing share of IT costs.
4. Sundry costs for customer negotiation, processing of orders and implementing despatches will vary in proportion to the number of units of each activity. Sundry costs for sales literature and general administration will be unchanged.
5. Amended volume of activity will be: total customers 2,600; customer negotiations 6,000; home orders 5,500; export orders 2,000; despatches to customers 18,750.

Recent industry average statistics for sales order department activities in businesses of similar size, customer mix and product mix are as follows:

Cost per customer per year	£300
Cost per home order processed	£50
Cost per export order processed	£60
Cost per despatch	£8
Sales literature cost per customer	£35
Average number of orders per customer per year	4·1
Average number of despatches per order	3·3

Figure 2.1

Activity Cost Matrix – Sales Order Department

Cost element	Total Cost	Customer Negotiations	Processing of orders Home	Processing of orders Export	Implementing Despatches	Sales Literature	General Administration
	£000	£000	£000	£000	£000	£000	£000
Salaries	500	80	160	100	90	20	50
Stores/supplies	90	16	6	8	60		
IT	70	10	30	20	10		
Sundry costs	80	8	10	6	20	10	26
Total	740	98	216	132	128	90	76
Volume of activity:	2,000 customers	3,000 negotiations	5,000 orders	1,200 orders	11,500 despatches		

Required:

(a) Prepare a summary of the amended activity cost matrix (per Figure 2·1) for the sales order department after implementing the proposed changes. **(8 marks)**

(b) Prepare an analysis (both discursive and quantitative/monetary as appropriate) which examines the implications of the IT initiative. The analysis should include:

(i) A benchmarking exercise on the effectiveness of the sales order department against both its current position and the industry standards provided.

You should incorporate comment on additional information likely to improve the relevance of the exercise. **(14 marks)**

(ii) An investigation of the customer negotiation activity where an analysis of the number of negotiations is as follows:

	New customers obtained	*No further customers*	*Existing customer problems solved*	
Original budget	300	1,800	900	
Post-IT budget	900	3,500	1,600	**(7 marks)**

(iii) Itemising FOUR strategic planning objectives of the company which may be aided through implementing the IT initiative and suggest why the IT initiative may help in each case.

(6 marks)
(35 marks)

66 (Question 3 of examination)

Assemblo Ltd is contemplating an early exit from the production and sale of PROD1 for which demand estimates are poor.

The following information is available:

(i) Assemblo Ltd has agreements with suppliers of the components for PROD1 at £20 per product unit on a JIT basis for the three year period to 30 June 2001. This agreement is subject to a termination fee of 20% of the cost of the supply of components for the year to 30 June in which early cancellation of the agreement is made.

(ii) Production and sales of PROD1 in the year to 30 June 1998 total 6,500 units. The estimated sales of PROD1 for each of the three years to 30 June 2001 is 1,500 units per year at a selling price of £100 per unit.

(iii) PROD1 is made under license on payment of a royalty of £5 per unit together with a fixed fee of £10,000 per annum. The agreement will run to 30 June 2001 and early exit would incur a penalty payment by Assemblo Ltd of £20,000 irrespective of the timing of the early exit.

(iv) PROD1 requires the lease of special equipment which was agreed on a five year basis on 1 July 1996 for a total fee of £400,000. This fee is payable in equal annual instalments over the life of the agreement. Early discontinuance of production of the product would require immediate payment of the outstanding portion of the lease.

(v) Sundry additional variable costs of £30 per unit are payable in respect of PROD1.

Required:

(a) Prepare figures which show for PROD1:

(i) the cash outflow due to a decision to cease production and sale at 30 June 1998

(ii) the cumulative net cash flow from 1 July 1998 to cessation of production and sale, where production and sale is ceased on EACH of 30 June 1999, 2000 and 2001. **(15 marks)**

(b) Comment on the choice of year end at which Assemblo Ltd may decide to cease production and sale of PROD1 and suggest additional information which may assist the decision process. **(5 marks)**

Assemblo Ltd is considering the addition of another product, PROD2 to its sales mix. A market has been identified for PROD2 with a three-year cycle to 30 June 2001.

Additional information is as follows:

(i) Production constraints will only permit the manufacture of a mix of 10,000 units of PROD1 and PROD2. Each product will use the same amount of production capacity per unit.

An advertising campaign for PROD1 is expected to considerably increase the level of demand for the product in the three-year period to 30 June 2001. The maximum sales estimates of the products are as follows:

Year to 30 June	*PROD1 (units)*	*PROD2 (units)*
1999	8,000	8,000
2000	6,000	8,000
2001	4,000	6,000

Each product will be produced and sold at the maximum level of demand.

(ii) Advertising expenditure for PROD1 and PROD2 will be £100,000 and £60,000 respectively for each of three years payable on 1 July each year.

(iii) The production of PROD2 could be sub-contracted each year where a shortfall of production capacity exists. The price paid to the supplier of each sub-contracted unit would be £80.

(iv) Components for PROD2 can be obtained at a cost of £30 per unit of PROD2 with no penalty clauses in the agreement.

(v) PROD2 will require expenditure of £100,000 per year on computer software related to its production process. This is not payable in any year to 30 June in which the production of PROD2 is totally sub-contracted.

(vi) Sundry additional variable costs of £40 per unit are payable in respect of PROD2. This amount will be reduced to £15 per unit for which production is sub-contracted.

(vii) It is estimated that the selling price of PROD1 will be maintained at £100 per unit and that PROD2 will be sold at £120 per unit over the three-year period.

Required:

(c) (i) Determine for EACH of the years to 30 June 1999, 2000 and 2001 whether Assemblo Ltd should sub-contract production of ALL of PROD2 or whether it should only sub-contract that part of its production which cannot be achieved with its own production capacity. PROD1 will be produced and sold at its maximum demand forecast level. You should make the decision on financial grounds and show all relevant workings. **(9 marks)**

(ii) Name and comment on additional factors which may influence the decision to sub-contract the production of part or all of PROD2. **(6 marks)**

(35 marks)

Section B – TWO questions ONLY to be attempted

67 (Question 4 of examination)

The implementation of budgeting in a world class manufacturing environment may be affected by the impact of (i) a total quality ethos (ii) a just-in-time philosophy and (iii) an activity based focus.

Briefly describe the principles incorporated in EACH of (i) to (iii) and discuss ways in which each may result in changes in the way in which budgets are prepared as compared to a traditional incremental budgeting system.

(15 marks)

68 (Question 5 of examination)

The accurate estimate of total cost will require consideration of specific features of the resource inputs and production methods required for a product.

Expand on the appropriate sources and content of total cost estimation in each of the undernoted situations.

(i) Abatch of light fittings made to customer specification.
(ii) Chemical produced in a multi stage process cycle and sold per litre.
(iii) Construction of a bridge over a valley. **(15 marks)**

69 (Question 6 of examination)

Individual performance measurement is likely to be related to the aspiration level of the individual and the timing and level of the target set.

Discuss the above statement in the context of EACH of Tables 1 and 2 shown below. The tables provide illustrations expressed in terms of output, of the results of two separate studies linking targets, aspiration levels and achievement.

(15 marks)

Table 1

		Actual achievement (units)		
Target	Target Units	Aspiration level set by individual before knowing target	Aspiration level set by individual after knowing target	Average
Implicit	not quoted	53	57	55
Explicit: low	35	45	44	44.5
Explicit: medium	50	54	54	54
Explicit: high	70	40	60	50

Table 2

Target (units)	Aspiration level of individual (where target is known) (units)	Actual achieved (units)
70	80	80
90	90	90
110	100	100
130	120	112
150	110	90
180	nil	80

ANSWERS TO JUNE 1998 EXAMINATION

64 (Answer 1 of examination)

Examiner's comments and marking guide

Question 1: Part (a) required candidates to implement calculations in order to show nine possible outcomes of budgeted contribution from data provided. Part (b) required candidates to choose the most appropriate decision strategy from those calculated in (a) where each of three decision rules was applied. An explanation of each rule was also required. Part (c) required the calculation of the expected value contribution for each client fee strategy and hence the choice of the strategy which maximised this measure. Part (d) required discussion of ways in which each of four additional performance measurement areas could help instigate changes which would influence client demand, cost levels and profit.

In part (a) many candidates were only able to correctly calculate three of the nine required contribution outcomes. This was due to a mismatching of client fee rates and variable cost values. In part (b) few candidates were able to correctly apply the minimax regret decision rule. Marks were awarded for correct procedure even where incorrect answers to part (a) were used as the basis of the choice of strategy. In part (c) marks were allowed where a correct expected value calculation approach was applied, even where the data used was extracted from incorrect answers to part (a). In part (d) many candidates could have gained more marks by focusing more fully on alternative performance measurement areas such as quality and innovation and ways in which they could influence demand and profit.

			Marks
(a)	budget contribution (9 × 0.67)		6
(b)	basis of operaiton of each rule (3 × 1)	3	
	maximax and maximin choice (2 × 1)	2	
	minimax regre calcns, and choice	4	9
(c)	correct calculations and choice (on merit)		5
(d)	comment on existing model	3	
	additional performance measures and comment (4 × 3)	12	15
Total			35

Step by step answer plan

Step 1 Read the question again and make sure that you focus on precisely what is required. This appears to be a straightforward pay-off question for parts (a) to (c), with a discussion part (d).

Step 2 With three possible occupancy levels, and three possible cost levels, there are 9 possible outcomes for the year, to be summarised in your answer to part (a).

Step 3 In part (b), explain how you are applying each decision rule to arrive at the recommended client fee strategy.

Step 4 Part (c) requires you to calculate the expected contribution from each fee level and select the highest.

Step 5 Part (d) offers 15 marks and so deserves close attention after the routine calculations of parts (a) to (c). You are asked to do a number of things:

- discuss how to influence demand, cost levels and profit, other than through the fee rate. Examples might be improvements in quality, or advertising
- comment on the existing budget
- identify four new performance measurement areas. Examples might be quality, flexibility of service, resource utilisation and innovation.

Step 6 Now review your answer and ensure that it does precisely answer the question as set.

The examiner's answer

(a) Budgeted net Profit/Loss outcomes for year ending 30 June 1999

Client Days	Fee per Client day £	Var. cost per client day £	Contribution per client day £	Total contrib. per year £
15,750	180	95	85	1,338,750
15,750	180	85	95	1,496,250
15,750	180	70	110	1,732,500
13,125	200	95	105	1,378,125
13,125	200	85	115	1,509,375
13,125	200	70	130	1,706,250
10,500	220	95	125	1,312,500
10,500	220	85	135	1,417,500
10,500	220	70	150	1,575,000

(b) The maximax rule looks for the largest contribution from all outcomes. In this case the decision maker will choose a client fee of £180 per day where there is a possibility of a contribution of £1,732,500.

The maximin rule looks for the strategy which will maximise the minimum possible contribution. In this case the decision maker will choose client fee of £200 per day where the lowest contribution is £1,378,125. This is better than the worst possible outcome from client fees per day of £180 or £220 which will provide contribution of £1,338,750 and £1,312,500 respectively.

The minimax regret rule requires the choice of the strategy which will minimise the maximum regret from making the wrong decision. Regret in this context is the opportunity lost through making the wrong decision.

Using the calculations from part (a) we may create an opportunity loss table as follows:

	Client fee per day strategy		
State of variable cost	*£180*	*£200*	*£220*
High	39,375	0	65,625
Most likely	13,125	0	91,875
Low	0	26,250	157,500
Maximum regret	**39,375**	**26,250**	**157,500**

Example of the workings: at the low level of variable costs, the best strategy would be a client fee of £180. The opportunity loss from using a fee of £200 or £220 per day would be £26,250 (1,732,500 – £1,706,250) or £157,500 (1,732,500 – 1,575,000) respectively.

The minimum regret strategy (client fee £200 per day) is that which minimises the maximum regret (i.e. £26,250 in the maximum regret row above).

(c) The expected value of variable cost
$= £95 \times 0.1 + £85 \times 0.6 + £70 \times 0.3 = £81.50$

For each client fee strategy the expected value of budget contribfution for the year may be calculated:

* fee of £180 : 15,750 (180 – 81.50) = £1,551,375
* fee of £200 : 13,125 (200 – 81.50) = £1,555,312.50
* fee of £220 : 10,500 (220 – 81.50) = £1,454,250

Hence choose a client fee of £200 per day to give the maximum expected value contribution of £1,555,312·50. Note that there is virtually no difference between this and the contribution where a fee of £180 per day is used.

(d) The existing budget has linked demand in terms of percentage occupancy with the client fee rate. High, most likely and low levels of occupancy have been estimated as likely to apply for client fee rates of £180, £200 and £220 respectively. Variable costs have also been stated as likely to occur at one of three levels per client day. We are told that the range of cost levels reflect only the possible effect of the purchase price of goods and services.

Demand by clients, the efficiency of operation of the Health Centre and hence profit, will be affected by a number of factors. Additional performance measurement areas which may have an impact on demand and costs include quality, flexibility, resource utilisation and innovation. Some measures may lead to cost reductions with no significant impact on demand. Care must be taken to avoid cost savings which result in a fall in demand and an overall fall in profit. Others measures may lead to cost increases which result in an improved level of service and an increase in demand.

Specific examples of the possible effect of quality, flexibility, resource utilisation and innovation measures may be as follows;

1. Quality of service may be improved by upgrading facilities such as menu or accommodation services such as maid service, soft drinks cabinet or free daily newspapers. These may improve demand to an extent which more than offsets any increase in cost. Again costs could be reduced through sub-contracting the laundry service for the centre. If such sub-contracting results in a fall in quality, however, demand may suffer and hence profits fall.

2. Flexibility of service may be improved by hiring additional exercise consultants with specialisms not currently available. This may improve demand. This would have to be considered against it possibly reducing the efficiency of resource utilisation if the extra consultants were not fully utilised.

3. Resource utilisation may be improved through a decision to rationalise medical/dietary consultancy provision and hence reduce the number of consultants required. This could lower the quality and flexibility of this service with an adverse impact on demand and profit.

4. Innovation may take the form of new computer based systems for client bookings, information bulletins during their stay, and dedicated information sites providing access to general advice on various issues. Such measures would improve quality and should improve flexibility and utilisation of consultants. This may involve capital costs which would have to be recovered over the estimated life of the systems.

(Other relevant examples would be accepted.)

65 (Answer 2 of examination)

Examiner's comments and marking guide

Question 2: In part (a) candidates were required to prepare an amended activity cost matrix using the matrix provided in the question as the starting point and implementing the effect of a number of proposed budget changes linked to increased use of computer applications in the operation of a sales order department. Part (b) required an analysis (both discursive and quantitative) of the impact of the changes calculated in (a). This analysis included benchmarking against industry average statistics provided in the question. Candidates were also required to name four strategic planning objectives which might be aided through the implementation of the computer application changes.

Part (a) was generally well answered by candidates, although the presentation of the figures was often poor. In part (b) some candidates did not prepare a summary analysis which compared the unit costs of industry average, pre–IT change and post-IT change for each activity. Many candidates could have gained more marks through greater effort to comment on the comparison of the quantitative data for each activity. Many candidates were unable to identify strategic planning objectives which could be aided by the IT initiative and simply commented on general operational improvements.

				Marks
(a)	salary changes		1	
	stores/supplies change		0·5	
	software cost changes		2	
	sundry cost changes		2	
	Activity level changes and layout of table		2·5	8
(b)	(i)	data tabulation		
		– costs per customer, etc (7 × 0.5)	3.5	
		– activity measures (original and post-IT) all given in Q	1	
		– layout structure	1.5	
		comments linked to stats. analysis re-customers, orders and despatches, literature and activity changes (on merit)	8	14
	(ii)	customer negotiations - percentage stats.	2	
		cost per negotiation - original and post-IT	1	
		comments on above	4	7
	(iii)	planning objectives aided through IT changes and how IT will help (4 × 1.5)		6
	Total			35

Step by step answer plan

Step 1 Read the question again and make sure that you focus on precisely what is required. Acquiring the new computer software will have a significant impact on the company in the question; you are required to identify both monetary and non-monetary implications of the IT initiative.

Step 2 You are given the proforma to use for part (a) in the question. Work through the cost and volume changes described and slot the new figures into the matrix.

Step 3 Part (b) is worth a total of 27 marks ie, a quarter of your answer to the whole exam, so follow the instructions carefully. The benchmarking in (b)(i) should start with drawing up the required analysis of the industry, the company pre-initiative, and the company post-initiative.

Step 4 In (b)(ii) compare the performance of the department before and after the initiative, in converting customer negotiations into added value for the company.

Step 5 Part (b)(iii) asks for four strategic planning objectives, such as expanding the volume of overseas sales. Make sure that you only include strategic matters, and not day-to-day operational matters.

Step 6 Now review your answer and ensure that it does precisely answer the question as set.

(a)

Figure 2.1

Activity Cost Matrix – Sales Order Department

Cost element	Total Cost	Customer Negotiations	Processing of orders: Home	Processing of orders: Export	Implementing Despatches	Sales Literature	General Administration
	£000	£000	£000	£000	£000	£000	£000
Salaries	450	72	144	90	81	18	45
Stores/supplies	54		16	6	8	24	
IT	300	40	120	80	40	20	

Sundry costs	106	16	11	10	33	10	26
Total	910	128	291	186	162	72	71
Volume of activity:	2,600 customers	6,000 negotiations	5,500 orders	2,000 orders	18,750 dispatches		

(b) (i) Statistics may be prepared and summarised which compare the original and post IT budgets for the Sales Order Department of Cognet plc with industry average statistics where possible. The Cognet plc figures are obtained from the information in Figure 2.1 in the question and from the activity cost matrix solution to part (a).

We have:

	Industry	*Cognet plc Original*	*Post-IT*
Cost per customer per year (£)	300	370	350
Cost per home order (£)	50	43·20	52·91
Cost per export order (£)	60	110	93
Cost per despatch (£)	8	11·13	8·64
Sales literature per customer (£)	35	45	27·69
Average orders per customer (units)	4·1	3·1	2·89
Average despatches per order (unit)	3·3	1·85	2·5
Activity measures (numbers of):			
Customers		2,000	2,600
Negotiations		3,000	6,000
Home orders		5,000	5,500
Export orders		1,200	2,000
Dispatches		11,500	18,750

From an internal benchmarking viewpoint, the Sales Order Department of Cognet plc will achieve a fall of 5·4% in its average cost per customer. This is however, still 16·7% above the industry average figure.

Cognet plc will increase its number of customers by 30%. Home orders will increase by 10% and export orders by 67%. We are not provided with industry average figures for such measures. It would also be useful to have information which would enable us to calculate the estimated increase in contribution earned by Cognet plc and whether this would exceed the estimated extra cost of £170,000 for the year.

The proportion of export orders to total orders for Cognet plc will move from 19·4% to 26·7%. This may be seen as an appropriate move in developing the market base for Cognet plc. Similar information for the industry would be useful.

The costs per order comparison raises a number of points. Cognet plc cost per home order will rise above the industry average following the IT initiative. The cost per export order will still be 50% higher than the industry average, but will be 8·5% lower than the pre-IT level. We do know that the industry has an average orders per customer ratio of 4·1 compared to the post-IT level of 2·89 for Cognet plc.

The question indicates that the despatch of part orders has benefits for both Cognet plc and its customers in areas such as stock holding costs and work flow management respectively. The statistics show that the post-IT position for Cognet plc of 2·5 despatches per order is an ‘improvement’ on the 1·85 despatches per order which applied previously. The new figure is still below the industry average of 3·3 despatches per order.

The cost per despatch will fall considerably following the IT initiative from £11·13 to £8·64 which is very close to industry average of £8. Since many of the costs are indicated to be mainly fixed in nature, this improvement at Cognet plc may be a function of the increased volume of despatches.

The sales literature cost per customer will fall from £45 to £27·69 at Cognet plc. The level after the IT initiative will be below the industry average of £35. This may be viewed as an indication of the effectiveness of the new system insofar as it is linked to a 30% increase in customer numbers.

(ii) The customer negotiations may be analysed to show the percentage of each category in both the original and post-IT budget as follows:

	Total negotiations	*New customers*	*No further business*	*Existing customer problems solved*
Original	3,000	300 (10%)	1,800 (60%)	900 (30%)
Post -IT	6,000	900 (15%)	3,500 (58%)	1,600 (27%)

It is estimated that the IT initiative will yield an extra 600 new customers and that new customers will represent an increased proportion (15%) of all negotiations. The number of existing customer problems solved is increased by 78% (from 900 to 1,600). This may be seen as an improvement in the effectiveness of the SOD in helping improve customer satisfaction and hence adding value to the business. The negotiations resulting in no further business remain at approximately the same proportion of the total (60% to 58%). The increased activity resulting from the IT initiative may be viewed as a major factor in achieving the improved 'hit rate' of new customers.

The cost per negotiation is estimated to fall from £32·67 to £21·33 per negotiation. If the negotiations are viewed only in terms of new customers, the comparative figures per customer gained are: original budget £326·67 (£98,000/300), post-IT budget £142·22 (£128,000/900). This indicates a much improved 'value for money' in terms of the potential income stream to Cognet plc from each new customer.

(iii) The IT initiative may help in the achievement of strategic planning objectives as follows:

1. Improved competitiveness through an expansion of export business.

2. Improved customer relationships through, for example, the increased solution of customer problems.

3. Improved quality of business operations through wider and more frequent dissemination of sales literature/information.

4. Enhancing cost control compatible with maintaining/expanding the customer base through the increased level of activity which it helps achieve.

(Note: alternative relevant discussion and illustrations would be accepted).

Did you answer the question?

Look carefully at the objectives you itemised in part (iii). Are they genuine strategic matters, dealing with the big picture in the long-term, as required? Marks would not be awarded for operational objectives dealing with day-to-day matters.

66 (Answer 3 of examination

Examiner's comments and marking guide

Question 3: Part (a) tested candidates' ability to select and summarise relevant data in order that decisions could be made about early exit from the market for a product. Part (b) required comment on the preferred timing of exit from the product market and additional information which might assist in the decision. In part (c) candidates were required to determine whether to make and/or sub-contract an additional product in each year of its expected three year life cycle. In addition, candidates were required to name and comment on additional factors which might influence any decision relating to sub-contracting of the manufacture of the product.

This question was generally well answered and formed the foundation for many candidates for the achievement of a pass in this paper. A number of alternative presentation formats were used by candidates. In part (a) many candidates did not show the cumulative cash flows from 1 July 1998 to the chosen year end for the cessation of production and sale of the product. In addition, candidates failed to gain marks by incorrectly including penalty payments in the year to

30 June 2001 for royalty and lease payments. In part (b) additional marks could have been gained by candidates by providing more comment on additional information, such as the impact on company image of continuing to operate in a loss making market. Part (c) was generally well answered. A number of alternative ways of comparing the own production versus sub-contracting cash flows were accepted. In part (d), most candidates were able to suggest additional factors which might influence any decision to sub-contract the production of the product.

				Marks
(a)	(i)	component purchase penalty	2	
		royalty penalty	1	
		lease excess penalty	1.5	
	(ii)	cumulative net cash outflow to end of each year (3 × 2)	6	
		component penalty payment (3 × 0.5)	1.5	
		royalty penalty payments (3 × 0.5)	1.5	
		lease penalty payments (3 × 0.5)	1.5	15
(b)		comment on cessation 30 June 1998	1	
		comment on cessation in later years	2	
		comment on additional inforamtion	2	5
(c)	(i)	Relevant choice of sub-contract or produce PROD2 for each of 1999, 2000, 2001 (on merit) (3 × 3)		9
	(ii)	Relevant decision factors including appropriate comments (on merit) (4 × 1.5)		6
Total				35

Step by step answer plan

Step 1 Read the question again and make sure that you focus on precisely what is required. There seems to be lots of marks available here for a routine sort of question.

Step 2 Show your workings clearly for part (a). Note that (a)(ii) is asking for the cumulative net cash flow for each cessation date.

Step 3 In part (b), there are both monetary and non-monetary factors to take into account. Don't just accept the data given in the question. If sales are low, perhaps they can be increased by a new marketing initiative. If costs are high, perhaps they can be reduced by an efficiency drive.

Step 4 Part (c) is a standard sort of make or buy decision. With 6 marks available in part (c)(ii), try and make 6 separate points.

Step 5 Now review your answer and ensure that it does precisely answer the question as set.

The examiner's answer

(a) (i) Cash outflows due to decision to cease production and sale of PROD1 at 30 June 1998 are:

		£
Component purchase penalty 6,500 × £20 × 20%	=	26,000
Roalty penalty payment	=	20,000
lease excess payment 3 years × £80,000	=	240,000
Total cash outflow		286,000

(ii) Variable cost per unit:

	£
components	20
royalty cost	5

sundry variable cost	30
	55
selling price	100
Contribution per unit	45

Sales for each of the next three years = 1,500 units	£
Contribution per year 1,500 × £45	67,500
less: royalty fixed cost	(10,000)
less: lease charge	(80,000)
net cash outflow	(22,500)

For each of the years to 30 June 1999, 2000 and 2001 we also take into account the penalty payments which must be made according to the date of cessation of production and sale.

	Cessation as at 30 June		
	1999	*2000*	*2001*
Net cash outflow from production/sales	22,500	45,000	67,500
Penalty payments:			
component penalty (1,500 × £20 × 20%)	6,000	6,000	–
royalty penalty	20,000	20,000	–
lease penalty	160,000	80,000	–
Cumulative cash outflow	208,500	151,000	67,500

(b) Assemblo Ltd may wish to exit the market for PROD1 at 30 June 1998 because of the poor demand forecast for the next three years. This would mean payment of £286,000 in respect of penalty payments as shown in (a)(i) above. The company may have financial constraints which would make it difficult to pursue this course of action. The figures in (a)(ii) above show that by staying in the market for PROD1 a net loss will be incurred which will gradually fall as the effect of the penalty payments is reduced, particularly if production and sale is continued to 30 June 2001. It would appear therefore, that the company should continue to produce and sell PROD1 until 30 June 2001.

It may be felt that continued production/sale on the above basis will not be the most appropriate strategy. Continued operation in a loss-making market may have a detrimental effect on management morale and company image. It would be useful to consider alternative action which might improve the position. For example, could sales be boosted through a renewed marketing/advertising effort? Could profitability be improved through efforts to reduce costs through efficiency improvements or through changes in the product specification which would allow an increased selling price to be obtained and stimulate renewed demand for the product?

(c) (i) Contribution per unit for PROD2 may be calculated as follows:

	Own Production	*Sub-contract Production*
	£	£
component cost	30	
sub contract charge		80
sundry variable cost	40	15
total variable cost	70	95

selling price	120	120
contribution	50	25

For each year we may choose to sub-contract all of PROD2 or alternatively we may use the production capacity left over after PROD1 has been produced and sub-contract the balance of PROD2.

	Make and sub-contract £'000		*Sub-contract only* £'000
1999:			
produce 2,000 × £50	100		
less: computer cost	(100)		
sub contract benefit 6,000 × £25	150	(8,000 × £25)	200
net cash inflow	150		200

Choose to sub-contract all of PROD2.

	Make and sub-contract £'000		*Sub-contract only* £'000
2000:			
produce 4,000 × £50	200		
less: computer cost	(100)		
sub contract benefit 4,000 × £25	100	(8,000 × £25)	200
net cash inflow	200		200

Company will be indifferent to whether to sub-contract or produce PROD2.

	Make and sub-contract £'000		*Sub-contract only* £'000
2001:			
produce 6,000 × £50	300		
less: computer cost	(100)		
sub contract benefit	nil	(6,000 × £25)	150
net cash inflow	200		150

Choose to produce PROD2.

(ii) Additional factors which may influence the decision to sub-contract the production of part or all of PROD2 are as follows:

- problems with the quality of product from the sub-contractor. This could affect the probability of getting PROD 2 established in the market
- problems where the sub-contractor does not meet production deadlines. This could result in penalty payments to customers and possible loss of repeat orders
- problems of Assemblo Ltd being left with spare capacity where the combined demand for PROD1 and PROD2 falls and a sub-contract agreement has been made for the production of all or part of PROD2. Such spare capacity could result, for example, in industrial relations problems where insufficient work exists for the Assemblo Ltd workforce
- problems where the sub-contractor seeks an increased price per unit at a future date. Assemblo Ltd may be using its production capacity on other work which it is contracted to

complete for customers. It may also be that Assemblo Ltd has not retained the necessary skilled employees or the relevant production equipment where the sub-contracted work has been of suitable quality, delivery, etc.

(Other relevant points would be accepted)

67 (Answer 4 of examination)

Examiner's comments and marking guide

Question 4: Question 4 required candidates to describe the principles incorporated in each of total quality ethos, just-in-time philosophy and an activity based focus. In addition, discussion was required on the ways in which each of the areas might affect the preparation of budgets.

Most candidates were able to provide a description of each area. More marks could have been obtained by many candidates if they had provided a more comprehensive description of the principles involved. Most candidates did not provide sufficient focus on the impact of each of the areas on budgeting, in contrast to the operation of a traditional incremental budgeting system.

	Marks	
traditional budgeting features	3	
TQ ethos (on merit)	4	
JIT philosophy (on merit)	4	
ABB focus (on merit)	4	15

Step by step answer plan

Step 1 Read the question again and make sure that you focus on precisely what is required.

Step 2 For each of total quality, JIT and activity based focus, you need to:

- describe the principles involved, and
- compare with incremental budgeting.

This requirement gives the structure required for your answer.

Step 3 Now review your answer and ensure that it does precisely answer the question as set.

The examiner's answer

Traditional budgeting systems may be seen to incorporate a number of features which are incompatible with the impact of the total quality ethos, just-in-time philosophy and activity based focus which are features of a world-class environment. Features of traditional budgets include:

- They are incremental in nature. The basic assumption is that the existing budget model is still relevant. Adjustments are made to allow for planned changes in price levels, activity and efficiency changes relating to the existing model.

- The focus is on existing resources and changes to such resources, and on expense headings. For example the total salary budget for a department is compared with the total actual expenditure on such salaries.

- The budget analysis is departmental or segmentally based. This will be analysed for each department by expense type.

- The budgets tend to take a short-term view. This is indicated by the incremental nature of the budget process and the focus on existing resources.

A total quality ethos embraces the need for continuous improvement. It envisages change in the way things are done. A number of features which it will contain are:

- It aims towards an environment of zero defects at minimum cost. This is different to the incremental nature of traditional budgets.

- It requires an awareness by all personnel of the change factors compatible with supplying the customer with products or services of the agreed design specification. This requires greater employee involvement in the budget setting process.

- It recognises the need to maximise the ratio of value added to total cycle time and the elimination of non-value added activities such as stockholding costs. It seeks to incorporate methods changes which will assist in this process. The budget process must incorporate and quantify such changes.

A just-in-time philosophy focuses on customer demand for the products or services. It applies a 'pull through' approach. This aims at improved planning with closer dovetailing of the value chain from the inflow of raw material from suppliers to the delivery of the finished product to the customer. This will require moves towards the elimination of stocks of raw material, WIP and finished goods. It will also involve methods changes in order to facilitate smooth production 'on demand'. This will involve consideration of synchronised manufacturing systems which facilitate smooth production flow. It will require closer liaison with customers and suppliers with regard to the timing of requirements. All such factors will affect the structure of the budget model and the preparation of the budget.

An activity based focus attempts to rectify some of the weaknesses inherent in a traditional incremental budgeting system. The major focus in activity based budgeting is on strategies for change which aim at efficiency and continuous improvement. Activity based budgeting has a number of features which distinguish it from incremental budgeting.

- It forges closer links between planning and budgeting through identifying options for change. It will probably be operated in conjunction with a total quality programme.

- It focuses on activities rather than the expense focus of traditional budgets. This will require the identification of activities and their classification into primary and support activities and value added or non-value added activities as part of the budget preparation process. This links in with the just-in-time philosophy which aims to eliminate non-value added activities such as stockholding.

- It follows a total quality philosophy of involving all members of the workforce in the planning and budgeting process. Focus can be given to identifying cost drivers for each activity. The budget will be prepared after giving consideration to ways in which the incidence of a cost driver can be reduced and ways in which a cost driver may be more efficiently implemented.

It is evident, therefore, that the impact of total quality ethos, just-in-time philosophy and activity based focus are likely to be interrelated in the preparation of budgets in a world class manufacturing environment.

(Alternative relevant discussion would be accepted)

Did you answer the question?

The question is set specifically in the area of budgeting; your comments on quality etc, should refer only to budgeting, and not be general and unfocused.

68 (Answer 5 of examination)

Examiner's comments and marking guide

Question 5: Question 5 required candidates to expand on the appropriate sources and content of total cost estimation for each of three situations — a batch of light fittings, output from a chemical process and the construction of a bridge.

Answers to this question were generally of a very poor standard. Most candidates were unable to identify specific elements of total cost which would be relevant in each situation — for example that direct expenses such as special design costs might apply to the batch of light fittings or that an estimate of normal losses would be required in a process cost evaluation. Most of the analysis of the relevant elements of cost should have been brought forward by candidates from earlier studies. Very few candidates made any attempt whatsoever to discuss the likely sources of information for each element of cost, for example that materials content could be built up from a material specification as part of the design and planning information inc ach case, or that many costs would come from quotes by sub-contractors in the bridge building example.

	Marks
Comment on each of light fittings, chemical and bridge costs (including differences) (on merit) (3 × 5)	15

Step by step answer plan

Step 1 Read the question again and make sure that you focus on precisely what is required. You are asked to discuss the sources and contents of total costs in three situations.

Step 2 Identify the three situations: job costing, process costing and contract costing.

Step 3 For each situation, consider the sources of information for each cost element, as well as the types of cost elements that will comprise the total cost.

Step 4 Now review your answer and ensure that it does precisely answer the question as set.

The examiner's answer

(i) A batch of light fittings to be produced in accordance with a specification from the customer is an example of a job costing exercise. As many costs as possible will be identified as direct charges to the job. These will include:

- Direct materials: A design specification will be used as the basis from which a bill of material may be prepared. This will list the materials and components which are required and indicate which may be obtained from stores or specially purchased. Stock items should probably be priced at replacement cost and special purchases at prices quoted by suppliers.

- Direct labour: input may be estimated by comparison with similar tasks required for other jobs. Alternatively industrial engineering estimates may be used. It may be necessary to take into account any learning curve expected during the cycle. Wage rates will be known and any customer authorised overtime may be charged at premium rates.

- Direct expenses: there may be specific costs such as special design drawings or machine tooling requirements.

- Production overhead: this should be absorbed using appropriate cost driver rates. This may be a volume related rate such as per machine hour or may be linked to an activity based cost system.

- Other job specific costs: any job specific aspect of administration, selling or distribution cost should be identified. This could include special packaging or delivery costs.

(ii) The chemical cost per litre will be compiled on a standard or average cost basis for the output from a production run of the product. The cost will be arrived at after taking into account features such as:

- standard mix specifications of input materials which reflect current practice in the company

- estimations of normal losses which are expected to occur at each process. These may be due, for example, to moisture losses or chemical change effects and will represent current desired/expected levels of attainment

- estimations of the extent of re-cycling of work-in-progress which may reduce the amount of 'new' materials which must be input

- a charge for overhead costs in each process. This will include allocated and apportioned items.

Total costs will then be divided by the throughput quantity in a specified time period in order to calculate the estimated average cost per litre of output. This means that the throughput quantity is crucial in determining the share of fixed costs per litre.

It may also be that the chemical is one of a number of joint products which emerge from a final process and which may then require further processing. This would require the costs to separation point to be shared between the joint products. This may be applied using one of a number of bases such as quantity at separation point, sales value at separation point or final sales value. This is a further estimation exercise which reduces the accuracy of the cost per litre.

Once again any product specific aspects of administration, selling and distribution costs should be identified. For example sales promotion costs may have been incurred for the product in question. The estimate of such costs per litre will depend on the output quantity whose sale it is estimated will benefit from the promotion.

(iii) The construction of the bridge is a long-term contract which will be implemented by a main contractor with the support of input from a number of sub-contractors. A feature of this type of work is the very high direct cost element.

The cost is likely to be sub-divided into a number of aspects of the contract such as site preparation, preparation of foundations, work on access roads, main structure construction and erection.

Sub-contractor costs will be agreed after tenders from each sub-contractor including any profit element.

Acontract specification schedule will enable estimates to be prepared for materials, including concrete and other materials, timber, girders, sub-assemblies, electrical fittings.

Labour cost estimates will also be prepared including allowances for unforeseen delays and complications.

Heavy plant, machinery and specialist vehicles may be used at the site for weeks or months before being moved to another contract. The contract may be charged for such plant, etc. at a rate per day or week to include depreciation, running costs, repairs, administration and other relevant expense.

Miscellaneous site charges such as the hire of portable office and storage accommodation, power and water facilities must also be included as a charge to the contract.

Relevant charges from company central workshops and stores will be charged on a full cost basis using agreed charge bases.

The contract will probably be charged with a share of Head Office costs. This may be a standard percentage uplift which is applied to all contracts.

69 (Answer 6 of examination)

Examiner's comments and marking guide

Question 6: Question 6 required candidates to discuss ways in which individual performance measurement is likely to be related to the aspiration level of the individual and the timing and level of the target set. Answers were to be set in the context of data provided in two tables of data which summarised the results of two studies.

Many candidates did not provide sufficient references to the quantitative information contained in the tables. However, many candidates did attempt to carry out an interpretation of the tables. In addition, many candidates provided some background of behavioural theory as relevant to the situation for which marks were allowed.

	Marks
Discussion on timing and level of target and impact on aspiration level marking reference to the 4 targets in Table 1 (on merit) (4 × 2.5)	10
Interpretation of Table 2 in context of target and aspiration level (on merit)	5
	15

Step by step answer plan

Step 1 Read the question again and make sure that you focus on precisely what is required. You are required to discuss the relevance of aspiration levels to achievement levels by considering two tables of data.

Step 2 Consider table 1. Where individuals are given a testing target, they will generally aspire to reach the target. Both low and high targets can have an adverse effect on an individual's aspiration levels and actual achievements.

Step 3 Consider table 2. This also shows whether a challenging target will stimulate achievement, and produces consistent results. The highest actual achievement is reached where the aspiration level is highest.

Step 4 Now review your answer and ensure that it does precisely answer the question as set.

The examiner's answer

The study in Table 1 indicates that the formulation of a specific target improves performance. It also indicates that the precise effect is influenced by how the target influences the individual's own personal goal or level of aspiration.

Table 1 illustrates that the actual performance of individuals in the study was measured against four targets – an implicit target which was not disclosed (not quoted) and three levels of an explicit target – low, medium and high (35, 50 and 70 units respectively). The actual achievement was measured where the aspiration level of the individuals was set both where they had prior knowledge of the target and where they have no prior knowledge of the target. The average actual achievement was also calculated for each target level. For example, where the implicit target exists, average actual achievement = (53 + 57)/2 = 55 units.

The figures in Table 1 show that where aspiration levels are set after knowing the target, the individual tends to achieve the target goals or at least aspire to them. Where aspiration levels are set before knowing the target, the achievement levels fall dramatically at the high target level. Where an implicit target situation exists, that is no specific goal is set, the best average results are obtained (55).

Note that where a low level of explicit target is set (35), it is achieved easily, indicating that individuals expect to be able to exceed it. Note, however, that prior setting of aspiration will slightly improve actual achievement (45). This may indicate that being aware that the target is low will reduce individual aspiration level (44). Where a medium target is set (50), it is achieved irrespective of the timing of setting of aspiration level with an actual achievement of 54 units. This would appear to indicate that the medium target is approximately in line with the performance level which individuals feel they can realistically achieve.

Where a high target is set (70), the individual appears to make an effort (60) to achieve the target once it is known. This effort may be assumed insofar as the actual performance of 60 units is the highest achieved. There is, however, a significant fall in actual achievement (40 units) where the aspiration level had been set in advance of knowledge of the target. This may indicate a considerable adverse reaction to the high level of target once it is known.

Table 2 may be interpreted in the context of the level of challenge as a stimulus to achievement. There is a wide target range (70 to 180 units). The higher the target the higher the aspiration level of the individual up to a certain level after which aspiration level falls off and then collapses. The collapse is an indication of a perception by the individual that the target is totally unachievable and/or that he/she is unwilling to set an aspiration level.

Note that the aspiration level (80) is higher than target at the lowest target level (70). At 90 units we see that target, aspiration level and actual performance are all the same. This would seem to indicate a base equilibrium level.

Aspiration level and actual achievement each continue to increase in absolute terms for target levels of 110 and 130 units. This indicates that the higher targets seem to stimulate higher aspiration and achievement. At target levels of 110 and 130 units, however, aspiration level is only 100 and 120 units respectively. This indicates that individuals do not fully accept the validity of the target.

The actual results illustrate effort to achieve the aspiration level for targets up to 110 units. Thereafter actual achievement is lower than aspiration. Actual achievement falls off at higher target levels to the level achieved when a very low target was set (80 units). This indicates that the individual is likely to perform at a basic level even where no positive aspiration level is acknowledged.

(Alternative relevant comments and discussion would be accepted)

Did you answer the question?

Deal with each of the tables separately in turn. Don't try to combine your discussion by covering both tables at the same time.

QUESTIONS TO DECEMBER 1998 EXAMINATION

Section A - TWO questions ONLY to be attempted

70 (Question 1 of examination)

Manuco Ltd has identified a market for a new product at a selling price of £300 per unit. It has yet to finally quantify its estimate of the volume of the market in product units.

The estimated cost structure for the product per unit is as follows:

raw materials: 8·5kg at £5 per kg
special ingredient Z: 1·5kg
other variable costs are 60% of selling price

Manuco Ltd must place an advance order for the coming year with the supplier of special ingredient Z. It intends to enter into an advance contract for special ingredient Z for the coming year at one of three levels - high, medium or low - which correspond to the requirements of a high, medium or low level of demand for the product.

The level of demand for the product will not be known when the advance order for special ingredient Z is entered into. A set of probabilities have been estimated by management as to the likelihood of demand for the product being high, medium or low.

The amount of special ingredient Z actually supplied will always be equal to the actual demand level. However, because of the effects of unidentified volume on supplier costs:

(i) Where the advance order entered into for special ingredient Z was lower than that required for the level of demand which is actually achieved, a discount from the original price of supply is allowed to Manuco Ltd for the total quantity of special ingredient Z which is purchased.

(ii) Where the advance order entered into for special ingredient Z was in excess of that required for the actual level of demand achieved, a penalty payment premium in excess of the original price of supply is payable for the total quantity of special ingredient Z which is purchased.

A summary of additional information relating to the above points is as follows:

Estimated product demand			*Special ingredient Z – costs per kg*		
	Units	*Probability*	*Advance order* £	*Conversion discount* £	*Conversion premium* £
High	15,000	0.3	10.00		
Medium	12,000	0.5	12.00		
Low	8,000	0.2	14.00		
Special ingredient Z order discount or premium cost on conversion from:					
Low to Medium				1.50	
Medium to High				1.00	
Low to High				2.00	
Medium to Low					4.00
High to Medium					3.00
High to Low					9.00

Required:

(a) Prepare a summary which shows the total budgeted contribution earned by Manuco Ltd from the new product for the coming year for each of the *nine* possible outcomes which may result from the above data. **(13 marks)**

(b) Using figures from your answer to (a) as relevant, indicate the advance level order size which should be chosen for special ingredient Z and comment on the management attitude to risk where the decision is based on each of the following criteria:
(i) maximising expected value
(ii) maximax
(iii) maximin. **(9 marks)**

(c) Manuco Ltd has been offered supplies of special ingredient Z at a transfer price of £15 per kg by Helpco Ltd which is part of the same group of companies. Helpco Ltd processes and sells special ingredient Z to customers external to the group at £15 per kg. Helpco Ltd bases its transfer price on total cost plus 25% profit mark-up. Total cost has been estimated as 75% variable and 25% fixed.

Required:

Discuss the transfer prices at which Helpco Ltd should offer to transfer special ingredient Z to Manuco Ltd in order that group profit maximising decisions may be taken on financial grounds in each of the following situations:

(i) Helpco Ltd has an external market for all of its production of special ingredient Z at a selling price of £15 per kg. Internal transfers to Manuco Ltd would enable £1·50 per kg of variable packing cost to be avoided.

(ii) Conditions are as per (i) but Helpco Ltd has production capacity for 3,000kg of special ingredient Z for which no external market is available.

(iii) Conditions are as per (ii) but Helpco Ltd has an alternative use for some of its spare production capacity. This alternative use is equivalent to 2,000kg of special ingredient Z and would earn a contribution of £6,000. **(13 marks)**

(35 marks)

71 (Question 2 of examination)

A manufacturing company has a material handling department which provides a service to production departments and to other service departments. The material handling department has 40 fork lift trucks and charges users of the service at a rate per fork truck hour which is compiled using the following budget information:

- each fork truck attracts drivers' salaries of £26,000 per annum plus a bonus of 5p per cubic metre handled (all paid four weekly - based on thirteen four week periods per year)
- the fork trucks are powered by electric batteries. The charge to material handling department for keeping the batteries at full power is made at a cost equivalent to £1·50 per fork truck running hour
- fork trucks cost £26,000 each and are depreciated over five years on a straight-line basis with nil residual value
- maintenance per fork truck is implemented by the company maintenance department at an average cost of £120 per truck per four week period. This is considered to be a fixed cost
- each fork truck is expected to be used for 80% of company operating time. The budget for company operating time is 115 hours per week
- the average quantity handled per fork truck running hour is 10 cubic metres
- fork truck time is charged to users at a rate per running hour based on the above information

The actual data relating to the four week period ended 28 November 1998 is as follows:

- fork truck drivers' salaries £81,600, bonus £7,400

- total power cost £21,800. This is based on the actual time required to keep the batteries at full power where the time is charged at £1·50 per hour
- total fork truck maintenance cost £6,000
- depreciation charge is as per budget
- the company operated for 120 hours per week with each fork truck operating on average for 80% of the time. All fork truck running time was charged to users.

Required:

(a) Prepare a cost statement for the material handling department for the four week period ended 28 November 1998 which compares flexed budget with actual costs and shows: (i) variances for each expense type (ii) the total cost charged out to user departments (iii) the over/under absorption of cost for the period. **(12 marks)**

(b) Comment on advantages which may be claimed for the use of a charge rate to user departments for the material handling service which uses budgeted rather than actual costs. **(6 marks)**

(c) Power costs required for keeping the fork truck batteries at full power may vary because of the effect of the efficiency of the fork truck batteries on the time required. In addition, the cost of providing the facility to power the batteries may vary due to price and efficiency effects.

Required:

Using the data available and also using illustrative figures of your own choosing:

(i) Illustrate the method by which the power charge of £21,800 for the period ended 28 November 1998 has been calculated. In addition, illustrate *three* alternative methods which could also have been used. Illustrations should use combinations of standard and actual hours, actual costs per hour of £1·42 and a possible external cost of the powering of batteries of £1·75 per hour. **(6 marks)**

(ii) Comment on the motivational impact on the managements of both the providing and user departments of charging for the battery recharge service on the basis of the external price of obtaining the service.

(3 marks)

(d) Comment on the average maintenance cost per fork truck and provide examples of ways in which focus on each of the performance measures listed below could be used to help reduce costs and improve the maintenance service:

1. competitiveness, 2. flexibility, 3. resource utilisation, 4. quality, 5. innovation.

(8 marks)
(35 marks)

72 (Question 3 of examination)

Flosun plc makes and sells a range of products. Management has carried out an analysis of the total cost of production. The information in Appendix 3.1 reflects this analysis of budgeted costs for the six month period to 30 June 1999. The analysis has identified that the factory is organised in order to permit the operation of three production lines X,Y and Z. Each production line facilitates the production of two or more products. Production line X is only used for the production of products A and B. The products are manufactured in batches on a just-in-time basis in order to fulfil orders from customers. Only one product can be manufactured on the production line at any one time. Materials are purchased and received on a just-in-time basis. Additional information is available for production line X as follows:

(i) Production line machine costs including labour, power, etc., vary in proportion to machine hours.

(ii) Costs incurred for production scheduling, WIP movement, purchasing and receipt of materials are assumed to be incurred in proportion to the number of batches of product which are manufactured. Machine set-up costs vary in proportion to the number of set-ups required and are linked to a batch throughput system.

(iii) Costs for material scheduling systems and design/testing routines are assumed to be incurred by each product in proportion to the total quantity of components purchased and the total number of types of component used respectively. The number of different components designed/tested for products A and B are 12 and 8 respectively.

(iv) Product line development cost is identified with changes in product design and production method. At present such costs for production line X are apportioned 80%:20% to products A and B respectively. Production line maintenance costs are assumed to vary in proportion to the maintenance hours required for each product.

(v) General factory costs are apportioned to each of production lines X, Y and Z in the ratio 25%:30%:45% respectively. Such costs are absorbed by product units at an average rate per unit through each production line.

Required:

(a) Prepare an activity based budget for production line X for the six month period to 30 June 1999 analysed into sub-sets for activities which are product unit based, batch based, product sustaining, production line sustaining and factory sustaining.

The budget should show:

(i) Total cost for each activity sub-set grouped to reflect the differing operational levels at which each sub-set is incurred/controlled.

(ii) Average cost per unit for each of products A and B analysed by activity sub-set. **(24 marks)**

(b) Discuss the incidence and use of each of the following terms in relation to Flosun plc, giving examples from the question to illustrate your answer:

(i) hierarchy of activities
(ii) cost pools
(iii) cost drivers. **(6 marks)**

(c) Prepare a sequential set of steps which may be included in an investigation of activities in order to improve company profitability.

This should be a general list of steps and *not* specifically relating to Flosun plc. **(5 marks)**
(35 marks)

Appendix 3.1
Flosun plc - Budget data six months to 30 June 1999

	Product A	*Product B*
Material cost per product unit	£60	£45
Production line X - machine hours per unit	0·8	0·5
Production batch size (units)	100	200
Total production (units)	9,000	15,000
Components per product unit (quantity)	20	12
Number of customers	5	10
Number of production line set-ups	15	25
Production line X - maintenance hours	300	150

Cost category	*Production line X*	*Factory total*
	£	£
Labour, power, etc.	294,000	
Set-up of machines	40,000	
Production scheduling	29,600	
WIP movement	36,400	
Purchasing and receipt of material	49,500	
Material scheduling system	18,000	
Design/testing routine	16,000	
Production line development	25,000	
Production line maintenance	9,000	
General factory administration		500,000
General factory occupancy		268,000

Section B - TWO questions ONLY to be attempted

73 (Question 4 of examination)

Discuss the specific relevance of standard costs and variances in the application of each of the following areas of management accounting:

(i) target costing
(ii) backflush accounting
(iii) transfer pricing. **(15 marks)**

74 (Question 5 of examination)

'The structure and operation of a management accounting system may be influenced by internal and external factors. Accountability perspectives and contingency theory may provide relevant areas of focus when considering internal and external factors.'

Discuss the above statement with particular reference to:

(i) accountability and (ii) contingency theory. **(15 marks)**

75 (Question 6 of examination)

(a) Discuss ways in which benchmarking may be used by an organisation as part of a performance measurement and improvement focus. **(6 marks)**

(b) 'The measurement of performance in a not-for-profit organisation may have value for money as its focus.'

Expand on this statement incorporating comment on economy, efficiency and effectiveness into your answer.

Note: You should select a not-for-profit situation of your own choosing as the basis of your discussion.

(9 marks)
(15 marks)

ANSWERS TO DECEMBER 1998 EXAMINATION

70 (Answer 1 of examination)

Examiner's comments and marking guide

Question 1: part (a) required candidates to implement calculations in order to show nine possible outcomes of budgeted contribution from data provided. Part (b) required candidates to choose the most appropriate advance level order strategy for a material where each of three decision rules was applied. Comment was also required on the management attitude to risk where each rule was applied. Part (c) required bath the calculation of and comment on the transfer prices at which another group division should offer to supply a special material in order that group profit maximising decisions may be made.

In part (a) many candidates were unable to calculate the correct contribution for all nine outcomes. This was due to a mismatching of actual demand levels for special material Z and the advance order levels for material Z. In part (b) many candidates were unable to apply the correct expected value calculation procedures. A number of candidates did not refer to the risk attitude of management which corresponded to each decision rule. In part (c) many candidates had a good grasp of the basic transfer pricing principles but could have gained additional marks by recognising that for profit maximising decisions more than one transfer price might be required eg three prices in part (c) (iii).

			Marks
(a)	Calculation of contribution at each sales level (excl. SIZ) (3 × 1·5)	4·5	
	calculation of SIZ cost for each outcome (9 × 2/3)	6	
	overall layout and net contributions	2·5	
		—	13
(b)	for each criterion – choice of order level size (3 × 2)	6	
	– comment on risk posture (3 × 1)	3	
		—	9
(c)	(i) transfer **price** and comment	4	
	(ii) transfer **prices** and comment	5	
	(iii) transfer **prices** and comment	4	
		—	13
			—
			35
			—

Step by step answer plan

Step 1 Read the question again and make sure that you focus on precisely what is required. You have to calculate nine possible contributions from the combinations of data available to you in part (a) and comment on how these would be used in part (b) according to a manager's attitude to risk. Part (c) is an application of transfer pricing theory

Step 2 The system of penalty payments and discounts is confusing so make sure you understand how the advance order contracted price is adjusted before you begin.

Step 3 You can save a lot of time when answering part (b) if the answer to part (a) is laid out in a sensible format, so give some thought to how you are going to analyse the data once you have produced it. You will want to know the expected contribution for each advance level order size so for each order size calculate contribution at each level of demand. You do not need probabilities for part (a) but it may be useful to note them in your data table to make the calculation of expected value in part (b) easier.

Step 4 Calculate for (i) and state for (ii) and (iii) the order size which would be chosen. Explain the risk preference which is indicated by each choice.

Step 5 Part (c) requires you to state the general rule for a profit maximising transfer price and apply it in each situation

Step 6 Now review your answer and ensure it does precisely answer the question as set.

The examiner's answer

(a) Note: special ingredient Z = SIZ in table which follows.

Advance order size (SIZ)	*Demand for product*	*Probability*	*Contribution (excl. SIZ)* £000	*Total cost (SIZ)* £000	*Net product contrib.* £000
High	High	0·3	1,162·5	225	937·5
	Medium	0·5	930	234	696
	Low	0·2	620	228	392
Medium	High	0·3	1,162·5	247·5	915
	Medium	0·5	930	216	714
	Low	0·2	620	192	428
Low	High	0·3	1,162·5	270	892·5
	Medium	0·5	930	225	705
	Low	0.2	620	168	452

Workings:

1. Contribution excluding special ingredient Z:

	Product demand High	Medium	Low
Sales (units)	15,000	12,000	8,000
	£000	£000	£000
Sales revenue (at £300)	4,500	3,600	2,400
Sundry material (at £42·50)	(637·5)	(510)	(340)
Other VC (at 60% of revenue)	(2,700)	(2,160)	(1,440)
Contribution	1,162·5	930	620

2. Examples of workings for special ingredient Z:

– high advance level of order of SIZ and low actual requirement:

The purchase price of £10 per kg is subject to a penalty of £9 per kg. The cost of SIZ is, therefore, 8,000 units × 1·5kg × £19 = £228,000.

– low advance level of order of SIZ and medium actual requirement:

The purchase price of £14 per kg is subject to a discount of £1·50 per kg. The cost of SIZ is, therefore, 12,000 units × 1·5kg × £12.50 = £225,000.

Tutorial note:

1. The calculations can be carried out quicker by producing contribution initially on a unit basis. Thus, contribution per unit excluding ingredient Z at any level of demand = sales price – variable cost = £300 – 8.5kg × £5 – 60% × £300 = £77.50. The unit cost of ingredient Z (which will differ in each scenario) can be calculated from your data table. Unit contribution at each level of demand is then £77.50 – 1.5 kg × unit cost of demand. This can be multiplied by the demand level to arrive at total product contribution.
2. Although probabilities are shown in the answer table for part (a) they are not required until part (b).

(b) (i) The expected value (EV) contribution is calculated for each advance order size of SIZ by multiplying the contribution for each demand level by the probability of that level of demand.

For example, at the high advance order level of SIZ:

EV = 937·5 × 0·3 + 696 × 0·5 + 392 × 0·2 = £707,650

Similarly:

Medium advance order level of SIZ: EV = £717,100
Low advance order level of SIZ: EV = £710,650

Hence the maximum expected value contribution = £717,100 where a *medium* level advance order size for special ingredient Z is entered into.

This approach is adopting a neutral attitude to risk in so far as monetary values times the probabilities of all possible levels have been incorporated into the expected value calculation.

(ii) Maximax suggests that the decision maker should look for the largest possible contribution from all the outcomes. In this case it is a high advance level order size of SIZ where there is a possibility of a contribution of £937,500.

This indicates a risk seeking preference by management. Although it offers the possibility of the highest contribution, there is also a 20% likelihood that the worst possible outcome of a contribution of £392,000 will occur.

(iii) Maximin suggests that the decision maker should look for the strategy which maximises the minimum possible contribution. In this case it is the low advance order of SIZ where the lowest possible contribution is £452,000.

This indicates a risk averse management posture since the worst contribution is higher than that from the high or medium advance orders of SIZ.

(c) The general rule of transfer pricing to assist in profit maximising decisions is to set transfer price equal to marginal cost plus net opportunity cost to the group.

If we apply this rule to the three situations given we have:

(i) Since Helpco Ltd has an external market which is the opportunity foregone, the relevant transfer price would be the external selling price of £15 per kg. This will be adjusted to allow for the £1·50 per kg avoided on internal transfers due to packing costs not required.

The transfer price should be £15 – £1·50 = £13·50 per kg.

(ii) In this situation Helpco Ltd has no alternative opportunity for 3,000kg of its production of special ingredient Z. It should, therefore, offer to transfer this quantity at marginal cost. This is variable cost less packing costs avoided = £9 - £1.50 = £7.50 per kg.

(Note: *total cost* = £15 × 80% = £12
Variable cost = £12 × 75% = £9)

The remaining amount of special ingredient Z should be offered to Manuco Ltd at the adjusted selling price of £13·50 per kg as in (i) above.

(iii) Helpco Ltd has an alternative use for some of its production capacity which will yield a contribution equivalent to £3 per kg of special ingredient Z (£6,000/2,000kg). The balance of its spare capacity (1,000kg) has no opportunity cost and should still be offered at marginal cost.

Helpco Ltd should offer to transfer:

2,000kg at £7·50 + £3 = £10·50 per kg; 1,000kg at £7·50 per kg; and the balance of requirements at £13·50 per kg.

Did you answer the question?

In part (c) more than one transfer price is required in situations (ii) and (iii) to satisfy the profit maximising position.

71 (Answer 2 of examination)

Examiner's comments and marking guide

Question 2: In part (a) candidates were required to prepare a statement which compared a flexed budget with actual costs for a service department in a company; to calculate the cost absorbed by/charged to departments using the service and to calculate the over/under-absorption of costs. The service department used fork lift trucks in the handling of materials. Part (b) required comment on the use of budgeted versus actual costs as the basis for the charge rate for the service. Part (c) required the demonstration of the figures used in calculating the charge made to the service department for the re-powering of fork truck batteries. This required demonstration of the current method and the illustration of any three alternative methods which could have been used. Finally, part (d) required comment on the average maintenance cost per fork truck and ways in which focus on a range of performance measures could help reduce the costs of maintenance and improve the maintenance service.

The cost statement in part (a) was correctly prepared by most candidates. Few candidates, however, were able to demonstrate the calculation of the absorption rate for the service and the extent of any over/under absorption of cost. In part (b) many candidates did not consider the absorption basis used from the point of view of both the provider and the users of the material handling service. In part (c), most candidates were able to illustrate the calculation of the maintenance cost of £21,800 and also to correctly suggest three alternative bases on which the maintenance charge might have been made. In part (d) many candidates did not relate their answer to the improvement of the maintenance provision. Instead, they commented on the costs and efficiency of the operation of the fork trucks.

				Marks
(a)	Flexed budget figures (5 × 1)		5	
	actual cost figures		2	
	variances		1	
	charge to user depts.		2	
	over-absorption of cost		1	
	overall presentation		1	
			——	12
(b)	comments on benefit – at point of provision		3	
	– at point of use		3	
			——	6
(c)	(i)	current calculation method	1·5	
		three alternative methods (3 × 1·5)	4·5	
	(ii)	comments on motivational impact (on merit)	3	
			——	9
(d)	general comment on average cost of maintenance		3	
	comments on other measures (5 × 1)		5	
			——	8
				——
				35
				——

Step by step answer plan

Step 1 Read the question again and make sure that you focus on precisely what is required. The question is looking at performance in a service environment.

Step 2 Part (a) is straightforward but note carefully the time period each cost is measured over. As you are producing a flexed budget it is advisable to separate variable and fixed costs and remember to only adjust variable costs for changes in activity levels. Calculate an absorption rate based on budgeted costs and activity levels.

Step 3 In part (b) try to consider the advantages to the organisation as a whole of basing the charge rate on budget as well as to the user department.

Step 4 Calculate standard and actual hours for part (c) from the data given. Illustrate actual cost calculation and provide three other possible costs which could have been charged using pricing options given. When considering motivational impacts of using an external price consider both positive and negative points.

Step 5 For part (d) calculate the budgeted and actual average maintenance cost per fork truck and compare the two. Make some general comments about why the variance may have arisen and then give specific examples of performance measures in each area required relevant to the maintenance service.

Step 6 Now review your answer and ensure it does precisely answer the question as set.

The examiner's answer

(a)

Material Handling Department
Budget v actual cost statement period ended 28 November 1998

	Flexed	*Actual*	*Variance*
Total fork truck running hours:	15,360	15,360	
	£	£	£
Variable costs:			
Drivers' bonus	7,680	7,400	280(F)
Battery power cost	23,040	21,800	1,240(F)
Fixed costs:			
Drivers' salaries	80,000	81,600	1,600(A)
Maintenance	4,800	6,000	1,200(A)
Depreciation	16,000	16,000	nil
	131,520	132,800	1,280(A)
Charge to user departments:		135,905	
Over-absorption of cost		3,105	

Note: (A)= adverse (F) = favourable

Workings:

– Fork truck running hours = 40 × 120 × 4 × 80% = 15,360

– Flexed budget costs:
driver's bonus 15,360 hours × 10cubic m × 5p = £7,680
drivers' salaries (40 × £26,000)/13 = £80,000
power 15,360 × £1·50 = £23,040
maintenance 40 × £120 = £4,800
depreciation (40 × £26,000)/(5 × 13) = £16,000

– Charge to user departments: For fixed costs this is based on the original budgeted running hours i.e. 40 × 115 × 4 × 80% = 14,720 hours

Charge per fork truck running hour:
for variable costs = (£7,680 + £23,040)/15,360 = £2·00
for fixed costs = (£80,000 + £4,800 + £16,000)/14,720 = £6·848

Hence total charge per fork truck hour = £2 + £6·848 = £8·848

Total charge to user departments = 15,360 hours × £8·848 = £135,905

(b) Advantages may be claimed for the use of a budgeted charge rate both at the point of provision of the service and at the point of use:

It should assist in the control of the provision of the service. Any excess costs caused by expenditure in excess of that budgeted for the material handling department or caused by a reduction in the efficiency of operation of the trucks will be reported at the point of incidence i.e. in the material handling department. Excess cost or reduced efficiency of operation cannot simply be passed on to the user departments by charging an increased charge rate based on actual expenditure.

It should also assist in control at the point of use. The user department will be charged for the number of hours of handling work which it requests, charged at the pre-determined rate per fork truck hour. This means that any variance reported in the operating statement of the user department will reflect any change in the quantity of fork truck time used. The manager of the user department can investigate possible reasons for any increased level of requirement. It will not include any cost increases in the provision of the fork truck service. Such cost increases will be monitored and explained at the point of provision i.e. in the material handling department.

(c) **(i)** In the existing question, the charge has been made as:

hours required × standard charge per hour. The standard charge per hour is £1·50.

Actual hours required must, therefore, have been £21,800/£1·50 = 14,533·3 hours.
i.e. charge made = actual hours required × standard rate

= 14533·3 × £1·50
= £21,800.

The charge could have been calculated using alternative bases. Using the alternative combinations suggested in the question as necessary we could have:

1. Expected hours × actual rate per hour
   = 15,360 × £1·42 = £21,811

2. Actual hours × actual rate per hour
   = 14,533 × £1·42 = £20,637

3. Actual hours × external cost per hour
   = 14,533 × £1·75 = £25,433

(ii) Where the charge out rate is based on an external cost of providing the battery charging service we are treating the battery charging service centre as a profit centre. This may have positive or negative motivational implications for its manager. It may be positive where the cost of internal provision is lower and a notional profit is reported. It may be negative where the cost of internal provision is higher and a notional loss is reported.

The user departments may be positively motivated where a charge based on the external cost is used. They may feel that this will ensure that the internal providers are motivated to provide an efficient service at minimum cost.

(Alternative points could be made)

(d) The actual maintenance cost per fork truck is £150 (£6,000/40). This is 25% higher than the planned level of £120 per truck. This may be due to a number of factors including:

- relative inefficiency in the provision of the maintenance
- inefficiency of the fork truck operators in their use of the trucks
- problems due to the type of work which the trucks are being required to do e.g. carrying excess loads.

The reduction of costs and improvement in the provision of the maintenance of the trucks could be helped by focus on:

1. *Competitiveness:* comparison with outside sources of maintenance for this type of maintenance work.

2. *Flexibility:* what mix of maintenance skills are available? Is there an adequate mix to cope with the variety of repairs which may have to take place?

3. *Resource utilisation:* what level of idle time is there in the maintenance department? Can steps be taken to reduce this, for example, by better planning and scheduling of maintenance?

4. *Quality:* what records are kept about complaints about maintenance work? What records are there about fork truck reliability ?

5. *Innovation:* an example would be the provision of truck maintenance 'on site' during driver meal breaks in order to reduce truck idle time and to allow for the planning/scheduling of truck routine maintenance.

(Other relevant points would be accepted)

72 (Answer 3 of examination)

Examiner's comments and marking guide

Question 3: part (a) tested candidates ability to prepare an activity based budget which showed both total and unit costs for each of two products. The costs were to be analysed into sub-groups which reflected the operational levels at which each sub-group was incurred/controlled. Part (b) required discussion of terms relevant to the budget prepared in part (a). Part (c) required candidates to provide a sequential set of steps which may be included in an activity based investigation.

Many candidates made a very good attempt at the analysis in part (a). Others did not gain high marks through not providing analysis by cost unit, by sub-group, etc.

Many candidates were unable to explain the meaning of a hierarchy of activities. Candidates should note that this is explained in the core text - Management and Cost Accounting, Drury (4th edition) page 303. In part (c) many candidates did not relate their answer to an activity based focus.

Marks

(a)	Production line X totals – by item (12 × 0·25)	3	
	– correctly grouped (12 × 0·25)	3	
	product A – totals by item (8 × 0·25)	4	
	– totals by sub-group (5 × 0·25)	1·25	
	– cost per unit by sub-group (5 × 0·5)	2·5	
	product B – totals by item (8 × 0·25)	4	
	– totals by sub-group (5 × 0·25)	1·25	
	– cost per unit by sub-group (5 × 0·5)	2·5	
	overall totals and layout	2·5	
		——	24

(b)	discussion of incidence of each item (3 × 1)	3	
	discussion of use of each item (3 × 1)	3	
		—	6
(c)	list of sequential steps (on merit)		5
			—
			35
			—

Step by step answer plan

Step 1 Read the question again and make sure that you focus on precisely what is required. The question requires calculation of an activity based budget then explanation of background to activity based management terms and techniques.

Step 2 The calculations in part (a) are straight-forward and the key to the question is ensuring that you include all of the information required. Allocate each cost category to a sub-set then work systematically through the cost categories using cost drivers as detailed to apportion costs to product. Make sure you show a total cost and average cost per unit for both products for each sub-set.

Step 3 Part (b) requires a brief explanation of each term and an example to illustrate your explanation drawn from the question.

Step 4 Try to think of 5 steps in part (c) which describe general steps which may be taken in an activity based analysis of a company's performance.

Step 5 Now review your answer and ensure it does precisely answer the question as set.

The examiner's answer

(a) Activity based budget – Production line × six months to 30 June 1999

		Production line X	Product A Total	Product A per unit	Product B Total	Product B per unit
Total product units			9,000		15,000	
		£000	£000	£	£000	£
Activity sub-sets:						
Product unit based						
Materials	(note 1)	1215·0	540·0	60·000	675·0	45·000
Labour, power, etc	(note 2)	294·0	144·0	16·000	150·0	10·000
		1509·0	684·0	76·000	825·0	55·000
Batch based						
Production scheduling		29·6				
WIP movement		36·4				
Purchasing and receipt		49·5				
Sub-total	(note 3)	115·5	63·0		52·5	
Machine set-up	(note 4)	40·0	15·0		25·0	
		155·5	78·0	8·667	77·5	5·167
Product sustaining						
Material scheduling	(note 5)	18·0	9·0		9·0	
Design/testing	(note 6)	16·0	9·6		6·4	
		34·0	18·6	2·067	15·4	1·027
Product line sustaining						
Product line development	(note 7)	25·0	20·0		5·0	
Product line maintenance	(note 8)	9·0	6·0		3·0	
		34·0	26·0	2·889	8·0	0·533
Factory sustaining						
General factory administration	(note 9)	125·0				
General factory occupancy	(note 9)	67·0				
		192·0	72·0	8·000	120·0	8·000
Totals		1924·5	878·6	97·623	1045·9	69·727

Working notes:

Note 1: Materials per unit per Appendix 3.1 then multiply by number of product units.

Note 2: Total machine hours = 9,000 × 0.8 + 15,000 × 0.5 = 14,700
rate per hour = £294,000/14,700 = £20
e.g. rate per unit for product A = 0.8 × £20 = £16

Note 3: Product batches required: A = 90; B = 75
costs apportioned in ratio 90:75
e.g. product A = £115,500 × 90/165 = £63,000

Note 4: Machine set -ups: A = 15, B = 25
costs apportioned in ratio 15:25
e.g. product A = £40,000 × 15/40 = £15,000

Note 5: Components purchased: A = 9,000 × 20 = 180,000
B = 15,000 × 12 = 180,000
hence apportion costs equally between A and B

Note 6: Split costs between A and B in ratio 12:8 per question.

Note 7: Split costs between A and B in ratio 80%:20% per question.

Note 8: Split costs between A and B in ratio of maintenance time = 300:150 per Appendix 3.1.

Note 9: Based on 25% of budgeted factory costs per Appendix 3.1
Average cost per product unit = £192,000/24,000 = £8

(b) **(i)** *A hierarchy of activities* exists as used in the preparation of the activity based budget in part (a). This hierarchy identifies the level of activity which causes costs to occur. For example costs may be product sustaining. This implies that the costs are only avoidable if a particular product is discontinued. Others may be product line sustaining and are only avoidable if the entire production line is discontinued. Such a hierarchy has been used in the preparation of the activity based budget in part (a).

(ii) *Cost pools* are the summation of costs which occur at each level in the cost hierarchy. For example for production line□X the production scheduling, WIP movement, purchasing and receipt and machine set-up costs are all assumed to be batch related. This enables the apportionment of costs to particular products to be implemented more conveniently using number of batches as the apportionment basis.

(iii) *Cost drivers* are the factors which cause costs to be incurred. For example production sustaining costs such as design/testing costs are driven by the number of different components to be designed/tested. Identification of the cost driver will enable efforts to be made to cut costs by reducing its incidence and/or improving the efficiency with which it is implemented.

(c) A suitable sequential set of steps would be to investigate:

- What activities are being carried out and are they necessary?
- How effectively are activities being carried out and to what quality and standard?
- Which cost drivers determine the level of resources required for an activity?
- What is the relationship between an activity cost driver and its root cause?
- How can the activity model help in decision-making e.g. in budgeting for product costs?

73 (Answer 4 of examination)

Examiner's comments and marking guide

Question 4: required candidates to discuss the relevance of standard costs and variances in the application of each of target costing, backflush accounting and transfer pricing.

Many candidates were able to provide a basic description of each of the above areas of management accounting. A considerable number of candidates confused target costing with the setting of a standard cost against which actual costs could be compared. Explanations of backflush accounting were often very superficial. Few candidates made much effort at discussing the possible relevance of standard costs in the operation of each of the techniques. This was a core aspect of the question and relevant comment was required for high marks.

Marks		
Comment on each area of MA (on merit) (3 × 2)	6	
discussion of relevance of standards (3 × 3)	9	
	——	15
		—

Step by step answer plan

Step 1 Read the question again and make sure that you focus on precisely what is required. The question requires you to discuss the relevance of standard costing in three specific areas.

Step 2 In each area you should provide an explanation of the technique involved and then state clearly how a standard costing system may be used in connection with the technique.

Step 3 Now review your answer and ensure it does precisely answer the question as set.

The examiner's answer

(i) In target costing a market is identified for a product where market size and value are estimated. The required return by the company from the venture is quantified. Expected sales revenue - required return = target cost. It is at this point that standard costs may be usefully employed as part of the procedure. A standard or estimated cost may be prepared using the current expected specification for the product and incorporating current production methods which are envisaged. This standard cost may exceed the target cost and the cost gap of current standard cost minus target cost must be investigated. Efforts may then be made through value engineering and the use of cost engineering tools such as JIT and TQM to close the gap between the current standard and target costs. The current standard cost provides a start point from which progress can be made. Japanese studies have shown that evidence that a systematic approach in attempting to achieve the target cost has been undergone may lead to acceptance by the potential customer(s) of a compromise price increase in order to 'share' any residual cost gap. In this way both parties to the agreement have accepted that the most efficient possible procedures have been built into the price/cost equation.

(ii) The use of backflush accounting will be seen as relevant where the overall process cycle time is short and levels of material and WIP are low. Such conditions are likely to occur where a just-in-time approach to production and sales is in force. The backflush accounting system simplifies the accounting records by avoiding the need to trace the movement of materials and work-in-progress through the production processes.

The backflush accounting system is likely to involve maintaining a raw materials and WIP account and possibly a finished goods account. The use of standard costs and variances is likely to be incorporated into the accounting entries. Transfers from raw materials and WIP account to finished goods (or cost of sales) will probably be made at standard cost. Any stock of raw material and WIP which still exists will probably be valued at standard cost. The difference between the actual inputs to and the standard charges from the raw material and WIP account will be recorded as a residual variance. This will be written off to profit and loss account. The investigation of losses and inefficiences relating to material, labour and overheads is more likely to be implemented using non-financial indicators rather than detailed cost variances.

(iii) Transfer pricing is used for the valuation of goods moving from one division to another in a group of companies. In a divisionalised structure the issues of divisional autonomy, performance measurement and decision-making for corporate profit maximisation are all affected by the transfer pricing policy which is implemented. Transfer prices may be cost based, possibly with the addition of a profit mark-up to arrive at a notional selling price. The use of standard costs as the basis of arriving at the transfer price may be examined in the context of each of the issues stated above. Management at the supplying division may see the requirement to transfer at standard cost rather than actual cost as an infringement of their autonomy. The use of a planning and operational approach to standards and variances may help overcome this. The use of revised standards which incorporate any non-controllable planning variances may be seen as an acceptable compromise. Where a notional profit mark-up is added, the receiving division is more likely to accept a transfer price based on revised standard costs. In this way the profit mark-up will not be inflated due to inefficiency at the supplying division. Performance measurement in terms of reported profit at the receiving and supplying divisions is more likely to be accepted where standard costs are used as the basis of any transfers. To some extent the use of transfer prices based on standard costs will help in decision-making by receiving divisions which is in the best interests of the group. Where transfer prices are based on (inefficient) actual costs the receiving division may decide to purchase externally at what seems to be a lower price. The use of standards in this decision process would, of course, assume that the adverse variances (actual - standard) which exist will be investigated and eliminated.

74 (Answer 5 of examination)

Examiner's comments and marking guide

Question 5: required candidates to discuss the relevance of accountability perspectives and contingency theory when considering the structure and operation of a management accounting system.

Answers to this question were generally of a poor standard. Most candidates were unable to identify, define and comment on accountability. This topic featured in an article in the Students' Newsletter in August 1998.

Candidates are reminded that they are expected to read articles relevant to their current studies and to refer to additional reading references provided in conjunction with such articles. Few candidates were able to comment on the relevance of contingency theory to management accounting. This topic is treated extensively in Accounting for Management Control, Emmanuel, Otley & Merchant (2nd edition), which is one of the prescribed texts for this subject.

In order to give recognition for relevant general comments on internal and external factors affecting management accounting systems, marks were awarded even where no specific reference was made to accountability or contingency theory.

			Marks
(i)	Accountability - hard/soft; numbers/reports/ implementation; MA examples (on merit) (5 × 1·5)	7·5	
(ii)	contingency theory - contingent factors (3 × 1)	3	
	– MA examples (3 × 1·5)	4·5	
			15
			15

Step by step answer plan

Step 1 Read the question again and make sure that you focus on precisely what is required. The question is very general but states clearly that you should focus on accountability and contingency theory so this should provide the framework for your answer.

Step 2 For each topic you should

- explain the relevance to management accounting systems.
- relate the topics to internal and external factors

It would be useful to give specific examples to illustrate your points to avoid your answer becoming vague.

Step 3 Now review your answer and ensure it does precisely answer the question as set.

The examiner's answer

(i) Accountability in the context of the management accounting system may be viewed from a number of perspectives. The management accountant as the person in charge of the management accounting system may be seen as having both 'hard' and 'soft' accountability. Hard accountability involves consideration of the financial and quantitative information. Soft accountability involves consideration of the human input to the system.

Hard accountability may be viewed in three specific areas:

– Accounting for the numbers. That is the process of ensuring that transaction recording is correctly implemented and that information analysis is implemented as required in order that associated techniques may be efficiently and accurately carried out. For example the correct recording of costs and their analysis into fixed and variable elements in order that cost/volume/profit analysis may be implemented.

– Ensuring that the numbers are 'accounted for'. This will involve consideration of the number and timing of reports, their structure and dissemination.

– Being held accountable for the efficient implementation of the number processing and report preparation and distribution. Also for ensuring that relevant investigation, discussion and follow-up action takes place.

Soft accountability involves the human input to the shaping, evaluating and implementing of goals. The management accountant has a role to play in this process. Transferable skills in areas such as communication, negotiation and motivation must be effectively used in order that the soft accountability of the management accountant is seen to be achieved in an adequate manner.

The focus of the above accountability areas will need to be flexible in order to accommodate change in both the internal structure of the organisation and in the external markets in which the business operates.

(ii) There is a tendency to look for the single most desirable method of generating data to promote effective planning, control and decision-making. Contingency theory asks which contingency factors are important e.g. changes to the environment, the organisation structure or decision-making style. The question of the direction of causality is important. Do the contingent factors cause the accounting system to be as it is and to change as required? Alternatively is the accounting system itself a contingent factor in causing change?

The environment may, for example, be hostile or dynamic. A dynamic environment will increase the degree of uncertainty which will increase the need for the management accounting system to be able to respond. This could be through the use of quantitative models to evaluate the uncertainty or through the application of new techniques such as target costing.

The organisation may become more decentralised through growth, with more semi-autonomous divisions. This could increase the relevance of focus within the management accounting system on transfer pricing policy or on benchmarking as an aid to performance measurement and improvement.

The decision-making style may have to change. For example where a JIT system is implemented the management accounting focus for material cost will be on effectiveness measures such as percentage of faulty receipts from suppliers rather than on minimising purchase price per unit.

(Relevant alternative discussion would be accepted)

75 (Answer 6 of examination)

Examiner's comments and marking guide

Question 6: part (a) required candidates to discuss the use of benchmarking as part of a performance measurement and improvement focus in an organisation. Part (b) required candidates to discuss the relevance of value for money and to comment on economy, efficiency and effectiveness in a not-for-profit organisation of their choice.

In part (a) many candidates were able to discuss the meaning and use of benchmarking and also to provide examples of types of internal and external benchmarking. Some candidates, however, seemed unaware of the use of the term and its relevance.

In part (b) some candidates were able to provide reference to organisations such as higher education establishments and to illustrate examples of economy, efficiency and effectiveness. Many candidates did not focus on ways in which the measures may be in conflict with each other. This topic was featured in the article in the Students' Newsletter in August 1998, that was also referred to in relation to question 5.

			Marks
(a)	Benchmarking - basic meaning	2	
	– types of	2	
	– illustrative comment	2	
		—	6
(b)	not for profit - comment on each term (4 × 1)	4	
	– inter-relationship discussion	2	
	– housing or other example to illustrate	3	
		—	9
			—

Step by step answer plan

Step 1 Read the question again and make sure that you focus on precisely what is required.

Step 2 For part (a) briefly explain benchmarking then explain how it can be used effectively as a performance measurement tool.

Step 3 For part (b) explain the terms 'value for money', economy, efficiency and effectiveness and illustrate your answer with reference to a suitable not-for-profit example.

Step 4 Now review your answer and ensure it does precisely answer the question as set.

The examiner's answer

(a) Benchmarking enables organisations to learn about their own business practices and the best practice of others. It will help an organisation to identify areas in which it is not implementing best practice and to determine improvement programmes which will lead to the achievement of and improvement upon current best practice.

Benchmarking should focus on areas which are of significant strategic importance to the organisation. It will also be useful to target areas where it is envisaged significant improvement can be made. This will maximise the benefit in the short term from available resources for improvement. This is likely to create a positive motivational influence on staff and improve their commitment to the benchmarking ethos.

Benchmarking may have one or more areas of focus. It may, for example, be internal in nature where one internal unit (or division) learns from another. Alternatively it may be external in focus. It may focus on best practice by competitors where this information can be obtained. Again it may focus on customers by comparing current performance with the expectations of the customer such as the percentage of faulty goods amongst those reaching the customer.

(Alternative relevant discussion would be accepted.)

(b) The absence of the profit measure requires an alternative focus in a not-for-profit organisation. The principle of value-for-money implies that efforts must be made to ensure that the available funds are spent in the provision of services in a way which maximises the benefit to the users of the services. The value for money principle should be considered in conjunction with economy, efficiency and effectiveness.

- Economy implies the principle of frugality. What is the least cost method of providing a requirement?

- Efficiency implies the maximising of the output:input ratio.

- Effectiveness focuses on the achievement of the desired objectives through the spending of the available funds.

The three measures may be in conflict with each other and may sometimes complement each other. For example, purchasing a cheap version of an item (economy) may help maximise the number of units which may be obtained for a given sum of money (efficiency). This may be at variance with the desired objective of a high standard of performance from each of the units (effectiveness).

An example from a housing department viewpoint could be the desire to improve the quality of housing to occupants through a policy of installing double glazed windows. The purchase of cheap window units (economy) may help increase the number of houses which can be converted (efficiency) . This could possibly lead to dissatisfaction through poor performance of the units e.g. high condensation and poor sound proofing and hence the non-achievement of improved quality of living (effectiveness).

JUNE 1999 QUESTIONS

76 (Question 1 of examination)

Section A – TWO questions only to be attempted

A sports complex includes an ice rink and a swimming pool in its facilities. The ice rink is used for skating and for curling which became more popular after the 1998 Winter Olympics. The swimming pool is used for leisure purposes and as a venue for swimming competitions. The sports complex management is concerned at falling profit levels which are due to falling revenue and rising costs.

A proposal to change, and hence improve, the method used for heating the water in the swimming pool is currently being investigated as part of a quality improvement programme. A survey of the complex has been carried out at a cost of £30,000 to check energy usage. This has shown that the heat removed from the ice rink in keeping the ice temperature regulated to the required level for good ice conditions could be used to heat the swimming pool. At present the heat removed in the regulation of ice temperature is not utilised and is simply vented into the atmosphere outside the complex.

The following additional information is available:

(i) The expected costs for the ice rink heat extraction for the year ended 31 May 1999 are £120,000. It is estimated that due to rising prices, this cost will increase by 10% during the year to 31 May 2000. Heat extracted totalled 500,000 units of heat during the year to 31 May 1999 and this figure is expected to apply for the year to 31 May 2000.

(ii) The water in the swimming pool is currently heated by a separate system which is also used for a range of other heating purposes in the sports complex. In the year ended 31 May 1999 the swimming pool share of the system had operating costs of £150,000 using 200,000 units of heat. This was made up of 70% variable avoidable cost and 30% which is a share of general fixed overhead. On average all such costs will increase by 10% through price changes in the year to 31 May 2000.

(iii) In order to utilise the heat extracted from the ice rink for heating the water in the swimming pool, equipment would be hired at a cost of £75,000 per annum. This equipment would be supervised by an employee who is currently paid a salary of £15,000 for another post in the year ended 31 May 1999 and who would be retiring if not given this post. His salary for the year to 31 May 2000 would be £17,500. His previous post would not be filled on his retirement. It is anticipated that this system would help to improve the ice quality on the rink.

(iv) Only part of the heat extracted from the ice rink could be recovered for use in heating the water in the swimming pool using the new equipment. The current most likely estimate of the recovery level is 25% of the heat extracted from the ice rink. If the quantity of heat available was insufficient for the heating of the swimming pool, any balance could continue to be obtained from the existing system.

Required

(a) Prepare an analysis for the year to 31 May 2000 to show whether the sports complex should proceed with the heat recovery proposal on financial grounds where a 25% level of recovery applies. Explain any assumptions made and give reasons for the figures used in or omitted from your calculations. **(11 marks)**

(b) Calculate the percentage level of heat recovery from the ice rink at which the sports complex management will be indifferent to the proposed changes on financial grounds for the year ended 31 May 2000. **(8 marks)**

(c) In addition to the information provided in the question, internal studies carried out, together with feedback from customers, have shown that deteriorating quality of ice surface due to the problems with the cooling system used for its temperature control is a major contributory factor to excessive cost levels and falling revenue. Lack of ice skates and curling equipment for hire is also seen as a factor in falling revenue. In addition, it has been established that technical problems exist which contribute to difficulty in controlling the chlorine levels in the water in the swimming pool and in regulating the temperature of the pool water. These factors dissuade customers from using the swimming pool.

Required

(i) Discuss the meaning and use of the terms 'cost of conformance' and 'cost of non-conformance' in the context of a quality improvement programme. Your answer should include a graphical illustration of the matching of the two types of cost and discussion of its significance. **(10 marks)**

(ii) Give examples which illustrate the cost terms which you have explained in (i) in the context of the sports complex situation. Your answer should include specific examples from the information provided in the question and also examples of additional information which would be of relevance in each case. **(6 marks)**
(Total: 35 marks)

77 (Question 2 of examination)

Locorpo plc is currently preparing a budget forecast for the year to 30 June 2000 for one of its products. The product method of manufacture has been redesigned and the amended method has been operated from the beginning of quarter two, 1999.

Additional information is as follows:

(i) The production method is labour intensive and is estimated to be subject to an 85% learning effect. This is based on batches produced and uses batch one in quarter two, 1999 as the starting point. The budgeted labour cost for batch one, quarter two 1999 is £450. The learning curve formula is $y = ax^b$, where b = log(% learning)/log(2).

(ii) Production will be implemented each quarter on a just-in-time basis in order to satisfy demand for that quarter. Only whole batches are produced and sold. A production capacity constraint limits the quarterly output to 45 batches. The product is perishable and no stockpiling to overcome production constraints is possible.

(iii) The demand projections for 1999/2000 will be calculated using the following forecasting model:

$$D_q = K(4D_{q-1} + 3D_{q-2} + 2D_{q-3})/9$$

Where D_q = number of batches for quarter q
K = a constant which reflects the impact of a number of key variables on demand. The value of this constant is currently estimated at 1·2

(iv) Appendix 2.1 shows an extract from a spreadsheet model of the budget calculations. This shows the working calculations for:

– the production/demand estimates
– the working calculations for budget labour cost for each quarter.

Some of the calculations have been omitted and replaced with a question mark (?).

Required

(a) Calculate the total budgeted labour cost for each of quarters one and two, 2000, showing calculations to complete the appropriate cell values shown as (?) in Appendix 2.1. **(8 marks)**

(b) Explain the principles on which the learning effect is based and discuss its relevance and possible limitations to its use. **(6 marks)**

(c) Calculate the product demand estimate for quarter two, 2000 shown as (?) in Appendix 2.1. **(3 marks)**

(d) Comment on the structure of the forecasting model used to estimate the product demand in respect of:
– its incorporation of demand trend
– examples of TWO internal and TWO external variables which may affect the value of the constant K. **(6 marks)**

(e) Explain what evidence there is in the question that labour is a production capacity constraint and suggest FOUR ways in which this constraint may be overcome. **(6 marks)**

(f) Explain a method by which the budget versus actual results which are prepared for management may be presented in order to segregate differences due to poor budgeting from those due to efficiency of implementation of the budget.

Your answer should include examples of such segregation of differences in respect of

(i) production/sales batches and (ii) labour cost. **(6 marks)**

(35 marks)

Appendix 2.1
Budget demand estimates and labour cost calculations for product X

	1999 Qr2	1999 Qr3	1999 Qr4	2000 Qr1	2000 Qr2
Product demand estimates (batches)		38	42	46	?
Production/sales budget (batches)	35	38	42	45	45
Labour – product X budgeted learning curve calculations					
Cumulative batches – budget	35	73	115	?	?
Average labour cost/batch (y) – (all batches) (£)	195.52	164.56	147.93	?	?
Total labour cost – all batches (£)	6843	12013	17012	?	?
Total labour cost/Qr – budget (£)		5170	4999	?	?

78 (Question 3 of examination)

Cinque Division produces three types of wooden container which it sells to external customers and transfers to other divisions within its own group of companies.

Relevant budget information for the period ended 31 December 1999 on which the unit costs per container are based is as follows:

Container type:	*Uno*	*Due*	*Tre*
Total production/sales (units)	50,000	25,000	75,000
Direct material per container (sq. metres)	1·2	0·8	2·4

Material cost per sq. metre is £30.

Overhead costs for the division are:

	£'000
Production conversion cost	6,000
Administration cost	1,800
Selling/marketing cost	1,000
Distribution cost	1,400

The current policy in Cinque division is to compile unit cost per container on the basis of production cost plus distribution cost. Administration and selling/marketing costs are considered general divisional costs which are not product specific.

The budgeted unit costs per container are calculated as the sum of:

– direct material cost

– production conversion cost absorbed on the basis of an overall percentage on direct material cost

– distribution cost as an overall average cost per container unit

Product pricing is based on the achievement of an overall return on capital employed of 15% (ignore taxation). A single mark-up percentage applicable to all container types is applied to product specific unit cost in order to achieve this ROCE level. The resulting selling prices form the basis of selling and marketing strategy. Capital employed is taken as £16,800,000.

Required

(a) Prepare calculations which show the detailed unit cost and selling price calculations for each container type. **(9 marks)**

(b) Activity based unit costs are prepared for the period ended 31 December 1999. These differ from the original unit costs in a number of cost areas. The relevant amended elements of product specific unit costs are:

	Uno	Due	Tre
	£	£	£
Production conversion cost	42·81	30·69	41·23
Distribution cost	2·40	8·00	14·40
Selling/marketing cost (see note 1)	1·20	6·00	1·20

Note 1: 30% of the budgeted selling and marketing cost has been identified as product specific. This has been charged to container types after taking into account relevant activities. The balance of selling and marketing cost is still considered a divisional cost.

(i) Prepare a summary which compares original and activity based information per container for cost, profit and selling price for each type of container, where selling prices remain as calculated in (a) above. **(6 marks)**

(ii) A substantial proportion of sales of Uno are transfers to other divisions within the group. This business is obtained in competition with potential external suppliers. In addition, Cinque division is experiencing problems in retaining the level of market which it has budgeted for Tre.

Using this additional information together with the original versus activity based unit cost/profit/price analysis, suggest possible action by management for EACH of the three types of container in order to improve divisional and group profitability. **(6 marks)**

(c) Cinque division has a proposed strategy to redesign container Uno. There is some controversy as to the effect of the redesign on the number of cuts required per unit, which is seen as a key cost driver in the production process and also on the quantity of direct material which will be required per product unit. Probabilities have been estimated for the level at which these key variables will occur. Number of cuts and quantity of material are independent of each other. The estimates are as follows:

Direct material per unit (sq.m)	probability
1·6	0·3
1·2	0·4
0·8	0·3

number of cuts per unit	probability
40	0·3
35	0·2
25	0·5

(i) Prepare a summary which shows the range of possible activity based unit cost outcomes for Uno showing the combined probability of each outcome, using Appendix 3.1 as appropriate. **(6 marks)**

(ii) Comment on the likely impact of management's attitude to risk on their decision whether or not to implement the redesign strategy for Uno on financial grounds. You should include the calculation of, and comment on, the expected value of the product specific cost for Uno in your answer. **(8 marks)**

Appendix 3.1

Two Way data table to monitor the effect on the activity based product unit cost for product Uno of a proposed redesign. This may affect the direct material per unit – range 1·6 to 0·8 sq.m and the number of cuts required – range 25 to 50:

		Number of cuts				
		25	**30**	**35**	**40**	**50**
Material required (sq. m)	**1·6**	94·31	95·38	96·30	97·10	98·42
	1·4	87·00	88·08	89·00	89·80	91·12
	1·2	79·62	80·69	81·61	82·41	83·73
	1·0	72·14	73·21	74·13	74·93	76·25
	0·8	64·56	65·63	66·55	67·35	68·67

(35 marks)

Section B – TWO questions ONLY to be attempted

79 (Question 4 of examination)

Despite changes in the environment in which business operates, standard costing and variance analysis may continue to be used in a number of different ways in the operation of a management accounting system. An example of its use would be as a control aid in each accounting period through the investigation of variances.

Required

Name and explain *five* applications (other than as a control aid each period) of standard costing and/or variance analysis in the operation of a management accounting system. **(15 marks)**

80 (Question 5 of examination)

A traditional view of the environment in which goods are manufactured and sold is where stocks of materials and components are held. Such stocks are then used to manufacture products to agreed standard specifications, aiming at maximising the use of production capacity. Finished goods are held in stock to satisfy steady demand for the product range at agreed prices.

Required

(a) Discuss aspects of the operation of the management accounting function which are likely to apply in the above system. **(5 marks)**

(b) Describe an alternative sequence from purchasing to the satisfaction of customer demand, which may be more applicable in the current business environment. Your answer should refer to the current 'techniques or philosophies' which are likely to be in use. **(5 marks)**

(c) Name specific ways in which changes suggested in (b) will affect the operation of the management accounting function. **(5 marks)**

(15 marks)

81 (Question 6 of examination)

Discuss the advantages which may be claimed for Kaplan and Norton's balanced scorecard as a basis for performance measurement over traditional management accounting views of performance measurement. Your answer should include specific examples of quantitative measures for each aspect of the balanced scorecard. **(15 marks)**

End of Question Paper

ANSWERS TO JUNE 1999 EXAMINATION

76 (Answer 1 of examination)

Examiner's comments and marking guide

Question 1: part (A) required candidates to prepare a relevant cost analysis with explanations in order to determine whether an improvement proposal should be implemented on financial grounds. Part (b) required the calculation of the percentage level at which management would be indifferent to the proposed changes on financial grounds. Part (c) required discussion of the meaning of costs of conformance and costs of non-conformance in the context of a quality improvement programme, together with illustrative examples of such costs in the context of the question scenario.

In part (a) most candidates were able to provide a partially correct analysis. A common error was to treat the ice ring heat extraction cost as an incremental cost of the decision. In part (b) a minority of the candidates arrived at the correct indifference percentage. Most candidates were able, however, to show some relevant working towards the required solution. In part (c) many candidates did not provide sufficient explanation or examples of costs of conformance and non-conformance.

					Marks
1	(a)		Variable swimming pool costs (accept/reject) (2 x 1)	2	
			New equipment hire	1	
			Employee salary	1	
			Net increase and reject choice	1	
			Notes explaining figures used:		
			Variable swimming pool costs (2 x 1)	2	
			New equipment hire	0·5	
			Employee salary	0·5	
			Survey fee exclusion	1	
			Ice rink heat extraction cost exclusion	2	11
	(b)		Correct approach (on merit) – up to	4	
			Correct figures (on merit) – up to	4	8
	(c)	(i)	Costs of conformance – meaning and use (on merit)	4	
			Costs of non-conformance – meaning and use (on merit)	4	
			Graph and matching comment	2	10
		(ii)	Examples and comment on:		
			Internal failure costs	1·5	
			External failure costs	1·5	
			Appraisal costs	1·5	
			Prevention costs	1·5	6
					35

Step by step answer plan

Step 1 Read the question again and make sure that you focus on precisely what is required. The question has two major topics; the evaluation of a heat recovery proposal and a detailed consideration of the costs of quality.

Step 2 In part (a) you should decide whether each cost mentioned is relevant for decision making purposes and state clearly your reason for including or excluding the cost. Prepare a summary calculation and state your recommendation.

Step 3 Produce logical workings to support your answer to part (b).

Step 4 There are a lot of marks available for part (c) so ensure you leave sufficient time to answer the question in sufficient detail. The question requires explanation of the costs of quality and a graphical illustration of how they may offset each other. Part (ii) requires examples drawn from the sports complex scenario and additional relevant information.

Step 5 Now review your answer and ensure it does precisely answer the question as set.

The examiner's answer

(a)

Sports Complex – heat recovery proposal
Cash flows for year to 31 May 2000

	Accept proposal £	*Reject proposal* £
At 25% level of recovery		
Variable swimming pool costs	43,312	115,500
New equipment hired	75,000	
Employee to supervise equipment	17,500	
	135,812	115,500

The proposal should be rejected on financial grounds since there is a net increase in cost of £20,312 if it is accepted.

Notes:

1 At 25% heat recovery we have 125,000 units of heat available (500,000 x 25%). This is sufficient for 62·5% of the 200,000 units of heat required by the swimming pool. This means that 37·5% of the variable costs from the existing system will remain i.e. 37·5% x £150,000 x 70% x 1·1 = £43,312.

If the proposal is rejected, the total variable costs for 1999 are relevant i.e. £150,000 x 70% x 1·1 = £115,500.

2 The new equipment hire charge of £75,000 is an incremental cost of the proposal.

3 The salary of £17,500 to the employee is avoidable if the proposal is rejected. It is, therefore an incremental cost of the proposal.

4 The survey fee of £30,000 is irrelevant since the money has already been spent i.e. it is a sunk cost.

5 The ice rink heat extraction cost of £120,000 (plus 10% price increase) will remain whether or not the swimming pool new heating scheme is implemented. It is, therefore, irrelevant to the decision. It may be omitted entirely **or** shown to apply to both acceptance and rejection of the proposal.

(b) For break-even situation we require residual variable heating costs from the existing system to be £115,500 – (£75,000 + £17,500) = £23,000.

Hence units of heat required from the existing system = 200,000 x 23,000/115,500
= 39,827 units.

This means that units from ice rink extraction = 200,000 – 39,827 = 160,173 units.

This gives a heat recovery percentage from the ice rink of 160,173/500,000 = 32%.

Note: a number of alternative presentations could be used. For example:

If X = percentage heat recovery from the ice rink
We have heat extraction units from the existing system = 200,000 – 500,000X

Now, variable cost per unit of heat in year to 31 May 2000 from the existing system
= (£150,000 x 1·1 x 70%)/200,000 = £0·5775

For break-even position on financial grounds:

(200,000 – 500,000X) x £0,5775 = £23,000

Solving, X = 32%

(c) (i) In a quality improvement programme a number of factors may be identified which are causing costs to be higher at present than is desired. This means that there is non-conformance with the level of quality standards (and costs) which should apply if the quality programme had been implemented. These factors may be categorised as internal and external failure costs. Internal failure costs occur within the business during the production or implementation cycle. External failure costs occur when the product or service reaches the customer and standards are lower than required.

Costs of conformance are those incurred in ensuring that the level of quality standards required is achieved. Costs of conformance may be categorised as appraisal costs and prevention costs. Appraisal costs are incurred in ensuring that relevant checks on quality are implemented. Prevention costs are incurred in eliminating the causes of internal or external failure costs by implementing specific changes in procedure.

In principle, an organisation should continue to incur costs of conformance until they exceed the costs of non-conformance. This may be illustrated graphically as follows:

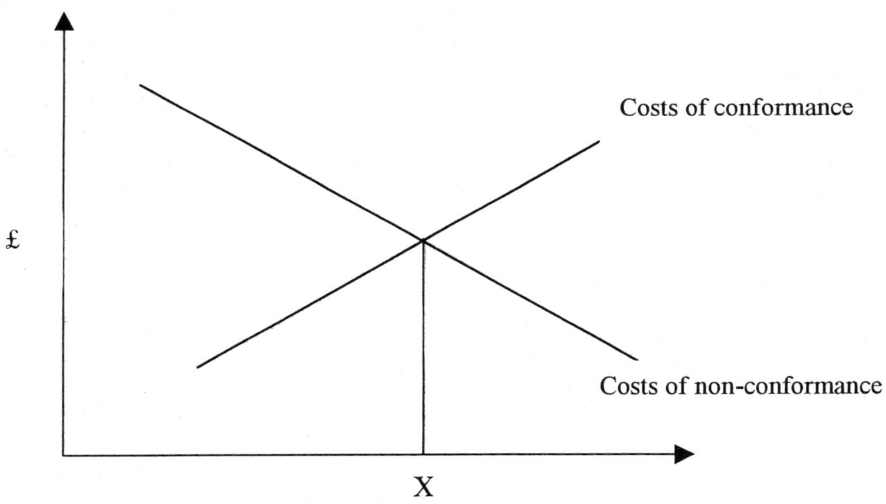

After point X the costs of conformance are greater than the costs of non-conformance and if the trend continues there will be a net cost to the organisation. It may be argued that it is unlikely that this level of improvement will be reached.

(ii) In the context of the sports complex, examples of the cost classifications may be:

Non conformance:
Internal failure costs: The cost of the existing system of heating the swimming pool because of problems with the efficiency of the heating process. Additional information is required on the make-up of the cost/unit of heat and how this could be reduced.

If the new system is taken up a 40% level of heat extraction from the ice rink is required in order to avoid any residual cost from the old system (500,000 x 40% = 200,000 units). How can the extraction level be raised from the current estimate of 25%?
External failure costs: The opportunity cost of lost revenue from customers due to factors such as lack of equipment for hire or problems from high chlorine content in the swimming pool water.

Conformance:
Appraisal costs: Specific checks which will incur costs are regular monitoring of the chlorine levels in the water and regular checking of the ice surface quality. Additional costs could come from approaches such as a questionnaire to all users of the facilities asking for their views on factors such as improving facilities or equipment availability.

Prevention costs: Items could be expenditure on additional sets of ice skates and curling equipment. Other expenditure could be on equipment to regulate the quantity of chlorine in the swimming pool water and equipment to improve the ice surface.

(Alternative relevant discussion and examples would be accepted).

77 (Answer 2 of examination)

Examiner's comments and marking guide

Question 2: part (a) required candidates to determine budgeted labour cost where a learning effect was anticipated. Part (b) required an explanation of the principles on which the learning effect is based and possible limitations to its use. Part (c) and (d) required the use of a forecasting model in the calculation of estimated product demand and comment on the structure of the model. Part (e) required explanation of why labour was a production capacity constraint and ways in which this constraint may be overcome. Part (f) required explanation of a procedure by which the comparison of budget versus actual results could be analysed to segregate differences due to poor budgeting from those due to efficiency of implementation.

In part (a) most candidates were able to implement the relevant calculations. There was evidence of some candidates having inadequate knowledge of the processes of learning curve calculations. In part (b) many candidates gave superficial explanation of the principles on which the learning effect is based and were unable to provide detail of possible limitations to its use. In part (c) many candidates substituted incorrect values into the formula provided in the question. Most candidates were able to comment on the forecasting model in part (d) and suggest examples of internal and external variables which might affect the value of the constant K. In part (e) many candidates did not focus on the quantitative evidence that labour was a capacity constraint. In part (f) most candidates correctly suggested the use of a planning and operational variance approach but were unable to specify relevant examples of its implementation.

		Marks	
(a)	Cumulative batch calculations (2 x 1)	2	
	Average labour cost per batch (2 x 1)	2	
	Total labour cost – all batches (2 x 1)	2	
	Total labour cost per quarter (2 x 1)	2	8
(b)	Learning effect principles (on merit)	3	
	Relevance and limitations (on merit)	3	6
(c)	Demand calculation		3
(d)	Structure of forecasting model re: demand trend	2	
	External variables in constant K (2 x 1)	2	
	Internal variables in constant K (2 x 1)	2	6
(e)	Evidence of production capacity constraint	2	
	Ways to overcome constraint (4 x 1)	4	6
(f)	Planning/operational split	2	
	Examples re- production/sales batches	2	
	Examples re- labour cost	2	6
			35

Step by step answer plan

Step 1 Read the question again and make sure that you focus on precisely what is required. There are six parts to this question addressing several different topic areas of the syllabus.

Step 2 Parts (a) and (b) require you to calculate budgeted labour cost figures given a learning curve model and then discuss the applicability and limitations of the model.

Step 3 Parts (c) and (d) require you to calculate a product demand forecast by inserting given data into a given formula and then to comment on the formula used.

Step 4 Part (e) asks you to provide evidence that labour is a scarce resource.

Step 5 An explanation of planning and operational variances is required in part (f) with specific examples to illustrate your explanation.

Step 6 Now review your answer and ensure it does precisely answer the question as set.

The examiner's answer

(a) The relevant labour cost calculations may be summarised as follows:

	Quarter 1	Quarter 2
Cumulative batches	160	205
Average labour cost/batch – all batches	£136·91	£129·18
Total labour cost – all batches	£21,905	£26,481
Total labour cost for the quarter	£4,893	£4,576

Working calculations:

1 Cumulative batches: Qr. 1 = 115 + 45 = 160
Qr. 2 = 160 + 45 = 205

2 Average labour cost per batch – all batches:
Using the formula $y = ax^b$
$b = \log(0{\cdot}85)/\log(2) = -0{\cdot}23446$
a = £450

Average cost for all batches (y):
To end of Qr. 1 = $450 \times 160^{-0{\cdot}23446} = 136{\cdot}91$
To end of Qr. 2 = $450 \times 205^{-0{\cdot}23446} = 129{\cdot}18$

3 Total labour cost for all batches:
To end of Qr. 1 = 160 x 136·91 = £21,905
To end of Qr. 2 = 205 x 129·18 = £26,481

4 Total labour cost per quarter:
Qr. 1 = £21,905 – £17,012 = £4,893
Qr. 2 = £26,481 – £21,905 = £4,576

(b) Learning curve theory recognises that where fairly repetitive tasks are being undertaken by employees, the time taken to perform a task will be affected by a learning effect until a steady state performance level is reached. The learning effect is represented in the formula $y = ax^b$ where y = average time per unit for all units; x = total number of units to date; b = the learning factor which is log(% learning)/log(2). A simple representation of the learning effect is that every time total output is doubled, the average time per unit for all units to date falls by the learning rate. For example choose a learning rate of 80% and the time for first unit = 4 hours. The average time per unit for two units is four hours x 0·8 = 3·2 hours; the average time per unit for the first four units = 3·2 x 0·8 = 2·56 hours, etc.

Failure to recognise the learning effect may result in incorrect labour costs both in the annual budget and in periodic budgets. This could, for example, affect the accuracy of the cash budget and the planning for short term action to overcome adverse cash flow forecasts.

There are a number of factors which may limit the accuracy and hence usefulness of the learning effect. These include:

- Inaccuracy in estimating the initial labour requirement for the first unit
- Inaccuracy in estimating the length of time for which the learning effect will continue
- The assumption that the rate of learning will be uniform throughout the timescale in which it is taken to apply
- The assumption that the tasks are sufficiently repetitive to allow a constant learning effect to occur
- The assumption that labour turnover will not affect the rate of learning

(c) Using the forecasting model given in the question we have:
$D_q = K(4D_{q-1} + 3D_{q-2} + 2D_{q-3})/9$

For q = quarter 2, 2000:
$D_q = 1{\cdot}2(4 \times 46 + 3 \times 42 + 2 \times 38)/9 = 51{\cdot}46$
= 51 batches, since only whole batches are allowed

(d) The forecasting model uses recent past performance or estimates as the basis for the forecast for the next quarter. The model in the question uses a weighted average basis of 4:3:2 of the demand estimate for the last three quarters. This may or may not reflect the demand trend.

The factor K is a key element of the forecasting model. Its value will affect the size of the demand estimate. It may be affected by many variables both internal and external to the company. Internal variables may include product price, advertising effort and product design changes. External variables may include degree of competition, changing customer taste and level of purchasing power.

(e) We are told that the quarterly output is limited to 45 batches. We are also told that the product is perishable and that no stockpiling is possible. The figures in Appendix 2.1 show that whilst budgeted demand in quarter one, 2000 is 46 batches, budgeted production/sales is only 45 batches indicating the production constraint factor. In addition, the budgeted demand for quarter two, 2000, calculated in (c) above is 51 batches and again the budgeted production/sales figure is restricted to 45 batches.

A number of approaches could be considered in order to overcome the production capacity constraint. Examples are as follows:

- Operate additional shifts e.g. change to 12 hour working for each shift.
- Recruit additional employees in order to allow increased output
- Try to reduce the amount of employee idle time and hence increase productive hours
- Change the method of production e.g. by eliminating unnecessary operations
- Sub-contract some of the production to a third party

(Other relevant examples would be accepted).

(f) The budget versus actual comparison may be improved by the use of a planning and operational variance approach. In this way the errors due to poor budgeting are recognised as planning errors and a set of revised standards is created which incorporates such errors. The revised standards are then compared with the actual results and a set of operational variances are reported. These variances will include those due to any inefficiency in the implementation of the budget.

(i) It may be estimated that the forecast demand in quarter four, 1999 using the forecasting model was understated because of a problem with the value of the constant K. Perhaps the revised forecast and hence budget for quarter four, 1999 is (say) 43 batches (instead of 42 as shown in appendix 2.1) and the actual sales are 41 batches because of marketing problems. In this case the planning variance is +1 batch (43 – 42) and the operational variance is -2 batches (41 – 43).

(ii) It may be discovered that the budgeted labour learning curve effect of 85% was overstated and that a 90% learning effect should have been used. The actual rate of learning may be measured as 92% due to insufficient training of personnel. In this situation, the change in labour cost due to the difference between the 85% and 90% learning effect is a planning variance and that due to the difference between the 90% and 92% learning effect is an operational variance.

78 (Answer 3 of examination)

Examiner's comments and marking guide

Question 3: part (a) required candidates to prepare calculation to show the unit cost and selling price of each container type using a traditional cost plus profit mark-up approach. Part (b) required the preparation of a summary, which compared the cost, profit and selling price as calculated in (a) with an activity based analysis provided in the question. In addition, a discussion of the comparison was required with suggested action for improvement for each container type. Part (c) required a summary of the range of possible outcomes where the redesign of one of the container types might require a range of different levels of two key variables. Comment was also required on the impact of management's attitude to risk on the decision to implement the redesign strategy.

In part (a) many candidates were unable to calculate the required mark-up percentage which has to allow for administration cost, selling/marketing cost and ROCE. Poor presentation was a common failing in answers to part (b). In addition, many candidates did not provide suggestions for action to improve profitability for each container type. The summary of outcomes was generally well prepared by most candidates in part (c). However, most candidates were unable to provide relevant comment on the impact of attitude to risk on any decision to implement the redesign strategy.

				Marks	*Marks*
3	(a)		Direct material cost (3 x 0·5)	1·5	
			Production conversion cost (3 x 0·5)	1·5	
			Distribution cost (3 x 0·5)	1·5	
			Profit mark-up (3 x 1)	3	
			Selling prices and layout (3 x 0·5)	1·5	9
				—	
	(b)	(i)	Summary for each product (3 x 2)		6
		(ii)	Comments on action for each product (3 x 2)		6
	(c)	(i)	Schedule for nine outcomes (9 x 0·67)		6
		(ii)	Calculation of EV	2	
			Comments on risk neutral/seeking/averse (3 x 2)	6	8
				—	—
					35
					—

Step by step answer plan

Step 1 Read the question again and make sure that you focus on precisely what is required. The question requires calculation of cost based prices, an explanation of management actions which can be taken to improve profitability and a risk assessment of a redesign proposal.

Step 2 In part (a) ensure you produce *unit* costs and prices. Remember to achieve the target return; general divisional costs must be covered as well as a profit mark up.

Step 3 Part (b) requires a table summarising the information calculated in part (a) and the data given in the question. This comparison is then used to suggest action which could be taken to improve profitability. Remember to comment on each product.

Step 4 In part (c) you are required to produce a summary of the nine possible outcomes with their associated joint probabilities and costs as shown in the two way data table given. You then have to calculate the expected value and compare the results with the existing cost for the product. State the action which a manager would take according to their attitude to risk.

Step 5 Now review your answer and ensure it does precisely answer the question as set.

The examiner's answer

(a)

Container type:	*Uno*	*Due*	*Tre*
	£	£	£
Product unit cost and price information:			
Direct material cost (note 1)	36·00	24·00	72·00
Production conversion cost (note 2)	27·69	18·46	55·38
Distribution cost (note 3)	9·33	9·33	9·33
Total product specific cost	73·02	51·79	136·71
Profit mark-up at 35% (note 4)	25·56	18·13	47·85
Selling price	98·58	69·92	184·56

Note 1: Direct material = sq.m x price per sq.m e.g. Uno = 1·2 x £30 = £36

Note 2: Production conversion cost = £6,000,000
Direct material cost = (50,000 x 1·2 + 25,000 x 0·8 + 75,000 x 2·4) x £30
= £7,800,000
Absorption rate (as % on direct material cost)
= £6,000,000/£7,800,000 = 76·92%
e.g. Du = £24 x 76·92% = £18·46

Note 3: Distribution cost = £1,400,000
Total product units = 50,000 + 25,000 + 75,000 = 150,000
Average cost per container = £1,400,000/150,000 = £9·33

Note 4: Mark-up on cost to include administration cost, selling/marketing cost and ROCE.

	£'000
Administration cost	1,800
Selling/marketing cost	1,000
ROCE = 15% × £16,800	2,520
Total mark-up required	5,320

Total product specific cost:

	£'000
Direct material (per note 2)	7,800
Production conversion	6,000
Distribution	1,400
Total	15,200

Profit mark-up required = £5,320,000/£15,200,000 = 35%

(b) (i) Original vs. ABC Unit cost comparison

	Product – Uno		Product – Due		Product - Tre	
	Original	ABC	Original	ABC	Original	ABC
	£	£	£	£	£	£
Direct material cost	36.00	36.00	24.00	24.00	72.00	72.00
Production labour and overhead	27.69	42.81	18.46	30.69	55.38	41.23
Distribution cost	9.33	2.40	9.33	8.00	9.33	14.40
Total product specific cost	73.02	81.21	51.79	62.69	136.71	127.63
Product specific selling/market		1.20		6.00		1.20
Amended product specific cost	73.02	82.41	51.79	68.69	136.71	128.83
Profit mark-up	25.56	16.17	18.13	1.23	47.85	55.73
Selling price	98.58	98.58	69.92	69.92	184.56	184.56

(ii) **Container type – Uno**: A major factor is that a substantial proportion of the units are transferred to other divisions within the group. Points which may require management action are:

- From a group viewpoint there is a need to focus on cost reduction. The ABC system indicates that overall unit cost is up by 11% even before the product specific selling and marketing cost is taken into account.

- Interdivisional profit on group transfers should be examined. Could such units be sold to external customers? If not, should transfers to other group divisions be offered at marginal cost in order to avoid more external purchases of similar containers from external suppliers?

- Possibly a dual system of pricing could be put in place. Cinque division may be allowed to report a profit based on the estimated selling price but should offer to transfer at marginal cost.

- It is important that the ABC costs are recognised. The marginal cost is not known. However, using total cost the problem may be examined. Under the existing system the total cost per unit (£73·02) is low. ABC cost is £81·21 (before selling/marketing cost). If an external supplier offered a product similar to Uno at £75 it would be rejected where the existing cost was used as the basis for decisions. The ABC cost of £81·21 shows that the external offer of £75 should be accepted on financial grounds.

Container type – Due: Relevant points are:

- ABC cost is 21% higher than the original cost (even before adding product specific selling/marketing cost). This must be investigated and cost savings sought.

- The product specific selling/marketing cost of £6 is much higher than for Uno or Tre (£1·20). The reasons for this should be investigated.

- At the existing selling price of £69·92 we are almost in a nil profit situation. Can a price increase be obtained without affecting demand?

- Can cost reduction be achieved in conjunction with a quality improvement programme?

Container type – Tre: It is known that Cinque division is having difficulty retaining its budgeted level of sales. Points of note are:

- ABC cost is approximately 6·7% below the original cost (approximately 6% after allowing for product specific selling/marketing cost).
- A price reduction of £8 could be allowed in an attempt to retain demand without affecting product profitability (as represented by a 35% mark-up). **or**
- An increased amount could be spent on marketing effort to 'sell' the merits of the product and company record on delivery, quality, etc.

(c) (i) A summary of the range of unit cost outcomes is as follows:

Direct Material Sq.m	Probability	Number of cuts	Probability	Combined probability	Unit cost £
1·6	0·3	40	0·3	0·09	97·10
		35	0·2	0·06	96·30
		25	0·5	0·15	94·31
1·2	0·4	40	0·3	0·12	82·41
		35	0·2	0·08	81·61
		25	0·5	0·20	79·62
0·8	0·3	40	0·3	0·09	67·35
		35	0·2	0·06	66·55
		25	0·5	0·15	64·56
				1·00	

(ii) For each row in the above table multiply the combined probability by the unit cost and sum the answers to calculate the expected value unit cost. The answer is £80·74.

Management may be risk neutral, risk seeking or risk averse. They may view the likely change from the existing ABC cost of £82·41 as the basis for their views. Note that the existing ABC cost was calculated in **(b)** **(i)** OR may be read from Appendix 3.1.

- A risk neutral manager may take the view that since the EV unit cost of £80·74 is less than the existing ABC cost, the redesign strategy is worth pursuing.
- There is a 21% likelihood of a unit cost of £66·55 or less which is approximately a 20% reduction from the current value. A risk seeking manager might see this as an attractive possibility.
- There is a 30% likelihood of a unit cost greater than the existing level of £82·41. This might be enough to lead a risk averse manager to reject the redesign strategy.

79 (Answer 4 of examination)

Examiner's comments and marking guide

Question 4: required candidates to name and explain five applications of standard costing in the operation of a management accounting system.

Many candidates provided a comprehensive list and explanation of relevant applications. Some candidates provided detailed descriptions of types of variance such as material usage and labour efficiency, which did not answer the question set. Many of the poorer answers indicated an inability to appraise the relevance of management accounting techniques which is a requirement of the syllabus.

			Marks
4	Five uses named (5 × 1)	5	
	Application of each use (5 × 2)	10	15

Step by step answer plan

Step 1 Read the question again and make sure that you focus on precisely what is required. The question requires you to discuss various uses of standard costing in a management accounting system.

Step 2 Your answer plan should centre around the various general aspects of a management accounting system e.g. planning, control, decision making, performance measurement and then give examples of how standard costing may be used in these areas as appropriate.

Step 3 Now review your answer and ensure it does precisely answer the question as set.

The examiner's answer

Standard costing may be used in a number of areas as part of a management accounting system including planning, decision making, performance measurement, pricing, improvement and change, accounting valuations. Examples of its use are as follows:

- It may be used in planning as a building block for budgeting. For example material specification standards may be used in constructing a material purchases budget when used in conjunction with planned levels of production and sales of products. Similarly labour or machine standard output rates may be used in the construction of wage and conversion cost budgets in conjunction with wage and expense rates and production quantities.
- It may be used in decision making in the evaluation of new product costs and profitability. Existing standards may be used as a starting point for the construction of an estimated cost for a new product. For example, the time taken to perform a specific task which is already performed as part of the manufacturing process for another product.

- Performance measurement may be enhanced by using variance analysis as an initial focus. This use may be enhanced through the use of planning and operational variances. In this approach the non-controllable (ex-ante) variances are segregated from the ex-post variances which measure the difference between the revised standard and actual events.

- Product pricing may be aided where it is necessary to tender for work and an accurate cost estimate must be calculated to which an acceptable profit mark-up may be added. In addition, in a target costing situation where the product price, market size and required return are known and hence the target cost is calculated. Here the target cost may be compared with the current standard in order to establish the size of any 'cost gap'. This gap may then be investigated with a view to its reduction or elimination through the application of techniques such as value engineering.

- Improvement and change may be aided through the monitoring of variance trend through time. Trends may be monitored in order to establish whether the situation is deemed to be 'in control' with variances fluctuating within acceptable limits. Alternatively, the variance trend may indicate an out of control situation which must be investigated with a view to improving and changing product design, production methods, etc.

- Accounting valuations for work in progress and finished goods are required for the preparation of periodic management accounting statements. For work in progress in particular, the use of a standard valuation basis avoids the need for the possibly complex calculation of valuations based on the actual costs, stage of completion and level of process losses.

(Note: Alternative relevant discussion and examples would be accepted)

Did you answer the question?

Did you provide five different applications of standard costing ? Avoid repeating the same application with different examples. Also detailed explanations of the operation of a standard costing system would not earn marks.

80 (Answer 5 of examination)

Examiner's comments and marking guide

Question 5: provided a brief explanation of a traditional view of the environment in which goods are manufactured and sold and in part (a) required discussion of aspects of the operation of the management accounting function in this environment. Part (b) required candidates to describe an alternative sequence from purchasing to the satisfaction of customer demand, referring to current techniques or philosophies, which are likely to be in use. Part (c) required candidates to name specific ways in which changes suggested in (b) will affect the operation of the management accounting function.

In part (a) many candidates focused on a description of the manufacturing sequence and not on the management accounting function which might be used. In part (b) the focus was mainly on JIT and TQM with little reference to the impact of features such as shorter product life cycles. In part (c) many candidates focused on a comparison of changes in the manufacturing process whereas the question asked for comment on changes in the management accounting system.

				Marks
5	(a)	Discussion of Man. A/c in existing system (on merit)	5	
	(b)	Alternative cycle suggestion (on merit)	5	
	(c)	Specific impact on Man. A/c system of change	5	15

Step by step answer plan

Step 1 Read the question again and make sure that you focus on precisely what is required. The question requires an explanation of the operation of a management accounting system in traditional and advanced manufacturing environments.

Step 2 For 5 marks you can only produce a broad overview for each part of the question. Do not be tempted to focus in great detail on any one aspect but provide a consideration of a wide variety of aspects of each topic.

Step 3 Now review your answer and ensure it does precisely answer the question as set.

The examiner's answer

(a) The traditional view stated in the question points to a number of aspects of the operation of a traditional management accounting system.

- Raw materials are purchased for stock. Such purchases are traditionally based on material resource planning based on a standard product specification and allowing for lead times from suppliers and estimated usage rates in production. Purchases may be in large quantities in order to take advantage of price discounts for bulk orders. This system requires the pricing of issues from stores and the valuation of stock balances which may be applied on a standard or actual cost basis.

- The production cycle will probably involve a number of sequential operations or processes. The management accounting function will be required to value WIP at various stages in the production cycle. It will also be required to operate an expense based control system for a number of cost centres. This system will focus on the absorption of costs by cost units, aiming at maximising the use of capacity. Acceptable levels of losses will be incorporated into the costs of output achieved and re-work or abnormal losses will be expected and valued.

- Production will be held in finished goods stock before sale. This must be valued for each product type.

- Selling prices for a steady range of products are likely to be known and profit monitoring may be, for example, by product range and/or geographical area. Profit margins will be measured against budgeted/standard levels.

(b) An alternative view more applicable in the modern business environment is likely to be related to a situation which relates to:

- Shorter product life cycles and the need to identify and obtain new markets.

- A 'pull through' production environment to meet demand from customers with minimum stock requirements.

- Flexible manufacturing facilities dedicated to the completion of a cycle of operations for a component or product during its life cycle

- A right-first-time philosophy focusing on total quality and continuous improvement

- The operation of a just-in-time system from supplier to customer.

(c) The management accounting system will be affected in a number of ways from changes such as those indicated above. Areas of change in management accounting may include:

- The need for a raw materials stock valuation and issue system will be significantly reduced.

- An activity based cost analysis system with a focus on the analysis of value added and non-value added activities is likely to replace an expense based system.

- The need for the valuation of WIP will be minimised through the use of dedicated production facilities. Focus will be on the trend of average cost per unit out of the dedicated facility rather than on the determination of normal and abnormal losses and their valuation.
- There may be increased emphasis on the use of techniques such as backflush accounting.
- There will be an increased level of use of non-financial indicators of performance.
- There will be greater focus on benchmarking as part of the control and improvement focus.
- Techniques such as target costing will be more relevant in negotiating new business and deciding on its financial viability.
- Customer profitability analysis will be more important in order to ensure that agreements for business which may be of a short term nature achieve an acceptable level of return.

(Note: Alternative relevant points would be accepted)

Did you answer the question?

Parts (a) and (c) of the question require specific comment on the management accounting function. General comments on the process would not gain marks.

81 (Answer 6 of examination)

Examiner's comments and marking guide

Question 6: required candidates to discuss the advantages, which may be claimed for Kaplan and Norton's balanced scorecard as a basis for performance measurement. Candidates were also required to provide specific examples of quantitative measures for each aspect of the balanced scorecard.

This was the least popular question in section B of the paper. Many candidates were able to name and give examples of the four points in Kaplan and Norton's model. Few candidates were able, however, to provide much relevant discussion of advantages which may be claimed for the use of the scorecard model. The balanced scorecard is a well-documented and topical concept. Candidates must try to broaden their study base in order to keep abreast of current developments in management accounting.

			Marks
6	Criticism of traditional focus (on merit)	5	
	Argument for balanced scorecard (4 × 1·5)	6	
	Examples of balance scorecard areas (4 × 1)	4	15
		—	—

Step by step answer plan

Step 1 Read the question again and make sure that you focus on precisely what is required. The question requires a consideration of the advantages of the balanced scorecard approach to performance measurement compared to a traditional approach.

Step 2 Begin by explaining the basis of the traditional management accounting approach to performance measurement. Then explain the various features of the balanced scorecard approach and the reasons it is considered to be a better technique. Finally give examples of relevant quantitative measures.

Step 3 Now review your answer and ensure it does precisely answer the question as set.

The examiner's answer

Robert Kaplan and David Norton carried out studies in several companies in the early 1990's. The studies aimed at investigating the need to balance short-term financial performance with the drivers of long-term growth opportunities. A number of advantages of the balanced scorecard over the traditional major focus on financial performance may be suggested. These include:

- Traditional measures tend to be dominated by financial accounting requirements. For example the need for stock valuation, including WIP for balance sheet purposes. Also the focus on short-term profit and ROI in order to ensure that short-term financial reporting was favourably received by stakeholders. The balanced scorecard is more broadly based. It argues that no single measure can provide a clear performance target or focus attention on critical areas of the business.

- Traditional measures are mainly inward looking. The balanced scorecard is more broadly based. It is more outward looking and focuses on comparisons with competitors in order to establish best practice and ensure that change is implemented in order to achieve it. It requires a balanced presentation of both financial and non-financial measures and goals.

- The balanced scorecard focuses to a greater extent than traditional measures on strategic planning for the longer term. It attempts to identify the needs and concerns of customers and the identification of new products and markets.

- The balanced scorecard attempts to overcome the over-emphasis of traditional measures on the quantifiable aspects of the internal operations of a company expressed in financial terms. It also considers a range of non-financial and qualitative measures.

The balanced scorecard views the business from four different perspectives which are internal business, innovation and learning, customer and financial perspectives. The questions asked in relation to these perspectives are:

- What processes must we excel at to achieve our customer and financial objectives?

- Can we continue to improve and create value?

- What do existing and new customers value from us?

- How do we create value for shareholders?

The balanced scorecard establishes goals for each of the four perspectives and provides measures that should assist in movement towards these goals. Its focus is both internal and external. Examples of measures that could be used are:

- Internal business perspective: cycle time, unit cost analysis including cost trends and VA/NVA analysis, engineering efficiency,

- Innovation and learning perspective: Time to market for new products; number of new products introduced.

- Customer perspective: % sales from new products, % on time deliveries, % orders from enquiries, customer survey analysis.

- Financial perspective: overall measures such as profit, sales growth, ROI; liquidity measures such as cash flow analysis ; evaluation of new investment opportunities.

(Alternative relevant points and discussion would be accepted)

DECEMBER 1999 QUESTIONS

Section A – TWO questions ONLY to be attempted

82 (Question 1 of examination)

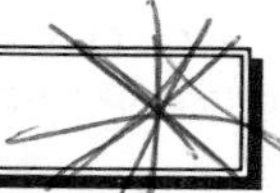

(a) Capella plc has prepared standard material specifications for each of products A and B as follows:

(i) Each finished unit of product A and product B contains 2 units and 6 units of component X respectively.

(ii) The standard input requirements for both products must also allow for losses during processing of 10% of the units of component X.

(iii) The standard purchase price for component X is £8 per unit.

Customer demand for period 2 for products A and B is budgeted at 2,280 units and 2,925 units respectively. It is budgeted that returns from customers of products A and B requiring free replacement will be 5% and 2·5% respectively of goods delivered to customers.

No stocks of raw material, work-in-progress or finished goods are planned.

Required:

(i) Calculate the material purchase budget for period 2 (units and £) for component X. **(4 marks)**

(ii) Comment on the usefulness of standard specifications in the compilation of the material budget for Capella plc rather than using the following actual information for period 1:

	Product A	*Product B*	
Sales to customers (units)	2,500	2,750	
Purchases of component X (units)	6,250	19,250	**(4 marks)**

(iii) Calculate the value of the budgeted 'external failure cost' for component X for period 2 and comment on the usefulness of this information. **(4 marks)**

(b) At the end of period 2, Capella plc revised the standard specification for component X. An alternative supplier will provide the new specification component X at £8·50 per unit. The standard of 2 units of component X per unit of product A will still apply. The revised standard input requirements will allow for process losses of 5% of input. In addition, customer returns of product A which will require free replacement should be reduced to 2% of units delivered to customers.

The actual data for period 3 is as follows:

(i) Sales of product A to customers remains at the period 2 level of 2,280 units.

(ii) Actual purchases of component X are 5,000 units

(iii) Free replacements of product A to customers were at the revised budget level of 2% of units delivered.

Required:

(i) Calculate the component X price and usage variances for product A for period 3 where a planning and operational approach to variance analysis is implemented. **(6 marks)**

(ii) Comment on the benefits which may be claimed for the use of the planning and operational approach to variance analysis. Refer to your calculations in (i) above. **(4 marks)**

(iii) Explain ways in which the acceptance of the variance results for period 3 may have dysfunctional consequences for Capella plc. Suggest TWO specific examples of such consequences. **(4 marks)**

(c) Capella plc is planning the production and sale of a new product C during period 4 which will use components X and Z. Each finished unit of product C will contain 4 units of component X and 6 units of component Z. Component Z is expected to cost £4 per unit. It is estimated that the process losses of component Z will be in line with the revised standard for component X (i.e. 5% of input). Returns of product C from customers requiring free replacement are also expected to be at the same percentage as the revised standards for product A (i.e. 2% of units delivered to customers).

Required:

(i) Calculate the standard material cost per unit of product C for period 4. (Show all workings) **(3 marks)**

(ii) Comment on the benefit of the availability of the standard material specification information in product pricing and also in target costing for product C. **(6 marks)**

(35 marks)

83 (Question 2 of examination)

Tannadens Division is considering an investment in a quality improvement programme for a specific product group which has an estimated life of four years. It is estimated that the quality improvement programme will increase saleable output capacity and provide an improved level of customer demand due to the enhanced reliability of the product group.

Forecast information about the programme in order that it may be evaluated at each of best, most likely and worst scenario levels is as follows:

(i) There will be an initial investment of £4,000,000 on 1 January, year 1, with a programme life of four years and nil residual value. Depreciation will be calculated on a straight line basis.

(ii) Additional costs of staff training, consultancy fees and the salary of the programme manager are estimated at a most likely level of £100,000 per annum for each year of the proposal. This may vary by ±2·5%. This is the only relevant fixed cost of the proposal.

(iii) The most likely additional output capacity which will be sold is 1,000 standard hours in year 1 with further increases in years 2, 3 and 4 of 300, 400 and 300 standard hours respectively. These values may vary by ±5%.

(iv) The most likely contribution per standard hour of extra capacity is £1,200. This may vary by ±10%.

(v) The most likely cost of capital is 10%. This may vary from 8% to 12%.

Assume that all cash flows other than the initial investment take place at the end of each year. Ignore taxation.

Required:

(a) Present a table (including details of relevant workings) showing the net profit, residual income and return on investment for each of years 1 to 4 and also the net present value (NPV) for the BEST OUTCOME situation of the programme. **(10 marks)**

Using the information provided above, the net profit, residual income (RI), and return on investment (ROI) for each year of the programme have been calculated for the most likely outcome and the worst outcome as follows:

Most likely outcome:	**Year 1**	**Year 2**	**Year 3**	**Year 4**
Net profit (£)	100,000	460,000	940,000	1,300,000
Residual income (£)	–300,000	160,000	740,000	1,200,000
Return on investment	2·5%	15·3%	47·0%	130·0%

Worst outcome:	**Year 1**	**Year 2**	**Year 3**	**Year 4**
Net profit (£)	–76,500	231,300	641,700	949,500
Residual income (£)	–556,500	–128,700	401,700	829,500
Return on investment	–1·9%	7·7%	32·1%	95·0%

In addition, the net present value (NPV) of the programme has been calculated as most likely outcome: £1,233,700 and worst outcome: £214,804.

It has been decided that the programme manager will be paid a bonus in addition to the annual salary of £40,000 (assume that this salary applies to the best, most likely and worst scenarios). The bonus will be paid on **ONE** of the following bases:

(A) Calculated and paid each year at 1·5% of any profit in excess of £250,000 for the year.
(B) Calculated and paid each year at 5% of annual salary for each £100,000 of residual income in excess of £250,000.
(C) Calculated and paid at 15% of annual salary in each year in which a positive ROI(%) is reported.
(D) Calculated and paid at the end of year 4 as 2·5% of the NPV of the programme.

Required:

(b) Prepare a table showing the bonus to be paid in each of years 1 to 4 and in total for each of methods (A) to (D) above, where the MOST LIKELY outcome situation applies. **(9 marks)**

(c) Discuss which of the bonus methods is likely to be favoured by the programme manager at Tannadens Division. You should refer to your calculations in (b) above as appropriate. You should also consider the total bonus figures for the best outcome and worst outcome situations which are as follows:

	Total bonus	
	Best outcome	**Worst outcome**
	£	£
Net profit basis	43,890	16,368
Residual income basis	48,150	14,624
ROI basis	24,000	18,000
NPV basis	60,323	5,370

(11 marks)

(d) 'The achievement of the quality improvement programme will be influenced by the programme manager's:

(i) level of effort

(ii) attitude to risk, and

(iii) personal expectations from the programme'.

Discuss this statement.

(5 marks)
(35 marks)

84 (Question 3 of examination)

Ochilpark plc has identified and defined a market in which it wishes to operate. This will provide a 'millennium' focus for an existing product range. Ochilpark plc has identified a number of key competitors and intends to focus on close co-operation with its customers in providing products to meet their specific design and quality requirements. Efforts will be made to improve the effectiveness of all aspects of the cycle from product design to after sales service to customers. This will require inputs from a number of departments in the achievement of the specific goals of the 'millennium' product range. Efforts will be made to improve productivity in conjunction with increased flexibility of methods.

An analysis of financial and non-financial data relating to the 'millennium' proposal is shown in Schedule 3.1.

Required:

(a) (i) Prepare a table (£m) of the total costs for the 'millennium' proposal for each of years 2000, 2001 and 2002 (as shown in Schedule 3·1), detailing target costs, internal and external failure costs, appraisal costs and prevention costs. The following information should be used in the preparation of the analysis:

	2000	**2001**	**2002**
Target costs – variable (as % of sales)	40%	40%	40%
– fixed (total)	£2m	£2m	£2·5m
Internal failure costs (% of total target cost)	20%	10%	5%
External failure costs (% of total target cost)	25%	12%	5%
Appraisal costs	£0·5m	£0·5m	£0·5m
Prevention costs	£2m	£1m	£0·5m

(4 marks)

(ii) Explain the meaning of each of the cost classifications in (i) above and comment on their trend and inter-relationship. You should provide examples of each classification. **(8 marks)**

(b) Prepare an analysis (both discursive and quantitative) of the 'millennium' proposal for the period 2000 to 2002. The analysis should use the information provided in the question, together with the data in Schedule 3.1. The analysis should contain the following:

(i) A definition of corporate 'vision or mission' and consideration of how the millennium proposal may be seen as identifying and illustrating a specific sub-set of this 'vision or mission'. **(5 marks)**

(ii) Discussion and quantification of the proposal in both marketing and financial terms. **(6 marks)**

(iii) Discussion of the external effectiveness of the proposal in the context of ways in which *1. Quality and 2. Delivery* are expected to affect customer satisfaction and hence the marketing of the product. **(4 marks)**

(iv) Discussion of the internal efficiency of the proposal in the context of ways in which the management of *1. Cycle Time and 2. Waste* are expected to affect productivity and hence the financial aspects of the proposal. **(4 marks)**

(v) Discussion of the links between internal and external aspects of the expected trends in performance. **(4 marks)**

(35 marks)

Schedule 3.1
'Millennium' proposal – estimated statistics

	2000	**2001**	**2002**
Total market size (£m)	120	125	130
Ochilpark plc sales (£m)	15	18	20
Ochilpark plc – total costs (£m)	14·1	12·72	12·55
Ochilpark plc sundry statistics:			
Production achieving design quality standards (%)	95%	97%	98%
Returns from customers as unsuitable (% of deliveries)	3·0%	1·5%	0·5%
Cost of after sales service (£m)	1·5	1·25	1·0
Sales meeting planned delivery dates (%)	90%	95%	99%
Average cycle time (customer enquiry to delivery) (weeks)	6	5·5	5
Components scrapped in production (%)	7·5%	5·0%	2·5%
Idle machine capacity (%)	10%	6%	2%

Section B – TWO questions ONLY to be attempted

85 (Question 4 of examination)

To focus on specific performance measures may lead employees or managers to take action which is not in the best interests of the organisation. Examples of problems which may occur are:

(i) Over-emphasis on the short term

(ii) Over-emphasis on the achievement of specific measures

(iii) Over-simplification of the meaning of specific measures

(iv) Deliberate distortion

Required:

(a) Expand briefly on each of the above problems, giving a specific example to illustrate how each may occur **(10 marks)**

(b) Name and comment on any FOUR actions which may be implemented in order to overcome problems in the operation of a performance measurement system. **(5 marks)**

(15 marks)

86 (Question 5 of examination)

At the planning phase of budgeting it may be recognised that there is some uncertainty about the achievement of the required annual profit.

Required:

Explain how each of the actions listed below may help in the formulation of the budget plan which will provide the desired annual profit:

(i) Application of feed-forward control.

(ii) Recognition of the committed, engineered and discretionary nature of planned expenditure.

(iii) Recognition and overcoming of production constraints.

(iv) Recognition of doubts about the accuracy of demand forecasting and consideration of the information which may affect such accuracy. **(15 marks)**

87 (Question 6 of examination)

(a) Alpha division has an external market for product A which fully utilises its production capacity.

(i) Explain the principle which would suggest that Alpha division should transfer product A to Beta division of the same group of companies at the existing market price.

(ii) Explain circumstances in which Alpha division may offer to transfer product A to Beta division at less than the external market price and yet report the same total profit. **(4 marks)**

(b) The transfer pricing method to be used for an intermediate product between two divisions in a group is under debate. The supplying division wishes to use actual cost plus a 25% profit mark-up. The receiving division suggests the use of standard cost plus a 25% profit mark-up. A suggested compromise is to use revised standard cost plus 25% profit mark-up. The revised standard cost is arrived at after taking into account the appropriate elements of a planning and operational variance analysis at the supplying division.

Discuss the impact of EACH of the above transfer pricing methods and their acceptability to the supplying and receiving divisions. **(6 marks)**

(c) An intermediate product is manufactured in limited quantities at three divisions of a group and is available in limited quantities from an external source. The intermediate product is required by four divisions in the group as an input for products to be sold externally. The total quantity of intermediate product which is available is insufficient to satisfy demand at the four user divisions.

Explain the procedure which should lead to a transfer pricing and deployment policy which will result in group profit maximisation. **(5 marks)**

(15 marks)

End of Question Paper

DECEMBER 1999 EXAMINATION ANSWERS

82 (Answer 1 of examination)

(a) (i)

Material purchases budget – component X – Period 2

	Product A	**Product B**
Number of components per product unit	2	6
Customer demand (product units)	2,280	2,925
Free replacements (% of units delivered)	5%	2·5%
Units delivered	2,400	3,000
Component X in units delivered	4,800	18,000
Process losses (10% of input)	533	2,000
Total input of component X (units)	5,333	20,000

Total component purchases budget = 5,333 + 20,000 = 25,333 units × £8 = £202,664.

(ii) The summary information from period 1 shows that average component input per product unit was A: 2·5 units (6,250/2,500) and B; 7 units (19,250/2,750). These figures do not attempt to show the factors which contribute to the overall average per unit. The standard specifications allow for consideration of each of three elements which contribute to the use of component X i.e. components per finished unit, process losses and free replacement levels. Each of these can be considered during the planning process. The standard specifications allow for consideration of the improvements that are planned which will reduce the actual level which occurred last period. The current standard can then be used when placing orders with suppliers of component X.

(iii) The external failure cost is that due to the returns from customers which do not meet their specification requirements and have to be replaced.

Abstracting figures from the budget in (i) above we have:
Free replacement component X (units) in the product units delivered

= 4,800 × 5% + 18,000 × 2·5%
= 240 + 450
= 690 units

Budgeted external failure cost = 690 x £8 = £5,520

Note: We could argue that the additional process losses on the free replacement units, while incurred internally, is caused by an external failure and is, therefore, a part of the external failure cost. In this event the total external failure calculation would be:

= 5,333 × 5% + 20,000 × 2·5%
= 267 + 500
= 767 units

Budgeted external failure cost = 767 × £8 = £6,136

This information represents the cost to the company (in terms of component X value) of allowing products to reach the customer which are not of the required quality standard. The information is useful as a planning and control aid. The cost of any action to reduce or eliminate the problem may be compared with the cost of failure at present. This may then be used in any decision-making about the financial viability of action to improve the situation. In addition, the trend of actual failure costs may be monitored and compared with budget in order to see if continuous improvement is being achieved in its control.

(b) (i)

	Original Standard	*Revised Standard*
Components in finished units (2,280 × 2)	4,560	4,560
Free replacement units (%)	5%	2%
Components in units delivered	4,800	4,653
Process losses (%)	10%	5%
Standard input of component X (units)	5,333	4,898

Planning variance (Usage)
= (original std. qty. – revised std. qty.) × revised std. price
= (5,333 – 4,898) × £8·50 = £3,697·50(F)

Operational variance (Usage)
= (revised std. qty. – actual qty.) × revised std. price
= (4,898 – 5,000) × £8·50 = £867·00(A)

Planning variance (Price)
= Original std. input × (original std price – revised std. price)
= 5,333 × (£8 - £8·50) = £2,666·50(A)

Cost variance = £ 164(F)

Note: The above approach values the usage variances at the revised standard price in order to give the current cost to the company of the change in usage.

The planning usage variance could be valued at the original standard price of £8. This would leave the price variance applying to the revised standard input quantity and the operational usage variance valued at the revised standard price of £8·50. The figures would then be:

Planning variance (Usage) = (5,333 – 4,898) × £8	=	£3,480(F)
Operational variance (Usage) = (4,898 – 5,000) × £8·50	=	£867(A)
Planning variance (Price) = 4,898 × (£8 - £8·50)	=	£2,449(A)
Cost variance		£164(F)

(ii) Planning and operational variance analysis provides additional information for use in forward planning and for control. The planning variances show the extent to which it is estimated profit will improve at the current level of activity because of the change in component X. The net component cost saving is £1,031 (i.e. £3,697·50 – £2,666·50). This allows focus for control purposes in the short term to be on the operational variances. In period 3, the operational usage variance of £867(A) shows the extent to which the revised standard has not been achieved. This may be investigated with a view to corrective action.

(iii) The period 3 results indicate that a net budgeted gain of £1,031 has occurred from the decision to change the sourcing of component X . There may be dysfunctional consequences of this interpretation of the change. The results do not attempt to take into account (and place a value on) factors such as:

– Lack of loyalty to existing suppliers. There may be reaction by suppliers to the loss of the right to supply component X.

– Cost which may occur due to inability of the new supplier to deliver the component as required to meet production/sales schedules (e.g. on a JIT basis)

– Costs which may occur due to problems with the quality of the new component X.

(c) (i) Using the information provided, the standard material cost per unit of new product C may be shown as:

Component X = 4 units × £8·50 × 1/0·95 × 1/0·98	=£36·52
Component Z = 6 units × £4 × 1/0·95 × 1/0·98	=£25·78
Total	£62·30

(ii) Existing standard information provides quantitative data from actual experience in similar products. It provides a benchmark which may be used in the estimation of costs for new products. It may also be useful, however, to attempt to obtain external benchmarks of best practice used by competitors (or other group companies) in respect of similar products to that now proposed.

The standard costs are useful in providing a realistic base from which to estimate selling prices where a cost plus profit mark-up approach is used in order to determine a quotation price.

Where a target costing situation exists, the price at which the product can be sold and the required rate of return will be known. The target cost (selling price minus required return) can be compared with the estimated standard cost in order to determine any cost gap which exists. Efforts can then be made in order to reduce or eliminate the cost gap, for example by reducing the estimated process losses percentage.

83 (Answer 2 of examination)

(a) Best outcome situation for the quality improvement programme

	Year 1	Year 2	Year 3	Year 4
Additional output capacity (Std. hours)	1,050	1,365	1,785	2,100
	£	£	£	£
Contribution	1,386,000	1,801,800	2,356,200	2,772,000
Less: training, consultancy, salary costs	97,500	97,500	97,500	97,500
Net margin	1,288,500	1,704,300	2,258,700	2,674,500
Less: depreciation provision	1,000,000	1,000,000	1,000,000	1,000,000
Net profit	288,500	704,300	1,258,700	1,674,500
Less: imputed interest	320,000	240,000	160,000	80,000
Residual income	–31,500	464,300	1,098,700	1,594,500
Return on investment (%)	7·2%	23·5%	62·9%	167·5%

Net present value (NPV) = £2,412,901

Working notes:

(i) Using year 3 as an example: extra std. hours = (1,000 + 300 + 400) x 1·05 = 1,785

(ii) Contribution (e.g. for year 1 = 1,050 hours x (£1,200 x 1·10) = £1,386,000

(iii) training, consultancy & salary cost for each year = £100,000 x 0·975 = £97,500

(iv) Depreciation provision per year = £4,000,000/4 = £1,000,000

(v) Imputed interest charge (e.g. for year 2) = wdv. x cost of capital(%)
= (4,000,000 –1,000,000) x 8% = £240,000

(vi) Return on investment (e.g. for year 4) = net profit/wdv. = £1,674,500/£1,000,000 = 167·5%

(vii) NPV= (Net margin x discount factor at 8%) for each year – initial investment
= £1,288,500 × 0·926 + £1,704,300 × 0·857 + £2,258,700 × 0·794 + £2,674,500 × 0·735 – £4,000,000
= £2,412,901

(b) **Bonus calculations – Most Likely Outcome situation**

	Year 1 £	Year 2 £	Year 3 £	Year 4 £	Total £
Net profit basis (note 1)	0	3,150	10,350	15,750	29,250
Residual Income basis (note 2)	0	0	9,800	19,000	28,800
ROI basis (note 3)	6,000	6,000	6,000	6,000	24,000
NPV basis (note 4)	0	0	0	30,843	30,843

Working notes: (giving an example for one year in each case)
1. Year 2: Bonus = (£460,000 - £250,000) x 1·5% = £3,150
2. Year 3: Bonus = (£740,000 - £250,000) x (0·05 x £40,000)/100,000 = £9,800
3. Year 1: ROI is positive (2·5%). Bonus = £40,000 x 15% = £6,000
4. Year 4: Bonus = £1,233,700 x 2·5% = £30,843

(c) The programme manager's choice of bonus method will be influenced by factors such as the timing of the bonus, its size, the relative ease with which it is earned and his attitude to risk.

The most likely outcome figures calculated in (b) show that the largest total bonus is £30,843 where 2·5% of NPV is used as the basis. The programme manager may, however, be influenced by the timing of the bonus payments. The NPV basis delays any payment until the end of year 4. The other bonus methods – ROI, net profit and RI – have initial bonus payments in years 1, 2 and 3 respectively. The programme manager may have a strong preference for early cash inflows from his bonus and choose the ROI basis which will yield £6,000 in year 1.

His choice may also be influenced by the relative ease with which the bonus is earned and the degree of control over the factors incorporated into its calculation. The RI and NPV bases are affected by the cost of capital percentage which is used. The programme manager may view this as unacceptable because of lack of control by him over the cost of capital percentage used in the calculation. The higher the cost of capital percentage, the lower the bonus paid even if the efficiency of implementation of the programme has been improved.

The ROI basis ensures a bonus of £6,000 per year so long as net profit is greater than £250,000. On the other hand, the net profit basis at a net profit of £250,001 per year will effectively yield a nil bonus.

The attitude to risk of the programme manager is also relevant. A risk-seeking manager may view the £60,323 bonus from the NPV basis where the best outcome occurs as very attractive. On the other hand, a risk averse manager may view as unacceptable the possibility of a bonus of only £5,370 from the NPV basis if the worst outcome occurs. He may then prefer the bonus of £18,000 from the ROI basis which is payable even if the worst outcome occurs.
(Other relevant discussion would be accepted)

(d) The outcome of the implementation of the programme will be influenced by the effort of the programme manager, his attitude to risk and the rationality of his decision-making. In the case of the programme manager, his level of effort and motivation may be affected by the bonus system or by promotion prospects. His attitude to risk may be related to the extent to which he feels he has control over the implementation of the programme and how it is monitored. It is also important that the manager is selected on the basis that he is suited to the job in hand and is capable of making relevant decisions about its effective implementation.

It may be argued that it is the individual who chooses actions and implements them. The strength of motivation to achieve the programme will be affected by the expectation that its achievement will result in some benefit and in the strength of preference of the programme manager for that benefit. His actions will be based on intrinsic and extrinsic factors. His motivation to achieve the implementation of the quality programme will be affected by both intrinsic and extrinsic factors and his preference for them. How highly motivated is he to receive a high bonus payment or possible recognition for promotion within the organisation? (extrinsic factors). How highly motivated is he by factors such as the 'feeling of achievement' or the driving force of 'professional pride'? (intrinsic factors)

84 (Answer 3 of examination)

(a) (i) Cost analysis – 'Millennium' proposal

	2000 £m	2001 £m	2002 £m
Target cost – variable	6·000	7·200	8·000
– fixed	2·000	2·000	2·500
Internal failure cost	1·600	0·920	0·525
External failure cost	2·000	1·104	0·525
Appraisal cost	0·500	0·500	0·500
Prevention cost	2·000	1·000	0·500
Total cost	14·100	12·724	12·550

(ii) Target cost is that which will provide the required return for the 'millennium' proposal. In order to achieve the target cost it is likely that Ochilpark plc will have to make some improvements over the current expected level of performance. This will include all areas in the cycle from product design to after-sales service to customers. The target variable cost is stated as 40% of sales. The target fixed cost rises in 2002 to £2·5m. This may represent a step-function increase due to increased activity.

The cost gap between target cost and current expected cost levels may be analysed into internal and external failure costs. Internal failure costs occur when work fails to meet the design quality standards and the failure is detected before transfer to the customer. Examples will include high levels of production losses or excessive machine idle time. External failure costs occur when the product fails to reach design quality standards and failure is not detected until after transfer to the customer. An example is the free replacement of defective product units returned by the customer. Internal failure costs are expected to fall from 20% of target cost in 2000 to 5% of target in 2002. External failure costs are expected to fall from 25% of target cost in 2000 to 5% in 2002.

Appraisal and prevention costs are incurred in an effort to reduce the incidence of internal and external failure costs in order that total cost may be brought closer to the target cost. Appraisal costs are those associated with the evaluation of costs and services in the cycle in order to ensure conformance with the agreed specification. Examples include checks on design and quality negotiation procedures with customers and checks that machines are performing to specified efficiency tolerances. Prevention costs are those associated with the implementation of actions to ensure that the company reaches the quality standards for the achievement of target cost. Examples include staff training costs or fees to consultants to improve operating procedures. Appraisal costs are expected to remain at the level of £0·5m over the three year period 2000 to 2002. Prevention costs are expected to fall from £2m in 2000 to £0·5m in 2002. This may indicate, for example, a reduced requirement for staff training or consultancy services as improvements are achieved.

(b) (i) Corporate vision may be seen as looking forward through the defining of markets and the basis on which the company will compete. Ochilpark plc has defined the 'millennium' proposal for one of its product ranges as a specific market opportunity. It envisages competing through the identification of key competitors and by close co-operation with its customers in providing products to meet their specific design and quality standards. The corporate vision is seen as being achieved through a focus on internal efficiency and external effectiveness. The 'millennium' proposal may be seen as illustrating a specific sub-set of the corporate mission since it:

- Has its own distinct business concept and mission – the 'millennium' focus.
- Has identified the key competitors
- Is a suitable area for the management of its own strategies – close co-operation with customers and the provision of products to meet their design requirements.

(ii) The 'millennium' proposal may be measured in both marketing and financial terms. Will it achieve market growth and improved market position? The projected sales (£m) in Schedule 3.1 show growth of 20% in 2001 (£18m:£15m) and a further 11% in 2002 (£20m:£18m). In addition, market position is anticipated to improve, with a market share of 12·5%, 14·4% and 15·4% in years 2000, 2001 and 2002 respectively. (e.g. 2000 = £15m/£120m).

The net profit: sales percentage is expected to increase each year. The figures are 6%, 29·3% and 37·25% for 2000, 2001 and 2002 respectively. The profit increase is partly linked to the projected fall in quality costs, both costs of conformance and costs of non-conformance. It is also linked to the increase in volume of business.

(iii) The marketing success of the proposal is linked to the achievement of customer satisfaction. The success will require an efficient business operating system for all aspects of the cycle from product design to after sales service to customers. Improved quality and delivery should lead to improved customer satisfaction. Schedule 3.1 shows a number of quantitative measures of the expected measurement of these factors:

- Quality is expected to improve. The percentage of production achieving design quality standards is expected to rise from 95% to 98% between 2000 and 2002. In the same period, returns from customers for replacement or rectification should fall from 3% to 0·5% and the cost of after sales service should fall from £1·5m to £1·0m.

- Delivery efficiency improvement which is expected may be measured in terms of the increase in the percentage of goods achieving the planned delivery date. This percentage rises from 90% in 2000 to 99% in 2002.

(iv) The financial success of the proposal is linked to the achievement of high productivity. This should be helped through reduced cycle time and decreased levels of waste. Once again Schedule 3.1 shows a number of quantitative measures of these factors:

- The average total cycle time from customer enquiry to delivery should fall from 6 weeks in 2000 to 5 weeks in 2002. This indicates both internal efficiency and external effectiveness.

- Waste in the form of idle machine capacity is expected to fall from 10% to 2% between 2000 and 2002. Also, component production scrap is expected to fall from 7·5% in 2000 to 2·5% in 2002. These are both examples of ways in which improved productivity may be measured. Both will be linked to the prevention and appraisal costs, which are intended to reduce the level of internal and external failure costs, (as shown in part (a) of the answer).

(v) The marketing and financial success of the proposal are linked to the achievement of customer satisfaction and high productivity. Increased flexibility of methods is expected to be achieved. This should help (internally) in achieving improved productivity and also (externally) in an improved level of customer satisfaction. High quality standards will improve customer satisfaction and in turn will assist in market retention and growth.

85 (Answer 4 of examination)

(a) (i) This assumes a short-sighted view leading to the neglect of longer term objectives. For example in the allocation of limited budget funds there may be undue focus on allocating funds to help improve short-term performance measures such as idle time percentages on existing machinery or sales levels of a product which is in the declining phase of its life cycle. A more useful allocation of budget funds may be on increased market research into new areas of customer demand or on research and development work into improved methods of production, perhaps focusing more on production layout dedicated to individual projects or products.

(ii) This implies behaviour and activity in order to achieve specific performance indicators which may not be effective. For example machine output efficiency may be measured as the ratio of output achieved (in standard hours of work) to total operating hours. Efforts to improve this measure from (say) 95% to 99% may focus on increasing machine speed in order to increase throughput rates. This may not be an effective course of action. The increasing of machine speed may create problems in maintaining the quality of output. This could lead to greater losses in process and/or problems with the finished product when it reaches the customer, resulting in returned goods and possibly the loss of future orders.

(iii) Oversimplification of performance measures may lead to their misinterpretation. It may involve failure to recognise the complexity of the environment in which the organisation operates. A fall in the volume of sales for a product may be seen as an indication that greater advertising effort is required. This interpretation ignores the likelihood that a number of other factors both internal and external may be contributing to the fall. For example internal problems with the quality of output, with meeting delivery dates to customers, with cultivating good relations with customers. External problems may include increased competition through alternative products or increased sales effort by competitors. Also factors such as a downturn in the level of purchasing power of customers or changing customer tastes.

(iv) The deliberate distortion of a measure in order to gain strategic advantage may be resorted to for a number of reasons. It may involve deliberate under-performing in order to avoid higher targets being set for a future period. For example the restriction of departmental consultancy earnings in a university department in order that the target for next year will not be increased and/or to hold back consultancy possibilities which are 'in the pipeline' in order to create slack.

(b) Examples of actions which may be implemented in order to overcome problems in the operation of a performance measurement system are as follows:

- Involvement of staff at all levels in the development and implementation of the scheme. It is important that staff are willing to accept and work towards any performance measures which are developed to monitor their part in the operation of the organisation and the achievement of its objectives.

- A flexible approach to the use of performance measures. It is best to acknowledge that they should not be relied upon exclusively for control. To some extent it should be acknowledged that improved performance may be achieved through the informal interaction of individuals and groups.

- Give careful consideration to the 'dimensions of performance'. Action here may include efforts to try and quantify all objectives. Such action should help to overcome a sub-optimal plan which omits some aspects of what is required. Also try to focus on customer satisfaction. This will help ensure an external focus which is vital to the level of achievement and future effectiveness of the organisation.

- Give consideration to the audit of the system. This may include expert external review of the system. An 'arms length' review will help avoid its incorporating inefficiencies due to the views of those operating the system. In addition there should be a careful audit of the data used. Any scheme is only as good as the data analysis and how it is interpreted.

- Focus on key features necessary in the system. These may include: nurture a long-term perspective among staff; hold down the number of performance measures to allow focus on key areas; develop performance benchmarks which are independent of past activity in order to focus on the way ahead and the achievement of plans for the future.

(Relevant alternative examples and comment would be accepted)

86 (Answer 5 of examination)

(i) Feedforward control is where the desired outcome is compared with that which it is estimated will occur if the current plan is implemented. Where any deviation exists between the desired outcome and the current plan, corrective action may be implemented in order to achieve the desired outcome. Where the initial budget will not allow the achievement of the desired annual profit, consideration may be given as to how to rectify the problem. For example it may be decided to adopt a policy of increasing demand through a combined increase in the budget for sales promotion and advertising.

(ii) Where the existing plan will not achieve the desired profit level, the feed-forward control investigation may focus on the recognition of committed, engineered and discretionary costs in order to close any gap which exists. Committed costs such as occupancy costs must be retained. Efforts may be made, however, to reduce the level of such costs. It may be possible to reduce such costs through the reduction in storage area required through the adoption of a JIT policy for incoming materials. Engineered costs are those which vary in proportion to activity levels. Changes in product design or production methods may allow some reduction in such costs. For example through the use of a less expensive component or the elimination of an element of the required production cycle.

(iii) The achievement of the desired profit may be hampered by the existence of one or more production constraints. There may be a shortage of available materials, machinery or manpower. It may be possible to overcome these in a number of ways. For example a shortage of machine capacity may be overcome through a longer working week, hiring extra machine capacity or sub-contracting some of the production. A shortage of materials may be overcome by seeking alternative sources of supply or a substitute type of material or component.

(iv) Demand forecasting may be affected by the sources of information used. Will past performance and trends be used as the basis for future projections? This may be inaccurate in that it does not take into account the stage in the product life cycle. To what extent do we intend to enter new product markets? To what extent are some products in the declining phase of their life cycle?

How accurate is market research information? What pricing policy will be required in order to penetrate new markets? How will competitors react to actions which we propose to take? The uncertainty of the answers to such questions will affect the accuracy of any budget which is prepared.

It may be decided to use quantitative modelling techniques to help in the forecasting process. If a price/demand model is used, how accurate is the price/demand elasticity which is incorporated into the model? Is the assumption of a linear relationship between price and demand acceptable?

The formulation of an accurate budget will be affected by the extent to which such problems are recognised and efforts made to allow for them.

87 (Answer 6 of examination)

(a) (i) The general rule of transfer pricing is that for the most efficient decision-making to be made from a group viewpoint, transfer prices should be set at marginal cost of the supplying division plus the opportunity cost to the group. Since Alpha division has external sales which utilise its entire production capacity, the contribution which it earns from external sales is the opportunity forgone if it transfers internally. For example a selling price of £20 per unit may include a variable (marginal) cost of £12 and a contribution earned of £8.

(ii) Alpha division is likely to have costs which it incurs for external sales which will not apply to internal transfers to another division. It may, for example, be able to save on transport costs and on packing costs when goods are transferred. If such costs make up £3 of variable cost, the contribution of £8 shown in (i) above can still be earned by Alpha division with a selling price of £17 instead of £20.

(b) The use of a standard cost based transfer price is argued to be effective in that the supplying division is not allowed to pass on to the receiving division any inefficiencies in operation. Such inefficiencies are left as adverse variances at the supplying division. This is useful where the transfer price is being compared to any quotes from external suppliers in order to choose the most effective strategy from a group viewpoint. The supplying division may, however, be faced with cost increases due to permanent and non-controllable changes from the original standards. For example, the level of material usage may have been underestimated or the wage rates finally agreed may have been understated. Such permanent changes may be reported as planning variances and incorporated into a revised standard. This revised standard will reflect current efficient costs at the supplying division. In this way the transfer price reflects current efficient costs to the group and the residual operational variances are reported and controlled at the supplying division. If properly explained, the receiving division is likely to accept this approach to transfer pricing. The use of actual cost plus a profit mark-up would maximise the reported profit at the supplying division but would not encourage cost control and could lead to sub-optimal decisions by a receiving division to buy externally.

(c) Where there is a shortage of the intermediate product, a linear programming model may be formulated centrally which incorporates all relevant information about selling prices and conversion costs of the four divisions which wish to use it in products for external sale. In addition, the marginal cost and the external opportunities (if any) of the intermediate product at one or all of the supplying divisions, will be built into the model. For example, it may be that one or more of the divisions has a partial external market for the intermediate product. The solution to the linear programming model will show to which divisions the available supplies of the intermediate product should be directed in order to maximise group profit. The model will also show the shadow price of the intermediate product which indicates its scarcity value. The shadow price shows the extent to which profits can be increased if one additional unit of the intermediate product is made available.

Professional Examination – Paper 9
Information for Control and Decision Making

Marking Scheme

				Marks	Marks
1	(a)	(i)	Calculation of free replacement product units	1.5	
			Calculation of component process losses	1.5	
			Calculation of total input (components)	0.5	
			Calculation of total value (£)	0.5	
					4
		(ii)	Reference to quantitative data	1	
			Discussion of uses of standard specification	3	
					4
		(iii)	Calculation of external failure cost	2	
			Comments on usefulness of information	2	
					4
	(b)	(i)	Planning variance (usage)	2	
			Planning variance (price)	2	
			Operational variance (usage)	2	
					6
		(ii)	Use in forward planning and control (2 × 1)	2	
			Reference to variances in (i) (2 × 1)	2	
					4
		(iii)	Dysfunctional consequences comment	2	
			Two specific examples (2 × 1)	2	
					4
	(c)	(i)	Standard material cost – component X	1.5	
			Standard material costs – component Z	1.5	
					3
		(ii)	Use in product planning	3	
			Use in target costing	3	
					6
					35
2	(a)		Additional output capacity	2	
			Contribution	1	
			Training, consultancy, etc	1	
			Depreciation	1	
			Imputed interest	1	
			RI	1	
			ROI	1	
			NPV	2	
					10
	(b)		Annual bonus calculations – method A	3	
			Annual bonus calculations – method B	3	
			Annual bonus calculations – method C	2	
			Annual bonus calculations – method D	1	
					9
	(c)		Name relevant discussion factors (any three)	3	
			Discusion of factors (3 × 1)	3	
			Reference to figures in (b) (3 × 1)	3	
			Reference to best/worst outcome bonus	2	
					11

	(d)		Comments relating to effort and risk		2.5	
			Comments relating to personal expectations		2.5	
						5
						35
3	**(a)**	(i)	Target variable cost		1	
			Internal/external failure cost (2 × 0·5)		1	
			Appraisal/prevention cost (2 × 0·5)		1	
			Overall layout and total per Schedule 3·1		1	
						4
		(ii)	Cost classification meanings and examples (5 × 1)		5	
			trend and interrelationship		3	
						8
	(b)	(i)	Corporate definition and millennium proposal as part of this (on merit)		5	
		(ii)	Quantification of marketing measures	3		
			Quantification of financial measures	3		
					6	
		(iii)	External effectiveness and quality	2		
			External effectiveness and delivery	2		
			(data and comment in each case)		4	
		(iv)	Internal efficiency and cycle time	2		
			Internal efficiency and waste	2		
			(data and comment in each case)		4	
		(v)	Links between internal/external measures (on merit)		4	
						23
						35
4	**(a)**		Discussion of each problem (4 × 1·5)		6	
			Specific example of each problem (4 × 1)		4	
						10
	(b)		Actions to overcome problems (4 × 1·5) Max of 5			5
						15
5			Explanation for each action (on merit) (4 × 4) up to max of 15			15
6	**(a)**	(i)	General rule principle explained		2	
		(ii)	Application of general rule in situation given		2	
						4
	(b)		Impact and acceptability of each of actual cost, std cost and revised std. cost methods (3 × 2)			6
	(c)		Explanation of LP approach to transfer pricing and deployment policy (on merit)			5
						15

Present value table

Present value of £1 ie, $\frac{1}{(1+r)^n} = (1 + r)^{-n}$

where r = discount rate

n = number of periods until payment

Discount rates (r)

Periods (n)	1%	2%	3%	4%	5%	6%	7%	8%	9%	10%	
1	0.990	0.980	0.971	0.962	0.952	0.943	0.935	0.926	0.917	0.909	1
2	0.980	0.961	0.943	0.925	0.907	0.890	0.873	0.857	0.842	0.826	2
3	0.971	0.942	0.915	0.889	0.864	0.840	0.816	0.794	0.772	0.751	3
4	0.961	0.924	0.888	0.855	0.823	0.792	0.763	0.735	0.708	0.683	4
5	0.951	0.906	0.863	0.822	0.784	0.747	0.713	0.681	0.650	0.621	5
6	0.942	0.888	0.837	0.790	0.746	0.705	0.666	0.630	0.596	0.564	6
7	0.933	0.871	0.813	0.760	0.711	0.665	0.623	0.583	0.547	0.513	7
8	0.923	0.853	0.789	0.731	0.677	0.627	0.582	0.540	0.502	0.467	8
9	0.914	0.837	0.766	0.703	0.645	0.592	0.544	0.500	0.460	0.424	9
10	0.905	0.820	0.744	0.676	0.614	0.558	0.508	0.463	0.422	0.386	10
11	0.896	0.804	0.722	0.650	0.585	0.527	0.475	0.429	0.388	0.350	11
12	0.887	0.788	0.701	0.625	0.557	0.497	0.444	0.397	0.356	0.319	12
13	0.879	0.773	0.681	0.601	0.530	0.469	0.415	0.368	0.326	0.290	13
14	0.870	0.758	0.661	0.577	0.505	0.442	0.388	0.340	0.299	0.263	14
15	0.861	0.743	0.642	0.555	0.481	0.417	0.362	0.315	0.275	0.239	15

	11%	12%	13%	14%	15%	16%	17%	18%	19%	20%	
1	0.901	0.893	0.885	0.877	0.870	0.862	0.855	0.847	0.840	0.833	1
2	0.812	0.797	0.783	0.769	0.756	0.743	0.731	0.718	0.706	0.694	2
3	0.731	0.712	0.693	0.675	0.658	0.641	0.624	0.609	0.593	0.579	3
4	0.659	0.636	0.613	0.592	0.572	0.552	0.534	0.516	0.499	0.482	4
5	0.593	0.567	0.543	0.519	0.497	0.476	0.456	0.437	0.419	0.402	5
6	0.535	0.507	0.480	0.456	0.432	0.410	0.390	0.370	0.352	0.335	6
7	0.482	0.452	0.425	0.400	0.376	0.354	0.333	0.314	0.296	0.279	7
8	0.434	0.404	0.376	0.351	0.327	0.305	0.285	0.266	0.249	0.233	8
9	0.391	0.361	0.333	0.308	0.284	0.263	0.243	0.225	0.209	0.194	9
10	0.352	0.322	0.295	0.270	0.247	0.227	0.208	0.191	0.176	0.162	10
11	0.317	0.287	0.261	0.237	0.215	0.195	0.178	0.162	0.148	0.135	11
12	0.286	0.257	0.231	0.208	0.187	0.168	0.152	0.137	0.124	0.112	12
13	0.258	0.229	0.204	0.182	0.163	0.145	0.130	0.116	0.104	0.093	13
14	0.232	0.205	0.181	0.160	0.141	0.125	0.111	0.099	0.088	0.078	14
15	0.209	0.183	0.160	0.140	0.123	0.108	0.095	0.084	0.074	0.065	15

Annuity Table

Present value of an annuity of 1 ie, $\frac{1-(1+r)^{-n}}{r}$

where r = discount rate
n = number of periods

Discount rates (r)

Periods (n)	1%	2%	3%	4%	5%	6%	7%	8%	9%	10%	
1	0.990	0.980	0.971	0.962	0.952	0.943	0.935	0.926	0.917	0.909	1
2	1.970	1.942	1.913	1.886	1.859	1.833	1.808	1.783	1.759	1.736	2
3	2.941	2.884	2.829	2.775	2.723	2.673	2.624	2.577	2.531	2.487	3
4	3.902	3.808	3.717	3.630	3.546	3.465	3.387	3.312	3.240	3.170	4
5	4.853	4.713	4.580	4.452	4.329	4.212	4.100	3.993	3.890	3.791	5
6	5.795	5.601	5.417	5.242	5.076	4.917	4.767	4.623	4.486	4.355	6
7	6.728	6.472	6.230	6.002	5.786	5.582	5.389	5.206	5.033	4.868	7
8	7.652	7.325	7.020	6.733	6.463	6.210	5.971	5.747	5.535	5.335	8
9	8.566	8.162	7.786	7.435	7.108	6.802	6.515	6.247	5.995	5.759	9
10	9.471	8.983	8.530	8.111	7.722	7.360	7.024	6.710	6.418	6.145	10
11	10.37	9.787	9.253	8.760	8.306	7.887	7.499	7.139	6.805	6.495	11
12	11.26	10.58	9.954	9.385	8.863	8.384	7.943	7.536	7.161	6.814	12
13	12.13	11.35	10.63	9.986	9.394	8.853	8.358	7.904	7.487	7.103	13
14	13.00	12.11	11.30	10.56	9.899	9.295	8.745	8.244	7.786	7.367	14
15	13.87	12.85	11.94	11.12	10.38	9.712	9.108	8.559	8.061	7.606	15

	11%	12%	13%	14%	15%	16%	17%	18%	19%	20%	
1	0.901	0.893	0.885	0.877	0.870	0.862	0.855	0.847	0.840	0.833	1
2	1.713	1.690	1.668	1.647	1.626	1.605	1.585	1.566	1.547	1.528	2
3	2.444	2.402	2.361	2.322	2.283	2.246	2.210	2.174	2.140	2.106	3
4	3.102	3.037	2.974	2.914	2.855	2.798	2.743	2.690	2.639	2.589	4
5	3.696	3.605	3.517	3.433	3.352	3.274	3.199	3.127	3.058	2.991	5
6	4.231	4.111	3.998	3.889	3.784	3.685	3.589	3.498	3.410	3.326	6
7	4.712	4.564	4.423	4.288	4.160	4.039	3.922	3.812	3.706	3.605	7
8	5.146	4.968	4.799	4.639	4.487	4.344	4.207	4.078	3.954	3.837	8
9	5.537	5.328	5.132	4.946	4.772	4.607	4.451	4.303	4.163	4.031	9
10	5.889	5.650	5.426	5.216	5.019	4.833	4.659	4.494	4.339	4.192	10
11	6.207	5.938	5.687	5.453	5.234	5.029	4.836	4.656	4.486	4.327	11
12	6.492	6.194	5.918	5.660	5.421	5.197	4.988	4.793	4.611	4.439	12
13	6.750	6.424	6.122	5.842	5.583	5.342	5.118	4.910	4.715	4.533	13
14	6.982	6.628	6.302	6.002	5.724	5.468	5.229	5.008	4.802	4.611	14
15	7.191	6.811	6.462	6.142	5.847	5.575	5.324	5.092	4.876	4.675	15

HOTLINES	AT FOULKS LYNCH LTD
Telephone: 00 44 (0) 20 8844 0667 Enquiries: 00 44 (0) 20 8831 9990 Fax: 00 44 (0) 20 8831 9991	Number 4, The Griffin Centre Staines Road, Feltham Middlesex TW14 0HS

Examination Date: ☐ June 2000 ☐ December 2000	Publications				Distance Learning	Open Learning
	Textbooks (Pub'd July 99)	Revision Series (Pub'd Feb 2000)	Lynchpins Pub'd Feb 2000	Tracks (Audio Tapes)	Include helpline & marking (except for overseas Open Learning)	
dule A – Foundation Stage						
Accounting Framework	£18.95 UK IAS	£10.95 UK IAS	£5.95 UK IAS	£10.95	£85 UK IAS	£89
Legal Framework	£18.95	£10.95	£5.95	£10.95	£85	£89
dule B						
Management Information	£18.95	£10.95	£5.95	£10.95	£85	£89
Organisational Framework	£18.95	£10.95	£5.95	£10.95	£85	£89
dule C – Certificate Stage						
Information Analysis	£18.95	£10.95	£5.95	£10.95	£85	£89
Audit Framework	£18.95 UK IAS	£10.95 UK IAS	£5.95 UK IAS	£10.95	£85 UK IAS	£89
dule D						
Tax Framework FA99 - D/J00	£18.95	£10.95	£5.95	*£10.95	£85	£89
Managerial Finance	£18.95	£10.95	£5.95	£10.95	£85	£89
dule E – Professional Stage						
ICDM	£18.95	£10.95	£5.95	£10.95	£85	£89
Accounting & Audit Practice	£22.95 UK IAS (£23.95)	£10.95 UK IAS	£5.95 UK IAS	£10.95	£85 UK IAS	£89
Tax Planning FA99 - J/D00	£18.95	£10.95	£5.95	*£10.95	£85	£89
dule F						
Management & Strategy	£18.95	£10.95	£5.95	£10.95	£85	£89
Financial Rep Environment	£20.95 UK IAS	£10.95 UK IAS	£5.95 UK IAS	£10.95	£85 UK IAS	£89
Financial Strategy	£19.95	£10.95	£5.95	£10.95	£85	£89
			P7 & 11 Pub'd 7/99	*Available Feb 2000		
P + Delivery UK Mainland	£2.00/book	£1.00/book	£1.00/book	£1.00/tape	£5.00/subject	£5.00/subject
NI, ROI & EU Countries	£5.00/book	£3.00/book	£3.00/book	£1.00/tape	£15.00/subject	£15.00/subject
st of world standard air service	£10.00/book	£8.00/book	£8.00/book	£2.00/tape	£25.00/subject	£25.00/subject
Rest of world courier service†	£22.00/book	£20.00/book	Not applicable	Not applicable	£47.00/subject	£47.00/subject

GLE ITEM SUPPLEMENT FOR TEXTBOOKS AND REVISION SERIES:
u only order 1 item, INCREASE postage costs by £2.50 for UK, NI & EU Countries or by £15.00 for Rest of World Services

'AL					
Sub Total £					
Post & Packing £					
Total £					

lephone number essential for this service *Payments in Sterling in London* **Order Total £**

LIVERY DETAILS

Mr ☐ Miss ☐ Mrs ☐ Ms Other

als Surname

dress

Postcode

ephone Deliver to home ☐

mpany name

dress

Postcode

ephone Fax

nthly report to go to employer ☐ Deliver to work ☐

PAYMENT

1 I enclose Cheque/PO/Bankers Draft for £__________
Please make cheques payable to AT Foulks Lynch Ltd.

2 Charge Mastercard/Visa/Switch A/C No:

Valid from: Expiry Date:

Issue No: (Switch only)

Signature Date

DECLARATION

I agree to pay as indicated on this form and understand that AT Foulks Lynch Terms and Conditions apply (available on request). I understand that AT Foulks Lynch Ltd are not liable for non-delivery if the rest of world standard air service is used.

Signature Date

ase ow:	UK mainland - 5-10 w/days NI, ROI & EU Countries - 1-3 weeks Rest of world standard air service - 6 weeks Rest of world courier service - 10 w/days	***Notes:***	All delivery times subject to stock availability. Signature required on receipt (except rest of world standard air service). Please give both addresses for Distance Learning students where possible.

n effective December 99 ***All details correct at time of printing*** ***Source: ACRS00***